CHARLES LIS

LETTERS AND RECOLLECTIONS

WITH A MEMOIR BY HIS FATHER, LORD RIBBLESDALE

Edited by Paul Foster, FRSA

Published by Minutecircle Services Limited

ISBN 978-1-908345-16-5

Design and typesetting by Minutecircle Limited, 12 Conqueror Court, Sittingbourne, Kent ME10 5BH.

By the Same Author

Other Books In The "I Was There" Series Include:

visit: **www.remembering1418.com**

This book is dedicated to my beloved

and faithful companions, Woofer and Max,

who accompany me at all times.

In memory of my grandfather
Sergeant Frank Heesom
1893 - 1974

Charles Lister

Letters and Recollections

With a memoir by his father,

Lord Ribblesdale

… throwing a jam-pot grenade during the Gallipoli campaign

Editor's Introduction

Charles Lister was the second son of Thomas, Baron Ribblesdale and Lady Charlotte. He had a typical upbringing for a member of the aristocracy and was educated at Eton College before going up to Balliol College, Oxford.

A highly intelligent young man Charles decided to make his life as a diplomat. He passed the Civil Service examinations then served in Rome and Constantinople. Through his family and friends he was also able to spend considerable time in India and Europe. His knowledge of the diplomatic situation and personal insight during the build up to and outbreak of the First World War is fascinating. As soon as it was possible Charles volunteered and joined the army. He first worked as an interpreter before joining the Royal Naval Division and being sent to serve at Gallipoli. During the voyage he was with his great friend, Rupert Brooke, who died *en route* and Charles was responsible for the burial party. He was wounded shortly after arriving on the beaches but refused the offer to return to a desk job in the Foreign Office. Charles rejoined his men at the front where he was slightly wounded however he made light of it in his letters. Charles was wounded for the third time and he died on board the hospital ship, the *SS Gascon*. He now lies in East Mudros Military Cemetery.

Lord Ribblesdale published *'Letters and Recollections'* a year after Charles' death. I have re-set the original book and, where appropriate, added contemporary illustrations to compliment the text. The third section of this publication contains additional information and cameos on some of the events and those who were mentioned in the original publication.

I hope that you enjoy reading the insight to Charles's life as much I have.

... sailing from England

CHARLES LISTER, Gisburne, August. 1899.
By J. S. Sargent, R.A.

When Mr. Sargent was paying a visit at Gisburne, he was impressed by a
fidelity to type conspicuous in this mid- seventeenth century portrait and the
Charles Lister of 1899. This accounts for the background of his drawing.

... views of Mudros Harbour

CONTENTS

PART I

PART II - RECOLLECTIONS

PART III — ADDITIONAL INFORMATION

LIST OF ORIGINAL ILLUSTRATIONS

PREFATORY NOTE

I am indebted beyond words to the Vice-Provost and to Mrs. Warre Cornish for their sympathy, counsel, and active help. Further, I am glad and it seems to me befitting that this little book should have found its origin at Eton under the shadow of College buildings. Eton, in the hour and circumstances of this great War, is signally the meeting-place of many memories of high promise. My thanks are due to Charles's ambassador, Sir Rennell Rodd, for his recollections — these seem to me to touch the routine of Chancery work and life with the true impressionism of the poet and the friend; — to the Master of Balliol and to Mr. Lindsay, tutor of that College; to Mr. Cyril Bailey, to the Rev. H. T. Bowlby, to the Rev. Ronald Knox — all good friends of Charles's — for their valued assistance. I am also most grateful to those who not only wrote to him constantly but who kept his letters with affectionate care.

Notes to letters in a collection of this kind are a matter of taste and opinion. As a reader of a good many books of this variety I, personally, like notes: I mean notes which cross or even transgress the frontiers of explanation and which so venture to supplement or amplify the text. But to the best of our ability we, Mrs. Cornish and I, have kept ourselves in control, and I hope that there is little in the way either of head or foot-notes which can be considered diffuse or irrelevant.

Charles always dated his letters, and, mindful of Dr. Johnson's dictum that Chronology is the eye of History, we have done our best to present them in their proper order.

R.

Master Thomas Lister and his pony.
By Dobson.

Charles Lister was born in Grosvenor Square on October 26, 1887. Dr. Roberts, of Manchester Street — a great friend of the family's — brought him into the world and looked after the childish ailments of his earlier years. He often declared that he was an unusual and most clever little boy, and devoted extra meditation to the lengthy prescriptions of the old-fashioned reassuring sort which he devised for Charles. I cannot remember him not able to talk distinctly, and he assimilated very quickly long words, which told with excellent effect in the lingua franca of the nursery and school-room. He liked sonorous and eccentric words — this taste he may have got from me — and from the first pronounced them with clearness; this knack he certainly got from his mother, who had an excellent gift of purity and poise of enunciation. Mr. Gladstone, who paid us a visit at Ascot in 1893 or 1894, at the time I had charge of the Buckhounds, was much pleased at this accomplishment of Charles's. "Ornithorhynchus" was, on this occasion, the particular word which elicited approval; Charles was showing Mr. Gladstone a natural history book with fine coloured plates, and explaining the habits of the more obscure animals. [*He had, from very early days, considerable facility for drawing, and before he went to Eton had filled two or three scrap-books with bold, strong-coloured water colours on foolscap paper of the larger and more ferocious fauna. His elder brother also drew easily, but relied chiefly upon the comic incidents of the hunting field, whereas Charles's pencil was usually inspired by Indian jungles and African plains. Both boys when so minded got fun and action into their drawings and were quick and handy with colours and brushes.*] These they discussed at large together, and they became quite friends. On Mr. Gladstone's departure his mother asked Charles how they had got on. He replied, "He seems to be a clever man". This taste for words and for the collection of pretentious words did not last long. Now and then he might employ one with success, but his letters, and I think anything he wrote later on, are in good sterling English and free from elaborateness. They go straight up to and hit off the meaning. A good example of this I shall refer to presently. At the time it was written the back premises of the stable-yard at Gisburne were occupied by a polity of well-bred rabbits, guinea-pigs, and mice of varied colours and sorts. These were administered as a working Utopia and subject to all kinds of strictly defined eugenic and dietary by-laws and regulations. They were very tame, and Charles certainly appeared to have a sort of Androcles effect upon any wilder member of the community, but he soon got tired of them. The mice were, at heart, Bohemians, and were always escaping. The rabbits proved heedless of well-ordained marriage laws. As to the guinea-pigs, Charles himself on one occasion said to Lady Ulrica Buncombe — a close friend of his at this time — that although they were nice little fellows they exhibited traces of the worst human characteristics — dirt, greed, and cowardice. The letter I have just spoken of was written to my agent, Mr. Charles Starkie, who has preserved it all these years, as at the time he was impressed by its thoroughness and clearness. [*Writing from school at Rottingdean in 1896, he says: "I did not quite understand your statement of the number of Flemish Giants. I am glad you have sent two to Mrs. Cayley. Don't gull them Belgian hares when you are talking about them to people who seem likely to buy." Then follow some minute instructions as to the feeding of "the young Flemishers" and as to "keeping down the price of food". He concludes by urging Mr. Starkie to keep a close eye on Tommy, a farm boy attached to Charles's special service. Tommy — a poultry proficient — was not fervent in business and reckoned naught of guinea-pigs. The Flemish Giants were a new "line". What happened in Belgium in August 1914 gives this letter a de l'epoque flavour, — R.*]

As far as I recollect he wrote pretty regularly to his mother and to me during his early and later school days, but seldom at any length, and on facts, not thoughts. Every now and then he described the greater occasions of private school-life at Mr. Stanford's at Rottingdean— a cricket match [*Charles wrote fully to his mother about the St. Aubyn (Rottingdean) cricket matches, explaining such terms as leg-byes, caught and bowled, stumped, and so on, rather than dwelling upon the mere incidents of the game. He and I became — later on — staunch lookers-on at first-class cricket, and he was anxious that his mother should share our leisured joys. Alas! a willing but inattentive disciple, she made no progress in appreciating cricket values, and one day, at the Oval, at once pleased and displeased her instructor by asking whether the bowler made the runs. — R.*] or a concert. I remember one when he saw the local harriers casting themselves on the neighbouring downs as good as could be. In the same way I remember with pleasure two or three of his holiday letters: for instance, the novel experience of a spring hunting day with the New Forest hounds, which terminated in an emerald bog and the green fracture of his left arm; or it might be a day's shooting away from home, the methods of the keepers and the retrievers, the performances of the guns, and the quality of the luncheon. But I do not think he ever wrote to us at any great length from Eton.

An old Eton Cloisters friend shall describe him for me in his Eton days. She writes: "Let me give you a pen-and-ink portrait of Charles at this time. He was seventeen. His figure was tall and slender. The head, which may be described as pear-shaped, was framed by closely curling hair. The complexion was uniform and pale, the features delicate. The eyes, which were blue, were both frank and observant — the frankness was for the person he spoke to, the observation was turned outward;

when speaking his eyebrows went up. His chief distinction among the scholarly band of his friends was to be totally free from self-consciousness. The priggishness which often accompanies a schoolboy's first approach to civilization was entirely absent. From the first he was the embodiment of comradeship in whatever society he found himself. The way men lived filled him with curiosity. Like the Celt of old, who awaited at the cross-roads the passers-by to compel them to tell him something new, so Charles interrogated his companions."

One thing I may here note about the very early years: an almost Red Indian-like acquiescence in things as they came. His mother declared with joy that his mind was so superior to ours that he did not notice whether the water in his bath was hot or cold, or the weather pleasant or disagreeable; certainly he never minded or deemed such things worthy of comment. In the same way with the various ailments of childhood and boyhood, of which he had his share, he never complained — almost as a baby "Soon be better" was an invariable formula — and it was almost impossible to get at where and how he felt pain and discomfort. This high inborn quality of refusing to be disquieted by any physical adversity or discouragement endured to the end. By way of illustration let me quote this passage, from a letter to Colonel Freyberg, dated July 30, 1916, from France; it appears in full later on:

"I think we began to shape ourselves into real Hoods the day that Lister — his wounds hardly healed — returned joyously to that sun-baked camp with its twin plagues of flies and dysentery, and declared that everything was very jolly and that this sort of picnic was one of life's richest slices."

In these very early days Charles was either unaware of, or unmindful of, fear. Probably the latter: everybody is aware of Fear; its effect, and the degree and nature of its perception is temperamental. He got this gift of courage from his mother, who for herself was never afraid — later on in the larger occasions of war, I believe that Charles's indifference to risks was recognized and borne witness to by brave men who were his fighting comrades in the Gallipoli operations.

Charles attached very little importance to honours, or to the world's tokens of success, yet I often wish he could have seen the wording of General Sir I. Hamilton's Honours dispatch of October 5, 1915, in which he recommends him for a decoration.

Here I avow myself in some perplexity as but a prentice hand at memoir writing. Is it or is it not a good thing to say something of the outdoor amusements and the indoor tastes of one's subject? That Sir Robert Walpole opened a letter from his keeper or his huntsman before he even looked at his official correspondence;

that Mr. Gladstone was an eager and catholic reader of novels, are — for me — comfortable reflections. So, thus emboldened, I shall now examine Charles as a rider and as a reader.

Charles picked up riding quickly. From the first he had excellent hands, but never acquired the balanced ease and elegance of his brother Tommy's seat on a horse. This seat and its look — highly commended to Sancho Panza by Don Quixote — largely depend on long thin legs, and his brother had the pull over him in this respect.

His first pony was a roan, with black points and a tan muzzle. I bought him at Norton Conyers of Sir R. Graham, his own boys having grown out of him. A good if rather lazy hack, Joey had no pony tricks, and, though a hearty feeder, never seemed to get over-fresh. His record as a hunter is insignificant and without merit. Joey could and would climb up and down a bank, but cared little or nothing about hounds and jumped with extreme reluctance. Still, he was a character and a favourite. The photographs of him and Charles are very like both of them at the time. His first real hunter was by Escamillo, and came from Mr. James Darrell of Ayton, a great ally of the family's. This was a very good 15.2 horse, narrow, with fine shoulders and several crosses of East Riding blood.

The knack of sitting properly over fences was not acquired without some discouragement and even tribulation. This accomplishment seldom matures all at once with boys. But Escamillo stood away and really delivered himself over his fences, so he taught Charles the real thing. They used to enjoy themselves very much together with our two packs of harriers, the Pendle Forest and the Craven. The country is all grass or fell, plough we don't know by sight, the few gates seldom open amiably, and most of the fences appear to have been made to jump. After that he had a charming horse called Whirlygig. I saw this bay horse going in front during a long hunt late in the season with the Cottesmore, and I bought him the same afternoon of my friend and brother officer of Rifle Brigade days at Gibraltar, Colonel Dawson of Launde, who was riding him with evident confidence and security. On this horse Charles jumped two or three really high fell walls. He always liked high places. Whilst posted as attaché at Rome he hunted regularly with both packs, deer and fox, and on my arrival there I found that he had earned and sustained quite a reputation for performances over the singularly upright and uninviting timber of the Campagna. Slow paces and the minuet airs and graces of manage riding he never practised, and he never cared to make a horse bend or show himself. As a little boy he liked to gallop his ponies along, and allowed no difference to exist between macadam and the springiest old turf. His mother shared this preference for speed. On the riding excursions we frequently took *en famille* his sister Barbara and I funking along behind admiring the scenery, used to tremble for their animals' legs as they pounded along the dazzling white limestone roads on a hot August afternoon. [*In an amusing passage Swinburne asserts that Jowett would have made a foxhunter of merit had he devoted his talents to that pursuit. One reason for this was that the Master of Balliol's love of Nature was so "temperate" that he would not have drawn rein to look about him, though hounds had been running up the Vale of Tempe or across the Garden of Eden. Craven — where we live — is designed by Providence for the sudden and violent effects of wild weather. There is enough hill for its scowl; enough sweep for its smile. Charles was equably aware of all this, but seldom called attention to these phenomena, whereas his brother Tommy, the late Sir Mathew Wilson, and I myself were overfond of doing so. — R.*]

It is a question whether anybody cares to know what anybody else reads. I personally like any passage in a biography which refers to the books and the reading tastes of its subject. So let me here say something about Charles's ways with books.

As a family — without reaching Mr. Gibbon's [*Gibbon's "Autobiography"*] mark, who avers that he would not have exchanged his invincible love of reading for the treasures of India — we were all as much attached to desultory reading as to regular riding. I remember, when I was young, a Sunday with Mr. Jowett at Balliol. At that time he wished me to take more pains with myself and more advantage of my opportunities; thus we had some correspondence as to the possibilities of my becoming "a serious-minded peer". This was, as it were, the cliché [*This definition of aspiration was mine. It seemed to amuse him, and in the two or three letters he wrote me he diverted himself and me at the expense of any such transformation. — R.*] of the inquiry. At the outset I remember Mr. Jowett asked me in a letter whether I was prepared to read for two full hours a day — not two hours at a time, but that reading should take up that space of time daily — whatever the weather, whatever my inclinations, and whatever my circumstances. This, he wrote, sounded easy enough, but that it was a covenant or a stipulation by no means so easily carried out. I forget what I replied at the time, but, a sufferer from an unchartered freedom, I am afraid I have not achieved the gentle task he proposed. But let me get away from this personal digression and the recollections it has induced of Mr. Jowett. [*As a visitor to Balliol, not an alumnus of Oxford.*]

As quite a little boy of five or six Charles and I became agreed upon a common liking for the same sort of subjects. Our especial favourites were books about Indian shooting; we preferred, above all, the literary society of man-eaters; then

Charles Lister on Joey.
Circa 1895-6.

came pig-sticking and the habits of elephants, and the manners and customs of aboriginal tribes such as the Bheels and the Gonds. I remember reading aloud to him — he cannot have been more than seven or eight years old — the tribal and tradition chapters of Forsyth's most admirable "Highlands of Central India". It may be remembered that Gibbon discovered in the Dynasties of Assyria and Egypt "his top and cricket ball", and on the very morning of his return for the holidays from his private school, I remember that Charles made a careful digest from the Whitaker's Almanack sketch of our Indian Empire. The Mogul Empire and Akbar Khan were at this time his prime favourites, but minor states and ephemeral chiefs held an equal place in his affections. In M. de Lisle Adam's phrase, *Il gardait au cœur les richesses steriles d'un grand nombre de rois oubliis*. These early tastes or instincts held good, "thus, writing to his friend Tommy Lascelles, in August 1911, he says," I am feeling rather unambitious just at present, and inclined to chuck the Service [Diplomatic] in favour of anthropology and hunting"; and on one of my visits to Rome somewhere about this time, he desired me to read some chapters of the "Golden Bough", and more especially of Miss Mary Kingsley's travels in the hinterlands of the Congo, reminding me at the time of these very early readings together.

His mother possessed the gift of reading aloud in a most lucid, pleasing, and untiring way: thus during the period of his earlier schooldays at Rottingdean and at Eton, and during the last year or two of his brother Tommy's life, a good deal of reading aloud went on at home at odd times, both at Gisburne and in London. But I do not think Charles was as avid a listener as either Tommy or myself, though I remember distinctly his enjoyment of bits of Pickwick and the Legend of Montrose and Waverley — this amounted to delight or even transport; but it was always rather a case of "bits" with him — as, I imagine, with most people. Thus in Waverley I remember his pleasure — we all shared it, being fond of and used to horse-dealers — at the bit when Lieutenant Jinker (the horse-coper) transfers, with indignation, all the blame of Balmawhapple's catastrophe [*All Scottites know that at the battle of Preston the Laird of Balmawhapple was carried where he would not — into the enemy's fire — by the mare he was riding getting the better of him.*] from the mare to the Laird himself, who had insisted, against the Lieutenant's advice, in riding her in a martingale instead of with a running ring on the snaffle rein; and he was always on the look out for the Baron of Bradwardine's dissertations on feudal tenures and ancient law. In the same way he valued the tactical canons and commentaries of Captain Dalgetty and his martial affection for his model, Gustavus Adolphus. But Charles got on regrettably well without either Thackeray or Dickens. I don't think that he had ever read any of the former until the time of his convalescence at the Blue Sisters Convent at Malta. He then wrote to me and to Mrs. Cornish discriminating appreciations of Pendennis and Vanity Fair: Sir Pitt Crawley's ways and his establishments in London and in Hampshire pleased him especially.

On the other hand, his loyalty to Surtees, dating almost from the nursery, was all that could be desired. Alas! his mother never cared about Surtees, though she delighted in and often re-read "Market Harborough," so Charles read this author to himself or with me; we constantly discussed and considered together the teaching of those admirable novels. Upon the whole we agreed in preferring Surtees's quieter treatment of life and character to the Hogarthian or Rowlandson manner which the author manages with success indeed, but with exaggeration. Thus we liked best the by-products and sidelights of his close serio-comic observation — his description of the look of a landscape, the feel of the weather, of country houses and country gentlemen or their horses and their habits. In short, we felt more at home with Mr. Jawleyford and Mr. Sponge than with Lord Scamperdale and Mr. Jorrocks.

Coming back for a moment to "bits": in the days I am thinking of I was — and am still — fond of reading Biographies [*Charles and I both read too much from the "Index" i.e. the bits we fancied or wanted. However, in the family I held the record of having read the whole of Archbishop Benson's Life from cover to cover. This feat was held to be in the nature of an exploit.*] and Letters, and I sometimes administered a dose all round from this sort of book. He usually approved of my selection, but seldom discussed or elaborated the point or the argument as his mother would, and he never read that sort of book himself.

I do not think he meddled much with English Poetry: though he had a haphazard sort of acquaintance with its notables. Pope he neglected, and when he was about thirteen dismissed as an ingenious writer. When at Rome he was absorbed in Dante and read it in Italian, but as we were not on common ground I paid little attention to several things he said to me about this. I got on better when, as he often did, he commended to me the adventures of the Odyssey and the justice and vitality of its epithets and figures. Passages from Greek plays, too, of the more cheerful sort — not fateful or tragic — he sometimes called my attention to on the same grounds of beauty, truth, or charm. Times of instant loss and sorrow are the common heritage of most families. On one of those occasions — when it seems difficult to plead justification and impossible to furnish assent — I remember reading him with admiration and some sense of healing Johnson's lines on the trite thesis that what is decreed is best. The poet eulogizes the hard task of cajoling comfort out of any human theories of consolation. He seeks and finds it elsewhere:

> *Yet when the scene of sacred presence fires,*
> *And strong devotion to the skies aspires,*
> *Pour forth thy fervours for a healthful mind.*
> *Obedient passions and a will resigned:*
> *For Love, which scarce collective man can fill;*
> *For Patience, sovereign o'er transmuted ill;*
> *For Faith, that panting for a happier seat*
> *Counts death kind Nature's signal of retreat —*
> *With these Celestial Wisdom calms the mind.*
> *And makes the Happiness she does not find.*

They left him cold; indeed he never shared my views of eighteenth-century taste. Dealing himself in simple and unfurbished ideas, the eighteenth-century formal treatment of the emotions — laying them out, as it were, in avenues and groves and gazebos — was not to his liking or, at all events, found no room in his philosophy. In the same way he cared little or nothing for the Essayists of the *Spectator*. Their dignity and classicism he respected, but he thought their regard for equipoise and elegance often whittled away and denaturalized the real thing. I now come to his relations with the Independent Labour Party, but cannot fix with any exactness their beginnings; anyhow he took to this kind of thing — at least to Socialism— whilst he was still at Eton. An Eton friend of his writes that as he first remembered him in 1902, he did not realize him as a "budding Socialist"; it was not until 1905, he writes, that this side appeared and shone out fully. "Then came the intense sympathy with the Russian people— that £75 collection after a public meeting, portraits of Father Gapon all round his room — half in joke and half serious — and Tolstoi always to the fore." At this time I found it difficult to account for this new departure, having regard to his Quietest aptitude for making light of the best and worst of things as they came his way. But still, I was always aware of an extreme and eager susceptibility to Causes. In 1911 he writes to his friend T. Lascelles, from the Villa Rosebery at Naples, "I am a great exponent of the Doctrine of Divine Economy, and I do not quarrel when I see no chance to convert"; but in the earlier phases of his I.L.P. associations nothing of this appeared: Divine Economy was in flagrant disgrace long before that — so was a very old friend of mine who owned property at Hoxton. When Charles was still at his private school he became much interested in a Hoxton mission and Hoxton affairs, and "property" came in for serious censure. Yet his Socialism — I use this meaningless word for lack of a better — was of quite a good-natured sort. Mr. Goldwin Smith predicted that the triumphs of plutocracy and of Grosvenor Square would end by making him an American citizen; but Charles had no quarrel with plutocracy, or with Grosvenor Square; they were in themselves Causes, and so respectable; nor did he ever bother about persons or their views. For instance, in the days when he favoured nationalization of the raw material of industry — including our few family acres — and a comprehensive reconstruction of society, he never weakened in his liking for the landed gentry, the amusements of the leisured, and the Anglican clergy. Even the one or two important nobles who from time to time he encountered did not appear to make any disagreeable impression on him; indeed he often commended their spacious ways of providing outdoor pleasures and good fare for themselves and others. At one time Charles was alleged to have flown the red necktie of extreme opinions; but a revolution would have had to proceed in due course of law — so I understood, and at the time he most favoured the nationalization of land he told me that he approved of some form of material compensation for the landlords — not indeed as a matter of abstract right, but of conventional equity. In short, Charles would never have agreed with Bernhardi that law was only a makeshift.

In our conversations about Labour he never seemed much concerned with the economics of the problems; for instance, the relation of Capital to Labour, cutting of prices, underselling, margins of profit, etc. Nothing of this sort seemed of any essential concern — he was pervaded with the notion that something or other might be evolved from nowhere in particular and applied to Labour conditions, which would anticipate the contingencies and remedy the ills inseparable from the vicissitudes of our present industrial system. This conjecture never seemed to derive from Mill and the Utilitarians — it had its origin in some counsel of perfection, at times so little palpable in his own mind as to be not easily defined in conversation, nor, as far as I know, did he ever seek to appease his discontents at the nature of things as they were, with his pen. Yet he never seemed bewildered either by the variety or by the magnitude of his tasks. I enjoyed this Socialist or Fabian period, and was sorry in a way when its blood-heat passed off. But this inability to solidify notions by words was certainly a bar to the fuller comprehension of his ideals. However, Charles was eminently practical. I felt that he had things in his mind which were capable of practical expression, which some day he would express.

But the day came when he abandoned these Castles in Spain and resorted to the Sidney Webbs. I use the term generically. The remedies for the race— at this time wholly comprehended and involved in Labour — were to be prescribed regulations, by-laws and returns, based on statistics and worked out to decimals. I was able to lend him two or three books of this dismal gospel, and I got him more from the London Library. Yet, curiously enough, I do not remember seeing him read this sort of book, though I suppose he did. Mine still have a few unintelligible marginal markings and notes, but he added none — they are my own. Nor did I ever see him taking notes, or come across notes of his; although at the time he was reading hard and successfully for Greats he did a great deal of it in my sitting-room at Gisburne, which he much favoured when at home. But let me return to his relations with the I.L.P. The day came when he elected to be received into its bosom; we were neither pleased nor displeased. His mother thought it a mistake to contract himself out of being helped by the machinery and caucus support of either of the two great recognized parties — at that time a condition of adoption and grace — but she was reassured by Mr. A. J. Balfour, who was mildly interested and approving. Indeed, he pointed out to her that Charles would get all sorts of experience and some sort of special knowledge which might be of more use to him in after-life than if he kept Selling Platers or ran an actress. I was present and I heartily concurred. The ceremonies took place at Blackburn, and I rather think Mr. and Mrs. Snowden were his hosts for the occasion; anyhow, either then or very soon after he enjoyed their hospitality. True, he returned to Gisburne with the measles, but he made lighter of this testimony of zeal for the real thing than his mother or an apprehensive family circle did. He always spoke with great pleasure and satisfaction of the interest and experience of his sojourn at Blackburn. After this initiation, for I dare say a year or so, he appeared to be conducting a regular correspondence with various "Comrades". He lived and moved encumbered with papers, returns, and leaflets; received and wrote many letters, and set up a business-like yellow leather dispatch-box of the shape and size now standardized by serious-minded persons. This *vade mecum* was constantly being mislaid or left in trains, but it bore a charmed life. This was not a cheerful phase, and he often seemed to be brooding over the intractable anomalies of a troublesome world. Still, there was light as well as shade. One day a reception of the I.L.P. and a tea-party took place at Gisburne; speeches were made by leading Extremists slightly cramped in style by their courteous reservations in favour of one particular park and one particular proprietor. Mr. Clough, the Member for our division, made a capital, if unexpected, speech, all but rebuking Charles for having acted hastily in cutting himself off from the traditions to which it had pleased God to call him.

Why he left the Independent Labour Party I never discovered — "Wise men change their minds — fools never" is a good Yorkshire adage, but I can hardly think it was on the alleged ground of an attack in some silly paper on Lord Lovat's or our own family at the time of his sister Laura's marriage. Anyhow, he changed, and he certainly came to disapprove of their more recent methods. Latterly he said I was more of a Socialist than he was, and I remember his telling me when he elected to spend four months' leave from his diplomatic post at Rome in Indian travel, that his interest now was to see the working of the Imperial machine, and to get to know some of the men who worked it. The same friend whom I quoted writes, "I last saw him in Rome after his Socialist views had changed, and found him immersed in anthropology." Possibly he never lost his early interest, but it became platonic and critical. Thus he writes to T. Lascelles, August 25, 1911, on the Labour situation at home: "It is appalling. I feel the Labour grievance as strongly as ever, but I've lost faith in most of the remedies I used to believe in. If only they could get back to the old sober trade unionism and to collective bargaining on the same lines. But a change of spirit in most of the trades unions is required before this is achieved. They are shockingly out of hand — except the miners and the great cotton trade organizations."

Sir Rennell Rodd in his impressions of Charles, which come later on, is of opinion that he would have done well in diplomacy, and I believe his resignation would have been viewed with regret on public grounds by one or two others competent to judge of his merits and possibilities. After his first wound Charles was given the opportunity of returning to Foreign Office work. They were short-handed in Downing Street, and I was told that the suggestion that he should return — his year's fighting leave being nearly up — was conveyed to him in kind and even complimentary terms. He never mentioned anything of this to me; but an Eton and Balliol friend of Charles, Captain Bruce Ottley, A.S.C., writes me that the Foreign Office letter offering him special and interesting work reached Charles at Alexandria. Then and there he sat down and declined it.

"It happened in this way. Charles and I had made friends with the Assistant Provost-Marshal, and we had arranged to go together in search of some native ammunition stores which had been located close to my camp at El Zahiria. When Charles arrived about 7 p.m. I had just received orders to return to England on the next morning. I told him this, and he told me that he had just been offered a job at home, but that he felt he could not accept it. As far as I can remember his actual words were: "I feel I ought to see this thing through, and I can't bear to think of leaving the wonderful fellows of my battalion. He then asked me if he might write some letters for me to take back with me. I took him to my tent, which was pitched on the sand outside the mess-house, and he wrote by the meagre light of a hurricane-lamp that flickered in the cold wind that always blows in the evening in the desert." Yet I am certain that he liked his work at Rome, as I visited him there in two successive years. And in 1911, when he was beginning to learn his business at the Foreign Office, he writes to one of his most regular correspondents, "I love my work and am thrilled by *Weltpolitik*; I am not very good at it, but it is routine work up to the present and what excites me is not what I actually do but what I read and the papers I see".

All this is now but idle speculation. The War had taken possession of him with all the intensity of the Crusades of his younger days. Perhaps even with some of their glamour — not much of this, though. This War was a very different affair and occasion. In Hooker's phrase, he looked upon our going into it as "the strong and invincible remonstrance of sound reason." He was no longer a boy liable to the Tolstois and the Gapons and the Fabians. The Call had come upon him as the Holy Ghost came down upon the apostles — as a sudden great sound in the likeness of fiery tongues.

In his last letter to me, written from the hospital ship Gascon on August 26th — he died on the 28th — his only complaint is of this third and tiresome interruption of the business in hand. From the nature of the wound I think he must have been in suffering, or anyhow in discomfort equivalent to suffering, but this letter is as clearly and freely written in respect of point and clearness as any he ever

HMHS Gascon

wrote me, and the envelope is addressed with unusual distinctness and vigour of pencil. He speaks of the hours going slowly and of his not feeling up to much reading — though he stuck to his books throughout — owing to the monotony of the fixed supine position enforced by his surgeon, but beyond that there is no word of complaint, only regret that this last wound may prove a longer job than the others.

This is what Mr. Mayne, the Chaplain of the Gascon, wrote me at the time; it is dated August 29, 1915. Charles had died at 7 o'clock in the evening on the 28th, after being taken aboard from Cape Helles somewhere about midnight on the 25th. "He had very skilled attention and very careful nursing while on board, and was, I know, a wonderful patient. He never complained or even spoke of his wound, and if he had pain he bore it very bravely and patiently. But I believe that he did not have too much pain. We talked together sometimes, but he was easily tired, and one could not stay with him long. My great regret is that I did not know yesterday that he was so much worse until rather late, and when I went to see him he was unconscious. It is seldom comparatively that one sees a man in such command of himself, and so controlled. The books at his bedside spoke for his literary taste, [*Amongst these— I have the list— were the Purgatories of Dante, the Koran, a Turkish grammar, the Oxford book of Italian verse, the Life and Works of Goethe, a d'Annunzio novel, and the Imitation of Christ. — R.*] and the day before he died I lent him a copy of the poems of Rupert Brooke whom we both knew, and who was in the Howe Battalion with your son.

As I write we are waiting for the boat to take his body ashore at Mudros, where the burial will take place tomorrow. He will lie almost within sound of the heavy guns." It is very difficult to hit on the seemly balance of anything of the kind I am trying to write, especially having regard to our close relationship and to our always having been great friends and a good deal together. Memory takes me tightly by the hand and leads me back to all kinds of scenes and incidents and places in his company: to the flat horizons and the tulips and the picture galleries of Holland; to charming Munich, its opera and its Bach-abends, its overheated but excellent hotel, its superlative caviare and beer; to the grey-green sweep of the Roman Campagna and hounds running over the *stationatas*; to Milan and to Bergamo; to the steep hills and stones above Helmsdale; to Ross's Hotel and our symposia with Mr. Ross himself— lovely August weather; liver- and-white pointers of beauty and staunchness; to many talks and rides and walks; to London theatres and pavements; to the uplands and rough pastures of Wigglesworth and Bowland. But I am exceeding and straying outside the confines of my task, and I must let his letters speak for themselves, and rely upon some of his friends to deal with other things outside my own experiences and knowledge of Charles. It would not be possible, and I do not think it would be becoming, for me to attempt any estimate of the higher quality and value of the few years of his mortal life.

So may it be, that so dead yesterday.

No sad-eyed ghost, but generous and gay.

May serve your memories like almighty wine.

I know not where these lines come from or whose they are; their grammar is certainly not unimpeachable. Years ago I copied them on to a foreign envelope, and came across it again the other day. As far as a few words can assert that the memories of Life dispute with success the supremacy of Death they seem to manage a good deal.

RIBBLESDALE.

October 1916.

The following letters, chiefly to Eton and Oxford friends, mark the close of Charles's Balliol life. The examination for Greats at Oxford was over and he had got his First. To this success perception as well as knowledge of Greek history had contributed; but, perhaps, the chief factor all along was his anxiety about his mother's health and his great desire to give her the pleasure of his First. He now went to read in Germany, but still clung to every association formed at Eton and at his University. Mr. Lascelles was a great friend who graduated at Trinity, Oxford, and then prepared to go up for the Foreign Office examination. Their correspondence lasted for years. — R.

To A. F. Lascelles.

Gisburne,
July 23, 1909.

My viva was as follows:

On July 22nd, Lister entered the schools punctually at 9.30, and repaired to lecture-room No. 7, where the Rev. J. Walker and F. C. Schiller were closeted. Lister was ordered to return at 9.45. At 9.45 he was put through five rather awkward minutes by Walker, on the distinction between chattel, slave, and apprentice knave. His triumph was only partial. Walker beamed and was affability and kindness itself. I don't think it can have made very much difference to my class, whatever that might have been.

The best of luck to you, dear Tommy. [*Baffling in this respect as the boy Ascanius, Mr. Lascelles, whose baptismal names are Alan Frederick, is and has always been called "Tommy".— R.*] I shall feel quite hipped if you don't get your First.

To the Same.

Grand Hotel Continental, Munich,
August 2, 1909.

Many thanks for your delightful letter. It is very kind of you to think so well of me. I fear your confidence in my powers is rather misplaced. I seldom feel anything like a great man, or one who will in any way particularly justify his existence. I am glad it was "all right," because (1) it gave pleasure to me, my relations, and friends; (2) it gave annoyance to some who think of me — if they think of me at all — as generally good for nothing. I'm afraid such things as Firsts are largely matters of luck. I got questions that suited me, though I didn't think so at the time of the exam. I wish I had the power of feeling more thrilled, and more confident in myself, like Julian. Still, I am very happy. The odds against Firsts are more or less what you say, I think; and you certainly did capitally in getting your Second, seeing your Oxford life was so full in other ways, and that you did not work much till last year. I wish you had got a First, and thought you might, when you knew so much Greek history. We got such good papers in the Greek history and it would have been pleasanter, after we'd talked over so much Greats shop together, to be in the same class. Still, it is no use repining. I have just been at Bayreuth. I saw Parsifal and Lohengrin. Parsifal well done, but bad singers in the leading parts; Lohengrin is probably the worst he wrote, but as performed at Bayreuth it was perfectly glorious. The choruses made one weep — they were so beautifully done. [*When quite a little boy Charles was often unable to restrain himself at passages in plays which he admired or objected to. I remember his being profoundly stirred at Bernard Shaw's 'Major Barbara'. On these occasions he would get up in his seat and loudly express his admiration or censure — though he kept himself in better order at concerts or opera. Yet music had the same kind of effect upon him. He forgot himself, with most of us a difficult thing to do. — R.*] I went with my landlady, who showed me all her relatives. I took her into a sort of supper, and on coming out was confronted by her husband, who asked me some question

GBS

in German, to which I replied *"Ja"*. Lord knows what the question was — it might have been whether I was trying to supplant him, for all I knew. This sort of thing, however, improves one's German. Munich is in the throes of a Mozart Festspiel. You come out too late for the Festspiel, but will see the Ring as often as you please in the normal course of events. Do come out sooner than the 25th.

To the Same.
Grand Hotel Continental, Munich,
August 3, 1909.

I only got your kind wire yesterday owing to change of address, etc. Yes, it is satisfactory. A First is a kind of unknown quantity - those who get it are told it is of great importance. Those who don't are consoled with the thought that it doesn't matter what sort of degree one takes, etc. — such is life.

I heard Parsifal and Lohengrin done at Bayreuth. Lohengrin, a most magnificent performance, quite perfect, except for a rather poor Ortrud. Parsifal not so well performed, but what an opera! The choruses were magnificently sung. The orchestra not so good as the Munich Orchestra, but very fine. I didn't find any particular "atmosphere" at Bayreuth. Just the same sort of thing as you get at the Festspiel at Munich. Save that at Bayreuth there is an immensely powerful cult of the Wagner family, and the railway officials are inordinately stupid. There is a good old Opera House at Bayreuth, seventeenth century and perfectly preserved. Well worth seeing. More anon.

To the Same.
Ohmstrasse I, Munich.
(No date—prob. mid-October 1909.)

How I liked your letter, but how it roused regrets in me. I'll tell you why. It is very unlikely I shall winter in Munich — I *can't* learn German in Munich. Nothing but English and Americans in pensions, and such-like, and also even if you get out of pension circles, you always meet people who talk English or French better than one talks German oneself, so it comes to the same thing; and German is a helpless talk for the ingenuous if he remains here.

It is too sad. My plans are to go in for the Merton Prize Fellowship; if I get it (!!!) to stop in Oxford for a year reading for All Souls, and try and get something of a Donship at the Alma Mater, which I want badly to do, as I am very interested in book-learning just at present. If I *don't get it*, to come back to the Fatherland, and grub up the language in some small, boring place where one don't see English — I contemplate the latter alternative as practically certain — and then try to pass my diplomatic in August 1910. It's bloody because I love Munich.

I've made a few acquaintances, whom you are sure to get to know — a Graf von Leyden and his sister, Lady Blennerhasset, the English Minister and wife — pretty well; and the Austrian and Italian Ministers' wives — only sort of card-leaving terms; also an opera singer, a Miss Maud Fay, who will be away till the middle of November. There are no Germans here at this time of year, as it is the *saison morte*. I may be in Munich on my return to the Fatherland, for a few days, but I don't even know that. My town will probably be Cassel, of all places. How sad about Ned Lawley! I hadn't seen it. It is curious how all these lads who are our contemporaries die violent deaths. Dicky Gibbs was a tragedy.

I sail on the 25th for the Merton P.F. [*Prize Fellowship*] exam. So I shan't see you unless I get a glimpse previous to departure. But I've made up my mind to be thoroughly bored for this winter, and Cassel seems unavoidable.

I have just read the *au secours* incident in Anatole France's "Pingouins," and laughed much. Julian *will* not write to me. I have been frightfully happy here. English friends through the whole time. Eddy here now. Have seen Kaiser to-day. I cry at the thought of not meeting you here, but feel I *must* learn German. Please take this as a tear-stained epistle from a strong man greatly unstrung.

Kaiser Wilhelm II

To the Same.

Gisburne,
October 12, 1909.

I have written to my mother to write to a certain Graf von Leyden about you. I knew him at Munich and loved him — the best of men, but I don't feel I am in a quite strong enough position to give you a letter to him, as I was but an introducee myself. Mother, however, is a great friend of his, and he would do anything she would ask him. Leyden lives with his sister, a certain Lady Blennerhasset, an *esprit fort*, who will frighten you at first, but whom you will ultimately like very much. …

I did not get the Merton touch; my History paper was the best. This is pleasing, as one Giles was competing, who has for two years lectured at Edinburgh on Greek history; but my Philosophy only second class, as in Greats. So I shall be coming out to Germany again, and will see you all right for a day or two, which will be delightful.

I am living quite a Julianesque life here, alone in the house, and hunting and shooting wild pheasants in-the-hedgerows sort of business, which I always find fun enough for a modest performer like myself.

I only hope Leyden will be in Munich; anyway you will see Lady Blennerhasset. She wants fearless handling — not after the patrician fashion, viz. rather liberal conversation, as she is old-fashioned — but quiet and persevering gentlemanliness. …

To the Same,

Hoherweg 12, Göttingen,
December 4, 1909.

I am sorry you can't do a Berlin. Life is really remarkably grossartig in that city. … Reginald [*Benson*] I think wants to go to Berlin rather than Munich for his Ausflug from his studies, because it is the Haupstadt, and he is more likely to see more of the soldiers he will have to confront in the coming German war. Oscar Fernsemer I know well: he is the son of my pension lady, and a very good fellow. I saw little of him because I was grinding like a galley-slave the whole two months I was there, but liked him very much. My feelings are also that I ought to see Berlin. … I am reading much newspaper matter here, and getting quite an expert in Triple Alliances, etc.

I rather agree with Elcho on the four-poster question, but then I am an old-fashioned moralist, and not always in sympathy with the spirit of my age. [*This refers to some amateur tableaux which were given at the Court Theatre about this time.*

Passages in the life of St. Ursula were portrayed. Miss Cynthia Charteris played the St. Ursula of Carpaccio's picture, notwithstanding her — on this occasion Roman — father's disapproval. — R.]

To Edward Speyer.

Hoherweg 12, Göttingen,
December 22, 1909.

Thank you very much for your last letter, which I delayed to answer till I had been to Berlin. I went and I saw the "Leonardo" Bust. It is certainly not by Lucas. I think it is quite out of the question when one looks at Lucas's other work; whether it is a Leonardo is another matter. In my poor judgment I don't think it is, as it has not the Leonardo smile, and has the hair done in a way not usual in Leonardo's, and in general has not the charm one would expect from a Leonardo. Bode has been much chaffed, and has taken the matter very much to heart. He apparently spent £8,000 entirely on his own responsibility and unassisted by the advice of any committee; it seems a curious position of affairs that so much responsibility should be in one man's hands. I thought the Kaiser Friedrich Museum a wonderful collection — the most wonderful I have seen, I think, as all schools are pretty adequately represented. I expected to find Berlin very much more ugly than it is. It is a modern and rather mushroom growth, like the Hohenzollern dynasty; but there is a certain air of efficiency about it which pleases me a good deal, and a general impression of work and good management. The Sieger Allée is not a thing of beauty, and the Royal Family is somewhat lavish with the statues which meet you every turn you take; but they compare favourably enough with the gentlemen in frock-coats and trousers outside the House of Commons, who hold scrolls in their hands. There is a grand ice rink in Berlin, where I performed with the skates and much interfered with the people practising elaborate figures. From all I heard the *hohe gesellschaft* is confined to a very small circle — some eight or nine great families and one or two embassies. The professors and artists have their own circles. This seems curious to the English. I don't think the Berlin Opera is anything very much out of the common. We heard the Walkyrie poorly given, and a good level performance of Siegfried — very fine, really. Also a good performance of La Tosca — remarkably good for a German company in a subordinate opera-house. We didn't go to any plays, as I have to read a play before I can see it appreciatively. I have seen "Moral" again, which, if you remember, we saw together at Munich.

To A. F. Lascelles.

174 Rue de la Pompe, Paris,
March 27, 1910.

Please excuse pencil and delays in replying to your first-class letter of Friday, 18th, which filled me with delight. … I am afraid I shall have to go to Scoones. I quite agree with what you say about Tristan not "gripping". I don't think, however, I put it "top of all". I think it worse than the Meistersinger and the Ring, though the Liebestod and other little bits are the best things he ever wrote.

My life here is very hard-worked — an occasional play, and Faust last Wednesday, and Samson et Dalila next ditto — otherwise uneventful. I don't like my philological studies and loathe the grammar and pronunciation difficulties, which are always cropping up. In spite, however, of the dullness of the work I've been very happy, on the whole, abroad — both in Germany and here. In Germany I was with a really charming family, though very pious, and met heaps of people I liked; and here I am also having fun. Madame is an excellent woman, and the most gaulois talker about the mistresses of the divers French kings and the misdemeanours of the past and present rulers of France. I think she likes me; she is certainly lavish in her compliments, and says I am handsome, well-conducted, and likely to be much desired. This is not a prospect that refreshes me very much. My misogyny is still burning with a bright and pure flame.

I am rather in a phase of a sort of melting-pot scepticism all round, which I fancy will last for some time. I am not, however, very troubled about it. I like Philip Sassoon much and he really quite amuses me.

If you see Twiggy [*Anderson*], you might give him my address; if he can spare any of his time from the dissipations that are the duty of visiting football teams, as I should like to see him. Well, this is a dull letter, but written in a palpitation of excitement at me prospect of seeing you at the end of the month.

To the Same.

New Milton, Hants,
July 12, 1910.

I don't know if I shall be able to manage 20th to 25th, as I may be doing a riding-tour with Julian Grenfell those days.

… I am reading Ferrero, who is a great artist. I am all alone in a gloomy hotel, as I have been smitten with cold, and I can't turn into my mother's mansion yet as I may be infectious for a day or two. Ferrero on Cæsar makes me weep. It is a much more human presentation than Mommsen's, and I am feeling rather sad. …

Julian Grenfell

To Mrs. Speyer.

38 Bedford Mansions, W.C.,
August 28, 1910.

Just one line of very warm thanks for my delightful week-end at Ridgehurst. [*Mrs. Edward Speyer introduced Charles in many ways to the best traditions of modern music. He especially admired the songs of Brahms, some of them expressly written for her. Charles often enjoyed the hospitality of Ridgehurst with his friends Ferdinand and Edward Speyer — Eton and Balliol friends — the latter was Mendelssohn Scholar at Oxford in 1909. — B. W. C.*] It was most enjoyable and very refreshing to the poor jaded worker. It was most kind of you and Mr. Speyer to ask me. Thanks to my iron constitution, I don't feel exhausted after my labours at tennis and croquet, but quite like a giant refreshed. Eddy had lunch with me in town and was sped as a parting guest to Waterloo, where I hope he caught his train to the New Forest. Please give my respects to any of your charming family who may yet be with you, and not scattered by the general break-up that takes place on Monday. Thank you again, and Mr. Speyer too, for all your kindness to me.

To A. F. Lascelles.

Gisburne,
September 30, 1910.

Thanks awfully for your epistle. I am very much afraid there will be no one at Gis. all these days after Tuesday, till the wedding is over. [*His sister Laura's wedding, which took place in October. — R.*] I have to worry about medicals, etc., though to judge from the physique of the diplomats known to me, I don't fancy that stern demands will be made on my soundness. … I hope you have been enjoying your Scotland. I saw Guy B. [Benson] at the Inverness meeting ball. He said you had been unlucky with the stags, but later reports of your deeds ring like the account of a triumphal progress. I have been having quite fun with my Scotland. I have been shooting with varied success, and making further acquaintance of my new in-laws, all of whom I like very much. Heavens, what a dull letter! Alan Parsons is here and in very good form.

To the Same.

24 Gloucester Place, W.,
October 18, 1910.

*Harold
Nicholson*

... I am very happy, in full swing at the Foreign Office, effectively impeding the work of my department, under the patient rule of Nic., [*The Hon. Harold Nicolson.*] who is a most excellent man, and whom I find capital company. I am busy, and tied down, which I like. I *loathe* being at a loose end. ... Well, good-bye, old friend — a line abt. Thursday night, if combined action is in any way possible. I am a member of the St. James's Club, so fear nothing of what man can do unto me.

To Alan Parsons.

Cavendish Hotel,
January 2, 191 1.

This is how to treat Madame —: [*The mistress of a French pension.*] (1) Treat her as a marchioness, capable of unbending, but still very high in the social, moral, and intellectual hierarchy. (2) Laugh at her Rabelaisian stories, even if you don't understand. (3) Feign affection for the house cat, which stinks. As to the dpg, you can take your own line, (4) Don't ever find her out in conversation; she is very glib on many questions, historical and literary, but wildly inaccurate. She has to be treated as infallible. (5) Try and check her talking about the exam, at meal-times. She can be a bore on this subject. Buddha is decidedly preferable. (6) Madame loves conversation, so be talkative, but avoid too much blasphemy. It goes down with Madame, but not with Madame (7) Tolerate Madame *mère.*

To the Same.

I am staying at the Trinity Mission House with G. L. in his new sphere of influence. There is a programme of the day neatly framed in every room.

Breakfast	8 a.m.
Matins	8.30 a.m.
Prayers	9 a.m.
Luncheon	1 p.m.
Evensong	6.30 p.m.

I like the meals and hours of orison sandwiched in together. One might spend the whole day between the Lord's table and one's host's ditto. It is very characteristic of organized English churchmanship. ...

If I am a great exponent of the doctrine of Divine Economy, and do not quarrel when I have no chance to convert.

Laffan is in No. 38 for several days. I trust his yoke will be easy and his burden light. [*Some chambers where the regulations as to hours, light, and food were austerely conceived. — R.*]

To A. F. Lascelles.

Foreign Office,
February 18, 1911.

Many thanks for your delightful letter, which sent a ray of sunshine into our rather grey official lives, and cheered us up wonderful. I am glad you like Madame, and get on with her so well. She is a great dear, and a capital talker — wildly inaccurate whenever she makes a statement, but clever as a monkey. I should have loved to have seen Madame's passage at arms with Mr. — I quite agree that he is not very formidable, owing to the spread of brain-rot over his system. Except for father's leg, [*Broken out hunting with the Duke of Beaufort's hounds, but most successfully plated and restored to me by Sir W. Arbuthnot Lane.— R.*] my life has been very happy lately. I love my work and am thrilled by *Weltpolitik*. I see the usual sort of people, and like my fellow-creatures. Nic. is quite the best man, and we get on like a house on fire. … I am not very good at my work, but it is routine up to the present, and what excites me is not so much what I actually do, but what I read and the papers I see, etc. We are flooded with *Weltpolitik* just now, and in a perfect orgie of secret papers. I am always finding secret telegrams in the trouser-pocket of my dress-clothes, and feeling a perfect fool; but it is no use minding — one must just do better next time. The thing thrills me, and I mean to go on. Besides, I'm not the only *gaffeur* in the office. I am sorry to be so bucking and tedious; but my gods live in Whitehall, and it is very much my centre; and one can't help talking about a place where one is a fixture from 11 to 6.30 every day. … I have been living down at the Trinity Mission House, a very jolly sojourn, though I use the place rather as a hotel. It is very cheap. It is so curious finding anybody for whom women in any shape or form simply don't exist. I always feel very fish-like myself, as compared to others, but I am a positive Don Juan compared to , who takes no sort of interest in the business, and is hardly on speaking terms with any woman outside his family. … Father, I am sorry to say, is going to be operated on to-morrow, but there is every chance of the show being a success. It is a question of wiring the bones. Give my love to the boys, and to Madame, and to Madame *mère*.

To the Same.

May 8, 1911.

Your letter has helped me very much. Also your being cheerful at breakfast. It was just what I wanted. Yes, it was horribly sudden. I was dancing up to within an hour of mother's death; [*Lady Ribblesdale died at Wimbledon on May and after a long illness, fought out with courage and patience and unselfishness, which Charles constantly extolled and recalled. — B. W. C.*] it is a sickening thought. One comes out of all this feeling for the moment like a whipped cur — full of remorse for shortcomings in one's sonship and with all one's comfortable groovey life knocked out of its lines. Even the fact that mother was ill so long does not seem any adequate preparation. Still, there it is — come back soon, and see me.

... Berlin at the outbreak of war

An Appreciation By
The Rt. Hon. Sir Rennell Rodd, P.C., G.C.V.O.

Rennell Rodd

Among those of the younger generation who have served with me, or whom I have had the interest of launching on their diplomatic career, there have been few as able and more wholly lovable than Charles Lister. I feel sure that none of his own contemporaries would grudge him such an appreciation, and that all of them would be ready to endorse it.

In the little families which are constituted by our missions abroad life is as a rule very intimate, and the members learn each other's virtues and failings very quickly. The head of the mission is the father of his family and relations are almost always very cordial. He has exceptional opportunities of studying the character of his staff, which forms a small group isolated in alien surroundings. This is particularly the case in the Embassy at Rome, where the summer life at Posillipo is one of constant camaraderie. I feel therefore that I am qualified to speak with due knowledge of a very dear friend.

Charles Lister joined my staff in the spring of 1911. He was the son of old friends and the nephew of a colleague and almost a contemporary, to whom I had always been greatly attached. I remember making rhymes and pictures for his elder brother, who also gave his life for his country, in the grim Somali wastes. He came, moreover, from my old college at Oxford, and there is no stronger link than that which unites Balliol men all the world over. He was therefore at once adopted into the family, and we made his more complete acquaintance on a short yachting cruise from Leghorn to Naples in the opening of the radiant Italian summer, visiting Elba and one or two of the islands on the way south. In the Villa Rosebery at Posillipo, near Naples, thanks to the generosity of the giver whose name it commemorates, the summer quarters of the Embassy are established. The Secretaries' house stands on the wall rising straight up from the sea above a little landing pier for bathers, and there the children who are in or on the water all day long at once made him their own. The verdict of children and their intuitive perception of character is quick and unerring. There was not a moment's shyness on either side. The fine open face, the kindly voice, the unflinching honest eyes and the warm-hearted humorous smile made them at home with him at once. One little boy, then seven or eight, always endeavoured to sit next to him at meals, and their conversation ranged over the strangest and most abstruse subjects. Peter propounded unanswerable problems, and Charles considered them with the gravity of an affair of state, discussing them with professional earnestness and inexhaustible good humour. It was good to listen to them. Mister Lister was soon quoted as an oracle. Those children have seen many members of the staff come and go and retain their friends in affectionate memory. Certainly there is no one of them all more fondly remembered. When I asked Peter if he was not distressed to have lost his old friend — it was more than two years since he had left us — he said truthfully, with a retrospective smile, "He was a real nice fellow — he was always asking my advice and taking his". Charles Lister displayed two characteristics which are but rarely found in combination — the spirit of the sportsman and the lover of adventure with the instincts of the scholar gentleman. He was of the type which would have found its right environment in the large-horizoned Elizabethan days, and he would have been of the company of Sidney and Raleigh and the Gilberts and boisterously welcomed at the Mermaid Tavern. He would sometimes pretend that he was divided in his mind whether the life of the fox-hunter or that of the college don would have most tempted him if he had only had to follow his instincts. But in reality he was much too deeply imbued with the sense of duty and the higher obligations of life to have devoted himself to the former to the exclusion of graver things. He was, however, seriously drawn towards the student's life and was a deep and thoughtful reader with a very retentive memory. No doubt he was also a hard and fearless rider, without the graces of the natural horseman, and here in the Roman Campagna with its long deceptive reaches of grass and its sudden and unexpected obstacles his impetuosity often alarmed his friends. But there, as in the sea in the bay of Naples, where currents ran strong and seas were high, as afterwards in the deadly battle area of Gallipoli, he was physically the most fearless of men. In the more difficult tests of moral courage I have known no braver soul.

At college and after college he had strong Socialistic leanings, and I do not think he ever discarded the appreciation of human destiny which his generous heart inspired. He only outgrew the atmosphere of the exponents of the Socialistic creed with whom he had at one time associated, the limitations and even prejudices which he felt had become as fetters to them, and ended by believing them to be not very practical people. A young man, said the late King Oscar of Sweden, who has not been a Socialist before he is five-and-twenty shows that he has no heart, a young man who remains one after five-and-twenty shows that he has no head. It is high testimony to his lovable character that at the time when he was identifying himself with the extremer votaries of Socialistic propaganda he made no enemies among the most reactionary of his contemporaries, who never resented his earnest opinions and always recognized as his due the *aqua potestas quodlibet audendi*.

Whatever he undertook he endeavoured to master. And so when he entered the Diplomatic Service he quickly became absorbed in his profession, and at that early age, when other interests are crowding in, he quickly acquired a perception and a grasp of foreign questions. Here in Italy he at once endeavoured to get into touch with the more serious as well as the social elements, and showed an ambition to be familiar with all the many facets of life. I have no doubt he would have been a very successful diplomatist had he lived, though he might not have appeared to be specially adapted for the profession. But he had a strong power of sympathy and a capacity for seeing things with the eyes of others, and he was conspicuously free from prejudices and preconceptions. His temperament was not, I think, so much creative and imaginative as reflective. He never shirked thinking a question out, and he thought for himself, not in grooves and under the limitations of convention; thus arriving at conclusions which were essentially his own and had the force which is conferred by sincerity. He not infrequently revised them, and was always the first to admit a mistaken appreciation which maturer experience had enabled him to correct. He was, moreover, most scrupulously conscientious in his conception of his duties, even in carrying out the duller and more mechanical ones. Most of us have had the experience in our earlier posts of the brilliant young colleague who could work with admirable application at what interested him personally, and in the lines where merit is acquired, but who was disposed to leave the routine and the orderly working of the official machine to others, Charles Lister was brilliant and capable, but he gave the same devotion to the lesser as to the greater things. He even made a strenuous but unavailing effort as an attaché to overcome a certain constitutional disability of harmonious movement, and master the accomplishments of the ball-room. His sense of humour was keen but always kindly, though he could be roused to generous indignation, and his enjoyment of life in all its phases was intense. After some two years of continuous service he became entitled to a long leave of absence, and devoted it to a visit to India. On his return he was appointed to Constantinople, to the sincere regret of his many friends in Rome, and especially of myself.

On the outbreak of war he volunteered for active service, to the great loss of the Civil Service, for men of his ability and sense of duty are rare, and can ill be spared. But it was characteristic of his generous and adventurous spirit, and he took his chance of sacrificing a brilliant career. His example would have been followed or anticipated by nearly all the younger members of the service, but authoritative steps were taken to prevent them from volunteering. Alas! he found the means. The toll of the Dardanelles has been a very heavy one, but of all the gallant souls who gave their lives in a forlorn hope on the disastrous shores of the Thracian Chersonese none died more deeply regretted, none sacrificed a fairer promise. As I myself draw nearer to the close of a long career abroad, with its numberless vicissitudes, friendships, acquaintances, and reflect on my many experiences, I realize that our two years of association in the Embassy at Rome have left me with a singularly bright memory of one of the largest natures and warmest hearts I have ever known. Of all the sorrows and the infamies which those who are responsible for these disastrous years have brought upon us, few have touched me personally with such bitterness of resentment as the loss of this most gallant soul and honourable gentleman, cut off in the flower of his days, who made the holy sacrifice to his country and the cause he felt so deeply.

Rome,
March 1916.

To A. F. Lascelles.

British Embassy, Rome,
August 17, 1911.

[The Roman letters are full of gossip, and an Editor consequently finds himself up against a host of living and justifiable susceptibilities. Besides many of the names of the illustrious Romans involved are more or less illegible or undefined. Mistakes in names or styles are always to be condemned. Further, some of all this refers to agreeable acquaintances I made when at Rome myself, and one or two are noted duellists. But, on the other hand, Charles's letters are so much himself that I have let some of the gossipy bits stand and have resorted to the paltry expedient of misleading initials as a way out of if not over a Pontine marsh of perplexity. — R.]

My life here is all it should be — just enough work to make one feel one is not a cumberer of the ground, pleasant colleagues, and a nice chief, full of go and interest. The "boys"? I feel very old; they are, of course, older than me. I long for one of you. I hope the diplomats are jolly in your year. I think one appreciates one's past much more if removed for some little time. I like my colleagues most awfully, though, they can't in the nature of things come up to the old times. They don't smile as much, or argue as loud, or make as many loose jokes, or rejoice in simple innocent pleasure like the old Balliolic Satyrs and Fauns. But one is melancholy on paper, and I am really radiantly happy out here. Just back from a wonderful yachting trip in the Ambassador's yacht. This week we go to Naples, though I feel anxious as to the prospect of too much sea-bathing, a form of amusement to which I have never been very partial.

I am much excited by Frazer's "Golden Bough" — magic, and that sort of thing — you must read it as soon as you've a moment's time. And I am looking about for some sort of outside subject to take up, and do some decent work on. It is vital, as one's brain is bound to go, in this kind of hack-work, which I don't think adds to the brain, though it sharpens the wits in just the way I want them sharpened. The efficiency of the Service appals me. I don't know where to turn, so many things here and in my books interest me so much. The hunting here will be first rate, great expanses of grass country, high timber, and little walls, and nailing hirelings. I am looking forward to it I wish you were here; you'd love it, and do it much better than me.

To the Same.
Villa Rosebery, Naples,
August 25, 1911.

Many thanks for your capital letter. I have always thought the Veto Bill a "politicians'" question, and I expect a good many other people think so too, now it has been dwarfed by Morocco and the strikes. I can't say I feel very happy about either of these last. The French Government is clearly very nervous, and the unfortunate Préfet de la Seine must be sweating with fear. I think they will be kept straight by French public opinion. The German game seems to be to wait for something to turn up — and it did to some extent in the shape of our Labour troubles, which I see The Times connects with the reluctance of the Germans to come to any terms, and to give German public opinion — roused to extravagant hopes by the opening moves of Wilhelm — time to subside, so as to permit said Wilhelm to climb down from his high horse with comparative safety. Unless he is prepared to face a war, he is bound to come out of the negotiations with rather less of a triumph than was expected by the pan-Germanic Press.

The Labour situation is appalling. I feel the Labour grievance as strongly as ever, but I've lost faith in most remedies I used to believe in. If only they could get back to the old sober trade unionism, and to collective bargaining on sane lines. But a change of spirit in most of the T.U.'s is required before this is achieved.

They are shockingly out of hand — except the miners and the great cotton trade organizations.

How horrible Civil Service logic sounds! I'm glad I didn't take it up. I thought of doing so at one time. Bunt Goschen, I hear, has contrived to escape Burlington House again. Did he hurt himself falling out of his balloon? How you would laugh at our bridge games here. … I do play badly! Auction bridge — the only sufferable card game. I am assured, however, that I am getting better.

To the Same.

Villa Rosebery, Naples,
August 31, 1911.

My colleagues are appreciative, and I'm very fond of them; but their vitality is at times rather low. Of course I've always been used to living with tremendously vital people, who all talk at once, and they are a little different from that class. I find I like sea-bathing much better than I thought, albeit I'm a very slow swimmer. The water here is marvellous, and keeps you up like a cork. I bathe twice a day with the children. I am ducked by the children and by the eldest girl, a great dear twelve years old, but the recent arrival of the naval attaché has distracted attention from myself, and he, poor man, spends most of his time under water. The museum in Naples, as Baedeker puts it, "repays inspection". I went over with the Ambassador, and was thus only able to cast a roving eye all round it. I was slightly compensated by a visit to the aquarium, where we gazed on the octopuses for about half an hour. They have all the grace of skirt-dancers, and wicked little eyes like the devil. Watching them is almost a vice in itself.

We live here *en famille*, and have lunch with the children. The youngest lately had his sixth birthday. He was informed by Lady R. that he couldn't really be six, as he was still unable to swim or read He was then informed by his little sister that he had no ambition. I think this a very false method. Lady R. has very different views from mine. But I am a great exponent of the doctrine of Divine Economy, and do not quarrel when I have no chance to convert. Well, good-bye my dear Tommy; mind you serve the examiners as they deserve.

To the Same.

Rome,
September 13, 1911.

I am glad you liked the Gisburne life, which sounds ideal. It is a good place, if only the shooting was better. How cruel to put Pat on the Boer pony! But he has not written to me, so it serves him right.

Morocco is bloody, however it turns out. We have saved our bacon — but the French? The Germans will get a damned sight more than they ought to have, without fighting, so Lord knows why they should be bellicose.

We shall be very soon leaving this place, which is sad. I've enjoyed it very much on the whole, and am very fond of the Ambassador and Lady Rodd. The Italian butler ought to spend a month or so at Oxford and learn how champagne should be handled — otherwise I've no cause for complaint.

They are having, possibly, an inter-Parliamentary conference at Rome in October, and Macaulay will be on us. It may be put off because of the cholera. Funny time to have conferences; in this season of distrust all round. I wonder what they will say. I am sure there was much more European solidarity in the twelfth century than there is to-day, for all their conferences and talkey-talkey shows. I hope you will get out here sometime before I leave, you will have two years, nearly, to do it in, as I don't so much as get home till October year at earliest. This isn't a bad plan, as one gets used to long spells abroad straight off. I have seen a dispatch from Bones [*R. T. Smallbones, of Trinity. On one occasion the Proctor would not believe that his name was authentic until it was spelt out for him over and over again.* — R.] — only think — about the Registration of Domestic Servants at St. Paul Loanda. He is now in charge. No more for the present. This is a poor letter in comparison with your purple emperor of a letter. Write to me about your Scotland, and give my love to George Vernon.

I have a piece of news for you. Cyril Bailey is going to be married to Miss Creighton, the daughter of the Bishop.

To the Same.

Rome,
October 1, 1911.

It is the very devil you're having been defeated by Burlington House, and I am indeed sorry, as I had hoped to have a friend in high places, whilst I was eating out my heart at Caracas, and longing to be sent to Christiania, to end my days in a clime where my flesh would not rot away so soon. I am sorry — it must be so — for you, and the feeling that our labours have been in vain is always a bitter one. Still, a vacancy may turn up, so there is still hope. And the divers platitudes about the value of honest effort has no salving power in connection with an examination. Still, I don't know that you'd have liked the quill-driving life at the F.O. much, and I think I can say quite honestly that there is the "well out of it" aspect.

Riding about in the Campagna is the best thing about this place. The atmosphere is full of excitement, and I am thrilled by the thought of being in a country at war. Public opinion here is very confident, and on the whole in favour of the war. I should feel sorrier for the Turks if their conduct generally had been more deserving of sympathy, and if they had shown themselves more accommodating, in particular to ourselves, less so to certain other gentlemen. I don't think the Italians will definitely annex. They will establish themselves in the same way that we are established in Egypt.

To Edward Speyer.

British Embassy, Rome,
September 21, 1911.

We live here in the middle of rumours of wars. I write with no special knowledge, but I suppose we have to some extent saved our face over the Morocco business. But in any case I fear the German coup will be successful to the extent of adding to German territory and causing grave anxiety to be felt for the future of our Central African possessions, now that Germany has got to the Congo River, and that she will insist on a say in the future of what was once King Leopold's happy hunting-ground. The French, by the time they have rounded-off their African possessions, will have paid a very fair instalment of blackmail. I say "instalment", because I fear recent events will encourage a repetition of Agadir tactics. Still — this is all rather depressing.

Rome is a charming place, though I have not been there much lately, as the Embassy summers near Naples in Lord Rosebery's villa, where we have had a pleasant lotuseating two months or so with talking, reading, and a little quiet Chancery work now and then. Italy is supposed to have sinister designs on Tripoli, but otherwise little disturbs our peace.

To Ferdinand Speyer.

British Embassy, Rome,
April 14, 1912.

[*There is a gap in the correspondence from Rome. This is due partly to the difficulty of getting hold of Charles's letters to friends who are now serving at the Front, partly to the fact that Charles was devoting much of his time to the study of Anthropology, Ancient Religions, Fetish Worship, Magic, and their kindred subjects. Further, in October 1911 Charles was at home, — R.*]

Many thanks for your most interesting letter. I don't, of course, see how we could have acted otherwise than we did in Morocco. We were bound to be in the French diplomatic camp by the terms of the Entente, and we were bound to prevent

Germany getting a part of the Atlantic seaboard. Also, as a matter of principle, I think it is undesirable that the Germans should make the French pay twice for what they had already obtained under the 1909 agreement. It is quite true that the French behave abominably as far as the commercial interests of other nations in their possessions are concerned. They have no notion of an open-door policy; and I dare say in this matter the German intervention had happy results. I quite agree the F.O. should be more up to date in commercial matters, but financiers have very often been indifferent counsellors, and men like and the other big people who have really a chance of getting the ear of the Secretary of State, take a very denationalized point of view, and ignore the political aspect of questions, such as the Bagdad Railway. But I have never been a believer in Parliament, and certainly Parliamentary control would not help the F.O. to a more intelligent attitude in commercial matters. Your Parliamentary expert in Foreign Affairs is either a sentimentalist of the Philip Morrell-Arthur Ponsonby type, or a wiseacre who thinks he knows all there is to be known because he has been two years honorary attaché at Constantinople. The latter is, if anything, the greater danger. In both cases there is blissful ignorance of commerce. Under pressure of public opinion and the Board of Trade, certain hybrids called commercial attachés were appointed. Ours has a pretty wife, and times his arrivals and departures so as to fit in with the principal golf competitions on the Roman links. I should suggest some compulsory subject in the examinations in banking, finance, and trade, but probably some Hawkins would come along and put it all into a book in the form most easily learnt and most easily forgotten, and little would come of it The Commercial Department of the F.O. is simply a post office between the Board of Trade and representatives abroad. I don't think it very educative. So it is difficult to know what to do.

It is remarkable that the coal strike passed off quietly and was so little felt. It hardly seems to have made people think enough. I remember we used to say what a good thing it would be if people did think. I'm not sure about that now — most people's thoughts as to remedies are not worth very much.

I am at present very sceptical; I don't see any hope in Socialistic legislation or in the Socialist vision as a whole. Yet I am quite conscious of the force of the destructive criticism Socialists have levelled against present-day society, and find it difficult to take up a conservative position,' as from the point of view of most people there is precious little worth preserving. I remember in the old days we used to say that if you had organized capital on one side and organized labour on the other side, *sufficiently strong to be afraid of each other*, we should have no strikes. This was one of the more "respectable" arguments advanced at Oxford C.S.U. meetings to convince the more stodgy members that trade unions were not unlike branches of the Y.M.C.A. But certainly in the case of the coal strike the opposite has occurred. Of course Syndicalism is the inevitable result of the failure of the Parliamentary party; in a way it is a good thing that the work-people are having their minds turned away from hopes of grandmotherly legislation to a good hearty wages movement, though the Syndicalist way of "the sewers for the sewermen" is *kindisch*.

I love Rome and am happy here in a quiet way. Many interesting people in nearly all lines of life, save politics; it is difficult to meet politicians. But of course a rather lotus-eating post as far as work goes.

To the Same.

Rome,
April 30, 1912.

It is true, I fear, that I have been remiss in correspondence. The flesh is pretty weak out here. My father has been here, also Viola Tree has been in Rome, and we had the jolliest of times together. Viola was very jolly and in great looks and spirits — a very good woman. Patrick has been here too. I imagine he is quite keen about his City work, which, while it hardly sounds enlivening, is just as enlivening as most things of that sort. I suppose everybody is bored with their professions at the earlier stages — perhaps more so those in official employment — and one must just recognize the fact. I am very happy here, and prevent myself running intellectually to seed by stiffish reading, though this is interfered with by social activities. The right policy here is to make a few friends and specialize in them; and these friends, once made, never to go out and make useless acquaintances. I fancy one would always enjoy one's second year more than the first, as one has no circle and is always nervous with people, fearing either to love or be loved.

To Edward Speyer.

Gisburne,
December 29, 1912.

[*The autumn of this year, 1912, was marked by a loss which Charles felt very keenly: Sir Reginald Lister, his uncle, died at Tangiers of malarial fever while serving there as H.M. Envoy Extraordinary and Minister Plenipotentiary. He had been His Majesty's Minister Plenipotentiary at Paris from 1905 until 1908, when he had been transferred to Tangiers. He died when Charles had been only fifteen months in the service. — B. W. C.*]

Much water has flowed under the bridges since I got your last letter, and I must admit that I was perhaps a little hard on the German Government in our previous correspondence. Germany has certainly, exercised a sound influence during recent Balkan events. I wonder what the betting on peace is? I have lately seen a member of *The Times* staff" fresh from London — I've been a country mouse since my return and hunting all the time — and he seemed to be rather hopeful. I should be happy if the Austrians stopped moving troops about and sabre rattling. I take it the Austro-Serbe difficulty is more or less settled. Berchtold is supposed to be an indifferent performer — *un dilettante elegante* he was called by the Italian Foreign Office authorities after his recent visit to Italy. The Italians must be thankful they haven't been made to toe the line by Austria to the extent of going to war. And this might have happened — even looked like it when I was last at Rome. Such a war would have been frightfully unpopular in Italy — impossible, I think. I'm sorry to have missed Ferdi this time, but shall make a point of seeing him in London. With best wishes for the New Year.

To Mrs. Edward Speyer.

British Embassy, Rome,
February 12, 1913.

I wish I hadn't had to leave England so soon owing to my sudden change of plans. But one must be ruthless about going to India. 1 must say the February weather here is marvellous — dry and sunny but rather cold. The golf here is very good just now, and we play on a wonderful links within sight of the Via Appia and the aqueducts. There is a good deal of *va et vient* this year, which there wasn't last, owing to the war. I went to the opera last night — "Isabeau", the new Mascagni opera. I personally did not care for it. The music is not melodious and pleasant like the old Italian opera — neither is it atmospheric, dramatic, extravagant, or any of the things modern opera is. It is very laboured and *Operosa* and the duets are hectic beyond words. It was well given on the whole, with a young Canadian tenor. Mascagni oughtn't to try for ponderous efforts. But opera is largely a question of mood, and I dare say I wasn't in a suitable frame of mind. I am to be the Indian Bacchus at a fancy dress ball on February 27th at the Embassy *mi-carime* night— and am much exercised about my tights and my other appurtenances. Tights apparently take ages to make, but I must hide a large stretch of bare legs between the end of my tunic and my leopard-skin buskins.

To Mrs. Warre Cornish.

British Embassy, Rome,
April 20, 1913.

Many thanks for your charming description of the wedding at St. Margaret's. [*This refers to Percy Wyndham's and Diana Lister's wedding at St. Margarets. — R.*] It was a kind thought of yours to write to me. We shall be a very small family now, just me and father. This is rather a sad thought, as we always have so much fun together, and after one has passed one's collegiate stages, where friends are very much to hand, one begins to feel there aren't too many in the world and to value one's family more as a social centre.

Here we are just past the season, and all of us rather tired of the festivities to which we have been subjected. Roman society is small, and one meets the same people ever so many times, yet without that consciousness in many cases of getting "forrarder". Still they are nice here. The Italians are certainly the most *naturally* intelligent people of Europe. I don't think a stupid Italian exists. They *will* always know, and are put to miserable subterfuges at times to hide their ignorance. But this, like their other faults, is a fault inherent in extreme youth, and they certainly are great babies — especially the "smart" ones — and with all the freshness and charm of babyhood. Gossip about one's friends is one of the main forms of conversation, but it is not ill-natured, as no one attaches any importance to it and it is very amusing. There is never what one finds so often in England, the phenomenon of people trying to talk about things they know nothing about, and putting up hares which they can't follow. Altogether the Italians, especially the Naples and Sicily people, are very charming, friendly, and agreeable persons. They are kindness itself to foreigners.

Lady Rodd has a passion for organization, and has been making our lives rather hectic by giving a fancy ball of a very elaborate and historic character. Many of the Romans appeared as their ancestors, and looked really marvellous in Cinquecento dress, which is the costume Italians ought always to wear. The poor Secretaries were all turned out as Greek gods and heroes, and looked rather silly and theatrical. I was the bearded Dionysus. Later we had all to figure in a theatre for a charity.

We are all glad to be gods no more.

You will be glad to hear I play golf now — unlike Arthur Benson! No time for more. Write to me again, dear Mrs. Cornish. It gives me great pleasure. I will be home in November and come and see you. My love to the Vice-Provost and Mrs. Desmond MacCarthy.

To Lord Ribblesdale.

British Embassy, Rome,
June 6, 1913.

I am off this afternoon to Caprarola to stay the night with Mrs. Baldwin and *fille* who is now there. I then go on to Diana Manners and then to Reggio, where Tyrwhitt is staying with the Pansas. We go to Naples on the 20th. The Ambassador has at last got off on his yacht, and will be with us again about the end of the month.

Rome has been pretty quiet lately. I have been seeing the usual sort of people. Princess Teano is shortly going to London, and told me she would write to you. She was quite *en beauté* and sunburnt from the country. The Casatis have, I think, been at Venice. I never got to Lady Helen after all, but it really couldn't be helped. The R.'s are, I believe, reunited by the kind offices of Percy Drexel, and the R.'s house will next winter be a monument of respectability and a veritable temple of Vesta for the chaste virgins of Rome. The old Princess R. has succeeded in marrying off their youngest daughter to a Marcheggiano nobleman of some wealth, but obscure and provincial. R. *père* at the time when he announced this piece of good luck to his friends did not know the young man's Christian name. It is said that the A.'s are separating, also the B.'s — the latter with better reason. I fancy A. can't do without his wife's *dot*, and as a liquidation of the dot is a corollary of separation, I should think the house will be kept together. The B.'s, I fancy, are in a different case, as he was pretty rich always. P. when they married took little notice of his wife, and unhappily fell in love with her some six years later, by which time she had made a life of her own. She would not modify her way of living for him, retorting that he hadn't cared for her when they began their *ménage*. Separations seem more common than *fiançailles*. Mrs. Granet has been in very good form lately, and expressed the view that the Italians did not understand boy and girl flirtations. I meant to ride to Caprarola this morning, but Mrs. Baldwin has sent over her motor for me, so I suppose I must take it.

To the Same.

British Embassy, Rome,
July 26, 1913.

I wonder how you're keeping and what your August plans are. We go on with our pleasant patriarchal life here and our simple pleasures. Invicta continues to grapple bravely with the arts, and to wear out her old picture hats with ostrich feathers in this haven of rest. X. is disturbed about the Turks' behaviour and makes periodical darts back to Rome, which are never very productive of information.

But I suppose embassies must be rather agitated at times. The papers say shares are going up, which looks more hopeful; but I am afraid that we shan't have peace just yet as the Austrians will encourage the Bulgarians to resist the terms demanded by the Greeks and Serbs. Austria has been the sort of *böser geist* over the whole thing, and it is her we have to thank for most of this slaughter. Still, it looks as if we were all rather fed up with fighting just now — though I should personally be bored with a return to the quiet life. ...

Rome must be uncommonly dull if there is not some crisis on and a real dead-and-alive post. Almost ever since I've been here there has been a crisis of some sort going on in which we are more or less interested.

To the Same.

Posillipo,
August 2, 1913.

Many thanks for your capital letter. ... I wonder how you'll like Dutch country life — I suppose there is some golf near the Hague. When I was there with you it looked as if the country-side was entirely devoted to tulips and dykes. The worthy Michiels is here now, flushed like the rosy-fingered dawn, courteous and at home. I don't know why the K.'s don't appreciate him. He is really very sympathetic. I don't think I shall ever go to the Hague *en poste*. I like the bloodthirsty Near East, where there are always stirring times. Our life here goes on very calmly with more sun, dry weather, and the pleasant prospect of a descent in force of the Stuart-Wortley family, viewed with mixed feelings by the Rodd children who have a healthy suspicion of their aunts and cousins. I have been *aux abois* lately with my inside, and have for the moment suspended peaches and other delights. But I fancy things will again soon be on a normal basis — like the City, though I am afraid this will take longer. Barbara says it's "worse than ever", but the papers here report improvement. I don't feel very hopeful at the present moment. Still, the worst feared has so often come off that it seems almost time for the luck to change. I'm not sorry has had a knock! Generally it is only the Christian supporters of the Jesuit protagonists who get the knock. I am reading Ariosto now — a very underrated writer who, I believe, was much admired by Byron. It is cheerful, fluent, skilfully written stuff, with an extraordinary gay and cheerfully cynical note running through it, and sometimes up to great heights. His improper cantos are especially satisfying. Scatters [*Sir M. Wilson*] has very handsomely offered me his rifles for my Indian campaign, which will be very satisfactory.

It might be worth considering buying one, as diplomats get a good deal of rifle-shooting in certain posts— not so much as they used to, I fear, owing to the increase of work. The new colleagues, a *jeune ménage*, are very agreeable, easy-going people, and quite cheer us up. The worthy Osborne, who saved Viola from the clutches of A— after the golf ball last year, dislikes America, where he's gone.

To the Same.

British Embassy, Rome,
September 2, 1913.

Adrianople seems now more or less settled and things seem going better in Mexico. Why the Americans burnt their fingers so I can't imagine; their policy seems to have neither rhyme nor reason. I'm told the chief reason for their wish to put a spoke into the Mexican Government's wheel was the fact that the Mexican Eagle Oil Company had had a considerable concession given to them which the Standard Oil looked on as their prescriptive right — *hinc ilia lachrynuæ*. Bryan is a godless man. The Americans go down steadily in manners, morals, decent feelings, and political skill, and will soon be Huns like the Bulgars without their manly qualities.

I have now got back to Rome, and the whole establishment will be here soon with the exception of Lady Rodd, who will go to Corsica in her yacht and come back again to England, a very child of brine and sunshine. My time at Rome has been rather strenuous, as I had to wrestle with a long series of queries about the Italian Parliament which our ninnies in the House of Commons want to know about — down to what coloured socks Italian deputies wear. Still, I like work, and should be dull without it. I saw Irene Lawley on her way through from Naples, where she had been with Lady R., and she spoke handsomely of you. Rome is otherwise rather dull and quiet, just a few colleagues. I go to the cinematographs with the Greek Chargé d'Affaires and the black Belgian and white Dutchman and Michiels. The latter, Michiels, is a great standby and a dear friendly fellow. I don't know what we should do without him.

You will be glad to hear our friend Peña has had a windfall — his mother dying. I don't know why you should be glad about that; but still! he has now about £100,000 a year. He has gone back to the Argentine and abandoned European amours, which, I think, shocked him profoundly. As you know, he was always urging Z, to return to her *sposo*. I saw *sposo* in the Grand Hotel, just off to shoot pheasants. He is standing for Parliament and may get in, but his tactics seem evasive. He is trying to hunt with the hare and run With the hounds, which he may be able to do with money. All the illiterates vote at the next election; their name is legion. Were there as many drunkards X. would be sure to get in.

To the Same.

British Embassy, Rome,
November 5, 1913.

News there has been but little here. Just over with our elections, which resulted badly on the whole for the Government. Numerous Socialist gains and a good many *ben pensanti* saved by the Clerical vote from defeat. Several of Giolitti's *bêtes noires* elected and of his trusted lieutenants soundly beat. At Naples things went disastrously. A popular obstetrician romped in in spite of all the efforts of the authorities for his opponent. This latter was a Town Councillor, and when he saw things going ill burst into one of the municipal offices which were polling booths and collared a few hundreds of his opponent's votes. This, however, was of no avail to stave off defeat. Here the Moderator got in for the two seats where the results were doubtful and went to second ballot. Leone Caetani was badly beat. The election was supposed to have been corrupt to an unprecedented extent. But I suppose bribery makes an advance along the path of constitutional progress; before people used to intimidate solely, and bribery was never heard of. The Government will probably be a broad-bottomed administration — no Giolitti and some members of the Right. Giolitti will take a rest for a little while and then come back.

The day before yesterday I went shooting with the worthy Mr. Young. We got one or two snipe. My marksmanship very defective, but the Italian snipe is not a bird to get the out-of-practice shot into form again. He rises very wild against brown landscape and flies low, especially if there's no wind. The place is lovely — great expanses of flats, rather marshy, with a line of dark-coloured scrub; then sand and then sea, and the woods of umbrella pines inland, and a little river. We lived the hut life, but very comfortable fare and most genial local *cacciatori*. The day closed with a fox-hunt. The fox was chevied about with praiseworthy energy by a pack of our dogs, but they couldn't get him up to the guns, I saw him several times — a fine, big chap. But they don't hunt down that way. The villages and houses are all built on sort of rocky excrescences from the soil fringed with ilexes, and look very frowning. I am very busy learning Turkish and getting on fairly well with the lingo, which is unlike anything you ever did before. The letters are fiendishly difficult. I have had one or two jolly rides, but the ground is still like a rock.

To the Hon. Irene Lawley.

In Train to Brindisi,
November 16, 1913.

Here we are, *en route*. Thursday evening, after writing to you, I dined at the Grand Hotel — whole British Embassy as Dering's guests — very impressive and a privilege for the world to see us all together, clean, gentlemanly, and restrainedly gay. After, who should I meet but old Z. [*This gentleman's family is famous for the evil eye. — R.*] He lunched with me Friday. He is a very nice man, and talks a lot about the morals and manners of the Royal Family, etc, and army politics, which are all mildly interesting to me. I think he will have a fairly good time here, as he is a friend of the Trabbias, and he also knows Serrestoris very well. Oh, he did catch his train to Lucca by a miracle — the train was in late — obviously delayed by the fact he was going to catch it. A perfect example! Hurried passengers delayed, perhaps, in matters of life and death, and the cause of the delay in no way inconvenienced! *Altro che.*

… And what do you think happened Friday morning? I was going out cub-hunting in my most aggressively hunting mood; on the road, for no reason whatever, my horse stumbles and breaks both his knees (don't tell any Italian friends). But I don't know that next morning counts.

The boys gave me a kind of farewell dinner at the Caccia, which was delightful, and the whole thing was very touching; and I am very fond of them, and I think they will remember me. I expect one's first post is the one that leaves most sort of social impression on one's mind. I shall never forget the agonies of my early struggles here. What I think was of most help was a failure with M. M. The first time I met her I talked very freely about Italy, etc., just as if it was Oxford and not Rome where we were. … Her good manners made me think I'd had rather a success. However, later I found out I had offended seriously. In fact it considerably delayed our friendship. It did me a great service in making my dull, unsupple mind realize that Rome wasn't Balliol. Italians are right to be sensitive about their country, and we ought to be more so. I'm always rather unduly upset by the *gaffes* I make; but I suppose, if one has a tendency that way, the only thing is to make an effort to cure oneself. So many things come hard to me which come easy to other people — such as packing. I now believe I've left my golf clubs behind. And think of India without golf clubs.

We are now creeping down the coast of the Adriatic, brilliantly blue to Brindisi, with a great feeling of melancholy that I shall see nothing of Italy for such a long time. It's all a great plain covered with vines, and the vine-leaves are turning brown — a good colour after the blue of the sea — with an occasional olive dotted about. What a country! I think I rather misspent my time in Italy, and didn't travel enough, being so much taken up with the hunting. The worst of life is, one can't do everything at once, and that's what one finds to be very much the case everywhere.

Victor Emmanuel III of Italy

Sir Rennell Rodd mentions in his monograph that after two years of continual service Charles became entitled to long leave of absence. In many ways, I think, he would have liked to come home to hunt and shoot — especially hunt — and to renew relations with friends at home; but the call of India and its varied opportunities supervened. Besides, Charles always had a lively taste for the universe.

Most of the letters that follow are written to Miss Lawley. Her father, the late Lord Wenlock, was Governor of Madras from 1891 to 1896. Her own impressions of India must have belonged to her childhood, but Charles's evident pleasure in recording his new experiences was increased by Miss Lawley's quick perception of all we associate with the East. — R.

To the Hon. Irene Lawley.

P. & O. "Osiris",
Tuesday, November 18, 1913.

SS Osiris

Brindisi was terrific at first. To our horror we were met, Mounsey [*Second Secretary at the Embassy at Rome. — R.*] and I, by a sort of deputation consisting of the British Consul, the pro-Consul, and several other notables, and finally given lunch. M. had to present to the ex-Consul that afternoon a C.M.G. The scene at the station was the more unwelcome to me as my luggage had not arrived by the same train but missed the *coincidenza*, and I pictured myself off to the East with one nightshirt. I made a *scenata terribile*, but my style was slightly too terrible to be effective. Lunch rather cheered me up and fortified us for the ceremony of presenting the C.M.G. to the ex-Consul. This took place at the latter's house, where all the smart set were gathered headed by the local deputy, and the Sotto-prefetto M., a modest young man did not make the most of the occasion, and took the heavily frock-coated hero of the hour — our host for the moment — into a corner, where he mumbled a few words and handed him two packets. This done, "God save the King" was played on the piano.

We then affixed the C.M.G. to the hero's coat-lapel amidst applause. I talked to the local deputy, who was a friend of the Frassos and Philipson, to the local deputy's wife, who had had the time of her life in London, to the sous-préfet, who knew all the ins and outs of S—'s liaison, so the time passed pleasantly, and when we got back to our hotel — the sort of "Grand" at Brindisi — I found my luggage had arrived and that about ten British subjects were ready to give me drinks. Before and after dinner we were plied with alcohol, and altogether made very welcome by the Grand Hotel set. Gambling is the forte of the Brindisi *jeunesse.*

They gamble away houses, floor by floor. They also have a roller-skating club. How well one could live in an Italian *ville de province*.

It is a fine harbour, coal stalks abound, black and angular against the palm-trees — *très Bakst*. White houses with flat roofs, quite the East already, and Albanians in the port. These last influenced Mounsey to change his plans and go to Albania instead of Lecca.

This boat is clean and comfortable— if small. Getting up is hell. No room to put one's things, so one's boxes and bags become a sort of bran-pie. Except at meals I am in a state of perpetual coma. I have, however, read some of the Italian verse book. The Dante lyrics on the death of Beatrice are marvellous — heart-wrung, exalted verse, and have all the thrill of great mystery about them. I've also read the Carducci selection — a grand man; such guts about him.

To the Same.

P. & O. "Egypt",
November 21, 1913.

SS Egypt

Here we are well down the Red Sea and due for Aden to-morrow. Ship life has on the whole been pleasant.

The great thing is that I have got a cabin to myself. A triumph. A man was in occupation when I arrived, but he has now cleared out. One sight of me, pale but determined, was enough, so I am really very comfortable.

Then Ned Lutyens is on the boat, who is very jolly and a real standby. He is a sort of lesser Harry Cust; inclined to tell stories about his children and to make puns, but be is for all that very rollicking and genial.

I miss a travelling companion on the whole more than I would have thought, as I've not the knack of getting on to terms with people at first sight. I am wanting in initiative; with a jolly man with me — or with you — it would have been fun; but when alone and timid like me, one don't feel inclined to plunge into quite new people, and I shan't be sorry on the whole when it's oven Between ourselves I'm afraid I'm getting a slight distaste for our race when I see them collectively and super-British. Of course knowing them individually, and so on, this disappears, and one always gets to like them; but I don't think a crowd of Englishmen together are as genial or sympathetic as a crowd of Italians, though man for man no doubt one would be better friends with them.

And what did you think of Port Said? What a place for unrelieved meanness. Shop after shop of Greeks. I'd a jolly native boatman who took me round — fat, black, in a blue overall and a green sash, who dealt with all others who offered themselves as guides very summarily: "No take him, he steal". I was shaved by a Greek, who handled my nose as if it was a Bulgarian, and I bought cigarettes from another. I don't like them. Maps of Greater Greece on the walls and portraits of the King, etc.

The canal is marvellous, with its sand and scrub foreground and the pink sand-hills in the distance, and the mirages and camels at the landing-stages under palms, and houses with flat roofs. It compensates for much that has so far been dull. But you've no idea with what a weary heart those who've done the passage say four to ten times look on the thing. My accounts are relatively delirious. Indian service is a stern business, I must say, and is taken as such by most of them. They are charmers [*Indian Civil Servants*], I must say, but this doesn't alter what I said about the crowd.

I wonder how it will all be when I land? Mrs. Benson is coming out to see Rex, which is a pity, and I shall disembark minus rifles owing to Scats [*His brother-in-law, Sir Mathew Wilson.*] carelessness — still, bless the boy, he's lent them me. The shooting tales are thrilling, and one wonders how any one comes back alive. Even snipe-shooting one is not safe — not that the snipe is violent, even in the rutting season; but many men, on picking up dead snipe have been bitten to death by cobras.

To the Same.

Bishop's Lodge,
Malabar Hill, Bombay,
November 28, 1913.

Aden is a grim tribute to the perverse energy of man — rocks unrelieved by a vestige of green, very sullen and jagged above the sand and sea, and dreary little buildings all round the port, with wooden frontages, verandahs on the highest stage. Hardbitten, well-yellowed, spare men in topees came on board to see their friends. In fact, the general note of severity was unrelieved. One poor man, who was doing the passage for the fourteenth time, told me he would sooner be at Perim or Aden than at any up-country station in India, because there at least you saw the ships passing. The Anglo-Indian is on the whole a sad man, and gives one a sense of one's inferiority physically and morally. He also expects much. I can't shake off the impression made by the Anglo-Indians, civil and military, and it depresses me to be such a poor creature.

You can't think of the thrill of delight one feels at touching terra firma again — even if one's morning is spent in rushing from hotel to hotel like the Holy Family, and bursting blood-vessels in angry arguments with Cook's Babu employees at the Bombay Customs. But the harbour's simply vast. I'd no idea of it. I expected a packed little Oriental port close under the city buildings. I shopped, etc., all the morning — the shops are marvellous — the shop-streets full of hideous sort of Indo-Gothic buildings varied by the verandah and trellis all-the-way-up type of house, painted light green, and strikingly plain, in the afternoon I drove through the bazaar quarter. I must say it surpassed my wildest illusions of colour and squalor, with those low little, mostly wooden houses — the room opens in front, where you see solemn old men lolling about on pillows and mattresses or sitting on their haunches and cross-legged, with great hairy chests showing through their cotton uppers, and mouths red with betel-nut, and their feet at almost Yogi angles, and the shawls of women and the depth of brown of the young men's legs, and the brilliance of their turbans. Not one smile the whole time did I notice, and no chattering. The impression was one of lurid brilliance combined with deep and age-long depression. Think what a Naples crowd would have been under the circumstances. The women I saw to-day were more saturnine and mirky brown than the men, and less sympathetic; but the appeal of the whole thing is not, somehow, to sympathy. Then it suddenly occurs to me that we're running this show, and the feeling of power makes one giddy. I suppose everybody notices these things.

To the Same.

Sharanpur, Nasik,
Western India,
December 4, 1913.

The Bishop took me to Elephanta Caves on Saturday after I arrived — and his Secretary, a Balliol man, full of the recollection of past triumphs and trials at the Oxford Union; curiously out of place on the vast waters of Bombay harbour, walled in by islands covered with jungle scrub and palms, and fringed with mango swamps.

I expect you've seen the Elephanta Caves. They are cut out of solid rock, the cave roof supported by colonnades of pillars with wall carvings at the end of the colonnade, or at the sides in recesses, of the various scenes of the married life of Sívá and Parbâti — what a thrilling appearance is given to the gods, especially in the depths of darkness, by smearing over with red ochre. They look like a sort of glowing coals. The sculptures are on the grand scale and finely unritual in feeling, and spirited, with quite a violence of motion and passion like the pediment of the temple of Zeus at Olympus. The centre piece of the Hindu Trinity is the most massive and awe-inspiring sight, and the heavy underlips of the three heads on one body, unlike the usual type on this side of the country, give the creature a look of gravity which would curb the most blasphemous in their sallies. Brahma is rather a rotter — degraded from the highest rank for a nameless offence, four-headed and always seated in a lotus flower supported by four swans. Gunpathi, the elephant god, is my friend. He is wisdom and good luck. He is given an elephant head because of this story. He was the son of Sívá and Parbâti, and one day saw his mother bathing. His father was so angry that he had the lad's head cut off. His mother, however, had no objection to being seen bathing and deplored her husband's action, and ordered the ladies-in-waiting to run out and cut off the head of the first animal they met to put on Gunpathi's shorn trunk. As it happened they met an elephant, cut off its head, and brought it along. It fitted the headless boy, and ever since he has had an elephant's head, the symbol of wisdom. If I put down all the stories I hear about Sívá and Parbâti they would take too long to write. Sívá is the "nut" here, and has beaten Vishnu hollow. He is at once destroyer and creator, but in this district suitably married. Elsewhere he is associated with the blood-goddess Kali.

Sunday there was a service in three lingoes in the Cathedral, and the hymns were sung at once in English, Mahratti, and Hindustani, the sermon being interpreted in those three tongues. It was really rather remarkable, and lots of men in church; and women in their bright shawls. I like their beady black pupils standing out against the white of the eye, equally brilliant, and their dazzling teeth,.

Monday I went round the Moslem quarters; it is the Mohurrum week now, and they will soon be in a state of the highest emotion and knocking each other's heads about. There was great preparation and much praying in the mosques — which is done with a dignity and order beyond belief and yet spontaneously, and gives no idea of being drilled. I fancy the Moslem has more sense of order and decency than the Hindu, whose temple is in a disgusting condition as a rule, and who has no sense of public worship. He also dots his little shrines about anywhere.

Tuesday I came here (Nasik). This is the second most sacred Hindu city in India — after Benares — dedicated to the god Rama, who is an incarnation of Vishnu. Here the river has been collected into tanks, where the people and pilgrims come down to wash in the sacred waters. The temples are not of a great age, about two hundred to four hundred years for the most part, but grand in setting. The shrines are dedicated mostly to Sívá. There were holy men in the passage of the temple of Rama — one very holy, absolutely sleepy gaga, and surrounded by Chelas cooking for him. The less holy and more active ones painted their foreheads in reds and whites and chattered round us likes apes, asking for money. By the tanks of sacred water there are men lying on spikes — not over sharp, I must say. They got off to eat, but they didn't look as if they thrived on it. Here were also people offering large leaves with little fruits on them and little piles of money by the side to their ancestors, while the Brahmans read the Mantras.

I went to see a temple built to the child Krishna by one of the last rulers of Nasik. This he did out of pique. He had intended to build a temple to Rama after attending R.'s birthday festival, but he was late for the ceremony and asked the god's birthday to be delayed. This the priests said they could not do. He therefore transferred the temple he meant to build from Rama to Krishna, and punished the god for his punctiliousness as to his birthday very properly. The present priest is a little boy — hereditary — managed by his mother— a fat widow, who gave me an offering of paddy and fruit. One temple in Nasik is erected to a Babu Civil servant who died in 1889. This gentleman, it is said, had squandered much of Government's money on the Brahmans, and was rather in a hole when the English collector came round to see how things were. However, all went well — the Sahib found all the money as it should be, and where it should be. For the gods had replaced all that had been squandered, ready for inspection. My guide and informant was a native parson— *padre* they are called — and knew all these priests.

What is striking is the fact that dress, cleanliness, etc., are no indication to a man's standing. The Brahmans of the highest kind are filthy, and wear baggy cottons like any one else. Their hair is all that's distinctive, and that's stuffed under a cap or a turban. It is very perplexing, this indifference in things material compared with our top-hat standards and mental habit of closely connecting rank and wealth. Little bits of history which crop up are thrilling; one of the temples has a Christian bell — to wake up the god, who is a sleepy cuss — taken from the Portuguese by the Moguls and from them by the Mahrattas. Nasik was their sacred capital.

To the Same.

Hotgi Station,
December 11, 1913.

My last was after my first day at Nasik. The second started with a drive out to caves — Buddhist, but then adapted by Hindus, and after the Buddhist movement reabsorbed into Hinduism — covered with rather rough sculptures of the Buddha in meditation. My host was an inefficient guide — it was difficult to make out where the Buddhist stopped and the later sculptures began. These caves are a great height up, so one always gets a grand view. In this case it was of glorious ghâts, sheer and clean cut on one side and of rolling plain running into ghâts on the other, with alternate stretches of brown and green and trees in the folds and dips of the ground.

After breakfast my native *padre* took me in charge. We first went into the Mohammedan quarter of Nasik, which is squalid, as the Nasik Mohammedans are poor and in a minority. We visited Saints' tombs — one of a worthy gentleman who drank milk all his life; cows are taken to his tomb and their yield of milk is thereby much increased. This should interest you as an agriculturist. We then went to call on a Brahman and family; in a small way but a fairly large house for Nasik — cow-dunged floors, and carpets and cushions against the wall to sit back against. My *padre* took off his socks and I inadvertently looked at his feet; he at once spotted this and said, "We generally take off our socks in the house". I felt I'd been rude, so hastily put him in the wrong by beginning to take off mine. He was all apologies at once. After a nearly interminable wait I was brought a Hindoo meal. Plantain leaf for plates, with little masses of chutney stuff and heavy, sickly sweets, some the shape of potatoes, others like indifferent pastry in shape, neatly arranged for me; everything tasted very hot or very sweet. My *padre* wolfed it all in ten minutes. I fear I made a poor show. I closed with betel nut wrapped up in leaves, which I crunched like a hero, without turning a hair. The Brahman was most amiable and the children darlings — the women waited on me but were silent.

The "spot" sight at Ahmednagar is the tomb of Chand Aibi — an Ahmednagar princess who married the King of Ajapore. On her husband's death she came back to Ahmednagar and became queen and mistress of a soldier, and died defending her city in its last struggles against the Moguls. The tomb is a fine monument, high up, commanding an immense view. She and her lover sleep inside the building — outside are two graves, a large one of her dog, and a small one of the legal wife of her lover; so the home is once more solid in death. The tomb is finely vaulted, but of that brown Deccan stone which is a bad colour, rather like the stone of which the Midland built their tunnels.

At the foot of the hill we met some Lamani — once the carriers of India. The women wear a gorgeous dress they are given at their marriage and never change. Ordinary sari stuff with gold and lots of glass sewn in, and ponderous armelets and anklets — jolly wild-looking people like gypsies. Ahmednagar was one of the Deccan Mussulman kingdoms, but the Moguls have left practically nothing except the fort. Then to Poona, where I stayed with the chief of the Staff— a charming man called

Colonel Gamble. I met a wonderful old Cowley Father, who lives in a village near, where he has an orphan school and where he has built a large church, though there is not a single Christian in the village. All the years he has been there he has not made a single convert, and his only congregation are these orphan boys; yet he is quite positive the whole village will come in sooner or later, and is sanguine beyond dreams about everything Indian — political, religious, and so forth. Overlooking his village is the ghat temple of Parbâti, and he sees there the site of the new cathedral he will build. He is the first saint I have ever seen, and as sane as you and me. I've never known such faith and good temper where you might expect the opposite.

At Byapur the little suggestion of gold and colour still left on individual monuments is perhaps even more effective than the buildings in their original glory, at least to our eyes; but what is a pity is that one sees dried-up ponds everywhere. These when filled with deep green water covered with water-lilies and reflecting roses planted along the edge like in the Vestal's garden in the Forum must have added much. But the atmosphere of departed splendours and living death cannot be conveyed in words, and the contrast between the little hospitals, high schools, and native dwellings we are putting up, sets us in a petty light as compared to the old kings.

We had the luck to come in for the Mohurrum procession, which is celebrated at Byapur in a general spirit as there were no Shias, only Sunnis — and everybody takes part in the dancing. There are a lot of criminal classes in Byapur, and each of these organize a sort of quadrille. The thieves came out with swords, and danced in a ring crossing swords. Then there were the coiners, who did a sort of club dance. The "Deerhunters", the worst criminals of all, dressed up, i.e. painted their nude bodies as tigers or carried great nets and did a sort of sham tiger-hunt. The last are Hindus, the coiners and the thieves Mohammedans. People also carried little models of the mosques on the tops of sticks made of coloured and gilded paper; they are the *tabuts*, supposed to contain the sins of the people. They are taken to the river, or, failing this, the rubbish-heap, and then thrown in to symbolize the putting away of sin. The coiners say that all men went to Allah to ask what their trade was to be — to one Allah said he was to be a carpenter, to another a black-smith, and so on. When the father of the coiners came, Allah said nothing but gave him a coin. On going home he found this coin to be a bad one, and of course palmed it off on some one else — since then he and his descendants have done nothing else. And the buffalo — Adam in the days of creation got tired of naming the animals, so he asked Allah if he might make one. Allah gave him the materials and told him to go ahead, and the animal Adam made was the buffalo. He was not allowed to make any more. I've now done with the Deccan and am going north.

To Lord Ribblesdale,
Khalsa College, Amritsar, Punjab,
December 18, 1913.

[*During his Indian tour Charles renewed his friendship with the family of the Rev. Richard Wright, for over forty years our vicar at Gisburne. He visited one of the Vicar's younger sons, then head master of Khalsa College, Amritsar. Here Charles enjoyed the experiences of inspecting with impartiality a large Native college. A bear hunt was thrown in to the Amritsar stay, and many old jokes were re-cracked whilst out in camp which carried both host and guest in spirit back to former days on the vicarage lawn, shaded by its heavy sycamore, when Charles, as quite a little boy, used to play bowls with the vicar. His host at Amritsar, Richard Wright, a Cambridge Blue, and capital shot and fisherman, is now head master at the Chiefs' College at Lahore.*

The Rajah of Chamba entertained the two young men handsomely, "He could not have done more for the Viceroy than he has done for us," wrote Dick Wright to me. "Chamba is right in the Himalayas, 75 miles from a station. The Rajah sent us a cavalcade, headed by two beautiful ponies for a six hours' ride through magnificent mountain passes and indescribable snows. The homes of the black bears were 2,000 feet up an enormous nullah. The Rajah provided attendants, and the signal was the rolling of boulders down the nullah." — R.]

Here I am staying with Dick to-night. He seems to have a most interesting, if somewhat controversial job here, and is much troubled still by the "beasts at Ephesus" from whom you saved him in 1912, and for which he is very grateful. As matters now stand he has been recommended by the Government of India for the Government of India Education Department. The matter is under the consideration of the India Office and being handled in the usual leisurely departmental fashion. You will remember Montagu's letter you showed me to the effect that the Government of India must take the initiative in recommending such appointment. It would be rather a good thing if you could write again to Lord Crewe, or to him asking how the matter stands. Dick would like the affair expedited in order to silence local criticism and set a seal on his work here (this will actually be finished two years hence — a five years' contract, two of which have been served); so I take it would the local commissioner and deputy commissioner. But here nothing can be done or made public till the I.O. move. And from what I know of offices they won't move in hurry unless they have their memory jogged. I suppose it is morally certain the I.O. will accept the recommendation of the Government of India — but the sooner the better. You're the best judge yourself of how much of these reasons should be given to Lord Crewe or E. Montagu; but I should be most grateful if you could take action.

All sorts of things, shooting, etc., are being organized for me by my worthy host. The less real care a man gives to the blasphemers the more he is attacked by them. I wonder if you went to Udaipur when you were in this country. It is a sort of fairy palace sloping down into a lake dotted with island palaces and peopled by real Rajputs, and every native house or shop is nearly four hundred years old. You would have delighted in it — the park filled with wild pig and the whole untidiness and profusion and squalor of Indian *grande seigneurie*. They have a fine contempt for what is "model", and I wonder what the agent at Welbeck would think if he saw these things. I'd sooner be an Indian maharajah than an English duke, I think. The Maharajah of Udaipur has shot one thousand tigers — more than I've shot rabbits. I had tea with the political officer. Colonel Kaye, who was captain of the Winchester XI and remembers you coming down to see Mr. Johns in the old days, and going to service in the cathedral. Then I stayed a day with the Agent-General of Rajputana — Sir E. Colvin at Ajmeer — a great man and a real charmer. One thing which has impressed me enormously is the amount Lord Curzon did for the buildings of India. Everywhere you go to is always Curzon "Lard" restored this or that, and so well done. It was a fine work of his viceroyalty. One day at Delhi *en route* for here, where I saw Lutyens and the new Delhi plans, which impressed me favourably. I also saw the Janra Meurjid Hûmayun's tomb, where Hodson shot the last Mogul then and there. I wish Shah Jehan was building the new Delhi. My bearer has fever; all well otherwise. Cold up here — I had to buy warm things at Delhi.

To the Hon. Irene Lawley.

Khalsa College,
December 24, 1913.

My host here has had an extraordinarily interesting job. The Khalsa College was built and started entirely with Sikh money, and was intended as a nursery for "advanced" Sikh thought. Result: it became a hotbed of sedition. Government had to take it in hand. Now that the King's enemies can't capture the place, they try to discredit it all they know and smash it up. My friend has kept his end up like a man, knocked out the seditionists and got it quiet. The Sikh is an interesting card and wants watching; the "politics wallahs" of the Deccan and Bengal are mice, but the Sikh is a man. That's the serious thing, and the present generation have forgotten the hammering we gave the Sikhs in the wars of the forties. He is extraordinarily good-looking — *d'une beauté presque vulgaire* — rather classical too, perhaps the effect of the presence of the army of Alexander the Great for some time, when he fought King [word illegible], very religious and a passionate intriguer whether on the right or the wrong side. He is wonderfully obliging and good mannered, and the way the people in the villages and outlying towns put themselves out for us on our shooting expeditions was amazing. A sort of royal send-off at the station, with garlands and accompaniment of the Sikh cry, "God is true," His religion is very pure — a schism from Hinduism started by Gum Nanule about four hundred years ago. "Sikh" is a religious, not a racial term — one god — ten gurus or teachers — no smoking, on earth at least. The Khalsa College boys, if the football team wins a cup, etc., go to the Golden Temple of the Sikh St. Peter and offer thanks to God. On one occasion the hockey captain asked, before an important match, that the assistant-clerk of the Principal's office should be let off work for the day of the match because he was such a first rate prayer, and would surely induce God to plump for Khalsa College! God is responsible for everything — the number of ducks one is going to shoot, whether one catches one's train, etc.

We had three capital days' shikar after ducks and snipe — a meagre bag for India, about fifty ducks and twenty snipe in the three days, but the jolliest shooting in great marshes with ten-foot high bullrushes and little waterways in between, the great open plain with occasional crops, then a line of trees, then the Himalayas in the distance. The best shikari you ever saw — Mohammedans. They made us shoot coot for them, and killed them by cutting their throats and breaking their legs, which is a salaam to Allah. The way they marked down the dead duck is a masterpiece. One can go anywhere here and find empty bungalows to stay in, shoot anywhere without asking My Lord's or His Grace's leave, and generally stretch oneself — which one can't do in England with its duke-ridden country-side — "a buck under every bush and no dukes", as Julian Grenfell said in praise of India. Then we went an armed picnic down the river Beas, one of the five rivers of the Punjab. Great sand river flats and grass-covered lagoons, with the Himalayas in the background, and fruitless stalks after black buck and fruitless searches after crocodile — but a never-to-be-forgotten picnic.

To the Same.

Delhi.
(No date.)

From Ajmeer I went to Delhi, where I saw Lutyens and the plans for the new Delhi. The Government House will have huge domes in the middle pillar fronting, fountains at the roof corners, built round courts, red sandstone up to top of steps, then white stone. The Secretariats will have smaller domes, and one big minaret at the corner. They will be more Indian in style. This may be conflicting.

I then went in Lutyens's motor to Hûmayan's tomb — where Hodson caught the last of the Moguls in the Mutiny time, pulled him out and shot him there and then; and then to the Nizam Uddin tomb, a Shah Jehan building of red sandstone inlaid, like most of the buildings here, with marble, entirely simple but vast. A huge court; fountain in middle; central mosque under large dome.

To Lord Ribblesdale.

The Guest House,
Chamba, near Dalhousie,
December 29, 1913.

One line to tell you that Dick and I have had a bear-hunt, organized by the Rajah, and killed two bears. We arrived here the day before yesterday after a magnificent two days' tonga and riding journey through the hills, and yesterday at 12.45 o'clock set out bear shooting. The Rajah had organized a "bonk" for us — which I'm told is a tremendous honour, as a rule only reserved for Viceroys and Commissioners. The bears had been located in a wood running up from a deep nullah into a pine-topped hill — extraordinarily thick cover. The men began beating practically from the horizon, shouting and throwing stones down. The bears were about three hundred yards below the horizon and took nearly an hour to move. We then had a merry fusillade. In my first four shots I wounded a big she-bear in the back — aft rather than fore — but must have broken the spine, as she was too weak to go on and came back and sat down, when Dick gave her the *coup de grâce* in the shoulder, *probably* also a shot in the nose, though I may have done this too. Her coming back made the others come back, and we had a second go, Dick cleverly killing another through the back. The bears were about two hundred yards off when we first shot, and difficult shooting, being hard to see for the scrub. For the later shots they were nearer — my fire was resultless, I regret to say. One bear, a cub, but about third to half grown, then advanced down the bottom of the nullah and came up towards us. At about fifteen to twenty yards off he stopped and looked at us through a bush, his head and neck visible. I delivered at him with seemingly crushing results, and he collapsed for the moment with a cry of pain, and, like the novice, feeling sure I'd accounted for him, I didn't fire at him on the ground. However, he was more frightened than hurt, and went on gaily running the gauntlet of the Rajah and *fils*, who had stayed behind. I got him in the neck, but lightly. Dick was magnificent, and I felt like Napoleon after Marengo, extricated from a nearly disastrous situation by Desaix. The Wrights are really marvels, and Dick, I'm sure, could be a real Selous with the time for it. I was much impressed by the way the beaters went for the bear — throwing stones at them at a very short distance. The kindness and charm of our host are wonderful. We were torch-lighted home. You Would like the Chamba ponies, little short-legged, sturdy beggars, who go up these "khud" paths like monkeys, and never put a foot wrong. I am asking the Rajah to Gisburne with warmth — I fancy he is a rather pious Hindu and won't come. He wouldn't eat with us at the guest-house for pious reasons, or rather for the pious reasons of his subjects. This is the only place in India where I've as yet found electric light generally used, and there are suspension bridges and every sort of modern tackle. It is rather a surprise in a place eighty-five miles by tonga and pony from Pathankote and served mainly by coolie transport.

To the Same.

Viceregal Lodge, Delhi,
January 8, 1914.

The only tidy place I've seen in India since I've been there has been the jail at Jerojepore. I went there after Amritsar to see an old Oxford I.C.S. man. He was pigging it like the rest of them here — sharing a bungalow with two others and sleeping in a tent, moving into the house occasionally when they went to camp; then out again when they came back. All life seems a camp here — one long camp — and the jail the only stable habitation of man. This, the jail, was marvellous. The summary justice of the civil surgeon who ran it; the mild industry of the prisoners and their well-fed, sleek appearance, the *spotless* cleanliness of the mud walls and floors, the absence of barbarities like prolonged solitary confinement and church services and chaplains' sermons — all made one very proud of the common-sense way the Englishman, if left to himself by cranks, or untroubled by religious lunatics and members of Parliament, can work things.

To the Hon. Irene Lawley.
Government House, Lucknow,
January 13, 1914.

I think this is the most distinguished address from which I have written. I came here with the Viceroy.

I suppose, as an old Anglo-Indian, that you have some idea of the greatness of the Viceroy. I hadn't, and I have been bewildered and left speechless with admiration at the special trains, and attentive and efficient A.D.C.'s, red drugget, bunting, and obsequious officials of every kind, caskets of silver, etc., in which he lives, moves, and has his being. There is no post like it in all the' world, and I would sooner be it than Prime Minister — or almost than Pope, and where one is hedged in by the many taboos. Lady Hardinge has a better time in some ways, in that she has all the men of highest precedence to sit next to at dinner, who are generally of the most interesting sort of Indian Civil Service men and Lieutenant-Governors. Her Excellency is very wide-awake and has picked up a lot. H.E. is a fine type of Englishman, with a simple direct way of going at things, a large fund of moral courage and a genial outlook on life. He talks very freely, though I've only so far talked diplomatic shop with him. He is most liberal minded. Personally I think he's very much in the right place.

One day we went to Cawnpore. This is one of the saddest places on earth, and when one is standing within Sir Hugh Wheeler's lines one cannot resist a feeling of despair for the future, and a conviction that no reconciliation between the two races can ever be attained. And I am afraid it is not only at Cawnpore that this feeling comes home to roost. One hears on some authority many dark stories of Rajahs insulted in clubs and first-class carriages by fiery young subs.; of ladies who complained at having to meet Indian "nuts" at Government House lunches; of the disastrous scandals, or rather one particular one in which an Englishman was involved with an Indian girl of high rank in public opinion. This apparently has delayed the movement to break down purdah for years to come, it was so much talked about. It seems a shame that all the patient work of men like M. should be ruined by an act of irresponsibility of that sort. The Englishman *must* live dead straight in India, both in manners and morals, and it is Bible and sword heroes like old Havelock, whose tomb I saw to-day at the Alum-Bagh, who have made us respected. I am told that in spite of every effort made in high places the cleavage between English and Indian is getting wider, that the Indians are asking for more and that the English are more on edge. Relations in native regiments, for example, are less cordial except in the cases of Gurkha and Pathan and Baluchi regiments. If true, this is all rather depressing — especially at a moment when the official world is striving so hard to carry out a policy of *apaisement* and to make people pull together.

An old I.C.S. man told me that India was a country of aristocrats governed by democrats — a very true remark, which sizes up a good many of our difficulties in getting into an Indian point of view. I suppose the British Raj is a stage in India's journey from chaos to chaos; for one is inclined to believe that Hinduism will absorb or shed us all — Hinduism impure and antique; I doubt any purified form of Hinduism long surviving. At present the Hindu is in the back seat, but the man in the back seat often sits longest. Then I expect the spiritually devitalized condition of Hinduism to-day almost vouches for its longevity. The less vital a body, the less it feels shocks. I suppose men are fast losing "belief", in the sense we use the word, in the dogmatic side of Hinduism; but that doesn't stop them from clinging to observance and to the whole solid system of Hinduism, and all-Hindu India with a government of Hindus will be chaos indeed — the most modest standard of efficiency would be quite out of its reach. India would become one huge Nasik, and money-changers would for ever defile the Temple. Well, at any rate, India has been a school of heroes for us — no one can come out of the Residency at Lucknow without feeling a braver man, and one more ready to believe in his country and face its perils. It has the same rousing effect as the presence of Lord Chatham.

To Lord Ribblesdale.

Viceregal Lodge, Delhi,
January 22, 1914.

My days have gone on here very agreeable, brightened by two mornings with the Delhi hounds. These are a pucka fox-hound pack lent by the Maharajah of Gwalior, and on both occasions provided quite good fun. The first day, Monday, was very cheerful; we were on the move the whole time, viz. 6.45 to about 8.15, and killed one jack after a short burst and ran another to ground after a very good chase, which involved crossing a canal and some stirring climbing of earthworks put up by our benevolent Government. This morning scent was less good, and we had about an hour and a half pottering after a good straight-necked jack, whom, however, we failed to hustle at all and who also went to ground. The hounds certainly worked very well, and the day was a jolly one. Otherwise I have sight-seen, played golf, and generally enjoyed life. The comforts of the place have, rather deranged my tummy, but it has been worth it. You would be much impressed by the huge work going on to make the new Delhi. Faith — assisted by some 9,000 coolies — is engaged in removing a mountain on which to rest the

Secretariats, and raising another on which Government House is to stand, and the roads have been levelled out right and left, and the whole place turned into an enormous dust-heap. It is extraordinary seeing how these people work and the way everything is done by manual labour, machinery being dear to import and coolies quite unable to work it. I imagine this cry about the relative cheapness of Oriental labour in Europe is rather bunkum. The. Indian is cheaper, I expect, but far less efficient, and you have to employ five or six very often where you would only require one white man or woman. The Delhi people come from some distance — very often Pathans — and are paid fairly high. The Viceroy thinks his estimate of £4,000,000 for the Government part of the business will meet the case. I'm told, *entre nous*, it was a pure shot, and that his confidence so far is far from being justified. Government House alone will cost over £500,000, specially with the imperturbable Lutyens to build it. The Rajahs will be turned loose over one area to build palaces of their own, which I should think will make a very curious medley. Every one is anxious to get as much done as possible so that it will be impossible for any new Viceroy to reverse the Delhi policy.

I lunched with the General to-day; he is in great conversational form. Dick [*Field-Marshal Sir O. M. Creagh's son, now a captain in the 9th Lancers.*] is generally beloved, and has a royal time as the guest of the gayer rajahs. The General stands for the out-of-date "silent" Indian who is fast disappearing; and one can't help admiring him as a man who really has got into touch with the people he is leading, and loves them like a father. This type of officer is, I fear, less common; the Indian is less trustful and more assertive than he was, and the so-called "fighting races", with the exception of the Pathan and the Gurkha, are disgruntled and degenerate. The whole nature of the struggle for existence has changed for the worse for them, and they think it hard that they are not allowed to cut the throats of the Bengalee competition-wallahs who beat them in exams, for Government billets. This seems rather the hour of the Babu-British, and men with foxy brains seem best suited to cope with the present-day problems. There was a Government House dance last night, to which Delhi rolled up in considerable force — all very well done. We danced in the dining-room, and you would have laughed at the way the sweepers prepared the floor, they ran up and down on all-fours with dusters under their knuckles, and had it all done in no time. The Viceregal Court is a strong supporter of morals, or supposed to be so, and the lighter ladies anxiously let drop the corner of their skirts to conceal their legs as they sailed past Her Excellency in the ecstasy of the valse.

I have also met Lady H., who from contact with Sir J. has acquired a considerable

The Viceregal Lodge

knowledge of affairs; this makes her an agreeable conversationalist. She is, of course, slightly *laudator temporis acti*, but not very much so. The daughter is most agreeable and clever and a dear — rather like the Barbara type of woman. She has her father's brains by inheritance. The question most discussed is Cawnpore and the rather public birching Lord H. gave the United Provinces officials. It is difficult to pronounce on the merits of the question. His action over the Indians in South Africa meets with general approval here, though it is recognized that Z, has exploited the whole question in order to embarrass the Government. He is of course as hot as mustard and a consummate vote catcher. Any other line, however, on the part of the Viceroy would have further helped his knavish schemes. G. ..., if you remember, had a great success with the P.M. To-day we went to see the house from which the bomb was thrown; it is a most appalling rabbit-warren — a fiery young policeman, full of convincing theories as to where the bomb was thrown from and how the assassin escaped, proved an excellent guide. A Parse lady in Paris is, it appears, the organizer of these atrocities, and the difficulty of the police is that when they do catch these terrorists they find they are babbling babes who hardly know what a bomb is and who could not possibly be the organizers of crime. The Delhi assassin has never been caught. It ,is regrettable to see how much the Viceroy has to be guarded — when he goes to Calcutta he enters a city of the dead. But another big bomb outrage would so seriously damage our prestige that we can't afford it. Must stop now.

To the Hon. Irene Lawley.

Viceregal Lodge, Delhi,
January 27, 1914.

Then there is the Jasmine Tower; here Shah Jehan died, his gaze fixed on the Taj. He had been kept a prisoner all his last years by his son Aurungzeeb in a cell, which can still be seen — on the plea that he was mad; like the King of Bavaria's building mania. He did indeed intend to build a tomb in black marble on the opposite bank of the Jumna which should be a great replica of the present Taj, and to connect the two monuments with a silver bridge, which would have been rather a job. From the Jasmine Tower there is a fine view to the Taj, and the old Emperor begged as a last boon that he might be allowed to die there with the monument of his love in view. One feels that the old man after all his disappointments and tragedies must have believed at that supreme moment that he had not lived in vain. Very few of us, after all, leave such overwhelming tangible results behind us. I feel the Emperor must have been his own architect, and that the Italians who did the inlaid work; etc., were workers in detail. The buildings immediately before and after Shah Jehan are so immeasurably inferior, and if there'd been some Government architect on the spot it is likely his work would have overlapped either into the reign before or reign after.

I think the view I liked best of the Taj was by the light of many stars before the moon got up through the gate. The stars were all , reflected in the water, which gives a perspective up to the monument, and there was a lamp dimly burning in the inside. The building looked like the outer shell of some deep inner mystery which just managed to shine through its walls, or perhaps like some great cloud through which the light of the moon has just begun to peep. You never saw anything so perfect as the proportions and the combination of quite plain shapes into synthesis of extraordinary beauty.

And then I must tell you about Fatehpur Sikri, which was the city built by Akbar and abandoned because of failure of water supply. It is the greatest monument to the personal grandeur of one man that I have ever seen, and a man who simply stands out in world history. Think of him dreaming of a Hindustan welded into one by a common religion, which he tried to evolve by making representatives of the various religions meet — carrying out a policy of tolerance, and race fusion, and he the heir of Jehad-preaching Tartar freebooters — and this at times when Christians were sending their fellows to the stake in every country of Europe.

Akbar himself soared into an ideality far beyond the understanding of the ordinary man. I admire the inscription on the big gate of victory built to commemorate his victories in the Deccan and his conquest of Ahmednagar and its Queen: "Said Jesus, on whom be Peace, *The world is a bridge, build no house on it.*" I forget how it goes on. But one feels now the dream of a united India in creed and government, and one is faced by the old tragedy of the great man who lives long enough, dying in disillusionment and in gloom of ideals unrealized. The man who could put up that inscription in the moment of conquest must have been on the grand scale. It's the old story — Jesus at the close of life asking only that the cup might pass from him; Paul pacing the sands of the Spanish coast in doubt; Napoleon at St. Helena. I suppose the big man alone realizes how much there is to be done, and is conscious sometimes of his own achievements in relation to what is left. By the time of Shah Jehan I fancy the Moguls realized how very little they could do politically for India on the lines sketched out by Akbar, and decided to pursue beauty alone and live only by their achievements in the service of Art.

Aurungzeeb tried to revive the Mogul Empire as an active and militant political power, and came badly to grief. At Fatehpur Sikri Akbar's Hindu decorations are all knocked about and mutilated. This was Aurungzeeb, the pious Moslem who objected to images of the Hindu sacred animals — the peacock, the elephant, and the monkey. The work of the wise in this country is always wrecked by the impulses of the fools, and it is a pathetic picture, the descendant of Akbar going round with his hammer like a militant suffragette, a pathetic end to the dream of the Empire and union. At Delhi, which is entirely Shah Jehan period — that is, earlier than the Taj and than the fort at Agra — one is vastly impressed with the sense that politics have taken a back seat, and that the ideal has been to construct a ceremonial capital and a seat of pleasure and magnificence.

The site of the new Delhi is of extraordinary interest, and one looks over the ruins of seven ancient Delhis which have one and all gone the way of ruin. The most interesting of these is the city of Hûmayun — Akbar's father and his tomb. Akbar and his son Jehangir never went to Delhi. The present Delhi is Shah Jehan's city — a fine, severe, robust style of architecture; only mosques and tombs left of it on a fine expanse of dusty and scrub-covered plain.

Lord Hardinge arriving in India on his appointment as Viceroy

To the Hon. Irene Lawley.
> *British Embassy, Constantinople,*
> *March 28, 1914.*

These are stirring times in which we live. I quite agree that a general election would do no good to any one now. If the Liberals come in again they won't find Ulster any more amenable. If the Tories come in they'll find the rest of Ireland in a similar condition of unrest. I don't understand how they failed to reach an agreement having got so near one, unless the whole idea of compromise was impossible from the beginning. The whole Irish business discredits party politics altogether, and the only people at all in a heroic light are the Ulster people, however local their point of view has been.

In this part of the world, too, we have our Ulster; the Greeks on the southern frontier of Albania whom the Powers have decided to assign to Albania have taken matters into their own hands and are having the time of their lives. They'll see themselves damned before they become Albanians, and wish to be independent or Greek.

I can't help liking people who really want a thing. Of course of our present troubles it may be said that the Prime Minister wanted to stop in office, or that Bonar Law wanted to get into office, but I'm old-fashioned enough to think these things don't matter so much as what the Ulster people are fighting for.

I went out a grand walk since writing, up on the down country above the Bosphorus. It is very treeless round here, wind-swept downs with occasional wooded valleys and sheltered bits where the peach-trees grow, and one can see little clouds of pink blossom. Then occasionally there is a dip in the ground, and there appears a bit of blue sea and a glimpse of the Asiatic coast and the road to Bagdad. There are some fine castles on the Bosphorus, [*The Crusaders (the Christians) built castles wherever they went, much finer castles than any in Europe. — B. W. C.*] great walled enclosures — walls sloping up and down hill in conformity with the ground, with round high towers at the corner and broken-down little Turkish houses in the middle with the same matchwood walls and red roofs. The peasants use the buffalo as in India. The Turk is a hopeless mongrel here; one can distinguish no "type", only occasionally one comes across the snub-nosed, slit-eyed, high-cheek-boned, highly coloured Mongolian, and one thinks of the original hordes that came into Europe and swarmed into India under Genghiz Khan and Timur, There is a great deal of Circassian blood in the modern Turk, as all the chosen women of the Sultan and the Pasha were Circassians, uprooted from the ends of the Black Sea and as white as snow. The Turks one meets in society have most agreeable manners and conversation. Sir Louis thinks the present sort are really anxious about getting things more into shape. The poverty of the State chest is appalling. Some weeks ago none of the officials were paid, and they couldn't go to their offices because they couldn't afford the tram fare and the price of the lunch. They could have got credit at the Greek shops, but the *mot d'ordre* had gone round that those were to be boycotted by good Ottomans owing to political differences. So you can imagine their suffering. Things are rather better now. I'm afraid the new Government will commit a serious crime, for they have just condemned one Aziz Ali to death on quite frivolous charges. This was the man who did all the fighting in Cyrenaica against the Italians. He is a hero, and looks like becoming a martyr. They may commute the sentence to one of life imprisonment, which is virtually equivalent. Aziz will probably "get ill in jail". The real reason seems to be that Enver, who is trying to be the Napoleon of Turkey, fears him as a possible rival. It will make a very bad impression in Egypt, which is seething with interest in Aziz All's fate.

To the Same.
British Embassy, Constantinople,
April 5, 1914.

I've had a very jolly time lately, take it all in all. Lots of work, Harold Nicolson having fallen ill, but some very good rides and walks. The down country from the city up to the Forest of Belgrade is really glorious; white heather and scrub all over the downs, then little valleys up which one rides and which end in woodland paths. There are everywhere violets and scarlet and purple anemones. The occasional villages with their wooden houses, a little mosque with its minaret and orchards in blossom, are most fascinating. Then below there are green hill meadows, and streams very much covered in with trees and scrub. Yesterday I went to Santa Sofia. From some distance off one thinks it quite small; as one gets nearer one thinks it quite big, and once inside one is really staggered by the size of it. It is immense. Great porphyry and grey marble columns, and great dabs of red and grey marble covering the walls like panels — a perfect Greek-cross shape. The Turks, when they came in, painted over all the mosaics on the ceiling with gold to obliterate the Christian pictures and crosses, and put up their "merab" out of line with the orientation of the eastern window. Also all the prayer-carpets which cover every inch of the floor are skew-eyed. This is because Christian churches are orientated towards Jerusalem, mosques towards Mecca. The nave of the church is covered with vulgar green plaques with gold Arabic lettering of huge size which look like patent-medicine advertisements. These are the names of the first few Caliphs, I think. Also, the roof is covered with a sort of silly design of no worth superimposed with the gold paint to hide the Christian symbols. The side aisles, where it is darker and where one is left with the marble walls and pillars, are most impressive. Here one sees less of the defacements of the infidel.

These are distressful countries; ever since the war there has been a continual *va et vient* of refugees from one state to another. Greeks had found life impossible under Bulgar rule, Bulgars under Greek rule, and so on, and they all seemed to seek soil under the flag of their own particular nation. It is a gloomy vision, and one can picture the arrival of these unfortunate victims of a racial hatred equally awake in time of peace as in time of war, and their homelessness. Mussulmans are now pouring into Eastern Thrace from Bulgaria and Greek territories.

And what of social Constantinople? I went on the night of April 1st — a fool indeed — to two parties at the Italian and French Embassies respectively. Such nice parties. You would have loved them. It is extraordinary how much politics are talked of an evening in the houses of the rich and the great, when you compare it with Rome. Sir Louis never leaves the side of Talaat Bey at social functions. The French Ambassadress is giving an 1830 ball shortly. I suppose the fancy-dress ball habit would follow one to Honolulu.

To the Same.
British Embassy, Constantinople,
April 12, 1914.

Here we are, still much concerned about Aziz Ali; it is a bad business — on a par with the murder of the Duc d'Enghien by Napoleon, and Maréchal Ney by Louis XIII — and I wish I could do something. I fear they mean to have his blood — Ugh — one has to meet these red-handed ruffians at parties.

Then we have had Easter, and I sang in the choir. The Ambassador went out to Broussa in the yacht and took all the sailors with him, on whom we mostly depend for our musical talent; so Jones (the butler) [*In a letter dated Alexandria, July 1915, Charles wrote: "Jones is longing to fight, and regretting his over-age"; and in other letters he often alludes to his efficiency and merits. — R.*] and I had to support the "virtuous females", as Mr. Jorrocks would call them, in the choir. It is tiring work, and I nearly burst a blood-vessel. However, the service rattled on very merrily, like an Irish jaunting-car. I gave the women no support in the "Alleluias" — a vulgar exclamation the Almighty must really resent — and always on a crackingly high note. I don't believe you can sing as well as I do. Not as loud, anyway.

I am very happy here and pleased with most things, except that I've lamed Gerry Wellesley's pony; don't tell him. And I've furnished my bedroom at dirt-cheap price — only £16, and that includes a bookcase. But it will be difficult to make my room at all nice. I have also to buy a pony.

I have been to bazaars and looked at carpets — what a complicated hobby. I feel I'll *never* know anything about them. But the really good ones are like great sheets of deep, glowing gems — a sea of them — and the shops here have stacks of them. And loot! think of it — think of the breach in those walls, white and brilliant against the blue skies, and the rush down the roughly cobbled streets with the dark bazaar arcades, and the trembling Greeks and Armenians on their knees, their faces pale and their lips quivering as they beg that something may be spared them. And the ride home with the spoils, each to his mistress, to lay the choicest at her feet.

To A. F. Lascelles.

Constantinople,
April 13, 1914.

L. Mallet is a most agreeable chief. He thinks George Lloyd will be Parliamentary Under-Secretary for Foreign Affairs in the next Tory Government. I think it is very difficult to make up one's mind which has behaved worst, during recent bothers, of the two parties. My impression is the Government did want to launch

Lloyd George troops on a perfectly orderly part of the Empire, as if it were an enemy's territory. It is quite true that the Ulster people were potentially disorderly. But the point is that they have given no provocation for such measures. In the case of strikes, troops are never sent till riots actually take place, and then on the distinct understanding that they are to defend property, etc. This cry of the army *versus* the people is quite absurd and won't catch on.

I cannot think the Prime Minister's plan of letting things rip until the Ulster movement got such purchase that he could turn to his supporters and Redmond and say that he must grant concessions has answered. This, I suppose, was his idea. However, the other alternative policy of preventing Ulster from arming might have had worse results, and made his own followers even less amenable to some settlement than they are now. Since you wrote things look rather better. A General Election now will do very little good as a solution. The parties should agree on a Federal

Prime Minister
Herbert Asquith

solution — a very un-ideal one, in my view — and have all vital points settled in advance *before* they go to the electors. Besides, *rebus sic stantibus*, whichever party gets in, the situation remains revolutionary.

To my mind the question, on its merits, has long been settled — no incorporation of Ulster into a Home Rule Ireland; Home Rule for the rest of Ireland.

I think A. J. B.'s estimates are unduly pessimistic. After all, the thing remains "much ado about nothing", considering the relative smallness of the interests involved.

To the Hon. Irene Lawley.
British Embassy, Constantinople,
April 16, 1914.

One approaches the "amusements" with high expectations, and one leaves them with a feeling of pleasant surprise that it wasn't worse. London amusements, with few exceptions, are not so. Expectations generally run high and fall short. Not in my mind, because I always liked the moment — *plus ou moins*. But one feels one would like other moments much better.

Here we had a cotillon at the French Ambassadress's: I sat unwisely in a rather prominent place, loosely attached to a pillar of the British colony. I was continually pulled up from my seat by charming and unknown damsels, and made to dance. You, who know how well I dance, can picture what this must have been. Generally I got through all right, and lasted out the figure — but not always. Dreadful having greatness thrust on me. After a rather unusual number of collisions I retired to a back seat. It was a jolly party, and I got out well at I a.m.; not so a poor colleague, who was collared by our formidable hostess and made to partner a *jeune fille* for the rest of the evening. The French Ambassadress said, *"On est Ambassadrice mais on est pourtant femme"*; and that at moments of great crisis, *"On cesse d'être Ambassadrice, on redevient femme"*. Wednesday next I shall confront this social potentate in 1830 costume. I like fancy balls to see other people's dresses for one moment, and one's own in the glass. But the idea of not being in one's ordinary clothes for a whole evening makes me shudder. I should like to get my fancy clothes *off at once*. My 1830 costume will be (1) whiskers, (2) Lord R.'s riding trousers, (3) hunting coat and waistcoat, (4) special jabot stock, (5) hunting top-hat.

I have lamed Gerry Wellesley's horse; sent his dog to the vet. for a little visit (in my charge she insisted on being sick every morning); hired a horse who is estimable if inelegant, and furnished my bedroom and much of my sitting-room. I feel no courage about buying things in a bazaar. They are all such experts here, from the Ambassador downwards, and I feel that for such a short time as I'll have here it's no use. I suppose I haven't the real collector's spirit. My Turkish goes on badly. The work has a compelling charm. I am pining to travel, but can't get away as we're so short, so I shall come home by a wonderful detour in the autumn late, or winter.

Aziz has got fifteen years, equivalent to a death sentence. He is bronchial.

To Mrs. Graham Smith.
British Embassy, Constantinople,
April 26, 1914.

[*Mrs. Graham Smith was Charles's Aunt Lucy, third daughter of the late Sir Charles Tennant and sister of Lady Ribblesdale. Easton Grey, near Malmesbury, was a second home to Charles in the holidays. — B. W. C.*]

Many thanks for your charming letter, which I should have answered before now. , I have been very pleased with life here, and I am sure I shall like this place very much. The work is, of course, very much more interesting than at Rome, and one has every sort of thing to do, what with bazaar riding and sight-seeing.

The chief political interest just now is Turco-Greek relations. They are very strained. An exchange of population is in progress between Macedonia and Thrace at present, and every sort of hardship is involved in the migration. Then there is the question of the islands. The Turks have a very active Minister of Marine, and the confidence inspired by his reforms in the fleet may tend to make the Turkish Government rather unyielding on the Mitylene and Scios question. Otherwise things are pretty quiet. The hunting here is quite amusing. A drag pursued by some twelve rather measly dog hounds over rather rough hill and heather country. The Master wears a pink coat and hunting cap of velvet — not hard. It is very comic. The Germans are very keen, and some Turkish officers come out, who are very agreeable. They talk French, and don't like talking German, which is the lingo one would think they would naturally know.

The Turks generally are more accessible now. The Ministers give dinner-parties of great splendour. Enver gave a very magnificent feast, I heard, with a band playing Wagner. He has married a royal princess, and plays the grand *seigneur* with great assiduity.

The society here is very official and political. Ministers and Ambassadors on every sofa talking high politics, very unlike Rome, which was frivolous and where the politicians never went out in the *monde*.

To the Hon. Irene Lawley.

British Embassy, Constantinople,
May 9, 1914.

How I envy your Spain and your drives to Sierra, and so on. … I've never been to Cameldoli — several places called that, one near Genoa, one near Naples — I never went to either. We were so d—d busy at Naples that we could never get out for expeditions. I think I rather misspent my time in Italy and didn't travel enough, being so much taken up with the hunting. Worst of life is one can't do everything at once, and that's what one finds to be very much the case here. The gun-running adventure must have been thrilling; but it looks now as if the crisis, as far as any real danger of civilians goes, was passed. I do not personally approve of "Federal" systems, but it seems that there is no way out except to give all turbulent persons (or potentially turbulent) exactly what they want and be done with it. I haven't read any speeches lately but I heard Mr. Birrell's was very good. The Government are very lucky not to have been hounded out of office with ignominy. I can't help thinking a more efficient Opposition would have got them out.

We had a delicious day — Harold, H.E., and me — at Therapia, about twelve miles up Bosphorus — it is the Posillipo of this place and lovely. It has a terraced garden, chock full of roses and stocks and irises and every sort of flower. Embassy has just been burnt down, but See's house is standing, a jolly old wooden house, whitewashed but generally Turkish style. The sea is at the door, we went up in the *mouche* and picked roses. Opposite Therapia is the bleak coast of Asia Minor, red soil, rock, bare scrub hills. It has a great charm for me, more so than the European side. Up and down the Bosphorus there are continual flights of little birds like petrels, little lost souls going up into the gloomy, windswept expanses of the Black Sea. There is always wind at Therapia and *always* colleagues, which makes it less nice than P. But there are always lovely flowers and garden ponds. We have had one or two jolly hunts, the last of them graced by the "flirt" of an important personage, a lady who is not received in polite society here. His lady was also at the meet So His E. had to steer a clear course. My poor little horse had a swollen knee as a result of the chase. I'd a jolly ride soon as the "flirt" had left me with a broken heart. And now I can't ride.

Then there has been a great *festa* here, St. George's Day, Elias's day for the Mohammedans. The whole people go out if the weather is warm, and have a picnic of roast lamb. This time there were not many as the wind was cold. But a good many people came over. It is an extraordinary thing to see them all squatting on the ground, perfectly happy doing nothing, and one is reminded of the women and children sitting round the camp-fires of Genghiz Khan, the real nomad spirit still alive. Perhaps they are still tired and quite happy simply to rest after their long marches. It is a becoming dress this black sort of nun's habit they all wear, but rather *triste* in this *ambiente* of cypresses. I doubt if I've yet seen a single real Turkish woman. On St. George's Day we saw a number of Imperial princesses and Circassians — in broughams — very pink and white but with black hair, dressed in light blue sort of bridesmaids' dresses and caps. We have all suffered bitterly from the cold, but it is now at last lovely, and I am writing this in the garden, so forgive pencil. It has great possibilities, this garden, and it absolutely overlooks the Golden Horn with the row of mosques beyond. There is an upper terrace lined with orange-trees, fine, but then lawns with dreary Russian-salad-like-sort-of-beds and no cypress avenue or jolly perspective of an avenue.

To the Same.
British Embassy, Constantinople,
May 15, 1914.

So you too are fired with the *wanderlust*. It is simply burning in me as the result of the presence of Miss Gertrude Bell, fresh from the heart of Arabia. She has been to a place called Hazzil, where you still find the East of the Middle Ages. It is ruled by the Amir Bim Rashid. He is a boy of sixteen, but he lives in the old-fashioned style. When Miss Bell arrived he was away raiding, leaving behind him his grandmother — Fatima by name; fairy story at once — and his wives, concubines, and eunuchs. It is an entirely women-run show, Fatima being absolutely *supreme*. The only other "European" in the place when Miss B. was there was a Circassian concubine sent to a former Bim Rashid by Abdul Hamid and passing from one head of the family to the next. The whole place smells of blood. They massacre each other in the traditional way, and the common people look with horror at the Palace code of morals, and the wives pass from one stage to another as the wives of David passed to his rebel son Absalom, Miss B. was lodged in a magnificent Arabian Nights colonnaded hall. She went to audiences given by the Regent, a cypher in Fatima's hands, and by the ladies of the harem; the ladies asked her what was the difference between Islam and Christianity, and she told them the words of the prophet Isa [*Jesus*]. There was a real Mogul atmosphere of gems and brocades, all come from India, and burning spices, and outside a silent town. Not a footfall can be heard, for all the streets are sand, and the camel's footfall is noiseless. The little Circassians sighed for the tramways of Constantinople. The Bim Rashid's are on the downward grade; the "man" of Arabia is one Bim Sand, Sheikh of El Hassa on the Gulf. He it was who was expelled from his city by a Bim Rashid, and reconquered it at the head of eleven men. He came by night to his wife, and she said as he knocked, "Who are you?" and he answered, "This is no time for love and kisses"; and then he went with his eleven men into every house where there were men of Bim Rashid's and killed them, and by the morning was master of the city. And to hear all this second-hand. It's *maddening*.

The Turkish provinces are in an appalling condition; in the most administered parts of the country the disorder is worst. There is not even the tribal sense of honour. Every single Arab has a rifle, and the Turks can do nothing. They have no troops; what they have are riddled with typhus. This is the great recruiting ground for the Turkish army, Asia Minor proper; there are no men for the wars in the Yemen, and the Balkans have thinned the population to an incredible extent The poverty is abject.

Things are shaping for war with Greece. The Greeks will come to no arrangement not based on the *status quo post bellum*; and the Turks can offer them nothing in exchange for the islands now in Greek occupation, except the islands in Italian occupation, which in Greek views are a very bad egg, as it is doubtful if the Italians will ever turn out (I think they will, but the Greeks don't). The Greeks, if they fight now, can by a single declaration of war stop the Turks getting the Dreadnoughts due to arrive this summer. If they temporize and let the Turks get these Dreadnoughts they will have to fight at a disadvantage. They *can't* get a Dreadnought for a long time. The only thing that may deter them is the fact that the Turks can bully Greeks living in Turkey. Even at this moment massacres of Greeks are feared at Smyrna, so incensed is the Moslem population against the Greek.

It is a tragic country, and we may have to play a big role in Arabia, where the Sheikhs are already virtually independent, and where it would be very easy for us to establish a loosely knit protectorate and keep them to some extent from each other's throats. The Turks have failed to do this. At this moment I suppose we should give the present Turkish Government a chance of getting things right; they are the only possible Government. The alternative is chaos leading to European occupation; and we are spectators at a distance — *such* a distance.

Turkish homes? I've been able to see very, very little of them. The Sultan Abdul, you will be glad to hear, has just got in another wife — one of his former second strings. He seems full of beans. It appears he had two children during the time

Sultan Abdul

of his exile — from 1909 to 1911 — one white and one jet black. This last wife has given us a lot of trouble, as the Turkish Government had given us assurances she should live in peace with her son, after she was chucked out from the Palace at the time of Abdul Hamid's exile; and the fact that she has been made to rejoin her former husband, has considerably inconvenienced her present "domestic" arrangements, consisting apparently in a life of unbridled orgies. The Imperial wives are recruited from any and every class, generally the lowest of the low, by sort of spies. The same applies to the wives of the big swells. Result: you get the blood quite spoiled, and the rise of any kind of aristocracy is rendered impossible. This must have had very harmful results, and now that the Turks are directing the Greeks and Armenians, they cannot find administration among their own subjects. Hence the progressive increase of foreign officials, etc., etc.

To the Same.
British Embassy, Constantinople,
June 8, 1914.

At a time when you write me long political letters, the crisis must be serious, and all things are possible. Write me another when you get home. We have not had much politics lately: mostly concerned with petty wrangles as to the size of the ship in which our Admiral is to visit the Sultan, This is a very material point; bigger ships have more officers, and this entails larger banquets for the Grand Vizier and Sultan and more expense. The former's face fell perceptibly when he was told that the British Admiral was coming to see the Sultan.

We hear less about war between Greece and Turkey, but things are shaping very badly. The Turks have a strong hand. If they fight they have nothing to lose. If the Greeks win the thing is not settled; either they fight before the big Turkish ships come out, in which case the Turks skulk in the Bosphorus where they can't be got at, and as soon as they have got their ships out press their demands again, or the Greeks fight while the ships are on the way or later, in which case they may destroy the Turkish fleet, and any way temporarily secure the islands; but the Turks won't give up the idea of *revanche*, and they always have in their hand so many Greek subjects whose lives they can make quite unbearable. The only way out is an exchange of islands. But this the Greeks will never consent to: they hold the Turkish naval power in utter contempt and don't care if their nationals in Turkey suffer. However, perhaps if the issue is postponed things may straighten themselves out.

On Wednesday we had the King's birthday garden party. The Ambassador stood on a carpet under a tree, and the Secretaries and Dragoman led down notable

HM King George V

after notable into the radiant presence and then conducted them to a superb buffet — Turks, English, Armenians, Greeks, and so on. Men in cowls like lamp extinguishers, in chimney-pot berettes, in turbans and flowing robes, came up and fired off little speeches at him.

Charles's long-standing interest in the perplexed affairs of the Near East suggested the ride through Macedonia and Albania described in the following letters. The "Durazzo crisis" discussed in the spring in the chanceries of Constantinople, and news of fighting in Albania — over a perennial Epirote grievance — added possibly the charm and invitation of a lost cause to the excursion.

First we touch the history of Serbia in its year of triumph over Bulgaria after the Second War. The first Balkan war of the Christian States against the Turks ended with the Peace of Adrianople 1912. In the Second War, Bulgaria attacked Serbia and Greece after they had formed an alliance to resist the claims of Bulgaria, discontented with the provisions of the peace.

The scene of battle visited at Kilkitsch is the field of Bregalnika, where the Bulgarian General fell on the Serbians suddenly, and where after two days' fighting the Serbs were victorious on July 1, 1913. Kilkitsch, burnt by their Greek allies, remained Serbian by the Peace of Bukharest, August 10, 1913. The scene at Kilkitsch described is typical of Serbia in the process of consolidating her new territories and moving her populations. On the other hand, the linguistic and political Babel of Albania is represented by Durazzo, the capital, too much agitated at the moment by a Greek revolt for the wise English traveller to enter.

Koritza in Albania, which was reached, is a city of great antiquity. It is the centre of much Anglo-Hellenism to-day. The Epirotes' cause summarized elsewhere by Charles as "the protest that they are Greeks and not Turks", was the supposed motive for the fighting which had recently dyed its streets red and that was still going on as Charles approached the scene which all along had been his goal.

But whatever passing sympathy towards an Epirote cause inspired his start, his journey in Albania was marked with prudence and moderation, even detachment towards "the revolt of Tchukes". Charles's description of the nature of the cause at issue draws a picture of a cause obscure enough to discourage active partisanship.

The Greek monastery visited on the way is near Karies, on Mount Athos. The Russian monks described belong probably to the great religious houses above the landing-places named Russovnik or Laura, on the Ionian Sea.— B. W. C.

To the Same.

Salonica,
June 14, 1914.

I am very flourishing; off; to Monastir to-morrow. I began my travels Monday and went to Mount Athos. Mount A. is like this, a long broken ridge running into this marvellous peak, the side of the ridge; its innumerable ravines are thickly wooded scrub and heather with wild holly on the lower slopes and chestnuts and oaks and pines on the higher. The convents are mostly within two or three hours at nearest of each other, and are only approachable by mule or boat. I expected a sort of huge monastic building, cloister on cloister, didn't you? — rather like S. Marco at Florence ten times over: or, perhaps more frowning and castellated. They are, as a matter of fact, great rambling country houses built in sometimes an English country house style, Lutyens, or the Stamboul style, round a sort of central court, most of which is taken up by a Byzantine church formed like the Greek cross and the dome in the centre. Inside there is a sort of covered loggia at first, then the church. The iconostasis dividing the inmost shrine (or sanctuary) from the rest. The inconostasis is a rood screen covered with icons, curious painted faces peeping out of an armour plating of gold and jewels, and an occasional brown hand visible. The gold and silver work is very wonderful, mostly tenth and eleventh century. Then the cups are things of wonderful workmanship, presented as a rule by some Byzantine Emperor or his particular community. One I saw was in silver with little figures in gorgeous enamel worked all round, and another was of some sort of opalescent marble with gold setting and handles. Then there was a fine silver crucifix with the Emperor Constantine's seal on it which the abbot told me he was going to take back to Constantinople. There are also marvellous relics, not so much the dirty old bones themselves as the gold cases in which they are shelled. Through a chink in a wonderful gold and jewelled gauntlet you see the hand of St. Luke or St. John, a withered brown substance, rather like Lady —'s personality, I should think, seen through her glowing outward form. The Greek Church have a strange tendency for "angelification". St. John Baptist is always represented with wings of an angel, and the angels who visited Abraham at Mamre and were chaffed by Sarah are supposed to have been the Holy Trinity. The Byzantine Church spent much energy in discussions on the sex of angels. I don't know what would happen if they came to Mount Athos, or if this question was ever settled. The monks were very hospitable and charming people; only one did I find who could talk French, and they did not seem to have any great cultivation. They were feverishly interested in politics. The ritual of a call was rather complex; on arrival one was ushered into a room — Axminster carpets and Maple armchairs of inferior quality, walls hung with portraits of all crowned heads, oleographs and photographs. One of them brought a tray with jam, liqueurs, and glasses of water; and the proper procedure was to take a spoonful of jam, then a glass of water, then a liqueur. I made several mistakes. I tried to combine the jam and the water as a sort of strop. I had to talk Turkish to them, my Albanian servant interpreting in Greek, so you can imagine what a brilliant standard conversation reached. They often took me to their libraries where there are lovely manuscripts and little golden-backgrounded angels and evangelists every twenty pages or so, and occasionally one comes across an Emperor's handwriting in purple, i.e. scarlet ink always; not many fine bindings. I didn't stay at a monastery; I was only there (Mount Athos) two days, and the headquarters, a place called Karies, is the most central. The scarcity which reigns there is remarkable; one evening our host could only find three eggs.

The monks seem to absorb all the eatables. My last day I went to see a Russian monastery, Moslem and organized on sort of Selfridge lines, almost two thousand people dependent on it. I saw the dinner the monks were going to have — one piece of salt fish with sauerkraut, not up to sample. Monasticism must be a vegetable sort of life tinged with discomforts no sensible man would accept.

From Mount Athos to this place (Salonica) on a dirty old boat, where the whole of the third class was taken up by Moslem refugees going to Salonica to get a boat for Turkey. They lay in the hold on their beds and mattresses, a heap of human beings one on top of the other, occasionally lit up by flashes of lightning from behind the mountains. The women wore black Turkish dresses and palest veils and head-dress in one. While they slept their troubled sleep a couple of Greek soldiers were dancing on the bridge, singing curious songs and rather drunk. You saw the whole discomfort of life here in one flash. This is the coveted city, which has been fought for and will be fought for yet again. There is a magnificent semi-circular sweep of harbour, and from the harbour rise red roof after red roof up to the Venetian castellated walls and the fort beyond, Genoese towers by the sea close up by the walls, and in the fort there are old Mussulman houses almost up to Stamboul, but in plaster instead of wood. The country around is barren down lands, cleared of vegetation, and a great plain on one side. The Jews are the real feature of Salonica. There are about 80,000 of them out of a population of 150,000. Most of the Salonica Jews are descended from Spanish Jews expelled by Ferdinand and Isabella. There is nothing else like it in this part of the world. There is no other town where the Jews are so much a community by themselves; they keep their old names intact also. Politics, I need not say, are the chief interest here, and, as connected with them, refugees; and I have seen heaps and heaps of them all saying more or less the same thing. They are just put into vast camps here, the arrivals from Turkish territory, till they can be settled, and they are given a loaf of bread a day per head by the Greek Government. Then there are Greeks from the Caucasus who have come here hoping to find the streets paved with gold, sitting on their baggage in the harbour; and there are Mussulmen leaving Christian territory, huddled into mosques, houses, anywhere till they get their boat.

To-day we went out to the battlefield of Kilki, where the Serbs beat the Bulgars in the Allies War, and we saw the trenches and stood where the Bulgar General Staff directed the action, and went over the burnt ruins of the tower fired by the Greeks *after* the battle in very cold blood. Near by, an enormous camp of Serb refugees from Asia and Thrace; the little boys tried to sell us bullets and shells, and the old women begged from us, and the calm of the whole scene was very impressive.

*Ferdinand
of Bulgaria*

To the Same.

*Tchukes, Albania,
June 20, 1914.*

After Salonica we got off to Monastir. It is a nice little Turkish country town in the middle of a large plain with mountains all round. I stayed there one day only, and in the morning went to see the battlefield. It is a very good sight, and the most of the fighting took place on a very high hill, wooded in its lower reaches and bare on the top. The Turks had nearly trenched it, and were driven from position to position by the Serbs. It is curious to see the trenches dug while the Serbs advanced. Sometimes they are little scrapings with the bayonet simply and just dug up by a man to protect himself for the moment, sometimes rather more elaborate. The fighting went on for about three days. Below in the plain there are very heavy marshes across which the Serb army had to advance. Some of them stayed there about twenty-six hours, in winter too. They are tough devils. From Monastir I headed my descent into Albania. This has so far consisted of two days' ride to a place called Koritza and two days' ride from Koritza on the way to a place called El Bassan, which I don't suppose I shall ever get to as the road is closed. The first day I had to make in a carriage with an attendant Serbian official who was to sort of bear-lead me — a rather tiresome little man. I don't like their jacks in office. The man of these parts if once he is educated is inclined to go downhill in character and more still in charm. He gets into the slouch-hatstage of civilization and loses his interest for the European sentimentalist busybody and also some real qualities. We went to a place called Stenia on a lovely crystal blue lake, Lake Presbra, with beautiful brown rocky hills all round except on the Monastir side, where there is a plain full of poplars like all the flat country here, and rather reminding one of France. We were met by a Serbian officer, in command of the little detachment there, and he made the soldiers do their little dances for us. They consisted in little crab-like steps with the men in a ring all round a gentleman who played bagpipes in the middle, and were very racy of the soil. The Serbian peasant seems a genial and very gay individual, always smiling and friendly. He is said to be capable of great latent cruelty. We had a very friendly meal. The Serbs do not, happily, try to commit one to political opinions. The next day I went on along the side of the lake through even more pretty country, first great oakwoods, then rocky hills covered with a lot of scrub and sort of wild box shrub, which is very pretty, and occasional great carpets of flowers. This day we had to ride practically all the time. I left my Serb friend on the Greco-Serb frontier, for we had to go through a little bit of Greece before entering the promised land. He wanted to come with me into Albania, but I knocked that on the head, saying that he would compromise me, which he would have done. I then, when it was a question of going through Greece, told him that he had better not, as he might compromise me there also. He was not a bad little fellow, but I had had enough of him.

At the frontier it was rather exciting. I wondered very much if I was going to get through. They sat me down in a little tent on a sort of floor of boxwood, and there I drank coffee and smoked cigarettes in suspense, while they had to go and find their officer, which seemed to be ages. It looked as if I would have to beat a humiliating retreat, which would have much pleased my Serbian friends, for they all said that I should be stopped for sure; they want to make out that this country is in high disorder and cannot run itself. After about half an hour I was let through amid tremendous demonstrations of Anglo-Albanian fraternization. They told me about "Sultan Wild", and what blighters the Greeks were, and how much they liked the English.

I rode into Koritza very happy, and stayed with a missionary there, a nice man full of politics with a jolly little wife. My head reels with all they told me about the linguistic question in Epirus and the state of mind of those unfortunate people who didn't want to be Albanians and thought they were Greeks, and so on. The next morning I saw the Prefect, the Bishop, the President of the Court of Appeal, and a curious old monk who had been at Mount Athos, a singular example of the infertile type of intellect produced by monasticism combined with that diseased nationalism which is a feature of every one's mentality out here. He also breakfasted with us next morning. The church at Koritza is lovely — built about 1707, but at first sight one would take it for a twelfth-century church. This is a real sign how far back this jolly country is. At first sight one wouldn't think so at Koritza. The country is flat; from the rock which forms the frontier into new Greece one sees a huge expanse of very well-cultivated plain. There are a number of very educated French- and English-speaking Albanians, full of modern notions; clever men, I should think. Then one sees lots of people unarmed, and the first impression is of a very quiet country-side. One can hardly believe that the Greeks were street-fighting in the town as lately as April; it is almost disappointing- one expects mountains rugged as one has never seen before, and so on.

From Koritza it was a jolly ride to a little place called Pogratetch, at the top of Lake Ochrida, which is a huge bit of water where they pull out very good trout, through the same quiet sort of country — oakwoods on all the hills, or rather oak scrub. They never let a tree grow here, it is always cut down for firewood. To-day another lovely ride along the side of Lake Ochrida. Our escort passed the time shooting the fishes from their horses, which we could see in the jolly limpid water as we went along. After about three hours along the lake, the wildest hills, rock and boxwood, with herons sitting on the tops of the "crags" in suitable attitudes, we went up and over a sort of pass into the plain of the Shumbi Valley. The Shumbi is a jolly river — rapid, with banks steep down into the water, red soil. We crossed the Shumbi, and are now in a little sort of rest-house. I am in a room like a prison and lying on matting, my bed for to-night. I am afraid I shall have to go back from here. There are insurgents within a few hours of us. I wanted to go on and made a scene. They said that I did so on my own responsibility and they will give me no escort. I think I shall funk it. They expect definite information to-morrow, and I shall act accordingly. I am sorry for this unfortunate country, still more so for those who love it. It has too many neighbours and too few friends. The hero of a Henty novel would no doubt at once take command of these people and lead them against the enemy's positions. But I shan't, and I am sure it is the last thing they would like. Letra and the rest of them wish to make out a case for the view that Albania should in the first instance have been partitioned between herself and Greece. Well, we will see.

Later. — They (i.e. the authorities) *begged* me not to go beyond Tchukes. My *kavass*, after kicking a good deal, expressed great hesitation, so I funked it Twenty hours' travelling yesterday finds me back here. Yesterday I started at four, got to the Serb frontier on horseback by 6.30, and to Straga about nine; carriage there to Monastir; two breakdowns and a walk or two, to and from places where fresh carriages available. It's the strenuous life. All over now. I am sorry. I am quite Albanoman, though I doubt their vaunted fighting qualities. These people at Tchukes and the insurgents opposed to them will sit opposite each other indefinitely. Then the authorities will bring a gun up and the rebels will scatter. The men I talk to of the Tchukes "force" said they, meant to impress the rebels by superior strength but not to fight them! The drilled peasant is really the best fighter, I should think, not the "wild man".

To the Same.

British Embassy, Therapia,
July 5, 1914.

Our life here has been very agreeable, with a lot of riding and not too much work. I nearly had one nasty jar: my horse, whom I was taking up a little bank, swerved into the fence, and I got my head entangled in brambles right round my neck. I was nearly pulled off, but not quite, and came back home with a line of blood round the neck as if some one had cut the head off and replaced it. The people I passed on the way home turned pale at this ghoulish sight.

The Admiral has now left us; his visit was a success, I think, and the Heir-Apparent went on board his ship. This was a score over the Germans, whom he did not visit. He was nearly drowned in endeavouring to get on board, as the sea was very rough, and his launch captain very incompetent I unhappily missed the Sultan at dinner; they did not know when I should be back from the "wilds". Sultey was in great form; he guffawed loudly when the Ambassador remarked the dining-room was very large, and a second time when the Ambassador asked him if he ever dined alone there. The food and wines were, I am told, mediocre. The Admiral got a 150-guinea watch for his pains and a portrait of the Heir-Apparent in a silver frame. Sultey is very interested in King George's health, and always asks for it.

The Gerrys last night gave a very notable *festa* in their wonderful garden. We went up through a beautifully lit tunnel on to a terrace high up, and sat on carpets under pine-trees by the light of Japanese lanterns, and listened to wonderful Greek singers, who sang songs in which they had to bleat like sheep; occasionally a basso very profondo gave tongue in fine style. Very like a scene from the Decameron, if not so lascivious, with nice little boys to play with. I think this was a sort of house warming.

The new Adviser to the Ministry of Justice is staying with us — a young barrister.

Eton and Oxford, a high mind, and a profound knowledge of the Insurance Bill. What other qualifications could you want for inspiring respect in the Turkish mind? He is a very nice fellow.

We have given dinner to the Ambassador. The German Ambassadress, who is a great friend of my housemate, Hugh Thomas, was the chief *clou*, and everything went very well.

I think this is all the Therapia news. I am afraid it is hardly scandalous enough for the jaded palate of the Londoner. I am principally kept informed of the London news by the "Letters of Eve" which appear in the *Tatler* weekly. I am much interested to hear that political feeling is running high.

To the Same.

Therapia,
July 12, 1914.

There is a writing paper famine in this house, so I shall have to keep a very straight line across the page. There is also a famine in events, as this place is very much the "cool sequestered vale of life", and the summer doings of a small, intimate, and not very interesting society require the subtle handling of a Jane Austen.

I have to sell my pony. There is no help for it. I am so full of work, as I have to know all about Kurds and Armenia, things which are at present the merest names to me; and I am also taking on *proprio motu* (?) an endeavour to get hold of what anthropological information our Consuls' possess. I am writing them a circular which they will, I am afraid, think a monument of insolence, and probably throw into the waste-paper basket, if such things exist in Kurdistan. So I won't ride enough to keep my dear pony, and as I rather want cash he will have to go.

I am reading Sir C. Eliot's work on Turkey. It is an extraordinary work, and the lucidity with which he deals with the various heresies in the Eastern Church, and the migration of the Turkish tribes is quite amazing. The riddle to me of the history of the East is the ethnical kinship, quite indisputable, of the Sultans of Stamboul and the Mogul of India. In things like appreciation of the arts they are as far apart as — say — the Southend-on-Sea Town Council of to-day and the Signory of Florence of the Middle Ages. However, they were both nomads and dwellers in tents, as can be seen from the Mogul buildings. Here they were such copy-cats, and simply added the minaret to the Byzantine church.

It is extraordinary to see their women-folk out on a day's pleasure, quite happy just sitting in the grounds in the shade resting from the long day's march over the hot desert in their subconscious selves, I suppose nomads still in spirit — a curious contrast to the English who on the occasion I'm thinking of were out also for a day's pleasure, and getting themselves hot and thirsty playing cricket in the glaring sun. I like the looks of the Turkish women with their soft darkling eyes and neat little features, and clean, clear complexions. They look so full of inward peace, and so cherished and cared for; they have also the charm of great seriousness — at least in appearance — and of that certain knowledge of what their part is in life. I don't believe you, any of you, have. They are a contrast to the Slav woman. The Slav looks on his womenfolk simply as drudges; they mayn't marry before they've given so many years of work in the fields. When they do marry they are wizen-like old crab-apples and haven't a trace of looks. The Turk, who is a gentleman, does look after his women, and if he isn't chivalrous at least, in a mild way, invests them with some kind of glamour. I'm not sure women aren't really happier if they live in the Oriental way. I doubt if the West is really much of a gainer from the freedom its women enjoy. However, I don't suppose you'd always like to be dressed like the women on that postcard sitting by the tombs. We have been much thrilled by an hour spent at one of the Sultan's mosques on the opposite shore, a glorious building of pink marble and stone, with great palatial rooms built on a little eminence by the sea covered with trees, with a wonderful view down the Bosphorus. It is about a hundred years old, built at the time of the treaty of [*illegible*] with the Russians. We are at present very *bien* with the German Ambassadress, who has twice dined with us. She is a charming woman, a master at tennis, and a tall, queenly, "perfect lady" type, which I rather like — a lot to say for herself. What an awful tragedy about dear Denny Anson. That rugged charm and Viking spirit and glorious laugh. I liked him because I also felt he was doing the sort of things I should have liked to have done, but hadn't the nerve and will to do — and he was such a powerful swimmer. One's circle grows constantly narrower.

To the Same.

Therapia,
July 20, 1914.

How curious it is that deaths nowadays always cause *embêtements* among the survivors. At least three recent ones that I know of have done so and been the cause of the breaking up of life-long friendships. I believe we have subconsciously harked back to the point of view of the witch-doctor, and that we also think if any one dies some one of his neighbours is personally responsible. If we accepted S. G.'s views on life and death, it would never be so. We, however, are an irreligious crowd, and have not even the fine fatalism of the Moslem. I am sure it is this want of religion which makes people so often squabble like ghouls at the grave-head.

Let us leave these sad subjects and get back to the wooded heights and brilliant blue of the Bosphorus. We all went a swimming party one day with the Germans, the Ambassador and Ambassadress. Some of us rode and the others went by *mouche*. It was a jolly day, and my first bathe since here. The Bosphorus itself is always agitated into tiresome little waves which fall into one's mouth, so one has to go out practically to the Black Sea for real pleasure. Also the current is so strong that it is impossible to swim up; one must go down. I have had several bathes since, and on one occasion nearly left my Chancery keys — VITAL to the Empire — at the place where I was undressing. As much as my place was worth. I should have then had to bury myself in Gisburne and to become a master of hounds.

I have dined with the American Ambassador, a spread of about fourteen courses, the aerated waters *coulaient à flots*, but the wine was less facile. Brotherly love was, howbeit, much in the ascendant. I sat next the Danish Minister, the fortunate husband of a lovely lady. He is like all Scandinavians, but we have identical views as to the value of exercise, and are both confirmed opponents of the cold bath: that is the type who has produced Ibsen. We have nothing so obvious to revolt against. After dinner I talked to his wife.

I must get up now, as I have to buy a cowboy hat for the bal costumi — it's the same world all over, and no far cry from the Tiber to the Bosphorus.

Charles Buxton mentioned in the following letter was the eldest son of Lord Buxton. At nineteen he inclined so strongly to Socialism as to be claimed as a convert. After devoted work for the working men's college alluded to he put his theories into practice on a small holding. He was farming at Wye when he died at twenty-two. To Mrs. Hamlyn Charles Lister confided at Constantinople his hope that his own experience of Socialism would bear fruit in his life, expanded as it was by life abroad. — B. W. C.

To Mrs. Hamlyn.

Therapia,
July 25, 1914.

Many thanks for your charming letter. I was very much attached to Charles Buxton, but had no idea he was so devoted to the simple life. He was always serious-minded, of course. I fancy his handling of the Ruskin College difficulties was very able and inspired great respect.

"We" in my letter was myself and my Albanian *kavass* — a jolly old fellow who had been with Aubrey Herbert.

Our life here has gone on very peacefully. We give occasional dinner parties, which have generally been fairly successful, and by dint of frequent *embêtements* we manage to keep our cook pretty well up to the mark. Lobster and lamb are rather frequent features in the bill of fare. But Therapia is not in itself a land of great plenty: and its lobsters are certainly almost, I should think, the equals of the Clovelly patriarchs.

I am now installed in my own rooms, with my books round me, but little more done: I feel a real nomad nowadays, and never think it worth while to do more than get the most hurried traces of myself into my surroundings. After all, "the world is a bridge, pass over it but build no house there"; much more so Therapia. I am in a state of continual dissatisfaction at the little I manage to get read and the little I get to know about this fascinatingly perplexing country, which I never want to leave, but am otherwise very happy and interested.

We are, by the time you get this, probably in the thick of a most difficult time abroad. Serbia and Austria *aux prises*, and a conflict raging which it will be most difficult to localize. Every one here seems to think war is certain. The Austrian Note is worded in such a way as to make its acceptance by Servia impossible. It is a very strong order. This moment, from Austria's point of view, is a good one. The longer she waits the worse it will be for her.

No more for the present, dear Mrs. Hamlyn. Write me some more gossip. I wish I had some here for you, but we are all so well behaved.

To the Hon. Irene Lawley.

Thekapia,
July 27, 1914.

Here our excitements have been principally political. It is a good moment for the Austrians. If they wait, Serbia will have time to consolidate herself in her new territories; Russia will be more ready for war than she is now; Serbia may manage to patch up an agreement with Bulgaria; their own internal difficulties may increase in other directions. It is the first time the Austrians have taken a really strong line since the beginning of the Balkan War. The Russians here were very much surprised. The Germans think the war will be localized, i.e. the Russians will accept their slap in the face and do very little for their Serbian friends. The Russian Ambassador's language has been so far very mild. I confess I do not see how the Russians can take it lying down, and if they once come in, the possibilities are endless. It will be curious to see whether the Germans will make use of these events as an opportunity for aggressive war against Russia. Anti-Russian feeling is at present very strong in Germany. The Austrians have got their tails up, and the Secretaries here seem very happy at the turn events have

HIH Archduke
Franz Ferdinand and his
assassination that was the
trigger for the
First World War

... in Sarajevo

Franz Ferdinand and Sophie with their children
Prince Ernest, Princess Sophie,
and Prince Maximilian

The car and the Franz Ferdinand's uniform can
be seen today in the Arsenal Museum in Vienna.

... the assassination

Above: lying in state

Right: the funeral in Vienna

taken. I saw the Austrian Ambassadress yesterday. She is English and charming; she will have three sons at the war. It is curious to see all our newspapers taking the side of Austria. I don't think the Austrians could have taken any other course, and on the merits of the case I am for the Austrians. We shall, however, look rather foolish if we have ultimately to range ourselves either diplomatically or otherwise, against Austria, and this is not unlikely, considering our general orientation, so our Press should have been more non-committal.

Otherwise life has been much as usual. We are now in Ramazan, the great fasting month. Moslems don't eat or drink all day, then at sunset they fall to and feast all the night. I fancy they sleep most of the day. I don't think this rule is very generally observed; but people like the caiquejev, the men who row one's boat, are inclined to be pious, and it is a bad thing to work them very much.

The Grand Vizier gave a party to celebrate an anniversary of the Constitution a little while ago. It was a very remarkable show. The American Ambassador rubbing shoulders with the Emirs of Mecca, and the villa by the Bosphorus, with its Western exterior, its pseudo-Arabesque Alhambra-like reception-rooms and its garden arranged like an open-air café concert. Nowhere else do you get these contrasts and this meeting of East and West.

I played cricket the other day, and made one run in the first innings and three in the second, four more than I expected to make, I can tell you. Even cricket, when little children in those delightful baggy trousers and their fezzes stroll across the ground, and you see the peasants working at the haystacks with their great red cummerbunds round their stomachs, and there are real buffaloes, like the Indian ones, cropping the grass hard by or cooling themselves in the water with only their shiny black flat backs showing over the surface, or perhaps the point of a curved horn, has a charm of its own. Tennis with the Germans is the great Sunday afternoon occupation; then the German colony is seen in all its glory. It largely consists of the daughters of former dragomans, fine wenches with a powerful drive down the court and honest *mädchen* features and colouring. One can imagine their seduction *seriatim* by Goethe. I wonder if he would have had such success in any other country. They have a lovely garden with little grass valleys and lily-covered ponds.

Charles was too ardent and energetic to endure patiently what he describes elsewhere as the "leaden calm of Therapia" during the fateful days of early August. War was a Fact. The sight of others leaving Constantinople to take an active part in the struggle was too much for him, and whilst seeing some friends off, homeward bound, he could not resist the impulse to remain on board. He regretted the rash step as soon as he had taken it, and returned by the quickest route to his post. His longing to get to England and into the fighting line was only strengthened by this escapade, and he did not relax his efforts till he had obtained the consent of the Foreign Office to his request for leave to join the Army. — B. W. C.

To the Hon. Irene Lawley.

Therapia,
August 4, 1914.

I wish I was you in the thick of it; we are very newsless and postless here, and have very little idea of what England is going to do. So far we seem to have sat on the fence rather, and to be very much offering pills for the earthquake when we put forward our little mediation proposals, etc.

Why this paper, you will ask? I am doing an enforced trip on this old boat, not having been nippy enough while seeing people off. It is rather a bore, but I shall see Smyrna and get back to Constantinople without loss of time. It is also nice resting, doing the journey third-class. Here they simply put up an awning over the bows and let the people shift for themselves then. The people have their luggage with them, consisting of bed-clothes and a little trunk, and they put them out anywhere. I, who did not take any clothes with me, find myself at a disadvantage and rather like the Son of Man; but I lead quite a pleasant pillar-to-post existence in this glorious sunshine looking at the coasts of the Ægean islands and the coasts of Asia opposite. It is an extraordinary mixed crowd, mostly Ottoman Greeks who are trying to escape the Turkish mobilization. They sing in a weary sing-song nasal tone all the day. They have some of them got gramophones which coin the same sort of sounds. A more picturesque element is provided by the numerous [illegible] who appear in a long voile sort of dressing-gown and with sashes, or striped white and yellow, white and red tunics, and then little head capes with great knotted strings round the top, in black and gold. Then there are Central Asians with their little flower-embroidered skull-caps and snub-noses and Mongolian eyes; and the sea and sun reconcile me to almost anything, even to sitting about in dirty little corners of a third-class. You should see the state of my white ducks after these adventures — discreditable in the main but with their lighter side. Don't retail them, because I feel culpably vague about the whole thing and shall get into hot water on return.

The people on this boat are most incorruptible without exception, and will do nothing for any one or anything. I have talked nearly all my languages to-day, including Turkish, with great fluency. The calm of all these people is very wonderful, and their cheerful submission to discomforts of many kinds; also their ability to sleep in almost impossible positions.

Therapia life has been peculiar; nothing to do all day, and a few little telegrams morning and evening which are very unsatisfactory and give us no real news. Food is very scarce and gold more so. I fancy a temporary accommodation is being made by the issue of bank-notes. Those who, like myself, have overdrafts will be in a jolly position, paying 11 per cent on them.

I wonder what the next of the chapter of accidents will be. No one feels very happy about the situation just now except our American colleague, a fine old German Jew, who declares that the Germans will be in Paris in a month's time. In that case it will be rather late for us to do anything by land. We should by rights have already begun landing.

I can write no more — I am depressed. Our position is, and always has been, unassailable, but we have not made the most of it.

> ### To the Same.
> #### British Embassy, Constantinople.
> #### (No date.)

I am much relieved that we have come in; and our state of suspense as to whether we were going to do the right thing or not was very acute. I believe the Germans thought we were for peace at any price and would never dream of chipping in, even if they violated Belgian neutrality, which we had always told them would constitute a *casus belli*.

I feel we are in a very strong position, and even if the Germans get to Paris, we and the Russians can continue the war till we have crushed Germany.

The Turks are very cross with us now, and we may all have to come home — if the Germans manage to rush them (the Turks) into war with Russia. That is now the game; a dirty one and played with characteristic cynicism.

It is manifest Turkey is faced with certain disaster if she makes war on the Triple Entente.

England rescues Belgium

Contemporary cartoons depicting the invasion of Belgium

To the Same.

British Embassy, Constantinople,
August 18, 1914.

I was glad to get your letter. You will, I think, regret going to America; the homing instinct is very strong if one's country is in danger, and you will be anxious and newsless over there. You can't imagine what a state of suspense we are in here — and how wretched we should be if we hadn't plenty of work.

SMS Goeben

SMS Breslau

You have no idea of what they have been doing here to compromise the Turks. They have got their warships in; *Goeben* and *Breslau* crews and German officers have been harassing our shipping in every possible way. [*Charles held strongly the view that our Government should not have recognized the transfer of the Goeben and the Breslau to Turkey. Once we had allowed the purchase of the German ships we could only work for a much-to-be-desired rupture between Turkey and the Central Powers. — R.*] Destroying our wireless apparatus, while their own are left intact by the Turks, who might by right destroy all wireless in this, a neutral port; requisitioning British cargo for supplies for their army; putting difficulties in the way of our telegraphy or of our getting news favourable to us published in the Press, and exciting public opinion against the Triple Entente and all Christians to such a pitch that the next phase, unless the tide turns, will be the preaching of a Holy War against all "infidels".

Sir Louis is just back. He gives an interesting account of things at home before Ministers finally decided to do the right thing, and of Kuhlmann's intrigues and suggestions that we should be content with an assurance that the Germans would not bombard Calais and Boulogne. I think no Germans are at this moment worth English tears, which I hear were so liberally shed by some over the Lichnowskys. Ever since the 1st of July Germany had decided on aggressive war against France and Russia, and the feigned innocence of the Lichnowskys should not find any believers. The Germans here seemed to calculate on our neutrality. They were equally confident the Italians would go in, and that there would be no difficulty with the Belgians. Three big mistakes. You can't imagine our feelings those days when it was doubtful what we were going to do. I believe the Italians will join us soon; here they talk as if they were at war with Germany already. Then the Roumanians will move. What a triumph for Rodd if this happens. We may have bad news for the next fortnight or more, as the big battles on the Rhine will soon begin, but later on, when the Russian steam-roller gets moving, our stock will be up again. The morale of the French is at this moment very high, but one must at least be prepared for their failure for the moment.

We have already gained a fortnight and no German soldiers on French territory, and the Russian mobilization has gone on quicker than was expected.

To the Same.
British Embassy, Constantinople,
August 20, 1914.

You will have all our bad news long before you get this: I was personally never very sanguine as to the French resistance, but I hoped that with ourselves to help them, and after the Belgian resistance, that the German advance would at any rate have been more delayed than appears to have been the case. I fear our part in the big battle has been fine but tragic, and I can hear the "beating, of the wings" of the Angel of Death very near. We have had black weeks before, and lived through them, and, as in the days of Napoleon, there is our fleet between us and a rapid fall to the status of a second-class power, so we can still hold our heads high, and I think we are rather at our best in this kind of situation. We are much where we were after Austerlitz, though the *débâcle* of our Continental allies is not nearly so complete: and we can look with faith to our Trafalgar.

Things here have naturally gone from bad to worse; German sailors arrive by scores, and German merchantmen are being fitted out from the German Embassy as auxiliary cruisers to have a go at the Russians in the Black Sea, it is thought. We are simply powerless, and expect to have to pack up any day. The Turks are quite *tête montée*. The Ministers say that they know nothing of these batches of German sailors arriving, and are in any case wholly impotent. The Bulgarian attitude is hitherto doubtful, but likely to incline to Germans after their successes.

If we stay here we are likely to be faced by a serious shortage of foodstuffs. We are all, however, very cheerful and busy.

We have, I fear, missed the chance of getting Italy in to join us. If the French had made a firm offer of Tunis at the outset we might have got them. The French, however, thought they were going to win, and made evasive promises, and the Italians are now going to get all they want from their past allies without stirring a finger — simply as the price of neutrality. However, "Come the whole world in arms".

It is a good thing that one hasn't much time to think and wonder what the tranquil existence of the subject of a second-class Power would be like. I shouldn't like it myself, because I feel my life very much bound up with my flag.

I am very anxious for Diana, whom I love second best in the world — what she must be suffering now. However, she's not the only one.

I wonder about the future — I do not feel this war will make any one better friends afterwards. We shall take the German colonies, I suppose, and as the Germans cannot forgive us for the colonies we have already got, it is doubtful if they will forgive us the more for having collared theirs. Then there is the embittering rôle that the Press plays in all mix-ups with its polemics as to atrocities and so on. I fancy no peace will be of a very lasting character. We shall go on fighting, and finally sicken the working classes of the whole performance.

The Germans now take the line that they will make peace with the French, conduct a "platonic" war with ourselves, and then unite us all against the Russians; this is very fanciful.

Europe an armed camp for years, broken up, dissolved in final ruin and revolution by those who have long suffered; it isn't a cheerful picture. But love seems for the moment to have fled the world.

To the Same.
British Embassy, Constantinople,
August 24, 1914.

One rapid line amid the hurry of these days, just before the mail goes in the middle of all this trouble — we never know when we have a post out and so on. ... The reports of a French reverse in the neighbourhood of Metz are, I fear, correct, but the French say it is an *incident de guerre*, and will not make any substantial difference to their plan of campaign. The Germans are happy and drinking champagne, but the Russians have begun their offensive and have invaded Eastern Prussia and will soon get the blighters on the run.

Yesterday I went to my first Baisans, the month of feasting after the fasting

The Russian steam roller moves forward

month of Ramazan. It is a great reception held by the Sultan in the big hall at the palace, an enormous high room, with a colossal chandelier hanging from the centre point of the dome all hideously painted with still life and perspective effects with great plaster pilasters. The Sultan sits on a large sort of seat like the woolsack, covered with cloth of gold, and the notables come up; some of them kiss a sort of stole with tassels held by the Master of Ceremonies; others, more distinguished, such as the Sheriff of Mecca's representatives and the Sheik al Islam, actually kiss his coat. As the Sultan comes in and goes out a shout is raised which means "Long life to our Sultan; yet there is God greater than him": it is now quite indistinguishable and all the time a band plays barbaric music, great clashes of cymbals and banging of brass. On the floor there are little strips of carpet for people to walk up, quite dowdy. The religious heads, the Sheik al Islam and the Mecca people are the real feature. The Sultan gets up for them, and for the Patriarch he advances about a yard towards the edge of a carpet, cloth of gold, in front of the throne. He is like a great egg, and sits half-right or half-left as the case may be, on the edge of the throne, with his hands tightly crossed in his lap. His whole chest and tummy are gold lace. He can walk slowly and get up on to his feet, but is otherwise not very mobile. The people who went up to him backed out of the presence, and then lined the sides of the hall.

The situation here since the Ambassador's return is rather easier. Enver has been laid up and the Grand Vizier is recovering power, but the military authorities, under German influence, continue to be most insolent. [*Enver Pasha, as everybody knows, was the dominant military authority in Constantinople and had received his military training in Germany. He became War Minister in Turkey at the time of the Young Turk revolution. To his influence more than any other we owe our rupture with the Turks in 1914. — R.*] They actually threatened to take down the wireless on the Italian and U.S. Embassy Stationnaires while they let German ships keep it up all the time. From the way they talk to the Ambassador one would think they were conquerors imposing terms on a conquered enemy. But we are being very patient. Otherwise we should be playing the German game.

Enver Pasha

To the Hon. Lady Wilson.

British Embassy, Constantinople,
August 24, 1914.

Many thanks for your last letter, which I had not answered yet owing to the wear and tear of these last few days, and the immense deal of work involved by the machinations of the Germans here. They are determined to drag the Turks in on their side, and through their military mission induce them to commit every conceivable breach of neutrality, with a view to forcing us to declare war on Turkey. We are very patient, and do all in our power to allow for the consolidation of the moderate element in the Cabinet which in distinction to Enver, who is the villain of the piece, is desirous, at any rate for the moment, to maintain a genuine neutrality.

The mobilization, Enver's work, has caused untold misery. The soldiers, called up for the fourth time within three years, cannot be fed, armed, or clothed. They openly state they will desert at the first opportunity — to be fed. They beat recalcitrants in the gendarmerie stations, and even flog their female relations if they suspect them of concealing their male relations from the authorities.

Anti-English feeling runs very high. It is sedulously fomented by the Germans, to whom our detention of the Turkish ships has given a great opportunity. Since Sir Louis came back the situation has been easier.

Elsewhere, as far as one can tell, German diplomats have drawn blank after blank, which is very satisfactory to my much abused profession. Events so far, except for the French reverse in Lorraine, have panned out better than we expected.

Our "bloomer" in not catching the Goeben is locally almost disastrous, but will not have much general effect on the course of the war. She is of course only Turkish

Empress Marie

HIH Grand Duke Constantine

in name. Our fear is that if the Turks become at war with us, the Germans will take her into the Black Sea with other merchant ships they are fitting out here as sort of privateers. How disgracefully they behaved to the Empress Marie and the Grand Duke Constantine. Serves the latter right, as he was leader of a pro-German party at the Russian Court.

We are all hard up here, but very happy.

To Lord Ribblesdale.
British Embassy, Constantinople,
September 6, 1914.

One line to say that I am well, happy, and very hard-worked whole day, and no time for riding or swimming expeditions. The work is entirely cyphering, and cheered only at intervals by news telegrams. Otherwise we only hear German news, and you know what that is. I much admired the Premier's speech at the Guildhall; it was a magnificent piece of real oratory, and most elevated in sentiment. I am glad he has been of the hauteur to see what we are really fighting for, and how we must win. We have, of course, a magnificent position.

I am afraid the war will last a long time, as we shall have to wear the Germans down by degrees. The German Ambassador here says they have food for three years. I don't think this can be true, but no doubt it will take a long time to starve them out. No time for more.

To the Hon. Irene Lawley.
British Embassy, Constantinople,
September 6, 1914.

Here we live in an atmosphere of lies and violently stirred up anti-English feeling. The prospects of actual war with Turkey seem to be rather diminishing, but the violations of neutrality are just as flagrant as ever. As the Prime Minister said, we must "take long views", as we can be satisfied with no partial victory. I fancy that the war on two fronts will by degrees force the Germans back within their frontiers. I think it will then be very difficult to make any serious impression on them, as their forts are strong and our artillery not so good as theirs. However, we shall wear them down and starve them out by degrees. I cannot speak of the sack of Louvain. Even if the population had fired on them they could surely have destroyed the houses where the fire came from and the principal culprits; but to sack all the churches, old buildings, etc., is a disgrace, even on their own showing, of the deepest dye. They are the Huns of Europe, and I only hope they will be treated as such and that the Cossacks will not forget. How can one reconcile these vile buccaneers with the kind of German one knows? What do they think in America? The Americans here are very *bien pensant* and anxious for us to beat the Germans. The German Ambassador runs about the quay and the hotels waving a newspaper and shouting victory. It will be a curious world after this war — very little money about, I should think, and hardly any to spend on fun; I don't see myself hunting for a long while to come — I don't, in fact, see myself home for some time. I simply can't be spared now; and while our relations with Turkey are uncertain they won't send out any one else, I don't suppose. The Ambassador is splendid; he learns up the names of his ships like a schoolboy, and he is going to take the Belgian Minister into the Embassy when we go back to Pera.

Cossacks charge the Germans lines

To the Same.
British Embassy, Constantinople,
September 13, 1914.

Six weeks of war, and are the Germans yet in Paris?

Here things go on much as usual. But the Turks are still convinced that the Germans will win, and they will stick to this conviction till the signing of the treaty of peace. They were just the same in their own war, and did not think they'd been beat till the Bulgarians were actually at Tchataldja. Of course it was different in the case of the Ministers, but the general public, I mean — and Ministers with regard to this war are more or less in the same position as the general public with regard to the other war.

The Turks are not even impressed by the reports of India's response — which is very remarkable; it must be due to the visit of the Crown Prince. One should organize tours of German royalty in England and the colonies, and then people get to know what the Germans really are. Did you see Goschen's dispatch reporting on his last days at Berlin and the Emperor's "apology" for the demonstration which took place outside the Embassy? It is an extraordinary document. I think our friend Jagow must be genuinely sorry for all this, and especially for the breach with England. The diplomacy of the war on the German side has been

Crown Prince Wilhelm

mismanaged — but not, I think, his fault; I fancy the Emperor did the whole thing during this big crisis. He is a marvel with his telegrams about God.

All my sisters by degrees will have their husbands fighting, and Percy must have already done a lot; I hope he will get a V.C. or something.

The Turks are less warlike; they have abolished certain commercial and judicial privileges of foreign subjects; and it is thought that this is in reality a peaceful move, as now they can show the public some results for their mobilization and are therefore not under the necessity of risking a war with some one — a war which only a few swollen heads like Enver really want, and which the civil element in general is determined to avert.

The Ambassador thinks about nothing but what he can do for the war and doing little kindnesses all round. Heaven knows one can do little enough in what is, after all, a backwater at this moment. It does not really matter if the Turks do go to war. It will only mean their own break up, or at best their becoming a sort of German dependency. However, here we are with our job, to keep them neutral, and we mean to see it through.

The Kaiser 'en route' to Paris!

Keir Hardie

How vilely all my old associates, Keir Hardie and Co., are behaving.

Our life here has been extraordinary — in German territory practically, and nothing but German news for a long time. After that awful fighting round Mons down to St. Quentin we really thought our army had been *vernichtet*, so you can imagine our feelings. Luckily we've had so much work that we haven't had time to think. Now we are a sort of *bureau de presse* and fill the Pera papers with our news. Why is it impossible to have a gentlemanly war with the Germans? The lies they tell in their foul Press, their low behaviour here — the German Ambassador running round to the hotels and shouting victory in the streets — the ungraciousness of their whole way of looking at things makes one feel very bitter. No one likes the Germans any better after having fought them. The French and Russians did like each other better after the Crimea. Ourselves and the French at least left each other's throats with a feeling of mutual respect. But these cads! I cannot reconcile them with the Germans I have liked. What a dreadful tragedy about Archer Clive. Really what that family has suffered: but it must in a way be a fine thing to have some link with the hosts of great spirits who have witnessed to our national greatness and are in a sense England triumphant while our warfare is still here; and at such moments *I* feel the oneness of the nation with its dead — and those who will die in this war die for righteousness and will be thanked for ever by the little nations for whom they have secured a free existence, unmenaced by powerful and interfering neighbours.

So you will be in London; think of me here sometimes: my plans are luckily very much fixed up — till they can spare me from here. Then — One feels here that one is doing so very little, and resents the sort of artificial denationalized position the diplomat has to submit to: it *is* merely position; one's character is more nationalized than ever.

The good news, our own and the Russian, has made us very happy — and happy for many things. One can hardly put into words the sort of thankfulness — that after all people are found whose policy is not simply a question of interest, and who value that intangible essence, unseen save at rare moments like the Holy Grail — the Nation's honour.

After all, what would the Belgians have suffered materially if they had let the Germans through? It is quite possible the Germans would have kept their word and retired after peace. It was the idea of the desecration of the streets of their beautiful old towns, where the guilds of the Middle Ages built their cathedrals.

To the Hon. Beatrix Lister.
British Embassy, Constantinople,
September 20, 1914.

Many thanks for your capital letter. I remember well what Reggy [*Charles carried on a faithful correspondence with his aunt, the Hon. Beatrix Lister. She had been trained, as few are, to appreciate the complex problems of European diplomacy. Her constant correspondence with her brother, Sir Reginald Lister, and her frequent visits to him at his various posts, had quickened her interest in the wide issues of world politics. Charles found in her sympathy and perception, and an understanding attention to everything that touched the career he had chosen. — B. W. C.*] and Mallet always said about Germany. We always imagined that the war would begin with an attack on England with the object of destroying the British Fleet: events rather show that England was not the first objective; more than that, the Germans, I think, did calculate on our neutrality. It is a mercy that we have done the right thing: I doubt if we should have, if the Germans had not violated Belgian neutrality. As you say, the whole thing was very badly stage-managed.

I gather from what the German Ambassador has said here, etc., that the Germans meant *as early as July* to declare war on Russia and all other comers. I suppose towards the end of September the German Ambassador used this sort of language after his return from Berlin, when it is probable that the whole thing was discussed: all the other Ambassadors had also been summoned home. Then came the Sarajevo murders. I think the Germans thought this would be an excellent chance to catch the Triple Entente more or less disunited — Russia torn between her Slav sympathies and her horror of regicide as a general principle; England sympathizing with Austria on this issue, etc.

She could then declare war on one of the Triple Entente, and find the others not ready to "march". The pace was therefore rather forced and a crisis hurried by the Austrian Note, a document largely drawn up in Berlin. I think Germany was out for war all the time, and not out for a mere diplomatic success. This was surely already secured — seeing the *abject* tone of the Serbian reply to the Austrian Note. And so we have war. I feel rather nervous as to the superior artillery of the Germans and this terrible 42-centimetre gun. Perhaps we shall not be able to make much impression against the German forts; otherwise, however, I think the situation very satisfactory. It will be a long job, and we may have to finish them by starving them out; but we've got them stiff. I sometimes almost wish we had not got Allies; there will be embarrassment when we come to making peace, and weak Allies may get beaten or give us other anxiety. However, I don't suppose an isolated fight against Germany would be practical politics — too many people dislike them. I think the war will last a long time as far as Germany is concerned. Constantinople is the one place where she has got sympathizers. Our holding up these Turkish ships and the arrival of the *Goeben* has created a strong feeling in her favour, and the military mission have been consequently able to get the whole thing into their hands. The Turks are *en mauvaise voie*. If the Germans win, Turkey will become a sort of German Egypt. If the Germans lose, Turkey will have to face the victorious Triple Entente Powers in no mood for trifling. The mot of a Belgian here now is worth repeating. One of the Ministers said, *"J'ai une nouvelle pour vous: les Allemands sont entrés à Bruxelles"*. He without a moment's hesitation said, *"Excellence, j'ai une nouvelle pour vous: les Allemands sont entrés d'Constantinople"*. It is the literal truth — they arrive train after train, they man the Turkish ships, arm their own merchantmen, sign all the Customs instructions, etc. They are, however, getting unpopular: Faust is beginning to realize that his bondage to Mephistopheles is not an unmixed blessing. I don't think the Germans have any definite plan. It is simply fishing in troubled waters; their idea is to hurry the Turks into war with some one so that they may ultimately get

involved against Russia and create a diversion. It is a cynical policy which quite disregards Turkish interests. Of the Turks, Enver is the villain of the piece. He is swollen-headed and crude, and the Germans have promised him Egypt and the Caucasus and Salonica.

P.S. — French strategy is hard to understand. I think that after his first failure to get through the Germans Joffre's idea is a retreat on the Marne, which is very defensible country and suitable to the kind of campaign he desires.

Joffre

To the Hon. Irene Lawley.
British Embassy, Constantinople,
September 21, 1914.

I don't know that very much has happened since my last. We have been through a phase of apprehension again, and the experts think war is more likely. The German officers are said to be making themselves very much disliked and to be even despised as not knowing their job: they have, of course, told the Turks that our officers taught them all wrong. Yesterday the German cruiser went out into the Black Sea, and returned in the evening. To-day the *Goeben* has gone out. It is an astonishing situation; the German captain, by molesting one of our corn ships *en route* from the Black Sea, could any day put the whole fat in the fire. As you know, our naval officers have gone. There have been the usual *potins* and

The Battle of the Marne

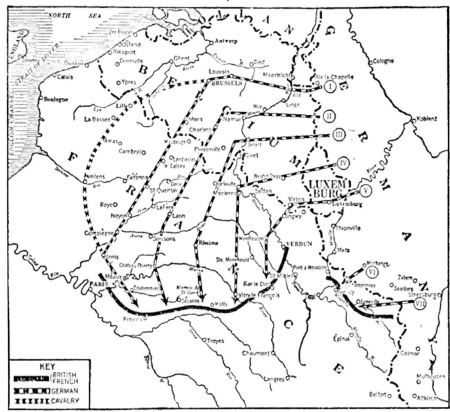

THE GERMAN ADVANCE TO THE MARNE

I Kluck	III Hausen	V The Crown Prince	II Heeringen
II Bülow	IV Würtemberg	VI The Bavarians	

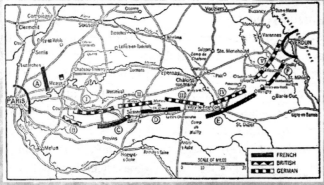

THE BATTLE OF THE MARNE, 5TH SEPTEMBER 1914

A Manoury   D Foch   I Kluck   IV Würtemberg

B British   E De Langle de Cary   II Bülow   V Crown Prince

C Franchet d'Esprey   F Sarrail   III Hausen

Note: The small black and white square above Meaux represents the Fourth Reserve Corps left by Kluck to cover his flank.

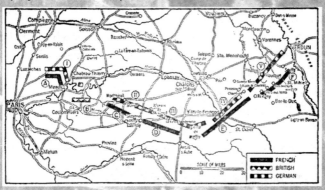

THE BATTLE OF THE MARNE, 8TH SEPTEMBER 1914

Armies distinguished by same symbols as on previous map. The small square north of the British represents the cavalry corps.

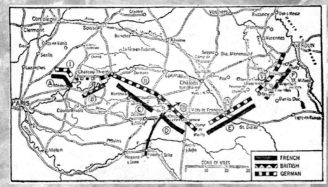

THE BATTLE OF THE MARNE, 9TH SEPTEMBER 1914

The arrow shows the attack by Foch's Forty-second Division which won the Battle of La Fère-Champenoise.

indiscretions in this connection.

It is curious to see how the people who most liked Germans before the war, and who were never out of the German Embassy, detest them now. I think they feel they have been deceived, and look on them as one looks on some cook who has swindled one. I must say it is very hard to reconcile the murderers of women and children and the destroyers of Dierick Bontses *ad lib.* with the Germans one knows — the mild art critics and inefficient tennis players and comfortable bourgeois and governesses. I always rather liked Germans, and was very fond of German food and drink; however, they have shown the cloven hoof with a vengeance.

A few days ago we sent off from here about nineteen volunteers, the English colony paying for their passages. Sir L. gave them lunch at the Embassy and made them a pretty little speech; we then went down to the boat and saw them off. It made one feel very much out of it. The honorary attaché has also gone. He was an old soldier in the Scots Greys, who have distinguished themselves. However, here we are, in fetters.

Did you see the *Daily Telegraph* account of Francis Grenfell's performances and the part Bender and Percy took in the affair? Wasn't it splendid — was it true? It sounded almost too good, and more like the list of names at some ducal week-end. I have taken occasional swims, and you will be pleased to hear I've got over the Bosphorus. This is not as good as Leander's performance; he swam the Dardanelles.

Forgive the dullness of this letter. I think the Italians will come in, but how far

Francis Grenfell in the action where he was awarded the Victoria Cross

they will go beyond occupying the Trentino and Trieste depends on many things. How is recruiting in the north of England? They are very anti-militarist, and none of them would join the Boy Scouts in old days.

To the Same.
British Embassy, Constantinople,
September 28, 1914.

Well, not much this week; things seem shaping for war, and it looks as if the Turks had decided to commit suicide. The excitements here leave me quite cold now, as is natural after what has been a two-months-long crisis at crisis pressure of work. It is not over yet. The Turks have closed the Dardanelles — where Leander swam over to visit Hero. I have been in a very golf and hunting mood lately, and am sure that the life of the "deserving" modern man, with his all-day office work, is a rotten thing — that we should have evolved this as our highest form of activity is not to our credit. Down with these big nations and organizations of business, etc., on the enormous scale, and let's have a lot of village communities, each run by the squire and the parson, with their heads meeting once a year to decide really urgent matters, and let's have no trains. Well, it's silly all this, I suppose, and the hands of the clock must sweep forward without remorse — unless there are cycles of change like Anatole France says in "L'Ile des Pingouins". There I think we finish up by internal combustion when the last word has been said in the organization of industry and the enslavement of the working class.

It has been exciting, that is to say we have been *plus ou mains* on tenterhooks all the time — and are still, though now one feels very stolid — but not interesting in the sense that a period of constructive diplomacy, concession hunting, or reform schemes are interesting, or that a period of things like Armenian massacres, which give you a real insight into the country and make you learn about its various rules, would be interesting. The appeal has been to the game-playing instinct rather than the intellect. But it has been splendid, and the Ambassador has shown extraordinary nerve and skill. He has told the Turks some home truths lately. They are, I think, beginning to repent their madness, but are more in the hands of the Germans than ever — and the Germans are getting impatient.

Has anything more been heard of John Manners? I saw he was "missing" in the papers. It must be dreadful not to know, and still worse to know if the worst has happened. We heard at first that Tommy was missing — and this was fighting Somalis — but then the next day I think, we heard he was killed.

What a fine performance our Mons retreat was. England is silent as the grave, and I get no letters — only hairdressers' bills of 1912 for five shillings.

The hour had struck. Charles's departure at this date from Constantinople was his conscious farewell to diplomacy. "Diplomacy is dead," he wrote to a friend; and to another who urged that he should remain at his post, he said, "The date of my birth determines that I should take active service." A via media offered itself repeatedly to Charles, that of the Interpreter Service, for which he would have been eminently fitted, but this, as will be seen, was three times eluded. He returned to England to learn the death in action of his brother-in-law, Lieutenant Percy Wyndham, Coldstream Guards, killed in their famous attack at Soupir on September 14th. No letters had reached Constantinople. And on his return to England Charles wrote none. — B. W. C.

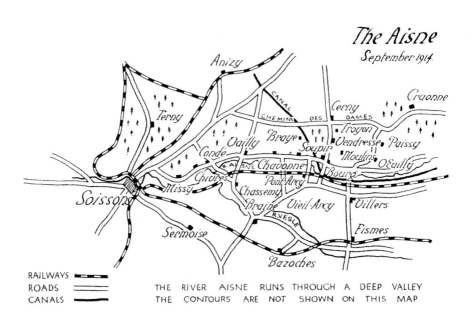

RAILWAYS
ROADS
CANALS

THE RIVER AISNE RUNS THROUGH A DEEP VALLEY
THE CONTOURS ARE NOT SHOWN ON THIS MAP

With the Middlesex Yeomanry

Note by Hon. Lady Wilson

Immediately on his arrival in England it was arranged that Charles should join the 1st County of London Yeomanry (Middlesex Hussars) as interpreter. Charles's brother-in-law, Lieutenant-Colonel Sir Mathew Wilson, C.S.I, had just obtained command of the regiment, and it seemed probable that they would shortly be ordered to France.

It took Charles three days in London in which to collect his uniform, kit, and charger, then he joined the regiment at Montsford, where its headquarters were luxuriously lodged in a brick riverside villa. Two or three weeks later, whilst Charles's dressing-table was loaded with books to enlighten him in the translation of the most obscure military commands, an order came from the War Office to the effect that interpreters would be provided for units on their arrival in France, so Charles secured a commission in the regiment.

The Adjutant, Captain Neilson, 4th Hussars, was an old friend. He had been at the Cavalry School in Rome whilst Charles was at the Embassy, and they had had many a good ride together across the stiff timber of the Campagna, Charles, according to Captain Neilson, not infrequently showing him the way, mounted on a fatigued hireling called Fernando. The 1st County of London Yeomanry was moved at a few hours' notice from their comfortable quarters at Montsford to the chilling asperity of the East Coast. At Montsford the regiment had a grey shoulder of the downs on which to manoeuvre, and the barns of the low-lying Caldecott-like villages afforded excellent stabling for the horses. The men had first-rate billets, in spite of the Thames valley mud, which motor-cycles and remounts churned up everywhere. The news that the regiment was to move was not received with enthusiasm. It was on a chilly morning in mid-November, after nearly twenty-four hours in a troop train, that the Middlesex Hussars reached Mundesley, a village five miles from Cromer. Here they settled down to their new rôle of defending the coast against all possible and impossible attack. Charles embarked with ardour on his new task. Some forlorn-looking trenches were dug on the sand cliffs, a machine-gun meanwhile doing some smart practice among the seagulls. A certain amount of spy-hunting gave spice to the early days at Mundesley, but later, when this flagged, the tedium grew intolerable. The different squadrons were scattered in surrounding villages, a narrow strip of grass which ran along the top of the cliffs was all the unenclosed country which could be used for squadron training. Here Charles could drill his troops, between the dreary back-gardens of seaside lodging-houses; sometimes, for better fun, his Colonel would be sergeant-major for him. The ever-retreating prospect of active service made Charles restive, and determined him to seek some way of getting out to the fighting zone. Yet, characteristically, he was able to make the best of a bad job: he hunted with the local harriers — the ploughed fields and cock fences did not come amiss to him, and he crowned a good *day with them by jumping his Colonel's best charger over a five-barred gate. Another day he was found gun in hand tramping after an elusive partridge; a wordy altercation followed, in which Charles succeeded by skilful dialectic in persuading the farmer that he was **not** poaching. — B. W. C.*

To the Hon. Irene Lawley.
Grand Hotel, Mundesley-on-Sea, Norfolk,
November 24, 1914.

There is much to amuse us here.

The local spy-hunter has been always with us, like the poor, and has laid all kinds of information against divers persons; the men are always seeing lights being flashed, and on one occasion they actually saw two men whom they chased down the cliff. Spy-hunting parties go out when these flashes are seen, and generally return empty handed. We put in durance vile the minions of a German who has a house ideally situated for signalling out to sea — he himself had been interned — and shut up their women in the kitchen; myself and Benn searched the house and read masses of correspondence, but with no result. It was a strange scene — the entrance into the house, the lower rooms of which were actually being *used* by one of our patrols; the men with fixed bayonets bringing to us a large smiling woman of the housekeeper type and a young wild-eyed girl with fair hair and a sallow complexion, a ward befriended in loneliness by this family, and the darkness outside. Then the search and scrutiny of the correspondence; our suspect was a Salvationist, and we found nothing but notes for sermons, also long family letters from relations in Canada and everywhere you please, very affectionate, with x x x at the end. The only incriminating thing was a picture postcard of the façade of Frankfort Station — coloured, too. They are jolly letters: tell you how the children are getting on, etc., when they are coming, and so forth; always say they are very busy. The ladies are now released; the men, I fancy, sent to the General.

To the Same.
Grand Hotel, Mundesley-on-Sea,
December 1, 1914.

You will be perhaps not surprised to hear that I have got the sack, quá interpreter. They have said that all the interpreters will now be supplied by the French General Staff, and would I accept a commission in the new armies. This I am most unwilling to do, as it would mean long waiting before getting out anywhere, and so I am trying to get myself a commission in this regiment. It is a bore after one had thought it all fixed up.

Last week we were rather hopeful as to our prospects of going out, but the latest news from the War Office is not very favourable. So we alternate between hope and despondency, and life goes on much the same, for now we have almost forgotten that there were such things as invasion scares or spies. The riding and jumping has on the whole been great fun, but I've been rather lowered lately by a cold and cough. The English winter, unless one is hunting all day, is a poor show, and I confess to a yearning for the sunny slopes of Rome's seven hills; Isa Chigi's last letter, too, describing the peasants going to and from the *fattoria* laden with grapes, called back pictures of days which I am afraid won't return. However, for us now England is a necessity. What I feel is that nothing will be the same after, and that our generation will live in a constant state of war's alarms and penury, and that fun of any sort or kind has left the world.

To-day I tried to learn the machine-gun. I don't feel that I am a very promising pupil, but it is a good thing that as many people as possible should know how to work it, and I dare say I could manage to get an elementary knowledge. My friends are very clever at it. I am not mechanically enough minded to be any use at modern warfare and look upon myself purely as *kanonenfutter*. But the East Coast is a long way from the German guns.

The newspapers have *nothing* in them now; it seems very much as if the winter, on the French side at any rate, would be a quiet affair.

I am going to learn Flemish from one of our troopers. It might be useful.

To the Same.
Grand Hotel, Mundesley-on-Sea, Norfolk,
December 12, 1914.

By the way, I'm practically a camp follower myself I hope to get my commission soon in this regiment. We are still waiting, and if it was a question of starting afresh I should have been a footslogger, but now I've made my niche and learnt a little about the job it would be a pity to switch off to something else — cavalry is more my stunt — apart from rather doing the dirty on the C.O., who looks to my languages. It's bloody for all that. I suppose we shall go as cavalry to Kitchener's army now. It's better for you, knowing you can do something for somebody, and you like that, I expect, but here one feels one is doing very little for anybody. *"La diplomatie est morte"* Cambon said, and I feel that will be very much the position of dips, for some time.

We go on in more or less the same rut, enlivened by occasional rides over leaps and days with the hounds, and depressed by inefficiency with the revolver and other weapons. They have competitions among the men — saddling and unsaddling, jumping banks, and going into action, i.e. galloping up over a bank *en route*, dismounting, firing, and then returning. They have been a great success, and the Brigadier is delighted with us.

Riding back from the day's finish, the setting sun behind, the stars overhead, and the little church-towers at intervals on the skyline, war seemed a distant dream and the world to be peopled with just one man and his tired horse. My khaki tunic and nothing else was there to remind me that the same stars looked down on hell let loose in France. Man is such a brute to man at this moment, that loneliness and isolation seem the only thing; he comes into contact with his fellows solely to inflict and suffer pain. This war knocks out the idea of progress as an inevitable concomitant of time, and I am afraid the world has shown that it has fallen behind the world that fought the Napoleonic wars in its ideals of chivalry, etc. Forgive these rather dull reflections; there may after all be something beyond the mountains.

To the Same.
Grand Hotel, Mundesley, Norfolk,
December 21, 1914.

I'm gazetted now, so my position is regularized. ... Saturday last I went out and had a day goose-shooting; no geese, but a lovely day out on a vast expanse of sand and salt marshes, and streams of these glorious birds over our heads right out of reach, circling and laughing at our impotence. You'd love the marsh with its brown, and greys, and greens, and creeks of oily mud, which we squelched in and out of in top-boots. We secured a few sea snipe, and ate and drank well of strange food, which I think is the chief charm of getting away,

I have read "Sinister Street". The Oxford part of it is excellent, very true to life, especially the Magdalen life, which I saw a good deal of. What unsatisfactory people! Alan of the sort *sans peur et sans reproche* settling down to be his wife's land agent, and Stella, after her cult of art and Bohemian swank, tediously happy as a châtelaine. Cellars could be filled with stuff similar to all those vignettes of the "Underworld", perhaps written with less art and realism, but it isn't really of much interest. Still, it is "some book", with a good deal of psychology.

To the Same.

Grand Hotel, Mundesley,
December 29, 1914.

I have had quite fun lately, looking after a troop in the absence of its proper leader. They must think me silly, and the sergeant knows everything about drill; he is so versatile, has a tenor voice and a fine notion of playing soccer. I am very fussy about the horses, and worry the men about grooming them. It is the only subject on which I can assert myself. It takes a long time to get their names. They are almost as difficult to make out as hounds, and do not wear distinctive dresses or paint themselves distinctive faces like the ladies of Rome. Khaki Is a leveller. I have just acquired a new horse, to my great satisfaction. He seems all he should be, in spite of a certain family likeness to a camel. The Colonel ramped twelve horses for us, and, Lord knows how, most of them £200 hunters; it seems a shame they should be under fire. I do feel for the horses, much more than for the men, except those I know.

We had a regimental drill one day before the Divisional General, a nerve-wracking affair. I was shepherded by my talented sergeant and got through fairly well, only once attracting the notice of the General.

To the Same.

Mundesley,
January 16, 1915.

We've had a very eventful and busy week here — full of drill and two days' hunting. First day very fair. I was on my good horse and did some good leaping; a harrier day slightly above the average but no more, a lot of "orficers" out. To-day, a very good day, I was unhappily on a horse that is a good jumper but has no great knowledge of banks. So I was put down twice; no hurt to myself, but my horse was once in the hell of a fix, his foreleg caught in a hard stub on the bank and his hindleg embedded in a deep, muddy ditch: however, with the help of one of the gilded staff of a neighbouring brigade we extricated him. We were rather often hitched by wire. I cycled to the meet nine miles against a very strong headwind, and before I started I had done two and a half hours' drill and about three-quarters of an hour grooming, etc. So it was a very full day. In the course of the drill we did a little sham fight. I delivered a finely conceived flank attack on an almost impregnable position and was shot several times myself and had to admit defeat, but the attempt was very glorious. The drill has not been a particular success, but my manners have become more confident, and I lay down the law on a great number of subjects I don't understand in the very least. I don't think the men can be very fond of me, as I am fussy about horses and like to see them groomed every now and then, but they did me the honour of asking me to figure in a group they were having done of the troop.

To A. F. Lascelles.

Mundesley,
January 17, 1915.

Still at Mundesley, and "the front" receding into the dim distance.

I *knew* Julian would do well: only think, last winter or so, he was wanting to be an artist and chuck soldiering. I only hope he will be lucky. I strongly dissuaded him from his artistic leanings, and with some effect, though every one else was doing the same. He is such an obvious soldier. I only wish I was — when I halt between two opinions as to which is my right, and am detected by irate generals making a muddle of off-saddling.

The Yeoman is a curious creature, but with a good music-hall sense of humour; his faculty for losing his kit makes me feel among friends.

To the Same.

Grand Hotel, Mundesley,
February 7, 1915.

We have had a pretty strenuous week, winding up with a day spent on the muck-heaps of our stables and clearing away masses of manure in pouring rain. So you see what Jacks-of all-trades we are nowadays. The day was a Saturday, so the men were not best pleased.

On Friday I directed a skeleton force — that is, two or three men with flags who represented armed myriads. I walked up and down the line on a prancing charger, not unlike Gustavus Adolphus. [*I again appeal to Scottites to remember gratefully Dalgetty's horse in the "Legend of Montrose".*]

Another day we did patrol work — a summer pastime in my view — as the officer has to stand stock-still near some object of note, such as a bridge, and wait till his men send in reports. He gets very chilly in the process, so does his horse. We have also had riding school and jumping on to each other's horses. Active little people like you might shine at this game, I confess I don't. However, once the stomach is well on the saddle it is simply a question of sprawling, and the horses stand any amount of this. I can manage the little troop horses, but not my own prancers.

The Brigadier's inspection was a success, and he liked our squadron very well, and this in spite of the fact that we were drilling with drawn swords, which lessens the control of the rider over his horse, as you can imagine. I made one egregious blunder — from ignorance, not loss of nerve — which I am rather getting over at drill. Drill is largely a question of swank and flourish — of a ringing voice when you are drilling and a theatrical wave of the sword when you are leading. I am supposed to have a fine word of command which shakes the rafters, and so on. I am taking an easy day to-day, as I was inoculated yesterday against — I don't quite know what! But you see how we cling to the belief we are going to the front. Touching, isn't it? I am sorry for the victims of such persistent fallacies, but error may sometimes be the mother of truth.

To Ferdinand Speyer.
Duke of Cambridge's Hussars,
February 8, 1915.

Many thanks for your letter — which interested me very much.

Sir E. Grey's only chance of averting war was to declare "solidarity" with Russia at the outset of the crisis. If he had said England would in no circumstances come in — the other alternative you suggest — he would have simply increased German determination to go to war with Russia.

You say we promised military help to Belgium. Do you refer to the correspondence published in the White Book, Grey Book, etc., which, as far as I can remember, shows that some of the things Grey said might be construed in this sense, or to some undertaking on the part of Grey hitherto

Sir Edward Grey in the House of Commons

unrecorded? I wonder how much anything we said might have influenced Belgium's attitude. Of course, I don't mean the *general* support, which we were to give, but rather promises of immediate military action. I rather fancy that the Belgians took the line they did, not so much with the idea that they could at once be got out of the wood by their allies, but because they thought a fine defence of the principle of neutrality, cost what it might, was for themselves the most farseeing policy to pursue; Belgian permission to the Germans to pass through their territory would have been a blow to all the smaller States of Europe. I believe, however, that it is the case that certain members of the Cabinet were only induced to vote for the sending of the expeditionary force to France because they thought it would clear the Germans out of Belgium. Curious how the right thing is done for the wrong reason, for by the time the expeditionary force was out the Germans were quite secured in their possession of the greater part of that country. I am on the whole inclined to agree with Vandervelde that Belgium did the most politic, as well as the most honourable thing in resisting. She is, after all, herself profoundly affected by this issue of neutrality, as a sanction that States are prepared to enforce by arms, and she would have created a precedent against herself by any other course of action.

I wonder what we should have done if Belgium had not resisted. I am rather afraid we should have missed the big issues — and come down on the wrong side of the fence, at any rate for some time.

I am surprised at the enormous reserve of men Germany appears to have. It is quite uncanny — but I dare say *The Times* has exaggerated.

It is great, your becoming a business manager already: you are a nut. I am glad. I saw F. McLaren a day or two ago; he came with his naval armoured cars and had a field day with us. He was in good form. He is under Wedgwood, the land-taxer, whom I liked very much.

I am having quite fun with the military life, though I feel my khaki is a sort of fancy dress, and that I am very much of a civilian all the time.

A few days were to bring a momentous change. Several Balliol friends of Charles had just obtained commissions in the Royal Naval Brigade, and a hurried visit to London decided that he was to sail with them. "It was difficult saying good-bye to dear Harry", he wrote of his Colonel from the ship Franconia about ten days after the date of the last letter, and again he expresses regret for the Middlesex Yeomanry and its Colonel. But he was glad to be off.

RMS Franconia

> *Now God be thanked who has matched us with His hour,*
> *And caught our youth and wakened us from sleeping,*
> *With hand made sure, clear eye, and sharpened power . . .*

These are the words of one of the band of new Argonauts — for so we must think of them — with whom Charles sailed from London port that February day, not in the same ship, but with the Divisional Staff. — B. W. C.

RECRUITMENT POSTERS FOR THE ROYAL NAVAL DIVISION

ROYAL NAVAL DIVISION
HANDYMEN TO FIGHT ON LAND & SEA

1ˢᵗ BRIGADE

BATTALIONS:
"BENBOW"
"COLLINGWOOD"
"HAWKE"
"DRAKE"

2ⁿᵈ BRIGADE

BATTALIONS:
"HOWE"
"HOOD"
"ANSON"
"NELSON"

RECRUITS WANTED   RECRUITS WANTED

VACANCIES for RECRUITS BETWEEN THE AGES of 18 and 38
CHEST MEASUREMENT 34   HEIGHT 5 FT. 3½ IN
PAYMENT from 1/3 per day   FAMILY ALLOWANCES
Besides serving in the above Battalions and for the Transport and Engineer Sections attached.
MEN WANTED
who are suitable for Training as Wireless Operators, Signalmen and other Service with the Fleet.
Apply to The Recruiting Office, 112 Strand, London, W.C.

Below:
A troop ship leaves dock

Below left:
Troops organise their kit on board the troop ship

With the
R.N.D
Royal Naval Division
ON BOARD H.M.S.
"CRYSTAL PALACE"
& ELSEWHERE
A Souvenir
Price ONE SHILLING

The Divisional and Brigade Staff of the Royal Naval Division were commanded by Brigadier-General Aston, K.C.B., Royal Marine Artillery. (General Paris, who had commanded at Antwerp, was afterwards sent out to relieve him on the Peninsula.) Charles was Interpreter to the Staff as "a Headquartersman". The battalions "Hood" and "Anson" and "Hove" sailed with the Franconia from Tilbury, and were not disunited until the whole flotilla reached Port Said.— B. W. C.

To the Hon. Irene Lawley.

Cunard R.M.S. "Franconia",
March 5, 1915.

... I suppose this is just wisdom, and that those who have lived would always like their lives over again. Well, I shan't regret this stunt, whatever happens. It is the most exhilarating feeling to be again on the sea of the ancient civilizations and dream of the galleys of Carthage and Venice — or farther back still — of the raft of Odysseus, and wonder why Dante put him in the Inferno (Canto XXVI). He is certainly a soul difficult to judge by moral. But I should have thought that passionate curiosity and yearning for knowledge would have counted for something with the All-knowing. I feel like a pinchbeck Odysseus — longing for the same things, but with the limits and valour of some little City clerk, and no power to return and slay the suitors of my Penelope — *in posse*. I am reading the Paradiso now. Canto XXXI; the end having the rather dry bit about the election of children to the heavenly heritage is simply stupendous, with all the Dantesque qualities of nervous description, mystic ecstasy, passionate seeking after the divine and bitter irony combined. He says of the Church triumphant that the Barbarians, as the Roman senators burst into their view as they advanced on Rome, could not have been more amazed than he at the sight of the redeemed.

> *Io, che al divino dall' umano,*
> *all' eterno dal tempo era venuto,*
> *e di Fiorenza, in popol giusto e sano.*

I love that last line, don't you? You ought to read all this when you get back to the hills and cypresses of Florence. It is a mistake to stop at *Siede la terra*, and so on. You might, however, in God's good time send me out a little Dante by post — Temple Classic is the best edition. ...

These are glorious times. I hope I shall like campaigning as much as Julian does. I *wish* you were here. You'd love it all so — why don't you try? — get out with Lady Paget's show to Serbia when you've had a real rest. Or why not here? but I don't understand our arrangements. I fancy they are pretty complete.

The following letter is from Malta. Patrick Shaw-Stewart describes elsewhere the meeting with Balliol friends."... When Charles caught the R.N.D., as one catches the last train, at the end of February, he was an interpreter and sailed on the Franconia with the Divisional Staff. The 'Hood' was in a poky little Union Castle boat called the Grantully Castle, and we only saw him now and then. At Malta he blew in on us, and we spent a noisy evening ashore." — R.

HMHS Grantully Castle

To the Same.

Cunard "Franconia",
March 10, 1915.

Things have proceeded pretty peacefully since I wrote, except for rather stirring times at a certain island. It does not look at all real — Malta — when you come into the harbour: there seems no way in and no way out of the great yellow walls that slope up from the sea, beaten by wave and sun and exhaling a sort of yellow dust into the southern air. Then it is so very seventeenth century — baroque without Bernini lavishness, under the restraint imposed by the original knightly uses to which the island was put as a bulwark against the Turks. The houses have often got flat roofs and bay windows with green shutters. They are nearly all built of the same yellow-whitish stone. No green to be seen till you have got well into the town, and then occasional ribbons of very bright verdure with a dry, stony background of hills. The outside walls of the fortress-city are grown over with bougainvillia and look on to neat little cemeteries —and the graves already prepared and stone-faced, and cypresses growing in the corners and down the central path. The people talk no known language. Italian worse than English. And the women wear an extraordinary head-dress. It appears they were over-complaisant to the French troops of occupation at the time of the Napoleonic Wars — so much so that they scandalized their own priests who devised and enforced this head-dress as an emblem of shame. It was to be worn for a hundred years. The hundred years are at an end, but this dress is still enforced. The Naval Division did not have long time enough to prove that humanity remains much the same. The ladies are with few exceptions plain. Patrick's ship was also in port, so we went and dined and to the Opera and generally razzled — "Jack on Shore" to the manner born. I did some laborious purchases on shore and left them all beyond retrieve on the quay, and for no legitimate excuse as we were as sober as you would have us be. We saw Ivor Windsor in fine dark blue uniform with silver chain epaulettes. He had been seeing the Captain of the Emden who was in chokey there. This hero is in real life rather glum and dry and not the Bayard of romance our newspapers said. I didn't see him. As we went out a French battleship *Léon Gambetta* came in, and we all cheered her and her band played "Tipperary "; we got tremendous cheering going out of port. This voyage alone is most heartening; to think of all of us going from end to end of this roguish old sea — unescorted — we only had torpedo-boats up till the end of the mine zone — just as if it was our territory — passing our strongholds on the way and seeing everywhere evidence of the great military and diplomatic conditions we have made — it's too good to be true. Malta was full of French ships and bristled with guns. You never get this sense of *power* at home.

Ship life has gone on its daily round. The rest of the ship count over its blessedness among ships in that it is honoured by a Divisional and Brigade Staff. And the mild radiance still lights our lives. I am neither fish, flesh, nor fowl, being viewed with suspicion as a Headquarters man and yet not sharing in the glories of the red hat and lapel tabs. But I am happy enough, as I've made several friends.

The Hood was in port at Malta when the Franconia, with the Divisional Staff, came into harbour. The first meeting of Charles with the battalion in which he had so great an interest strengthened the wish which he had already formed to be with the regiment, as one of its subalterns, in which were so many of his friends.

The Grantully Castle was a small Castle Line ship, and the subaltern officers' mess was afforded little space and few luxuries, but one of them had brought a piano on board,

Gisburne Park.
From a water colour by the Hon Beatrix Lister

and no record of the Hood Battalion on its way to the Eastern Mediterranean would be complete without mention of the rare pianoforte recitals and choice programmes given on those winter nights in more or less stormy waters. The musicians were Lieutenants F. S. Kelly and Denis Brown. — R.

To Lord Ribblesdale.

Cunard R.M.S. "Franconia",
March 10, 1915.

We are still at sea and more or less in the straight, and don't know when or where we are going to land.

We had a jolly time in Malta. That absence of green and the ramparts all round give an impression of artificiality; it is like a stage fortress or the great palace that the Magician drops from somewhere to conceal the princess he is guarding from the hero in a fairy story. And the sea never seems to have settled down since the descent of this Magic rampart into its depths.

I saw Patrick and Oc. Our whole flotilla was concentrated in the port; they have a very jolly battalion, which I should like to join in some capacity as soon as the Staff Intelligence Corps gets properly organized.

In a Divisional Staff all the men are so senior that one has always to be out with the "Sir". They are as nice as they can be, but a regiment is better fun, and it is more of a unity; a Staff is an amorphous body collected for no particular reason and with no particular traditions or tones, and a Divisional Staff is so large, and lacks the intimacy of a Brigade Staff, with its Brigadier, its Brigade Major and Staff Captain. Still, bless the Staff for getting me out here, and I'd sooner be a door-keeper, and so on, than dwell in Norfolk all the summer. So I feel I am as lucky as any one can be — so much more than I deserve.

Bless you. Did you enjoy your time in France? I suppose the Dunkirk heroine is back to her harness. [*This refers to the bombardment of Dunkirk, May 2, 1915, where his sister was serving in the Duchess of Sutherland's Hospital. Shells exploded close to the building, and the wounded had to be taken out on to the sea beach. Dunkirk, for hospital purposes, was evacuated after this. — R.*]

To Mr. C. Starkie.

R.M.S. "Franconia",
March 10, 1915.

I am afraid I never answered the letter you were kind enough to write to me about Gisburne doings, in which, as you know, I am keenly interested.

You will have heard that I am off — somewhere — and I write to you now from the high seas. I am glad to be out of Norfolk and for it at last, though I have now got a Staff job — interpreter attached to the Naval Division — which I do not like so much as regimental work, especially with my own regiment under Sir Mathew. Still, it is a good thing to get to the front as best one can.

We have had a very smooth voyage and been in no way disturbed by enemy submarines nor by storms. I fancy we go too fast for submarines, which can only take on a slow-going boat.

I am glad that the German blockade has proved such an egregious farce so far, and resulted in such heavy losses for them. Out here, seeing all our sea-power and the way we take troops from one end of the sea to the other — unescorted — has impressed me much. The Mediterranean is like our own territory.

What a run you must have had that Worthy Hill day.

The next halting-place was Lemnos. Neither the island nor its hero are very distinct amidst the allusion. Dr. Smith's Classical Dictionary tells us that Philoctetes, the famous archer in the Trojan War, was left behind by his men in the Island of Lemnos because he was ill from a wound which he had received from the bite of a snake. This is all that the Homeric poems relate of Philoctetes, but the cyclic and tragic poets have added numerous details to the story. Thus they relate that he was the friend and armour-bearer of Heracles, who instructed him in the use of the bow, and who bequeathed to him his bow with the poisoned arrows. According to some accounts the wound was not inflicted by a serpent, but by his own poisoned arrows. He was cured and soon after slew Paris, whereupon Troy fell into the hands of the Greeks.— B. W. C.

To the Hon. Irene Lawley.

R.M.S. "Franconia",
March 14, 1915.

This will not be a good letter as I am very hurried to catch our ship's post, which has come upon us as a thief in the night after a long expedition to the big town on this glorious island where we are for the time halted. This was the Island of Philoctetes, the Homeric hero, whom the Greeks found a disagreeable companion, as he had had his foot bitten by a snake, and been marooned on these rocky hills *en route* for Troy. Patrick and Oc. and I went to-day to the chief town and asked the natives who he was. They told us he was an Argonaut, and that the ladies of the island were so much *éprises* by him and his companions that they killed all their husbands, so that the handsome strangers might take their place. This is a very interesting mix-up of the story of Jason, who, on his return from the search after the golden fleece arrived here and found the place solely dwelt in by women who had killed all their menfolk — I forget why — and who had a rather serious flirtation with the Queen, whom he left, indignant at his treachery. Philoctetes, the natives added, lived two hundred years ago — hastily altered to eight hundred — and was a very good man who liked possession, and who liked all the building very well done. Oc. met a little Greek shopkeeper who had known him in Omdurman, and pointed him out to the duly impressed crowd of natives as "the son of Mr. Asquith". So you see what fame is. Here they talk every known language. I like getting back to these jabbering people in the costumes of all ages, one man with his bowler on his head and his great red sash and baggy trousers; another in perfect tailor-made clothes but with a dirty cloth wrapped round and round a wrinkled, sunburnt, crab-apple of a face. The various degrees of shaving were also interesting.

It was a dear little town we went to, with its turquoise harbour and frowning fort built high above the house on a great pile of rock, and another great mass rising next it to show God can always go one better than man. There was a little mosque in the centre of the main square, and near it a Moslem cemetery overgrown with purple wild irises and asphodel. We were very well received, and the police all turned out to make omelettes for us and order our wine — you never saw such wine — it tasted partly of liquorice, partly of turpentine. I think one would get to like it, but at the first contact one feels it would add a new terror to crucifixion. Then we had some white wine very like Muscat. Along the road we had glimpses of neighbouring islands. Samothrace, where Poseidon sat to look on at the fighting on the plains of Troy; and once we saw Mount Athos, snow-capped and beetling up into the sky, and where now sit thirty monasteries.

The fruit blossoms are just beginning to come out, and the village orchards will soon be one mass of pink and white. It is curious to think such an ideal spot should have been the cradle of so many cruel legends, and that Hypsilele's tears have watered the soil where the peasants grow their almond-trees. Jason, I think, was unduly criticized over this incident; the poor man was, after all, on active service — heroes were never off it. But heroes want watching. A nice fireside young man like me is the sort. Domestic — and no fire-eater. My Turkish is getting on very well, and if I light on a theme of which I know the vocabulary, I am almost impressive — but too quick speech rather flummoxes me.

P.S. — Have I given away our halting-place? Don't give it away to any one else — unless of course it is generally known.

The following is from Lemnos. A letter of Sir Ian Hamilton to Lady Wilson tells how

Sir Ian Hamilton

the news of the great battle in the Dardanelles reached the Naval Division. "As to your second question, ' Which G.O.C.-in-C. came on board the Franconia at Lemnos and brought news of first landing at Gallipoli? ' I was the only G.O.C.-in-C. in Eastern waters. J went on board the Franconia on the night of the great naval battle of March 18th when the Irresistible, the Ocean, and the Bouvet went to the bottom; the Inflexible and the Gaulois being very badly knocked about. I brought news of this historic engagement, and well remember the immense sensation it created in the Naval Division." — R.

To the Same.

R.M.S. "Franconia",
March 19, 1915.

I wish you were here. I'll tell you who *are* here — all the Staff of the newly appointed generalissimo — and the man himself. It is going to be a very big show, and the figures of troops one hears quoted increase by leaps and bounds. There are constant arrivals moreover; and you can see Australians and French jostling one another on the little quay outside the chief town. The opinions of our gallant fellows of the French are very funny — the sort of old Frenchman who appears with a goaty beard and spectacles whom one often sees excites much interest.

I am still in a condition of rather "unmasterly" inactivity, as I have nothing whatever to do on the ship, and am not turned on to any odd jobs; I've rather mixed feelings about this. I am sick of Turkish vocabularies, with which I never seem to make any progress, and get on shore as much as I can to talk to the natives, a lot of whom know Turkish and so give me good practice; and I think I am improving — I wish I was doing more; I am still full of fears that this may be a second Norfolk. I am afraid chafers like myself fret themselves too much. You will have our news before you get this in all probability. It is for the present not too good, and will probably lead to rather prompt action on our part.

To the Same.

S.S. "Franconia,"
March 22, 1915.

We are still here, marooned like the hero of the festering foot and expectant. When with the assistance of my housekeeper, who is to solace my declining years, I write up all this time, it will be interesting to see how Britain manages her affairs. First hustled out post haste. Stores all over the place, in the wildest confusion. Then held up in this spot for days — about to leave every afternoon, yet never leaving. Then a case of *reculez pour mieux sauter*. Then I suppose the final spring, I don't feel the Germans would have quite done it in this way. Priceless people aren't we? The horses have arrived only to be yoicked off *senz' altro*. No letters come here.

The Balliol men collected one evening and dined, and afterwards we sang the songs of our native heath with great gusto. The new Staff is brilliant but affable like the archangels, and applauded our singing efforts without stint. They are nicer than the Naval Division Staff; less conscious of dignity and the weight of office, and they've got some people who really do know what we're about, and have been in the Near East,

I went on shore yesterday and had a jolly walk among barren stony hills, windswept from end to end. Little peasants, their heads well wrapped round with nondescript cloths and brightly coloured petticoats, winding up and down the hill paths on their donkeys. I like to see sunburnt faces. I then came down into the town and talked Turkish with my friends at the little wine-shop. In the evening I talked with an old Constantinople friend of mine now on board. He is our great hope, and knows everything: talks Turkish like a marvel, and is sound, not a crank like most Balkan experts.

To the Same.

S.S. "Franconia," Port Said,
March 28, 1915.

We have left our island and have been whisked off ostensibly for Alexandria, then suddenly diverted here. I have seen a certain amount of this place, and it certainly has a character of its own. The naked and unashamed petty roguery and its unredeemed ugliness and ramshackleness are quite by themselves. It is all a huge joke at which every one is smiling, bearing with flippant calm all minor worries such as dust and flies. The latter are almost the "friend of man"; a man is quite unconcerned if they sit on the end of his nose or wriggle into his eyes, and there are flies even now. What will there be in August?

The natives wear a jolly blue overall and a fez sometimes wrapped round with a hoja's white duster. The ladies are often seen in the streets in black dresses like a man's habit veiled up to the nose and with a funny little brass ornament connecting the veil with the hood above. They don't look beauties: beauty is indeed rather absent among the people of this side, and the type is generally low. Every one talks Italian. It was rather a disappointment not going to Alexandria, but there may very possibly be some fighting here. There was a little fight a few days ago.

Our real object, however, in coming here is not to defend the Canal but to collect our armada and to straighten out our stores, etc., which in the case of the Naval Division are in a condition of some disorder. The Armada is still destined for the greater game. But many roads lead to Rome.

I can't help smiling at the boastful attitude of the papers of about a week ago as to Allied exploits in the Dardanelles. I am afraid we are rather quiet about our performances in that part of the world just now. I see the Admiralty have admitted in rather cryptic language that the attack on the 18th was not altogether a success. It dramatically synchronized with the arrival of a certain distinguished General Officer, who naturally witnessed the discomfiture of our ships.

Isn't the general note of optimism that prevails rather singular? I think we shall be through with the job by the end of the year, but July does seem rather early closing. Things seem going well for us in Italy. I am still more or less without occupation and have nothing to do besides working up my Turkish. For the time that we are here I shall try and get attached to Patrick's battalion. I am painfully getting this intrigue through now, lobbying and waiting for the great, who are to-day having an access of the work malady and not, as usual, comatose in the smoking-room armchairs. I think it will be successful, as my people have really nothing for me to do here. (*Later:* My intrigue is through.)

The chances of seeing a shot fired here are very slight but not absolutely nil, and we shall be safely behind our forts.

... shelling Turkish positions and forts

The story of the doings of the Naval Division is no longer told from the Franconia with the Headquarters Staff. The letters that follow are written from a Donald Currie steamer lying in harbour at Port Said. Charles was now gazetted to the Hood Battalion of the R.N.D. — and was meeting many Eton, Oxford, and Cambridge friends, all, like himself, full of eager anticipation of the vicissitudes and possibilities of war. — R.

To Lord Ribblesdale.

April 2, 1915.

I am now a fixture in my battalion. I would have sooner been a supernumerary in view of my inexperience of infantry work, but they wanted me to take a platoon and I could not refuse. My company commander, one of the best, can say *"Ejectum littore egentem accepi"* (I hope he won't have cause to finish the quotation). This is my first taste of camp life. The sand is the chief hardship — one day we had a horrid sandstorm, and it was impossible to go out without all the chinks of one's face being filled up with black sand: all our tents were finely dusted all over.

There is jolly bathing quite near and rude plenty; everything you get in the town is excellent, and we eat and drink like fighting-cocks. I am very fit. To-day we were inspected by the G.O.C.-in-C, and complimented on our appearance. I marched past with all the swagger of the rawest recruit; very self-conscious. My company has fine material, nearly all Naval Reserve men: hard nuts. I feel a sort of baby among them. There are many over thirty-five. The sun was brilliant, and the bayonets flashed like magnesium when it is burnt.

To the Same.

Mediterranean Expeditionary Force,
April 3, 1915.

This letter is written in *medias res* and the lavish disorder and glorious romance of the tented field with the transports in view that are to take us to —.

It has been very jolly getting into the battalion, there are so many likeable people. I have got a platoon and bellow out orders which I understand through a glass darkly, but which are carried out punctiliously by my men, who are old hands, having been mostly stokers.

I have taken to camp life with zest, and I bathe early every morning in the rather soiled sea of this place, and sleep out in a Wolseley valise, a Jaeger bag, and my fur coat. It is coldish in the mornings, but the angry dawn over the ships' funnels is a grand spectacle as is the moon that whitens great stretches of sand in the evening, and throws her light on the rigging of the fishing-boats, shaped like the ships of Odysseus on the Greek vases and black against their star-lit backgrounds.

We live in plenty — rude plenty — not too many clean plates, but heaps to eat and delicious prawns for nothing practically. My company commander is a topper and a champion swimmer, as hard as nails and a real fighting leader; not so knowledgeable as Wilson — bless him — but a grand man. I do not fancy this is going to be a second Norfolk: even if we stop here we have the enemy nearer to us than at Mundesley.

Patrick and Rupert Brooke are down with sun, but not seriously. I am marvellously well and in fine condition, thanks to these few days on shore.

To the Hon. Beatrix Lister.
Mediterranean Expeditionary Force,
April 3, 1915.

... I am afraid there is very little to say. We have been joy-riding about the Mediterranean under conditions which, up till now, made the idea of active service seem very remote. A Cunarder with its American bar, six-course dinner, and other accessories does not connect itself in my mind with anything but a transatlantic trip to Newport.

We were inspected by the G.O.C.-in-C. the other day, and really made a very good show. It is an exhilarating sense, marching in front of a line of strong men in step, their bayonets bright in the sun and the great adventure in their eyes. They all wear shorts now and step along very gaily. The G.O.C. was pleased with us and said so. The division, as you know, is fearfully and wonderfully made, and combines all the elements in its officers — the Guardsman, the Marine, the Balliol man, and the retired merchant service officer. It is remarkable how they have welded together. The war news looks very good, and I believe the end will soon be in sight. We shall now be able to reap the fruits of the battle of the Marne.

To the Hon. Irene Lawley.
R.N.D., M.E.F., c/o G.P.O.,
April 5, 1915.

One little line before the mail, after two days of purgatory on these sands — duststorm blowing all the time and not a chink of an honest, open countenance clean within half a mile of it. Tempers all rather ruffled, and food highly flavoured with sand. Were we birds our gizzards would by now be in the very best form and mastication a pleasure. I was Battalion Orderly Officer yesterday, so I had no relief from the attentions of the sand, having to stay in camp all day. I distinguished myself by ordering a sergeant-major of the battalion next us to turn out his light. I was not only *ultra vires*, but trespassing on a most cherished privilege. So my confusion was dire: otherwise the day was uneventful. All our mails we hear have gone to India — a very good place for them to go to, though some little distance from where we are now. Plans are still vague, and we are kept sitting on our haunches waiting for the *mot d'ordre*. It is, of course, impossible to give the men any work in this plague of Egypt. We had hoped yesterday that the sand might have been accompanied by locusts. One or two fine specimens, yellow and fat, flitted in to call on us. The men are in a state of cheerful grouse, and long for the quiet and peace of the Gallipoli Peninsula. We've had to chuck sleeping out as one would have been buried and dug out perhaps thousands* of years hence. I censor some of the men's letters. They all talk about their knees getting burnt by the sun — we have put them all into shorts — and that they can't say any more because of the Censor.

To Rev. Ronald Knox.

Hood Battalion, R.N.D., M.E.F.,
April 26, 1915.

The following more or less retrospective letter is written to a great friend of his Eton and Balliol days. It is dated from the Ægean, but properly finds its place here in view of the constant references to school and university comrades. — R.

No, I am not lonely at present, nor particularly uncomfortable. I am in a very jolly battalion — the "Hood". It is great fun having some small executive command as I have in the "Hood".

I fancy the original idea of the Admiralty was to force the Straits with ships alone. The R.N.D. were to come into the show as the force that was to do the dirty work of the ships, land occasional demolition parties, garrison forts the ships had cleared, and so on. Then came the gradual conviction that this was art impossible programme. Some marines were landed about the middle of March. My platoon got badly potted on ground which had been thoroughly searched by the ship's guns, and it was shown that ship's guns could not permanently rid ground of snipers or concealed trenches. Result: the gradual aggrandizement of our force with Australians, Frenchmen, and so on, and the addition of a General Officer Commanding-in-Chief. He arrived about March 18th, and witnessed the sinking of the *Irresistible* and the *Ocean*. After that all naval operations on the grand scale were deferred, and it was plain that so long as the Turks held the peninsula and the mainland of the Asiatic side they were in a position to drift floating mines down the current and prevent the passage of ships. So we were taken to Egypt and encamped at Port Said on a sandy stretch of the station. ... Port Said is a merry sink of the minor iniquities — sunny and unashamed.

Nothing there of interest except the people, a very low type of Arab, who accepts his degradation in a cheerful enough spirit, and has on the whole a very good time. [*From Port Said Charles sailed, to quote him, "to an island of marble, to brilliant blue landlocked bays, sage and balsam, and bees." The rest of this letter to Rev. R. Knox, which bears evidence of having been written at different times, finds its place with some letters written on the eve of actual operations in the Dardanelles. — R.*]

About this time Mr. Patrick Shaw-Stewart, of the R.N.D., thus describes Charles joining the Hood Battalion. — R.

"At Port Said Charles introduced himself by most subterranean methods into the Hood. He pulled as many strings to get off the Staff as others to get on to it — and in about three days he had a platoon. The four subalterns of the company were then Charles, Rupert Brooke, Johnny Dodge, and me. I had dysentery all the time at Port Said, so I missed the spectacle of Charles drilling stokers on Yeomanry lines — an entrancing one, I have been told. There is one particularly circumstantial story of how he marched a body of men on to the parade-ground before the eyes of the Brigade, and in his resonant parade tone ordered them to halt in words more suited to the evolutions of quadrupeds. When I staggered on board about April 10th he was firmly ensconced in the battalion, and evidently had no intention of leaving it. It became a very jolly family party on board ship. At the same table Charles, and Rupert Brooke, and Oc, and Denis Brown, and Johnny Dodge, and Kelly, and me. Rupert and Charles, who were great friends, were its pivots."

In the same way Lieutenant Denis Brown writes to Mr. E. Marsh of the unforeseen meetings in the new conditions of war: —

"Our party goes on happily. Charles Lister is a great gain even to those who don't understand him. He has the kindest heart imaginable, hasn't he? We laughed a good deal over the Divisional Notes on the character of the Turks, particularly at one which said they did not like night attacks because they hated the dark and invariably slept with a night light. Charles parodied them inimitably." [*These extracts from other folks' letters spoil, perhaps, the run of the actual correspondence, but still they give a sort of local colour — to use a horrible term. — R.*]

To the Hon. Irene Lawley,

April 15, 1915.

Written off Patmos. The ancient city lay on the eastern side of the island, with the harbour on the sea, rather lower than the modern town. The natives still show the cave where St. John wrote his Gospel in banishment. About April 12th the Hood Battalion had sailed from Port Said on the Franconia, — B. W. C.

We are still yachting in the Mediterranean, more remote from the feeling of war than when we were on the dustheaps of Egypt, and living the daily round of ship life, with its strangely made menus. You don't know what "cardoons" are — they sound like one of the degrees of black blood — yet we have them; not to mention hominies, and Yosemite girdle cakes, and Schoongesicht wine from Table Bay. I am trying to learn signalling, which is a useless accomplishment, I fancy, but I must above all give the impression of zeal, as I always feel my position is rocky and my accomplishments far behind those of my brother officers. They are so versed in machine-guns, physical drill, and all the other accomplishments of the foot-slogging soldier. I feel that anything I know is worth very little. Our best officer is an ex-cavalry man, but he has seen service in the Matabele and Boer Wars — and I have seen service at Mundesley.

I smile at these wishes for a rapid passage through the Golden Gate. [*The "Golden Gate" was one of the gates of the city of Constantinople. In the Middle Ages Constantinople was besieged by the Arabs soon after the Hejira, and we read that "from dawn of light till evening the line of assault was extended from the Golden Gate to the eastern promontory. And when the Greeks wrested Constantinople from the Latins in 1261, they broke an entrance into the city through the Golden Gate."— B. W. C.*] The nearest we have been to the G.G. is some fifty miles, and I feel the gilt of potential heroism wearing off amid the sands of Egypt as quickly as it was tarnished by the mud of Norfolk. I cannot write you any more about seas and sunsets, and shall not take up my pen till we have some tale of blood to our credit (at least, I suppose I shall, from what I know of the speed of our movements). But you would like the island of the Apocalyse. A city of dazzling white crowns it, and stands out brilliant long after the hills have been merged into the gloaming. I wonder if it existed in the time of St. John, and gave him the idea of the heavenly city.

To Lord Ribblesdale.

April 16, 1915.

This is again on board ship, bound for an "unknown destination". This, I suppose, is the *saut* after the *reculement*. But I fancy we shall wait about a bit more at our islands. I am very much happier in the Battalion than on the Staff, and there have so far been no contretemps with the platoon, which is tame and has good petty officers. The stokers look after themselves. You just tell a Petty Officer to get something or other done and it is done with unobtrusive regularity. It is impossible to do any drill on board ship except rather uncomfortable Swedish exercises, which, I suppose, are beneficial. They are certainly disagreeable, and done with little enough grace by most of us. Then there is practice in machine-gun work which I have continued since the *Franconia*, and semaphore signalling which I am trying to learn. This is difficult; a pretty thing if well done, but of doubtful advantage. I do not think that signalling is possible in face of an enemy — you would show yourself too much, certainly with flags.

We are sailing between wonderful islands of an opal colouring with cobalt blue shadows between the rocks and ravines. We passed the island of the Revelation, and saw a gorgeous white city on the top of one of the hills, which must have inspired the idea of the heavenly city. It remained in sight long after hills round had sank into the twilight. The sea under the setting sun is really wine dark.

We have got some horses on board, which have done pretty well and look very jolly in their boxes with their heads out. The men are having a fancy dress ball to-night, and we have to think of dresses, etc., for them, which is a business. As towels are about the only material available the problem is not easy.

I go on talking Turkish to our little interpreter. I acquire quite quickly, but do not make real progress, as he is very bad at English and never knows what I am talking about. What impression did the mishap to those ships about a month ago make on the English public? I see we made a clean breast of it. All love.

To the Hon. Irene Lawley
Hood Battalion, B.M.E.F., c/o G.P.O.,
April 20, 1915,
(Union Castle Line.)

This letter is from the Island of Scyros, known as the Island of Achilles. It lies with Lemnos and Imbros off the coast of Ancient Thessaly. A cycle of legends relate the conquest of Scyros by Achilles. There was a sanctuary of Achilles known to tradition, and the actual worship of the island is of a hero or god. Can this be St. George? The ancient city of Scyros is now the town of St. George. — B. W. C.

We are still waiting, in a neat bay formed by the Island of Achilles. Here he was hidden among a bevy of maidens, and dressed in female attire by his mother Thetis so that he should not be taken for the Trojan War. Thetis knew that he must die if he went to Troy. Odysseus, however, suspected this, and came to the island dressed as a merchant with draperies and female gewgaws, but amongst them was a sword, and Achilles at once gave himself away by showing interest in the cold steel. So he went to Troy and there died.

The island is made of pink marble, out of which sage and balsam and every kind of wild flower grows. It is humming with bees, and there are groves of olive- and thorn-trees in the ravines that run down to the sea from the mountain tops. In the middle of the island there is a little "nek" of brilliantly green cultivated land. The water in the island's bays is an extraordinary blue, and cold to swim in. Oc. and I and my company commander, who is a very fine swimmer, tried to swim back from the shore one day. Oc. and I had to chuck it, as we got chattering cold; my C.C. did the distance as easy as pot. It is about two miles, and we must have swum about a mile and a quarter. To-day we three all did a shorter swim from shore of about one mile. Patrick and I went a walk on the island, and we met the only inhabitant, a charming man in blue baggy trousers, who gave us lunch consisting of a sort of milk-cheese and some good damp brown peasant bread. We went home in a native boat, rowed by an old fisherman and his wife, who sleep in the boat and light fires in it. We have had two field days — one brigade, one divisional. The brigade day was pleasant We lay in the sun on a hillside and built ourselves little stone sangars. The divisional day consisted in aimless walking about over very rough country, which fed the men up thoroughly and spoilt their boots.

What have people at home made of the *Manitu* incident? [*The attempted sinking of the Manitu referred to was by a German destroyer which missed fire after magnanimously giving the crew five minutes to leave the ship. It carried guns for the 29th Division. The Franconia and several destroyers were at the time anchored off Scyros.* — R.] Curious that the Turks — well I won't say any more.

I doze over "Infantry Training", practise signalling, and read Anatole France. *Les Sept Femmes de Barbe bleu* is a fascinating example. *La Chemise*, the last story, of the search for the shirt of a happy man is charming. Then I have started on *Monsieur Bergeret à Paris*. I rather like the quiet, rather Christmas-numbery manner, with mild touches of the scabreux. It makes for better writing than the broader improprieties and far more subtle atmospheres.

The General Staff in an access of gaiety, have thrown six mail-bags into the harbour of an island which shall be nameless. So perhaps your last letter "shall suffer a sea change". I haven't had it anyway.

Life is so very quiet, and there seems no end to its peace. Our distance from active service seems to increase rather than decrease. But I suppose this cannot go on for ever.

I am every day happier at having left the Staff, and the sight of one's own men lying down in line among the stones and scrub of these jolly hills warms the blood. I hope I shall be brave; I am sure they will.

> **To Lord Ribblesdale.**
> **Hood Battalion, B.M.E.F.,**
> **April 20, 1915.**

One line to say I am still guiltless of blood and that the yachtsmen in the Mediterranean pursue their ordinary avocations and cruise from island to island. We had some excitement the day the *Manitu* was attacked and got a number of signals advising us in one sense and the other; we stuck, however, to our course and met with no mishap, hearing later in the day that the raider had been scuppered. There are one or two men-of-war about here, and occasionally we see dummies which would take me in but which deceive no one who is an expert at all, so I don't suppose the Germans get much hoodwinked. I have been swimming a certain amount twice since we have been here, an island smaller than our previous anchorage, stony, uninhabited, but with wonderful wild flowers and humming with bees. Its fragrance meets one as one comes into harbour. I like that smell of land. Platoon commanding is most amusing, and it is a very good thing that I have left the *Franconia* and the General Staff. Life is serene and war seems remote. No more now, as I must catch mail.

The following extracts from letters written by Denis Brown and Patrick Shaw-Stewart to Miss Lawley from the Ægean Sea, give some idea of their life during this time. — R.

"There's a fancy dress ball to-night for the men, and they're making wonderful confections out of nothing at all; the vain spark in my platoon is going as Queen Elizabeth. His skirt is my burberry, his stomacher my cabin curtains; his wimple (not historic, but one must wear something on one's head) is a boot-bag, and his veil a blue antiseptic bandage. Perhaps he's Queen Eleanor, but as he hasn't heard of her, we call him Queen Elizabeth. The rest are rather shy; they are too bashful to go as Greek athletes in a towel, which would be charming — and all the most magnificent want to go as old dames or niggers."

"We went to Scyros and lay in harbour there for a week — these were the weeks in which the Mediterranean Force lost its chance of doing something in the Peninsula — and there were days where we performed evolutions up those beautiful but stony hillsides, and there was one day when no one left the ship except by great ingenuity, and Charles and I exercised it and explored the whole barren southern half of the island all through the most perfect spring day, and ate bread and milk-cheese given us by a solitary shepherd. He was very delicious that day and very ardent — a frame of mind which always made me marvel (modern war has never had any attraction for me). Before we left Scyros, Rupert Brooke died and we were all very sad."

Rupert Brooke

> *To Lord Ribblesdale.*
> *Hood Battalion, R.N.D., B.M.E.F., c/o G.P.O.,*
> *May 9, 1915.*

At Scyros we had a blow in the loss of Rupert Brooke. He died of blood poisoning and we buried him in a grove of olives tucked deep in a rocky ravine under Mount Paphlee. αἱ δὲ ττaι ζώουσιν ἀηδονες.

[*Rupert Brooke died in a French Hospital off the Island of Scyros April 29, 1915. He was 27 years old. His letters, recently published with a preface by the late Mr. Henry James, speak eloquently for his reputation and character.*
Mr. Edward Marsh writes me: "Denis told me that Charles was one of those who turned the sods of Rupert's grave, and stayed behind after .the burial and covered the grave with great pieces of white marble."— R.]

> *To the Rev. Ronald Knox.*
> *April 1915.*

We are now at the last lap, waiting our turn. Our ship is anchored in a glassy, sunlit sea — enemy coast on every side — not a breath of air, not a sign of movement. It is still a sheer impossibility to believe that we are at war.

> *To the Same.*
> *Hood Battalion, B.M.E.F.*

Rupert Brooke died of blood-poisoning caused by a germ called the *pneumo coccus*. He had been rather pulled down at Port Said and suffered from the sea, so the *p. c.* had a favourable field to work in. There was no doubt as to his fate; he died

within twenty-four hours of the ill making itself manifest. He was buried in an olive-grove hidden in a ravine thick with scrub that runs from a stony mountain down to the sea. The grave is under an olive-tree that bends over it like a weeping angel. A sad end to such dazzling purity of mind and work, clean cut, classical, and unaffected all the time like his face, unfurrowed or lined by cares. And the eaglet had begun to beat his wings and soar. Perhaps the Island of Achilles is in some respects a suitable resting-place for those bound for the plains of Troy.

Rupert's was certainly a perfect death, and a very fitting close to a fine life; but it is rather a bitter thought that he should have seen none of the soldiering he had devoted himself to with such ardour, and that the gift made so gladly should have been accepted before Experience gave him any return. For any one with a mind alive, this war is primarily a search after the new, and appeals keenly to one's sense of curiosity.

On June 27th Sir Ian Hamilton wrote to Lady Wilson —
"The Hood Battalion made a feint of landing up at the head of
the Gulf of Saros towards evening on April 24th, and continued
threatening a landing until after dark on the night of April 25th.
As I wrote you yesterday, the only individual of the force who
really landed up there was Freyberg."

Freyberg, VC

This is what happens later as described by Mr. Shaw-Stewart —
"After several days hanging about we landed on April 29th. Then Charles began
to scent the battle and to be really happy. The third night the battalion went up to
the firing-line, and took part in the *manqué* advance of May 2nd. That day every
one who saw him says Charles was superb: he was hit by a shrapnel bullet in the
retirement and tried to conceal it, till he was given away by his breeches being
filled with blood — so his sergeant told me. That meant a long dreary blank for
me, especially as Oc. was wounded on May 6th and Denis on May 8th. (He came
back only to be killed on June 4th.)"

... an idealised view of the landing on the beaches

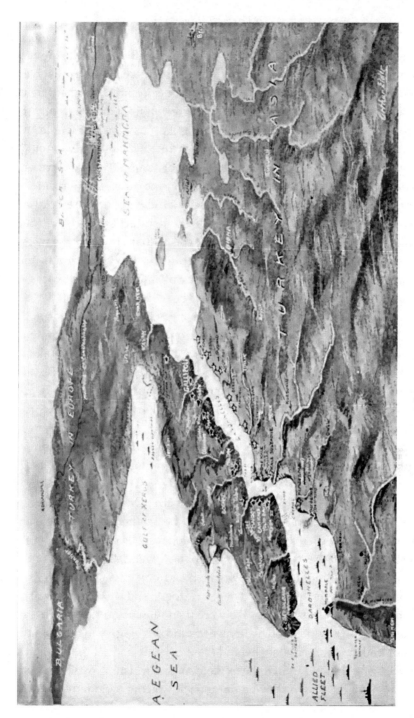

The Dardanelles

To Lord Ribblesdale.

May 9, 1915.

"The next evening (April 30th) the Colonel gave us a little address to the effect that now we were in for it, and on the morning of Sunday we found ourselves lying off the shore. For a day we sat and watched a rather leisurely bombardment of the little scrub-covered cliff sides and rounded green hills of an apparently tranquil coast-line. Not an enemy within miles: a sea like glass, and the whole notion of real war still remote and illusory, and all this time the landing was being made and our foothold on enemy soil dearly bought some fifty miles farther down the coast. The next day routine unrelieved was the order, and we did Swedish exercises in the sight of the enemy — rather sick at heart at these delays.

We were then moved down to nearer the scene of action, and for three days watched our ships pound the hills and woods that crowned them. It was a wonderful spectacle, the shrapnel going up like little white clouds and then bursting high up and sending down a spray of smoke like a firework, and the lyddite green and yellow which could only be seen when the shell had actually burst on the ground, and looked like some angry protest of the gods of the soil, in the form of deadly vaporous exhalation from the earth's inner chambers. The row of one's own guns is very deafening. The enemy shrapnel make a shrill ghostlike scream as it goes through the air overhead, but no more. Occasionally little ant-like men could be seen making their way up the cliff faces or creeping over the scrub-covered hillsides. And once or twice we saw Turks in retreat catching it from the ships' guns.

The night of Thursday we were landed and passed a chilly time on a wind-swept plateau-like field with the flare of smoking towns on the skyline, as red as a red dawn. The next day we passed quickly in digging and landing stores, and occasional shells fell in the water near where I was working. That night we drank rum and dug ourselves little nests in the heather, so we were warm and woke up fresh. We then dug trenches, occasional shells passing over our heads. I don't think we were ranged: one or two, however, fell just short of us. That night at about midnight we were woken by a tremendous volume of rifle and machine-gun fire which seemed at our very doors, and we passed about an hour in a state of more or less alarm. We were then marched out through a marshy ravine overgrown with lovely water weeds and olives, grey in the moonlight, to a line of trenches immediately behind the firing-line and sat tight, spent bullets from the firing-line and from rather remote snipers whistling over our heads. One of my men got hit. Dawn showed our men advancing and many Turkish dead.

... troops landing on the beaches under shell fire

One of our officers who advanced up a certain gully which was the critical point of the Turks' attack counted hundreds of dead. They must have lost *enormously*. We then advanced, my company in second line. When the leading company had got about 2,000 yards or so in front of the front line of fire trenches they got

heavily shrapnelled by the Turks. With no adequate trench cover and no time to dig themselves in and no support on either flank. Result: orders to retire. The same thing happened to other troops sent through and round us. My company being in the second line retired last, and by the time we were moving the whole of our front was being searched with terrible effect. One of the shrapnel burst on the ground about thirty yards behind me and a pellet ricocheted the ground and struck me in the off-buttock. I thought it was a piece of stone at first. I had already been hit by several spent pellets without any effect. One went through coat and shirt and hardly marked my skin; another knocked in my water-bottle, however, this third one found its billet, and I was soon bleeding like a pig and walking indifferent well — I never fell down. It was an irritating moment, as I should have been there to rally our boys after the retirement. They did well, considering the trying circs, and their relative rawness. I never saw a Turk within shooting distance: the other companies did, and did some execution; not much, I fancy. I was under fair shell fire for about one hour or so and light attentions from snipers. One bullet went between me and my petty officer as we sat together. The battalion has since been in the firing-line all the time and done very well, getting a bayonet charge on one occasion. I should like to get back quick, because I have seen just enough to tantalize. It is rather like love-making in this. The *mise en scène* was magnificent, and there is no sound like the scream of enemy shrapnel through the sky.

My return to the beach was easily accomplished for me on a stretcher, not so easily perhaps for the poor orderlies who had to carry me, and I had a feeling of great peace as I lay on my back and looked at the blue overhead. I was then put on to a lighter and then on to a trawler, which was full of wounded, slight cases for the most part, and there we were, rather toasted by the close proximity of

... carrying the wounded down to the beach

the boilers. Here I saw several of our people; we dropped about eight officers or so, slightly wounded in every case; as to men I don't really know, so I will give no figure — certainly not more than eighty and very few killed, but it happened all within an hour or so. From the trawler we went on to an Anchor Line ship, a dowdy old boat but comfortable enough. Rather a shortage of doctors to cope with the numbers on board — and to bed in our battle shirts. I found our adjutant here and one of our company commanders, so I wasn't lonely. I saw no very distressing case except a poor man who had been hit in the back of the head and had a compound fracture in the thigh and was quite off his chump — and my next-door neighbour. We did what we could for him.

I write from Alexandria, where we went, after a short wait, round the scene of action's vicinity for more wounded. I saw Letty and Mary Charteris here and Harry. [*Sir Mathew Wilson, in command of the and Mounted Division. — R.*] All the and Mounted Division are here now; and it was a great pleasure seeing the boys once more. Mary was in great looks. Letty rather pale. It is a Capua this place, and full of rank and fashion. So the wounded, no matter how slightly, have much sympathy. My injury was rather doubted, and I fear I was not in a position to give optical proof. But "Blessed are they who have not seen, yet have believed". Off we go to Malta now. I shall be back again soon — a week or so.

In the leisure and comfort of the Blue Sisters Convent Hospital at Malta, whilst recovering from his first wound, Charles wrote, in the form of a letter to me, a full and graphic account of the run of events and the varying phases of feeling at Constantinople during the months of July, August, and September 1914.

This MSS letter — much of it in pencil — worked out to over 15,000 words when I had it typed and suggested to me the possibility of getting together his letters, for he had several more or less regular correspondents besides his sisters and myself. The Vice-Provost of Eton, to whom I had shown the MSS, encouraged me to do so, and the Blue Sisters letter thus became responsible for this volume.

I should have liked to use the MSS, just as he wrote it, but this was not his own wish. Writing to me on June 3, 1915, he begged me to get it typed quickly, but added that he did not think it "could be used for a time", so I reluctantly defer and confine myself here to a few selected passages. On the news of the death of the Archduke Charles tells us "long faces were pulled by those who wished to appear knowing", but entertainments and dinners went on much as usual. — R.

We gazed on distant war-clouds through the light glow of Japanese lanterns. … The change came with the publication of the Austrian Note. The feeling that predominated at Constantinople at the outset was more or less a reflection of that which, as far as we could see, obtained in London; sympathy with Austria was considerable amongst diplomats, Austrians are generally liked as personalities, and from Constantinople the Serb can be observed rather too closely to pass for a chevalier *sans reproche*. I had just been a trip to New Serbia, and returned with unfavourable impressions. The Italians were upset about the turn of events. They had wanted that year to take their course and hatch out the Austria-Serb conflict in due time when Italy would be ready to play her hand. The premature announcement was not to their liking. The French had, from the outset, a rather clearer vision than ourselves of the German behind the scenes. The Germans in conversation were quite unequivocal in their approval of Austria's action, and were decidedly "out" to make us think that after all there would be no trouble. They sometimes said that the Austrians would climb down as they had done before. At other times they were full of stories of mutinies on the Black Sea front, Russian unpreparedness, and so on. The first and last time I dined at the German Embassy, Von Wangenheim was on this tack. As the crisis took its course we saw less of our German colleagues.

At this time, even amongst "the intimates" of the Young Turk Party, there seems to have been complete ignorance of Enver's intentions. Charles goes on to say —

The Turks, I fancy, in so far as they understood it all, were in the first phase not sorry that Serbia was to get a trouncing. Later, they rejoiced in the thought that thieves would fall out and honest men come by their own, and they calculated on a Turkish re-conquest of Salonica, for Greece was at that time their *bête-noir*.

On a long railway journey, from Smyrna to Constantinople — we had by this time come "in" as belligerents — Charles says —

My train was packed with soldiers answering the call. They seemed already rather German in their sympathies and not unwilling to be again called to the colours, but friendly to me as an individual.

Previously — that is before we came in — he says —

At Constantinople there had reigned the leaden calm which precedes a storm. The days of suspense when it was a question whether we would participate were very grim, and all that time we carefully avoided our French and Russian colleagues. We felt a sort of shame about meeting them. During the time that followed, after my journey from Smyrna, we at least knew we were men. Work grew brisk enough; reports from the provinces poured in. The Turks had viewed our entrance into the field with mixed feelings; they had hoped we should look on and, in company with themselves, play the part of the fox that sucked the bone for which the lions were fighting. They were rather impressed by our intervention; but I doubt if they thought we could really do much to benefit our allies, who in their view were certain to be beaten crushingly. The Turk has very little idea of sea power as a factor in war. He imagined that England could not come to very much harm, but he could not conceive sea power as an aggressive force in world warfare. In Government circles pro-German feeling was on the increase, and reached its climax with the arrival of the *Goeben*, following closely on the embargo we had placed on the ships Armstrongs were building for Turkey.

All these days the Ambassador was on leave; [*Sir Louis du Pan Mallet, K.C.M.G., became Ambassador to Turkey in the early part of 1913. He had previously been Private Secretary to Sir Edward Grey (1905-7) and Assistant Under-Secretary of State for Foreign Affairs (1907-13).*— R.] he returned soon after the *Goeben* arrived, to find the situation compromised beyond hope. The initial error had been in our impartial recognition of the transfer of the German ships to Turkey. Once that had been conceded; once we had failed to demand internment in a certain time, and, failing such internment, sent our ships up the Narrows — then but little mined — we could only work for the postponement of the final rupture between Turkey and the Triple Entente Powers. All sorts of rumours were rife as to the condition in which the *Goeben* had arrived; and for a long time she failed to make an appearance. We all thought Germany was waiting to see the *Goeben* restored to health before she finally pushed Turkey over the brink. The fateful date was to be September 11th; this was the date fixed for a great naval review in which the whole Turkish fleet was to take part. The review made less impression than was expected.

The Goeben appears to have done nothing to disturb the peace —

She used to sail up with her band playing, packed with German sailors — not a Turk in sight — and made a point of passing very close to the Russian Embassy at Therapia. The chief impression she gave was one of great breadth amidships. . . . The *Goeben*, however, was not the sole symbol of German domination. One day, on the polo ground, we met some apparently Turkish soldiers, who had obviously lost their way. They were spoken to in Turkish by the Zaptieh hard by, but without success. Then one of our Russian colleagues brought himself to speak the enemy tongue, and it transpired that these men had been deliberately brought in from Germany to garrison Turkish forts. Trainloads, in fact, arrived daily. After the taking of Brussels, David said to a Belgian friend of mine: *"J'ai une nouvelle pour vous — les Allemands sent entrés à Bruxelles."* He answered: *"Et moi, excellence, fai une nouvelle pour vous — les Allemands sont entrés à Constantinople"*

This is what he has to say of the German Ambassador at this time —

The figure which stands out amid the multitudinous detail and petty incident of these days is that of Von Wangenheim. He was a tall, well-made man with a dark, lowering face, somewhat marked by duelling scars, and a close-cut moustache. His features were well cut and their pose solid. There was a grimness about the clean-shaven chin and a cold stare about the sunken blue-green eyes. I liked the man. He was very fond of horses, and actually took the trouble to get hunters all the way out from Ireland for the Constantinople drag hunt. In his Junker way he

German occupied Brussels, 1914

liked the English, and was very hospitable to us in better times. He talked very freely to every one, and as early as June, after a brief visit to Berlin — where it was supposed he would take up Von Jagow's position — used to inform his barber every morning that "the war" would take place in the autumn or late summer. To the young he was full of chatter, and flattered them by his anxiety to hear their views. While German influence was stronger and more uncontested than in Marschall's time, I do not think Wangenheim ever bulked so large in the eyes of the Turks as his massive predecessor. He lacked the quiet strength, the awful silences of Marschall, and could never control his natural excitability. Morning after morning he used to sweep round the neutral Embassies like a tornado

with reports of German successes, which in due time kind friends repeated to us. ... The *Goeben* and *Breslau* used often to set forth under his orders, and his control of the Turkish military and naval organizations was complete, except in so far as he had differences with Liman von Sanders, a hot-head who managed to quarrel with every one sooner or later. Liman's temper was reported to be even less under control than Wangenheim's nerves. ...

Liman was certainly of the view, shortly before the war, that the Turkish army was quite incapable of taking the field, and

Liman von Sanders

he told Enver as much. When the fat was in the fire he had to box the compass, and has since been engaged in a task he has known from the outset to be hopeless. All the time I was in Turkey, members of the German military mission took the line that the task was impossible; they said they disliked the Turks, thought them stupid and unteachable, and despaired of any results. I have often wondered if the Germans at Constantinople were unanimous on the question of the advisability of bringing Turkey into the war. ... It is difficult for us to make out the Turks' attitude towards Germany. I don't think the Turk has any liking for the German; he looks on him as useful, and has boundless confidence in his efficiency. It was this conviction, that Germany was sure to win, which had to be met. ...

There is, after all, something to be said for those who were throughout convinced that it was in Turkey's interest to go to war on Germany's side, such as Enver and others of the soldiers. Turkey could alone hope from the Central European Powers for any reversal of the Balkan settlement arrived at in 1913; France was herself at war and therefore unable to lend Turkey money. This fact precluded any possibility of peaceful regeneration and raised the spectre of internal disruption and the fall of the Enver régime. Add to this the dazzling nature of the German promises.

Charles thus describes his impression of the Grand Vizier's attitude towards European intervention and advice in Turkish affairs —

He [the Grand Vizier] was a good French scholar and pugnacious in conversation, but a very oriental Oriental. He was never happy in the Stamboul frock-coat, and in the morning wore Arab costume. Before the Central Powers days he used to beg his Western friends to keep their enterprise and finance away from Turkey; Europe was trying to get the Turk to do things that were beyond his power; the Turk was too stupid to organize himself in any way: his only chance was to stagnate and remain in the East — speeding up he declared to be hopeless.
The rôle played by such a man in the present drama is enigmatic. He was, I think, sincere enough in his wish to keep the peace, for he saw the risks attending a rupture. He failed to realize the impossibility of playing with German influence, backed as it was by the *Goeben's* guns, and thought to the last that he could avert the inevitable. He remained in office, telling himself, perhaps, that *he* will be the influence for, moderation, and that *he* will enable Turkey to cut her losses by his diplomatic skill. Then he liked prominence. He realized that he could only appear equal to certain of his colleagues by retaining his tinsel trappings of high office, and that, German influence apart, he had never been really master in his own house. His devotion to Enver was almost doglike. My chief, in happier days, dined with the latter at a huge banquet and the Grand Vizier was also present. Throughout the repast he drew Enver out and made him tell stories of his marvellous escapes, asking him for his views as to Destiny, and other high subjects; listening to the oracle in speechless amazement.

In all these grave contingencies and complications it appears that —

the dogs of the enemy embassies refused to recognize the state of war; the Wangenheims had to pass our demesne to go for their evening ride, and their greyhound bitch Fly never missed the opportunity thus afforded of paying a friendly visit to an Irish terrier, Mike, of Nicolson's, and a bull-terrier pup then under my care. Fly was at times accompanied by a pointer, spotted, grim, and underhung, who was sometimes on the verge of blows with Mike.
Mike was equally without political conscience, and we sometimes had to enter

enemy territory to lure him from the Calypso-like charms of Fly.

This is also a passage of not unpleasing interest —

During the early days of the war Wangenheim rode for more than an hour with the huntsman of the Constantinople drag-hounds — Maiden by name — who had been huntsman to Sir Watkin Wynn and had fallen from this high estate to a measly £90 a year, plus a residence on an upland farm buried in the woods above the polo ground. His Excellency was full of commiseration for the poor English who had been bungled into the war against their will and interests; who had lost one army at Mons, and who were bound to go under. There seemed to be nothing of the "Hymn of Hate" spirit in him; nothing but pity "for his good friends". On more than one occasion, too, he talked to others of an early peace wrung from France, of a *guerre Platonique* with England, ending in the union of Western Powers against Russia as Kultur's arch-foe. As events developed his tone changed.

Charles's application to the Foreign Office for a year's leave of absence from his post was at last successful.

I left [*he writes*] about a month before the final rupture. Events took their course, and the Turk, as the successor to the Emperors of the East, took his place at the side of the man he believed to be the Emperor of the West, to divide with him the world's spoils. In the same spirit, moving along the same groove of historic fatality, the Turk of a former era coquetted with Napoleon, to be hauled back from the abyss by the strong hand of Sir Stratford Canning, but Sir Stratford had not to contend with the guns of the *Goeben*.

To the Hon. Irene Lawley,
Blue Sisters Convent, Malta,
May 16, 1915.

It is lucky this place has been built under Spanish influence and escaped the floridities of the Italian baroque, which was oozing into its most luxurious form about the time the knights came here and started to build, in about the sixteenth or seventeenth century. The part I like best is the little *Vittonosa* harbour, where the admiral lives. It is a narrow inlet of brilliantly blue water, like a canal of Venice, with great palazzos with pilastered façades here and there, and jolly little jutting-out flat-roofed houses with ship's images over the door. All the roofs are flat, and geraniums grow in the windows. My convent is not actually in Valetta, but on a hill called St. Julians, and I am most comfortable with the nuns. They are Irish and charmers, and wear little blue head-dresses — Eton blue — which hang down their backs like veils. My wound is practically healed up, but I was unfortunate enough to find the bullet, and the doctor is determined to have it out, and I have not sufficient strength of will to withstand him. It is, after all, hard luck. He has had scarcely a single case on which he could operate among our lot, and I should feel under a grievance at that if I was a surgeon — wouldn't you? My operation will not be a severe one, and I shall be back again in a short time — say a week. So write to the old address, if the fancy takes you.

I can tell you nothing of what is happening at the scene of action from here, and feel in a complete fog about it and dying to pierce the gloom and hear something. This sort of enforced absence feeds me up, and I'd give anything to know what the battalion was doing. Oc was hit about three days after me, I gather, and not very badly, though the Italian papers said *gravamente ferito*. I hear Princess Teano has been over in England looking over Red Cross things, etc. I suppose the Italians will be in by the time you get this. This new factor is in our interests on the whole, as the Adriatic question will not be solved in a sense so wholly favourable to the Slav if Italy figures in the conference after the war as a participant, and therefore more entitled to a hearing than if she were simply there as a neutral. It also cuts off another food supply from Germany. But we can win without her.

I saw Ivor Windsor [*A.D.C. to Lord Methuen*] at tea at St Antonio yesterday. He is in great form and very busy. They have done a lot for the wounded, on their own, organized accommodation for six thousand. It is badly wanted, as the actual accommodation on the spot has been lamentably deficient, and has entailed casting the wounded about on transports from port to port with a very inadequate number of doctors and orderlies on board.

Alexandria was Capua, *le tout Londres*. But here [*too*] there seem quite a number of people — though such tired warriors. The beauties here are for the most part floral; though the flapper *del popolo* is occasionally of dazzling beauty, she wears off as soon as the southern Italian, and becomes hunchbacked, wrinkled, and frog-like.

The Maltese come up between six and seven to our hospital, and crowd round the doors and are most effusive; funny black dresses, with black cotton gloves and toques. We are the sort of "lions" that don't bite. You would have laughed at our reception on the quay. *Le tout Malte* turned out covered with brassards and badges of the Red Cross, and the ladies lavished on us slabs of Fry's chocolate and glasses of rather tepid lemonade, and cigarettes. I never smoke cigarettes, but could not say "nay" to such a charmer as the young lady who made me the offer. She is almost as good-looking as you are. The Maltese are very pious — one hears bells going all the day long. I like it, it is soothing. You would like the Governor's [*Lord Methuen*] country palace. The garden is a paradise — orange groves and pergolas of geraniums and little loggias covered with creepers.

To the Hon. Beatrix Lister.
Blue Sisters Convent, Malta,
May 25, 1916.

Ever so many thanks for your letters, which gave me so much pleasure.

You will have heard from father of the details of my wounding.

I have had the pellet actually removed now — being subject to an operation about a week ago, and am now stitched up and a little gash near the groin. The pellet worked right round, I expect I shall be fit for duty shortly.

I am splendidly looked after at the convent by some delightful nuns, who are excellent nurses and angels of kindness. They put themselves to every sort of trouble, and are most anxious about our welfare. They make a marvellous open jam-tart, and their pastry generally is worthy of the highest encomiums. So with all this there is little to complain of.

I always thought that the Italians would come in, but I am rather surprised they have entered on war so soon, and at this moment the Russians are doing indifferently. Evidently the Salandra Government must have been determined on war for some time, and under the impression that longer delay would give the enemy more time to put his defence in order and recast his arrangement of forces. War is the only way the Italians will obtain the Trentino and Trieste, and the crushing of the Central Empires the only guarantee that they will retain any acquisitions they make. Were they to accept the Austrian offer, and remain neutral, they would find that after a few years of peace Austria would take back what she had given, if she were able to do so. She must therefore be really knocked out, and the best way for Italy to ensure this is for her to take a hand in the game. It is in British interests that Italy should voice her views at the conference which will end this war as a participant, not as a neutral. As a participant she has more claim to be heard, and if Italy is at the conference simply as a neutral, Adriatic questions will be settled in a sense wholly favourable to Slav aspiration.

Lord Methuen has been most kind to me, and as soon as my stitches are a little more healed than they are at present I shall go and stay at St. Antonio, [*The Palace of the Knights of Rhodes.— B. W. C.*] which is his country villa, a lovely spot, with marvellous geraniums in great masses all over pergolas. You would admire them. It is a great flower country, all over the fortifications there are lovely dollops of bougainvillea.

[*Writing to me May 1915 from the Palace, Malta, Lord Methuen says: "Having done my best to break your leg, the least I can do is to look after your son. Finding hospital accommodation for 7,000 men and all its attendant complications, makes me appropriate your son in a few days as extra A.D.C. He can remain until a wounded Scots Guardsman comes here for rest, and if your son is not well and is happy he can stay on. He has an old Eton friend in Windsor."*

Lord Methuen's horse kicked me with very considerable violence on my patched-up left leg in a gateway, out hunting with the Duke of Beaufort's hounds in March 1914. — R.]

To Edward Horner.

Blue Sisters Convent, Malta,
May 25, 1915.

I am so sorry to hear that you have been wounded, and I must write one line. P. got your letter *en route* for Scyros about your having got a load of earth on the torso, so I suppose this is a new injury.

My military history has been a record of futility. Two months' cruise in the Mediterranean, then three days watching the battle from afar off; then three days on shore, ending in an hour or two under shell fire and my wound in the backside, I shall be back again in about a fortnight, and I think I want to be, as I've had so very little show. If I'd been longer there I might feel differently. I hate being nursed.

I am at a convent . . . the atmosphere of piety — smiling and unruffled — is very congenial to me. They also make a very good tipsy-cake and an open jam-tart beyond praise. I have a jolly Maltese doctor who quotes Dante to me.

Leonie Leslie is here with Shane. She is, I fear, very sad, but wonderfully brave. He is very interesting about Parnell. I have just read Mrs. O'Shea's life of him.

It doesn't appear from the letters that P.'s intervention on behalf of O'S. in 1886 was a concession to blackmailing on the latter's part, as the Irish M.P.'s say, or that there was a real *ménage-à-trois*. Had there been the slightest suspicion of a *ménage-à-trois* at that time, it would have come out in the divorce and O'S. would not have got his verdict. Gladstone's trustees, it is supposed, suppressed what conversation passed between him and Mrs. O'S. This is a pity. She makes many statements to the effect that she was a go-between for Parnell with Mr. G., but cannot substantiate them. If Mr. G. knew of their relationship all along, his sudden horror in 1890, at the time of the divorce case, is rather a poser, though I do not of course see why he should have shown himself a moralist while O'Shea continued to be accommodating.

O'Shea is not at all the sort of loathsome, *souteneur*, book-maker type the ordinary "lives" represent him as, but a very intelligent observer and a gentleman, which was the reason for the dislike of the Irish members. His comments on the statesmen of the day are most illuminating. He sized up Lord Salisbury very well as "a really weak man". His friendship with Chamberlain seems to have been one of genuine comradeship.

Parnell turns into the strange, mist-enveloped silhouette of the mediaeval alchemist. His interest in astronomy, his efforts to get gold out of quartz, and his childish beliefs and superstitions make one even more conscious of his utter remoteness and intangibility. He thought much on death and its terrors, and yet was a man of marvellous courage — a mediaeval trait, I think. I can't make him out at all. I suppose his intense refinement and high-strung nervous system found just what was wanted in Mrs. O'S.'s liberalness. Parnell's mind seems to have been clear and comprehensive but not subtle, and his power of expression and turning a phrase limited except when dealing with broad issues.

I have also read the Koran — or rather most of it — and will let you know what I think of it. The Prophet is as insistent on the genuineness of his mission and the virtues of his book as the popularizer of a patent medicine, but has considerable lyrical gift. But more of him later. Bless you.

To the Hon. Mrs. Percy Wyndham.

Blue Sisters, Malta,
May 27, 1915.

What I meant by the Naval Division being a "washout" was that it is not being used as a division. The battalions are attached to other brigades of the 29th Division, and have individually done *very well* and suffered very severe losses. I think the chances of its being worked as a division were always slight, as it had no divisional artillery or cavalry. So long as this campaign lasts *I can't think* of going back. Now that more of our men are coming out it is possible that the Naval Division may again become a unit. The news of the *Majestic* is rather disquieting. I think the submarines have appeared on the scene just too late. Had they come earlier in the day — Even now it will be awkward if the ships have to discontinue

HMS Majestic after she had been hit

... a U-boat in action

their work in any way till the submarines are bagged. Operations on land seem to have settled down into normal trench warfare. Reinforcements constantly pass through here — including crowds of doctors and nurses. My pellet was extracted more than a week ago now, and the gash is not yet healed up. The operation was painless enough, as they froze the spot, and well done by my charming Maltese doctor. Even the stitch he put in a day or two later did not hurt. But I am immobilized and take no strong drink, so it is rather dull, and makes me so dependent on cabs. I have got through a lot of reading, including Mrs. O'Shea's Life of Parnell and the Koran, besides numerous novels of the lighter order. I have also nearly finished my retrospect, which I shall send you if you are still in England, or father or Laura, if you are not. I am sorry to say that my naval capacity has received acknowledgment from the naval hospital authorities, and that on Monday I am to leave my dear Blue Sisters and be put into the naval hospital, which is a sort of prison life. No leave to go out before two o'clock, and you have to be back before six o'clock. With the Blue Sisters we have perfect freedom, and are so well fed and looked after. They are all saints, but in some cases really wasted as spouses of Christ — pretty, fresh-complexioned, bright girls, nearly all. It is also a nuisance leaving my doctor, who knows my case, etc. But my bondage will not be of long duration, as I am fit now but for the silly slice in my thigh.

The Italian paper now publishes, day by day, snippets from the Italian *Libre Verde*, and it is of interest to see what efforts the Germans especially made to keep the Italians neutral — as it shows Italian intervention to be rather a serious blow. The Austrians seem to have been, as usual, *une pensie en arrière* and sceptical as to the extent to which Italy was prepared to make herself unpleasant. The Italians have up till now — I have read the *L. V.* up till the middle of February — conducted the argument with great skill and show of legality.

Mrs. Leslie has been a great standby, and introduced me to some nice Maltese. [*Amongst others whom Charles refers to especially as having been most kind and welcome friends at Malta are Mrs. Lawson and her two daughters, all of whom he admired. — R.*] A Roman archæologist — English — has been digging here lately, and I have seen something of him, which was a nice link with Roman days. Otherwise, except for its bookish side, life has been uneventful and dull. If I'd known I was going to be here so long you might have come out; but, alas, we never know, and I didn't want to suggest it in case I should be bundled off. Miss Maxine Elliott and Angela Forbes have done finely in this war. I suppose they have a prompt understanding of human needs. Father cabled me that Julian was still in danger, but better than might have been expected. I am very upset about him. I have written to him.

To Lord Ribblesdale.

No date.

Lord Methuen was most kind to me. I went about with him round hospitals in being or in preparation. He has worked like a Trojan, and his charm of manner to the men and nurses and doctors must hearten them up in their work. He is a marvellous walker, and if you lose sight of him for ten minutes, he is round the corner and three hundred yards down the street, and you have to be after him at the double.

I stayed about four days at the Palace, and was much pleased

Lord Methuen, Governor of Malta

with the Marsala there; but I am better without, I think, as it heats the blood and raises bumps, which I've lost since I got on board and put myself on to whisky and soda. As a senator I am sure you would have applauded Lord Methuen's eloquent harangue to the "Doblins" and "Munsters", many of whom are now convalescent, on the drink question. There is no holding these brave fellows; the Australians are like a young ladies' school in comparison.

Charles' friends Francis and Riversdale Grenfell with their uncle, Lord Grenfell, when Governor of Malta in 1901

To the Same.

Blue Sisters Convent,
May 29, 1915.

God! how sad it is about Julian. It's the bitterest blow I have had since this war and am likely to have. You must not make reservation about the "ultimately satisfactory issue". I'd sooner spend my life in trenches than have any other issue.

Julian Grenfell

You will see that I did not have very long of war's alarms, and that our performances that morning, through no fault of our own, were hardly brilliant. If the CO had not retired us we should have been annihilated — perhaps cut off, as the Turks were gathering on our flanks. Since then the battalion has done very well and seen a lot of fighting. That day they showed great steadiness for raw troops, but their situation was impossible.

To Lady Desborough.

Blue Sisters Convent, Malta,
June 3, 1915.

I can't write what I feel about dear Julian. The void is so terrible for me and the thought of it quite unmans me. I'd so few ties with the life I left when I went abroad — so few, that is to say, that I wanted to keep, and I always felt as sure of Julian's love as he did of mine, and so certain of seeing his dear old smile just the same. We did not often write of anything of that sort just for that reason, and now the whole thing has gone. How much worse it must be for you and yours. All of us loved him so, and I'm sure if I were back with father and Diana we should be in the depths and feel almost worse than I do now that one of our nearest and dearest has gone.

I suppose that if death meant wholly loss, all recollections would be wholly bitter; but the consciousness that we are recalling memories of one who may still be near us makes recollection precious, an abiding realization of what is, and not a mere regret for what has ceased to be.

I suppose everybody noticed dear Julian's vitality, but I don't think they were so conscious of that great tenderness of heart that underlay it. He always showed it most with you, and with women generally it was his special charm. I think now of the way he used to take my hand if he had felt disappointed with anything I'd done and then found out why I'd done it. I remember a time when he was under the impression I'd chucked Socialism for the "loaves and fishes", etc., and of course that sort of thing he couldn't abide, and he thought this for a longish while, then found out that it wasn't that after all, and took my hand in his in the most loving way.

I don't suppose many people knew of the ardent love he had for honesty of purpose and intellectual honesty, and what sacrifices he made for them, and sacrifices of peace of mind abhorrent to most Englishmen. The Englishman is a base seeker after happiness, and he will make most sacrifices of principle and admit any number of lies into his soul to secure this dear object of his. It is want of courage on its negative side, this quality — and swinish greed on its positive side — the man in his search for truth and in his search for what he believed to be his true self caused himself no end of worry and unhappiness, and was a martyr who lit his own fires with unflinching nerve. Out stalking he always wanted to do his own work, and he was just the same in his inner life. Surely the Lady he sought with tireless faith, the Lady for whom he did and dared so much on lonely paths, will now reward him? God, it is glorious to think of a soul so wholly devoid of the pettiness and humbug, the cynicism and dishonesty, of so much that we see. There is a story in one of Miss Kingsley's books of a West African medicine-man who found himself at death's door. He applied all his herbs and spells and conducted all his well-worn rites before his idols, and with his friend's intercessions, without any effect. At last he wearied of his hocus-pocus, and took his idols and charms down to the seashore and flung them into the surf, and he said, "Now I will be a man and meet my God alone". Julian from the time I knew him had flung away his idols and had met God. His intense moral courage distinguished him even more than his physical bravery from the run of common men — and his physical bravery was remarkable enough, whether he was hunting, boxing, or whatever he was at.

I think he found his true self on what we all knew would be the scene of his glory, and it is some melancholy satisfaction that his services received recognition. What must make you still happier must be the glorious glowing tone of those letters of his, and the knowledge that his last few months were crowded hours of glorious life, stronger than death in that they abide. I shall never forget how much they heartened me when I came to see you to get your kind offices for this show. The recollection of them will be a constant strength. No one wrote of the war like that or talked of it that way, and so many went from leave or after healing wounds as a duty, but without joy. Julian, apart from the physical delight he had in combat, felt keenly, I am sure, that he was doing something worth while, the thing most worth while in the world, and looked on death and the passing beyond as a final burst into glory. He was rather Franciscan in his love of all things that are, and in his absence of fear of all God's creatures — death included.

He stood for something very precious to me — for an England of my dreams made of honest, brave, and tender men, and his life and death have surely done something towards the realization of that England. Julian had so many friends who felt for him as they felt for no one else, and a fierce light still beats on the scene of his passing, and others are left to whom he may leave his sword and a portion of his skill.

You must have known all this splendour of Julian's life far better than I did, so I don't know why I should write all this. But I am so sad myself that I must say something to you, and because you knew how very fond I was of Julian.

One can seek comfort at this time in the consciousness of the greatness of our dead, and the work they have left behind them, and the love we have borne them: and such comfort is surely yours, apart from any larger hope.

To Lord Ribblesdale.

Blue Sisters,
June 3, 1915.

My own injuries are fast healing, and at the end of the week I shall see my naval people and ask for a berth back to Gallipoli. By dint of intriguing I have saved B. and myself from durance vile in Bight Hospital, where the naval authorities wanted to move me, and where 1 should have to have kept fixed hours and lived up almost two hundred steps in a sort of eagle's nest.

Ashmead Bartlett has been here, home bound. He was blown up on the *Majestic* and escaped, but without his notebooks, etc., which I believe contain scathing denunciations of all those in authority, and which, are just as well at the bottom of the sea. He will talk when he gets home. I hope he will get us more men sent out; but his tone is pessimistic and his statements exaggerations, which he qualifies by about 75 per cent, in his next sentence. So perhaps they will take no notice of him. The Turks are exhausting themselves by these attacks on our trenches and losing great numbers, and with a few more men we could do the trick soon enough. It would be hopeless loss of face if we chucked up now. I don't think we can. My only fear is Ashmead may paint in such gloomy colours that the Harmsworth Press may plump for a complete bunk. This would be *appalling* and, I think, impossible. Our hold is really *very* firm now, and it's simply a question of more men to effect our advance. I shouldn't write like this, only people at home have become such funksticks and seem only good for anti-German riots in Shoreditch. I should have thought there were other places where the readers of the Harmsworth Press could take part in anti-German demonstrations.

I always supposed the Government contemplated some unpopular measure like conscription when they called in the Unionist leaders for this Coalition, and am glad to see you think that may be the reason. I quite understand their wishing the responsibility to be shared. The same considerations would apply were it necessary for the Allies to conclude a peace falling short of popular anticipations, though I cannot conceive such a peace being so much as discussed at this moment. Madame * * * I am told, said the Italians contemplated three months' war, and they have subscribed to the London Agreement of some time ago, relative to the Allies not negotiating separately, etc.

To Mrs. Cornish.

Hood Battalion, R.N.D., M.E.F.,
June 11, 1915.

I have at last read Thackeray and must write to you, because you used to show me his drawings at Eton and tell me what a world was in store for me.

I read Pendennis and am now at Vanity Fair. I don't know which I like best Pendennis is on a more *tenuis avena*, and I think the satire, the little vignettes of literary London, of the London of servants, is better put in, with more subtlety and good humour, than in Vanity Fair. I think Thackeray loves old Major Pendennis, but really dislikes Becky, who I consider a much more likeable and admirable fraud. I spare much needless pity on Becky, and I'm sure I should have married her if she would have married me. But Pendennis is spoilt by the Fanny Bolton episodes, and the book is so largely made up of the telling of estrangements between son and mother, which one feels are of a kind that could not possibly have come into being on such slight occasions. I suppose we have all passed through the school of the larger charity taught by the Russians, and cannot understand Helen's readiness to believe the worst and treat her son's flirt so cruelly. I like the touch in Pendennis where Arthur, after having been most affectionate the whole evening to poor little Fanny, tells her that she must always call him "Sir" or "Mr. Pendennis", as their "stations in life were so different". In our greatest intimacies we still reach out over deep gulfs of class differences. Perhaps the dead of the war, side by side, may fill these up. Pendennis gave me such sheer pleasure from its remoteness from present days. The word "Przemysl" never occurred once in its pages. Vanity Fair in those Waterloo chapters is a poignant gripping emotion and gives one pain — the kind of pain one would not miss for anything — and one thinks of dear Diana, in Amelia Sedley's place, waiting for the news of the heroic stand of the Coldstreams at Landrecies. These chapters are self-contained, a piece of magnificent life drama, with all life's rapid passages

Landrecies

from laughter to tears, and smallnesses to epic valour. I wish Becky had liked her little boy. I feel Thackeray had made her so charming that he felt he must put something in to make her unpleasant and justify his own dislike of her. I think Sir Pitt is a masterpiece — both Sir Pitt senior and junior. I'm sure Sir Pitt junior only took to religion from want of occupation, or perhaps a desire to please Lady Southdown. How he rises in the canvas, like an El Greco saint in glory, when he turns Lady Southdown out of her predominant position in the *ménage*. There is no one in Vanity Fair so antipathetic to me as Arthur Pendennis. I suppose we are all very like him — by "we" I mean young men in general, but he is a very cleverly written warning — *Fabula de te narratur*.

I've been wounded lightly, and am now going back via Alexandria, which is our base. I was only three days on shore and about two hours or so under real fire. My love to the Vice-Provost and other Eton friends (especially Miss Margaret and Cecilia). What a period of sadness but glory it must be for all you who have watched Eton's life year in, year out.

To the Hon. Irene Lawley.

On Board Ship.
(Extract, undated.)

I have been reading some George Meredith. "Beauchamp's Career" I have always admired from a distance rather. But I must say his touch when he talks of love is so deep and subtle, so elusive and yet so true, that one lingers over the chapters and puzzles out each word. Not that it is so difficult, but the greatness of it all makes me always think I am missing something. I don't think the book is very readable apart from the love interest. Beauchamp as a politician is sympathetic but not interesting. However, the whole portrayal is that of a hero, and that end is most moving when he dies to save a little mudlark of a child, *chétif* and half idiotic. "This is all we have in exchange for Beauchamp." Read Lord Cromer's account of the ex-Khedive. It is massive, terse, and manly, and puts Lord Rosebery in quite a new light as Foreign Secretary. I always thought he was a bad one. But Lord Cromer says he practically settled our position in Egypt between 1892 and 1894 — periods of constant friction with the Khedive.

We take up the history of the Naval Brigade in the following letters after the battle of June 4th, in conjunction with the operations of our forces by sea, in which the Hood and Anson Battalions suffered severely. The Hood Battalion took a Turkish trench and bayoneted the Turks, but came immediately under fire from another trench, and they lost heavily. Colonel Quilter was succeeded by Colonel Stewart. Commander Freyberg as second-in-command. *Charles was company-commander, with three subordinate officers. The unit of the Naval Brigade and its battalions, the Hood and the Anson, had to be brought up to strength with new officers, new N.C.O.'s, and new men. After the battle of June 4th, the Hood Battalion was out of the firing-line. They were detailed for beach work, and, still underofficered, were employed in digging saps, beach fatigue work, sniping, and even unloading lighters and guarding G.O.C.'s. Commander Freyberg, who was seriously wounded in July, was now in command. Charles was in his company from the start and in all the advances under him. — R.*

To Lord Ribblesdale.

Cunard S.S. "Andania",
June 12, 1915.

I am now recovered and en route for Alexandria, with details of the R.N.D. to rejoin. We have about forty-two Naval folk and twenty-nine Marines, nearly all wounded and now better. I am very happy at the prospect, and quite as if I was going out for the first time.

SS Andania

I am still in the thrall of Thackeray, delighting in Vanity Fair; the Waterloo chapters read so living nowadays. But the pageantry and brightness of Brussels a week before the fighting must contrast rather with the businesslike look of Boulogne and its pathos. Mrs. Crawley did not don the nurse's uniform, which so well becomes M. and Lady —. Alexandria is probably more like the Thackeray Brussels. I shall never forget the change from our dowdy old steamer to the Alexandria racecourse. *Le tout Londres* and Lord — at dinner. This nobleman, from a safe seat in the club at Alexandria, said that he heard the — Naval Division always ran away; I hope he will revise this opinion. Certainly quite a number have not run away with sufficient expeditiousness to avoid the Turkish bullets. Our battalion now numbers about sixty men with four officers or so. Pat, I think, still well, though rumours are rather conflicting. However, most of us are in my case. Did you see our Brigade (2nd Naval) got specially thanked by General d'Amade, under whom we worked for several days? I hope we shall have silenced at any rate some of the criticisms and sniggers which have been our lot since Antwerp. I heard a bad account of Denis Browne. I saw quite a number of our boys hit in the June 4th fight. Their spirit

Denis Browne

was fine. My platoon has suffered very much, but has done very well. We were invited to "celebrate" June 4th at Malta, but I didn't, as I was not for organized guzzles at a time when better fellows were celebrating it in a very different way. Several Italians have been through from Constantinople, and they say that there are eighty thousand Turkish wounded there, that the Turks can only continue the war for a month. I think we have got them, shall wear them down, even if we make no advance. I wish I hadn't missed all this fighting, and that I had seen more of the battalion after it had really got into its stride. That first morning was futile, and we had such a foolish rôle to play. We did it as well as could have been done, but it wasn't the real thing. The division is now being worked as a division, and is no longer scattered. We have now one fine staff-officer who will pull us through. This ship has a Territorial battalion on board, and various other odds and ends, such as A.S.C. and doctors. I am the only officer who has been anywhere near the foe, and am asked for tips by staid old Colonels (formerly family solicitors like F— R— I expect) and blushing Staff captains. I have made many inaccurate and conflicting statements. My attitude to the Territorials is *trés digne*. I call my details to "attention" once a morning as the Territorial Colonel passes, but not a second time. I give my boys no work. We have lectures, and were informed last night by one of the medical officers that the female fly takes only ten days to attain to sexual maturity — a creditable performance.

> *To the Hon. Beatrix Lister.*
> *Hood Battalion, R.N.D., M.E.F., S.S. "Andania",*
> *June 12, 1915.*

Many thanks for your last, which was very welcome. I am waiting at Alexandria to get a ship back to the front. Our orders are so slow coming through, and we have to wait so much for other people. ... I have seen several other of our officers and heard the gup. The day I was hit the Brigadier of the brigade on the left of us came up to our Colonel and told him he thought our advance one of the bravest things. Then when we were with d'Amade we got a *most* handsome letter from him on our services, which appeared in all the French papers. On the June 4th fight our brigade was put up against a very stiff job and got heavily punished, but at one time was holding a whole brigade-front with three hundred and twenty men. We have about one hundred and fifty men left out of the battalion and five officers, including those returned after being wounded. My company-commander has got the D.S.O.

General d'Amade

We have lost two Colonels — Quilter killed and his successor, Stewart, hit in the jaw. We have altogether not done badly. I saw a number of my platoon at Malta wounded after June 4th, and they looked so jolly and bronzed in spite of their wounds. I am happy to get back. If we simply sit tight in our present position the *crac* is bound to come.

Will you send me Julian's poem published in *The Times*. I can't give you the date. The Egyptian papers quote it. Julian is an appalling loss to me. He was the most perfect of friends and heartening of examples, but I am relieved that E. Horner will be all right. I wish I knew more about Rex. Benson. News is so fitful here.

To the Hon. Lady Wilson.

Alexandria,
June 18, 1915.

I have been here now for about a week, and am sorry to say have been unable to see Scats [*Sir Mathew Wilson, late 10th Hussars, then commanding the Second Division at Ismailia. — R.*] who has been in hospital at Port Said. … Our base commandant is apt to send one off at a moment's notice, and Port Said is too long a journey to risk. Alexandria has been pleasant enough, with lots of old friends about and lots of our officers. Did you know a charming man called Major Bell, who was in Somaliland, and knew Tommy well? He is now a Sharpshooter. The Sharps and ourselves are still at Ismailia. The H.A.C. battery of Major got off one of his guns at the Turks — or rather at about one Turk — but the rest of Taylor's brigade have done nothing.

The Hood Battalion was finished on June 4th; we took a Turkish trench filled with Turks, whom we bayoneted. It was, however, under fire from another Turkish trench about fifty yards higher up, from which the Turks could throw hand grenades, etc., and we lost heavily, and did not get supports enough to go on. Out of nine officers who went with the charge, six were killed and three wounded.

We now number about one hundred and fifty men all told, I think, I think the battalion has done well. It has certainly earned a lot of official praise. Our new Colonel, Stewart, who was hit on the 4th, came back on the same ship as Scats, when he came back from India to marry you. Our Commodore and all the officers commanding battalions of our brigade are going to get Legions d'Honneur.

I like the poem of Julian's which they put into *The Times* — a real swan-song. And how very sad about Bill Tennant.

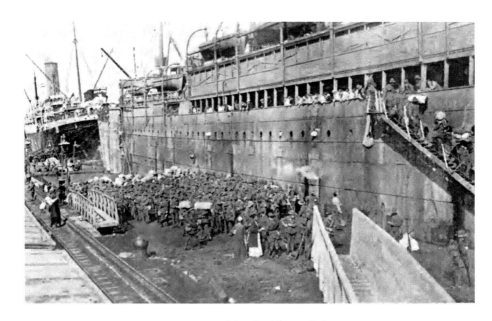

... troop ships in Alexandria

To Lord Ribblesdale.

Hood Battalion, R.N.D., M.E.F.,
June 23 or 28, 1915.

Just one line to say I am returning to duty now. They kept me waiting about a week in Alexandria, then put me on to the wrong boat, then kept me waiting ten days for the right boat; so you see they are not in a frantic hurry for the wounded to return. I shan't find my battalion much in the swing of it yet awhile; we are, I fancy, too reduced, and now getting ourselves together again under our ex-Second-in-Command. [*Colonel Freyberg.*]

Colonel
Freyberg

Stewart, by the way, who took Quilter's place, may be coming to see you. He is a charming fellow and a fine officer, and, while he will have little to tell you about me, he will be able to yarn to you about *les faits et gestes* of the 2nd Brigade and the battalion in general. The battalion, I fear, is a mixed lot now, filled up with odds and ends from new formations, etc. I saw Harry at Port Said, which was nice; he was there for a sore throat which they feared at one time was diphtheria. He was not looking famous, and rather fed up with canal guarding. Ismailia, however, is a very fine place from all accounts, bathing and good club. Am now back with battalion in rest camp. Big battle in progress, but we're out of it.

To the Hon. Lady Wilson.

June 28th.

... On this ship we are in a state of acute discomfort. Some forty-five officers in fifteen cabins — and a coal black ship. ... But I have been very lucky so far, and one mustn't expect Cunarders all the time. ... We have a subaltern on board who is in a corps of Palestine Muleteers, nearly all Russian Jews, who ran away from Jerusalem at the beginning of the war to Egypt, and enlisted, and have been made into "a transport unit. They have to be spoken to in Arabic and Yiddish-German. They are now going to the Dardanelles. We are having a jolly journey through islands, which we expect to complete to-morrow.

Lord Ribblesdale.

Hood Battalion, M.E.F.,
July 1, 1915.

I find everything very peaceful on my return [*Charles, after a tedious journey, now had about a fortnight in a rest camp. Two new battalions had been broken up to bring the Hood and the Anson up to strength, and the vexed subjects of brigade organization, always accompanied by some friction, are described. — R.*] — a new battalion brought again up to near its proper strength by accessions from other battalions, a line of trenches very solidly made reaching well up towards our goal, and well provided with drinking-water brought by pipes right into the firing-line, and an intermittent appearance of ships. It was tragic, the first arrival at dawn, to see nothing of the great fleet of men-of-war and transports that once was there, but the keel of the *Majestic* sticking out about four feet and lit by a solitary light, similar to the oil lamps put on the graves of the San Lorenzo cemetery on All Souls' night at Rome; but the beaches are busy with life and but little troubled with shell fire. The mischief is done by an elusive old lady on the Asiatic side nicknamed Annie. We can't discover her, as she moves on trollies. She sometimes drops a shell into our camp.

We haven't been in the trenches since June 4th, but will go soon. They are very safe and never shelled. The plan we follow now is to pound away at one little bit of the line and attack that. It answers better than general attacks all along the line, and the general tone is very optimistic and the Turkish shortage of shells very manifest. I am now a second-in-command of a company under a real type, Chalmers by name, whom I'm very fond of, but this will not last for long, when more of our wounded return. I am the baby of the "Hood". We have been subjected to pie-jaws on the subject of brigade reorganization, which has been necessary in our case and accompanied by some friction, as it involved the break up of two young battalions to make us up to strength. ... Soldiers, of course, have much practice in stump oratory, as the most junior platoon officer is supposed to lecture his men. I have studiously avoided doing so. I love our rest-camp life except for the dust storms. Soldiering is a grand life, and I never thought I'd like it so much.

I must now censor men's letters.

To the Hon. Mrs. Percy Wyndham.

Hood Battalion,
July 1, 1915.

I have got two delightful letters from you, darling, one describing your being shelled at Dunkerque and the other from Lilfeild telling me about the charge of the Essex. What a magnificent performance.

I have found the battalion in a rest camp — some miles from the firing-line — living comfortably enough and sleeping in pyjamas, except when we are standing by, which is rather our usual condition, especially if an attack is in contemplation. I have been in fine health since landing, except for slight *mal-de-mer* caused by an excess of rum last night. I look forward to the rum nights with all the zeal of an old sea-dog. It is a glorious liquor.

We have really got on well since I left, and while there may have been unnecessary losses, there is no ground for pessimism. The French are fighting splendidly, especially when they are on their own, and their bombardment of trenches is a masterpiece — marvellous rapidity of fire and accuracy. We are well round the Turkish flank on the Krithia side, thanks to a fine attack by the 29th Division, who have done marvels. It was well prepared for by artillery, and there were practically no Turks in the trenches, bay wounded and dead, when the men came up. If only the same had been done when we attacked on June 4th.

I went up into the fire trenches yesterday, and they gave me a great feeling of confidence. The Engineers are getting water right up to the firing-line by means of pipes. The trenches are for the most part bone dry, but they haven't always been so. Patrick is in great form. I, of course, did not see any of his activities in the field, but all say he is an excellent officer, very cool-headed and active. I am glad he gives me a *bonne presse*.

Patrick
Shaw-Stewart

To the Hon. Lady Wilson.

Hood Battalion.
(No date)

We each of us have our dug-outs, which are about two feet or so down from the surface. They would be a protection against shrapnel, but of little use against high explosive, which is what we are visited with from time to time. Luckily the Turks are very short of shells and so do very little "hating".

There is a gun called Annie on the Asiatic side which gives us now and then five or six about tea-time. I am told it was much worse last week. One unfortunate hero, who had been hit in the hand, came back and was hit in the ankle his first day *de retour* while lying in his dug-out. So his time in the Peninsula has been short.

It is a great difference from when I was last here, considering we are fighting a trench-war, like in France. We have pushed our line up very well, and made

our position very solid. The co-ordination of the various units' activities is far more efficient, and in my view we have the situation well in hand.

Our friends are all flourishing. Oc [A. Asquith] very fit after his bullet, and Patrick looking a holy man in his bright red beard, which might have been dyed with henna. He has done so well,

Oc Asquith and is *gai comme un pinson*.

To the Hon. Beatrix Lister.

Hood Battalion, M.E.F.,
July 1, 1915.

. . . Gallipoli has lost much of its charm of scenery since I got back. The place where we are camped has been changed from a smiling olive grove to a dust-heap. But everything is much better organized — splendid trenches, heaps of delicious water, and easy walking. The whole force is in great heart, and progress, if slow, has been considerable. The French artillery has quite found its length, has any amount of shells, and is doing magnificently. The new French General [Gouraud] is a great success and *some* thruster. Duststorms are our only grievance. We get very fond of our rum ration.

My brigade has not been in the trenches for some time, but is now fit for work again. We wanted a good deal of re-organization, but at this moment we are pretty strong. The only real discomfort I have had so far in this war was my passage from Alexandria to this place on a vile ship, where we were packed three officers per cabin, and which took about a week to do a forty-eight hours' run — what with dawdles and muddles.

To the Hon. Mrs. Wyndham.

Hood Battalion,
July 5, 1915.

Many thanks for three letters which I got all at once. I fear Julian was destined for a higher fate than hanging about Hazebrouck.

Rest-camp life I really find pleasant enough, and my dug-out is now fairly well organized, though I had two wet nights, owing to holes in my waterproof sheets which treacherously let the water-pool there find its way to the apertures and pour down on my devoted head. Shells come down from time to time. Yesterday three burst on our lines without doing any damage, bar riddling poor Patrick's best khaki tunic (luckily he was not in it, but it was hanging on a tree) and covering his sleeping-bag with soot. One fell in the lines next to us, killing two and wounding ten men. So it is purely a matter of chance.

I have had one or two amusing working parties. One of digging saps right up about sixty yards behind our firing-line and a hundred and sixty from the Turks' firing-line. It was at night, so I saw nothing but the usual fireworks and flares and rifle flashes, but very much doing. I went up yesterday to see where we had been working, and had a most interesting new and close, but perfectly safe position. I did some sniping at a Turkish loophole and had two shots hitting the iron round the loophole quite neatly. The men love sniping, but I think it is a safe enough pastime both for ourselves and the enemy, as the trenches are very solid. I fear I shall not do many more joy-rides for a little time, as we are on beach fatigue for about ten days or more. I am rather annoyed at it, but the general view seems that we ought to wait a bit longer. I have for the moment got a company. But this won't last long, as other wounded will be returning. I sleep in pyjamas now, as we are no longer standing by — so life is practically picnicking with little interludes of shell fire. I am getting a good judge of where a shell is likely to burst, as I expect you were also after your Dunkerque trials.

> *To the Hon. Lady Wilson.*
> *Hood Battalion, R.N.D., M.E.F.,*
> *July 5, 1915.*

Many thanks for your letter reporting on the last phases of Middlesex history at Mundesley.

My life since my return has been very peaceful, and I don't think there is any chance of our doing anything for some time, as we are detailed for beach work till further orders. We are still rather uncoalesced and we haven't a great number of officers. This is illustrated by the fact that I am *pro tem*, commanding a company, and for troops like us one really wants rather a full complement of officers. Our camp is really very pleasant, and the shade of the olive-trees and the breeze neutralize the fly and dust nuisance. At night our camp looks lovely with the little lights in the dug-Out shining through the sacking and waterproof sheets and the olive-trees in relief against the night sky and silvery in the moonlight. The darkness, moreover, hides the grassless state of our lines. We had shells in

yesterday — four into our lines which did no damage. But shelling is so much a matter of chance. The beaches are the most extraordinary places, full of dug-outs, etc., and just like London, for no one knows who his next-door neighbour is, and to find any one is practically an impossibility.

The Beach take themselves very seriously, and one would think that no one else on the Peninsula is in any danger whatever.

The Turks have pushed up a fresh army corps from the other side of Constantinople, who arrived here very exhausted after fifteen days' forced marches. They were at once pushed up into an attack, at which they made a very poor show, losing about three hundred men yesterday, and not pressing home an attack which might have rather shaken us. The Brigadier commanding in the trenches was suffering from the prevailing Peninsular complaint when he heard this attack was going forward, but acted with great decision. Picnicking and shell fire is not half a bad fire life, and I am very well and happy, though disappointed we are doing so little. K.'s fears about the ineptitude of shelling weeks before we have the troops for landing ready, and the fallacy that the R.N.D. and the French would suffice have been more than justified.

To Lord Ribblesdale.

Hood Battalion,
July 6, 1915.

Life continues to be peaceful and picknicky, and I have for the first time, fired a rifle in anger. This was in the course of a joy-ride to some advance trenches of ours, where we are within a hundred yards or so of the Turks, I fired two shots at a Turkish loop-hole and hit the iron immediately round the aperture. Sniping must be very good fun. The men in the trenches seemed most cheerful and pretty comfortable, though they don't get too much sleep, as heat and flies stop their getting it by day and rifle-fire and watches stop them at night.

I am rather annoyed at this continual state of inactivity, as we can't really get to know our men or train them if we are always doing fatigues and living under the eye of the Turkish gunners. Our new men want a lot of shaking down. We have not enough officers, moreover, and this is a bad thing in the case of 2nd home troops, which is what we are now.

F. Robinson is on the Peninsula now — at least, I suppose he is, but I have not had time to get at the Lancashire lines, and only been able to visit our lines rather occasionally.

Some offence has been caused by our new Eye-witness — a writer without an equal in describing Pimlico — likening the famous West Beach to Blackpool. Its inhabitants take the shells rather seriously and would resent this flippancy. The dug-outs on the beach are masterpieces of the sand-bag style, and very cool and safe. The very latrines are like the houses of the great.

To Mrs. Graham Smith.
Hood Battalion, R.N.D,, B.M.E.F.,
July 6, 1915.

I have just got two charming letters from you which gave me great pleasure. I am delighted to hear you are walking again. I expect you could do all the walking that is wanted on this Peninsula. Trench warfare has debased and made dull a noble science, and any one with a leg to stand on and a fairly sound stomach is fit for it. I went from Malta to Alexandria, where I was about a week before they found me a ship to take me on here, and from Alexandria it was about a nine days' journey. First we were taken down to a ship, about a thousand of us, which could accommodate three hundred. Then we were made to wait about three days till our new ship was ready to start. Then at Lemnos no one knew anything about us, so they had to improvise arrangements for us, which led to another three days' wait. No easy matter getting back to the front.

Our return to the Peninsula from Lemnos was a strange experience. When we first anchored off Cape Helles in May there was a huge collection of ships of all kinds, all lit up making an effect like Brighton Pier illuminated. At present all there is to be seen are a couple of hospital ships, a few destroyers, and a green shape protruding from the water, the keel of the *Majestic*.

... ships in Mudros Harbour

On land, however, the difference is tremendous. Considering how early operations developed into trench warfare, we have gained a lot of ground, and places which we thought reasonably near the firing-line earlier on are now rest camps. Our brigade has done nothing since June 4th, when it was very badly cut up, and we are likely to be on working parties for some time. The Turks occasionally shell us in this camp, and they are very assiduous in their attentions to the beach; but they do not do much damage, and the absence of the ships' guns to keep down their fire has not made so much difference as I expected. I suppose this is due to the fact that the Turks are short of shells. Our dinner was spoilt, as the dixy with the soup in it was riddled. So were two khaki tunics of Patrick's, luckily hanging on a tree and not on his manly form. These sort of things make us feel we are at war. The bathing here is very pleasant, though care has to be exercised in avoiding dead horses. Once out of their reach the water is deliciously cool and clear.

The Turks behave well to the wounded, give them first aid and sometimes return them to our own people after dressing them. Oc has been made lieutenant commander (same as a Major) and has got his company, a meteoric rise.

To the Hon. Irene Lawley.

Hood Battalion,
July 7, 1915.

It is delightful, having the Inferno by one again, as the most hard-hitting, poignant cantos are to be found there: they are in a sense more universal than the mystic ecstasy and transcendentalism of the Paradiso, to which one must be to some extent attuned and have steeped oneself in the spirit and spiritual theory of the Middle Ages. I think the finest thing in the whole Divine Comedy is the twenty-sixth canto of the Inferno, where Odysseus tells Dante of his last voyage and the wreck of his ship on the Mount of Purgatory.

We expect to go up to trenches very shortly, but I fancy we shall at first only be in support. The change since I was last here is enormous. We really have got on — have consolidated our portion in a remarkable manner. The trenches are splendid, and for the most part bone dry. The rest camp where we have our dug-outs is pretty quiet, though occasionally shelled. It would be untenable if the Turks had enough ammunition on the Asiatic side. I write under the shade of an olive-tree, reasonably cool, as there is generally a south wind blowing, but rather fed up with the dust. There are also lots of flies. But there is no real discomfort, and deliciously cool water. Patrick, who is practically the oldest inhabitant, never having been wounded, has grown a glorious red beard of the colour of henna. He is a thundering good officer and has quite a reputation. Since our last "push", on June 28th or so, we have marked time and the Turks have obligingly attacked us. They are supposed to have lost practically a whole division since that date. Gourand (O.C. French troops) will be a great loss. He was blown by a shell over a wall and broke both his legs in falling. He had got the French well together — and was a real Cœur de Lion.

To Lord Ribblesdale.

Hood Battalion, R.N.D., M.E.F.,
July 8, 1915.

Many thanks for two letters which I have just got, and for the cutting from *The Times* giving Julian's poem. It is a beautiful poem, and I like to think how fond he was of all his days of war. I saw it in Alexandria, but should like one to keep. I so liked the verse about the horses. It is very true of them here. They hardly turn their heads when the shells come, even if they burst quite near. They have not had such a bad time or lost any great numbers since I've been back. I've not seen one actually hit and maimed, though shells burst everywhere round them. They have made dug-outs for them behind walls, with mud partitions between — no overhead covers; and the battery horses all look fit, though on the fat side, as might be expected in this trench warfare, where they have relatively little distance to move. They seem a good stamp of horse. I have heard of one or two chargers having been killed, and am on the whole not sorry that Reynolds [*A very good bay horse of mine which went to Egypt with Sir M. Wilson. He won the jumping prize, beating a class of 87, at the Cairo Horse Show, 1916.*] is in Egypt, where he has a good master and is looking very well.

Lygrove sounds a charming place, if we any of us ever have money to hunt or own horses again. The return to settled life is very difficult to conceive at present. There are many rumours as to the future of the R.N.D., occasioned, I suppose, by the temporary removal from our section. This has never happened before, as there have never before been enough troops to admit of it. But in France I understand there are frequent choppings and changings.

To the Hon. Beatrix Lister.

Hood Battalion, M.E.F.,
July 12, 1915.

I have several charming letters to thank you for, which have in due time dribbled in. I am looking forward enormously to reading your collection of Granny's letters. All the time I have been back the battalion has been inactive, either in camp or digging trenches, unloading lighters, guarding G.O.C.'s, and other humble occupations, and I fancy we should all like a change. The working parties tire the men

and interrupt their night's rest, and the long time in camp gives them time to think of the food they are getting, etc., and leads them into grousing. If men have plenty of real work they haven't time to grouse. However, things are settling down pretty well. … It is distressing to look on the havoc modern warfare, with its trenches and dug-outs, makes with the kindly earth. I doubt when the soil here will recover its old look and these gaping wounds be healed. Also all the grass is trodden in and there is very little green. In the lines a little vineyard has been spared from the ravages of the spade and looks like a bright little emerald in the midst of the dirt and dilapidation.

Oc. Asquith and I went up into the French trenches one day. The trenches are built all round a great Turkish fort which they destroyed with shell fire and then stormed. They call it the *Haricot*. The Senegalais were in much evidence; they are marvellous sleepers, and do not mind the flies crawling all over their faces. Our men can't get sleep in the daytime in the trenches because of the sun and the flies. The French officers were extraordinarily nice and welcoming. They looked perfectly spick and span and were beautifully shaved. Our people don't keep nearly so tidy. They adore the 75 like a sort of goddess, and the French 75 may indeed become the new centre of French worship, now that they have got rid of God. They have had most difficult ground to get over.

We have had one night in the trenches since I've been back, well behind. We were shelled on the way home. My stick was hit by a spent piece of high explosive which had burst about two hundred yards away. It was of course absolutely done. They drop a few shells into our camp now and then, but they have not a sufficiency of ammunition to make themselves really disagreeable. We, I am told, will soon have plenty of shell both here and in France. This morning there was the very devil of a bombardment from about 4 a.m. onwards, and I think a considerable advance has been made both near Krithia and on the right of our line. The situation is well in hand. Whenever we concentrate gun fire on a little bit of the Turkish line and then push men up, we advance. We have a lot of troops coming out, and we have now contrivances by which our ships can anchor and shell the shore without fear of submarines. One of these last has been lately caught by nets. I think we shall be through with this job here by the end of September, if not before.

To Lord Ribblesdale.
Hood Battalion, R.N.D., M.E.F.,
July 18, 1915.

We are now in the trenches. We went in about three days ago. They are old Turkish trenches, with one or two admirably protected dug-outs, which we suspect the Turks have been made to hollow out for the German officers. It is fairly whiffy, and there are quite a number of dead in the neighbourhood, and the tell-tale stocking or end of boot is now and then seen protruding from the trench wall. We get our share of sniping, even in the support trench, which I have seen most of. One has to drop nimbly past certain critical corners. But there is no need for any one to get hit if they keep down. The Turks are sniping from a long way off and fire on the chance. The communication trenches are rather ticklish by day, though safe enough by night. There are occasional dead bodies where people have been killed, and it is an awful job getting our men past them: they have a sort of supernatural fear of trampling on their own dead; this kind of feeling of awe is felt also by the men in the case of the Turkish dead.

We get all we want to eat. The Eastern tea and biscuits and jam are excellent, but for a jam variety known as the Sir X. Y. brand, with a picture of the inventor on the label. He is a characteristic Millbank type, with the urbane glance of the sweating mill-owner of the forties. He gives us away, because the French used to give us wine in exchange for jam, but are now tired of doing so, as they always get this sample foisted upon them. What a good example of Gresham's Law.

Trench life means a good deal of repose but very little sleep. This is not so much due to the enemy as to the torrents of raw levies coming up to do working parties or to relieve pals or to look for their proper *places* in the line, and so on. I have had my toes trodden on by every officer and man of a Scotch Territorial Division. They come up in driblets, carrying the most weird cooking utensils, and with every sort of impedimentum. They never know how many of them are coming, and if you ask them each man says he is the last. Then after about ten seconds' interval fresh men come up, carrying what appear to be portions of bagpipes. They are always getting lost and held up. Last night I *had* to get them out by dint of jumping on the top of the communication trench parapet and kicking dust on to their heads, and at the time using the most violent language. The humours of trench warfare are really delicious. Our men are in fine fettle and have worked awfully well, taking things up to the firing-line with hardly any rest.

Patrick keeps a most lucid grasp of affairs, even with the Scots standing on our toes, when the trench is a seething mass of humanity. I had no idea the difficulty of getting men in or out of the trenches would be so great. The trenches are bone

*"There was the Turk — a great heat-swollen figure,
stinking in the sunshine."*

dry just now, rather hot and dusty, but there is always a breeze, I am very well and happy. The trench soil is limestone and chalk, rather white and trying to the eyes.

To the Same.
Hood Battalion, R.N.D., M.E.F.
July 22, 1915.

We have now done with our time in the trenches and emerged from four days' very hard work with great credit. This is due to our acting C.O. Freyberg, who will come and see you when we get home.

Our digging operations, carried out at night within about two hundred yards of the enemy's trenches and under a certain amount of rifle fire, have not only made our own position quite secure but rendered untenable for the Turks a small portion of our sector which they still held in between our extreme right and our right centre. They have also given us a point of vantage from which we can enfilade Turks retiring before the French on our extreme right. Oc. has been extraordinarily dogged, and is practically responsible for all this corner, which will be known as Asquith triangle. He hadn't a wink of sleep all the four days, and Patrick and Kelly also distinguished themselves and in one night dug a long trench connecting Asquith triangle with our main support. Six men of this company were killed and wounded, and I think the company of another battalion working with them lost about as many. Patrick and Kelly remained above ground the whole time, and it is a wonder they were not hit Their petty officer who was doing the same got killed. This trench will be called Shaw-Stewart Street.

Our last two days my company joined Oc. in the fire trench. The fire trench is heavily sniped, and before I had been in two minutes I got a bullet through my helmet, which was a salutary warning and made me keep my head well down. My company was chiefly occupied in operations against a little advanced post the Turks had pushed up against our lines like this. There was a sandbag barrier separating us from the Turks. One night we took this barrier down and pushed it about ten yards up the Turkish communication trench. As things were before, the Turks could have come up quietly and dropped bombs into us.

The next day we were more ambitious. The artillery — an Australian battery and the French — shelled the advanced Turkish post for about twenty minutes while we massed, with a covering party of men with bombs and bayonets and a main body of men with sandbags, in the trench, ready to rush out up the old communication trench and push our sandbag barrier still farther forward. It was not feasible to take the Turkish advance post, as it could not be held in face of Turkish guns on the hill slope opposite. Our shelling was magnificent. We realized the importance of rushing in immediately our shelling ceased. But as it turned out we were rather too close, for a shell fell among our people and buried six of them, who were, however, dug out unhurt or only slightly wounded. The shell luckily did not burst. This was followed by a Turkish shell which fell right in the middle of us as we were all crouching for the rush, hit Freyberg in the stomach, killed another man, and covered me with small scratches, which bled profusely at the moment. We had by now got our original barrier, so I got our covering party out and rushed them up the trench over quite a number of dead Turks, while my company commander, a grand fellow called Egerton, most valuable organizer, did the same with sandbags. We stopped our men just short of the Turkish advanced post: threw bombs in which did not light and would not burst, and at once started the new barrier; not a Turk in sight. The snipers, however, soon came back and made work at this point difficult, so we moved back and contented ourselves with a gain of about forty to fifty yards on our old position. The men, once they had recovered from the shaking they had got from these two shells, behaved very gallantly. We had only one man killed, and the East Lanes (Kitchener's Army), our neighbours, who helped us very cordially, lost their company commander; sniped because he put his head up.

General Paris

General Hunter-Weston

Our Commodore, General Paris, and General Hunter-Weston are all delighted with us. The latter now feels quite easy about his line.

The serious thing is Freyberg. He was sure to get the battalion and is such a splendid soldier. He got a D.S.O., you know, for swimming ashore at the Gulf of Xeros and lighting flares. I told him to look you up when he comes home. A stomach wound is always dangerous, but I think his chances of getting over it are good. He has been awfully good to me. I have been hit in about six places, but all *tiny* little scratches, so they will send me to Imbros for a fortnight or so. It is a delicious place. Buy me a wedding present for Violet — I should suggest *Storia di Mogor*, a translation from the Italian of the Memoirs of Minucci, a Venetian who was a doctor at the Court of Aurungzeeb. I have had no pain, only slight discomfort, in this clearing station on West Beach, where one can get nothing — not even a second cup of tea.

Above: officers resting in a dressing station

Below: the wounded being taken to a hospital ship

To the Hon. Beatrix Lister.

Hood Battalion,
July 24, 1915.

My injuries are very slight and do not even want dressing now, and the operation was a great success, as we got our barrier at least forty to fifty yards farther on and have quite secured our trenches from the danger of being bombed by the Turks. The position was like this, and we advanced our barriers from point X to Y. When I went out there were no Turks about: the artillery had scattered them to the four winds; but they soon came back, and we had only just time to get our sandbags up. Our days in the trenches were very hard work, what with garrison duty, getting water and ammunition up to the firing-line and improving our fire trenches themselves, and we hardly closed our eyes all the time. It is hard to sleep in the daytime owing to the flies. But it was never very hot, and we always had heaps to eat and drink. I have never, however, been so conscious of the uses of a water-bottle.

The battalion worked awfully hard and emerged with great credit in the highest quarters — all our friends, Oc, Patrick, and so on, are the most excellent officers. I am in the hospital at Imbros, a most delightful island, full of lichen-covered grey rocks, trees, and orchards — every sort of delicious fruit — and a glorious blue sea. It is much cooler even down here near the beach than the Peninsula, and a real land of plenty. The hospital people are most kind and put themselves out in every way. I get Guinness's stout for dinner.

I am reading d'Annunzio's *Trionfo della Morte* — apart from his luscious and eloquent treatment of the passion he is supreme at describing the drear life of the provincial *noblesse* of Italy and its underlying dramas of squalor and pathos. He is tedious when he goes too deeply into the morbid psychology of his heroes.

To Lord Ribblesdale.

Hood Battalion, R.N.D., M.E.F.,
August 1, 1915.

I am afraid you will have thought it very odd my not wiring about being wounded, etc., but it was quite impossible, as the authorities would allow no private wires to go through. The wires are retained for official messages only.

My wounds were very slight — mere scratches. So now I am back to duty again. We are still in our old rest camp, acting as Army Corps Reserve, and likely to be used in the coming fighting, but not as first line of attack, which will be undertaken by new troops. The division was told they would be taken off the Peninsula at the end of the month, but it has now been decided that not a man can leave, so I suppose there will be something doing.

We get fish for our breakfast, as we have an enterprising officer who goes and bombs them, then dives and picks them off the bottom.

As to my convalescence, I was first of all in hospital at the clearing station on the beach, where I wrote to you. It is a vile place. The men only get bread and cheese, and officers can't get a second cup of tea or sugar with their bread and milk. I then went over to Imbros with a sort of "world's fair" boat, with Sikhs and Turkish prisoners. The Turks told me all the Germans had left the Peninsula, and that they were fighting alone now — this is true of the higher command, but not of the machine-gun section. They praise the Heir Apparent, who when he went round the wounded said to them, "Inshallah, you will go home when you are well". Enver said to them, "Inshallah, you will go back to the war when you are well".

George Brodrick took me to lunch while I was at Imbros, and Sir Ian was most kind and affectionate in his inquiries after you and the rest of the family. He lives very simply, though well. We had excellent fish and potatoes and stewed plums. I should be rather more luxurious if I were G.O.C.-in-C. Sir Ian chatted pleasantly on the demoralized state of the Turks and on Egyptian antiquities, notably a cat-goddess with a lovely young woman's body he saw at Luxor — his recollections in our present conditions of monkery filled all with anguish.

Sir Ian Hamilton

The hospital at Imbros was rather congested with pale-faced officers whose tummies had been upset by the suns of the Levant. So I got into the interior as soon as possible, and went up to a charming village called Fanaghia, where I stayed with the resident British. I gorged on fresh vegetables excellently cooked by a handy Greek. I used to go jolly rides all over the island on pack-ponies, brushing through masses of Persian lilac and oleander on either side of my stony path. I went to one or two little monastery churches, kept tidy by one or two old monks who do damn all, and once a year give the country-side a "jolly" out of the endowments of these little churches, and I did one famous climb to a shrine of the rather controversial St. Athanasius. The highest hill in the island is crowned by a little shrine of St. Elias, built of shell and red tiles. St. Elias for some reason is the great saint of thunderstorms, and I suppose connected with the old Aryan sky-god, whose holy places were always on hill-tops.

I am now returned to duty, flourishing and very happy to get back to the battalion.

We are still Army Corps Reserve, but likely to be employed — *Parturiunt montes.* We have lately been common objects at Divisional Headquarters, and sat round Staff officers discoursing to us, like the disciples of St. Francis and Savonarola round their masters, and we had one very amusing morning making and firing off bombs. They are most undependable, and the fuses either ignite practically before they are lit or never at all. The bombs I saw were so remiss in going off that I feel they are almost suitable toys for children. I lit one and threw it with a catapult. I disclosed my lack of deftness in striking matches, a characteristic of very early days. General Paris talked to us to-day. He looked most young and cheery — brighter than I have ever seen him. He has a little poultry-yard at Headquarters and two roosters, a white one called Hindenburg and a buff Orpington called the Grand Duke — Hindenburg never allows the Grand Duke any play with the hens, but drives him away.

To the Same.

Hood Battalion,
August 10, 1915.

Many thanks for your letter and the Gis [burne] news . . . I should think Jock's fondness for hunting will make Mrs. Y. friendly, but I dare say a visit would help matters. Hunting seems so very remote now.

I approved your comments on Lord —'s scheme. He must be off his rocker. The soldiers, I hear, say the war will last at least another two years — particularly the French. I think if we are to go on for this time we shall have to run things in a different way to what we are doing now, as it seems agreed we are, at this rate, financially good for only one year. How we are to take our horns in I don't exactly see, so it is a pretty dilemma. Here we hear every day that Warsaw has fallen, which must mean a further prolongation. Apart from financial considerations, a long war is not altogether against our interests. It gives us time to pull up a number of unconsidered trifles in different parts of the world, which we should otherwise not have time to look at. Of all the Allies we have so far been the only gainers. The smashing up of German influence in the Far East, in the Persian Gulf, in the Pacific, in South-West Africa and in West Africa is an enormous gain.

... the Germans in front of Warsaw

I have written Diana at length about recent fighting here. Results are so far shrouded in mystery. I don't think no news is always good news. The Hood Battalion, acting as Army Corps Reserve, have done no fighting. We are not even sleeping in our clothes. The men get instruction in the "use and care" of the rifle and receive rather halting lectures on how to dig latrines in trenches, and other topics of martial interest. So all is pretty peaceful. We are so very callow just at present and our drafts so raw that it is not a bad plan some initial ignorance should be dispelled. The men's health is not quite as bad as it was, but is distressing us all a good deal. They cannot get rid of this mild dysentery. ... It affects their spirits and makes proper feeding an impossibility. However, we've been here

... fatigues

since May 6th, and should be thankful nothing worse has made its appearance.

To the Hon. Irene Lawley.

Hood Battalion,
August 11, 1915.

Many, many thanks for your letter, which I loved getting. The Prophet is much given to self-repetition, but he has a glorious power of making his clouds into angels with sweeping wings, and giving nature a soul, and great lyrical fire. He is also an old fox, and the skilful use he makes of Gabriel and Allah to get him out of domestic difficulties commands respect. It is a pity Gabriel is not at the disposal of the modern husband — or wife. He is an "affable archangel" as far as the Prophet is concerned, and makes special exemptions for him not accorded to other believers. The Prophet was not too humanitarian, and was at times inclined to compromise with idolatry; but there is a fine statesmanship of the patriarchal type about the man. And he generally must be admitted to point out the evil consequences of unbelief as coming from God, not from his own armies. I can't find any positive order to kill the non-Moslem, and to the "People of the Book" he was, administratively, most lenient. Mary in the Koran conceives under a date-tree near a stream of running water — a graceful image.

I have been wounded again since I wrote, but it has been a very light affair and only kept me away for about a week, giving me the chance of going to Imbros, a dream island, where the mountain paths are choked with masses of Persian lilac and the mulberry-trees are almost dark blue. I did little rides on pack-ponies all over the island the two days I was there and soaked myself in mulberries. I wonder there is not some Islamic legend making of the mulberry a transformed nymph; the juice of the fruit is the nearest thing to blood in trees and flowers. You can't think how delighted one is to guzzle in fresh vegetables cooked by Greeks. Except for onions and potatoes they are the great dearth here. We get plenty of fresh meat, and I haven't eaten bully beef — which I don't like — since I have been on the Peninsula. I like all the other ration things, especially the men's stews and desiccated vegetables, etc. The form of bully beef is repellent.

Annie has been very quiet lately, and altogether we get precious little shelling now. I feel we are not going to do any fighting for some time — we are such a long way short of strength, both in units *quâ* Division and in officers — so you can be sure we are pretty safe. I believe we are being sat on by a commission which is to decide our fate. It is about this struggle against dissolution, which can only end one way, and to feel one is more or less out of it.

Patrick, alas! is not with us *pro term*, as he is Army Corps *liaison* officer, but we see him quite often and the job gives more scope for his abilities than the little hack-work we do here in the way of instruction. I am, *vice* him, a company commander, which is rather comic. I leave all to my second-in-command, who is a sort of Dugald Dalgetty and was himself a C.P.O. and can jaw on any subject under the sun. Asquith is battalion second-in-command and a most distinguished and respected figure. The men even take his advice about investing in War Loan.

To the Same.

Hood Battalion, R.N.D.,
August 13, 1915.

You will have got my letter telling how it all happened. "It" is really the two vaccination marks on shoulder and one on arm. It is now practically well, though I still have it dressed, and it has done just as well in camp as it would have done in hospital, where I should have been much more bored. Sick men are the last kind of company one wants if one is sick oneself, and yellow faces give me the pip.

We have done nothing since I got back to the battalion. But time has gone pretty fast, as we have an agreeable mess. The fighting on this side has been in itself costly and unproductive, but I fancy our attacks of the 6th and 7th (I forget dates) did have the effect of keeping Turks on this front who would have otherwise gone to the other front and opposed the new landing. We may have even done more. ... The new landing, intended to lead up to a "threat" at Maidos, is so far a partial success. It appears we got to all the critical points, but were not in sufficient force to hold them. A landing operation is like getting men over a bridge — you can't pass more than a certain number over within a certain time, so at the outset you have always strictly limited forces confronting unlimited forces on the enemy side. The last information to hand is to the effect that both sides are digging like badgers. We have, however, more troops to land, so it is possible that we may be able to break the Turkish line yet. But once we settle down into trench fighting it becomes a slow business, and additional divisions dropped in don't make very much difference. I don't know what troops we've got to play with. At present it looks rather like a game of noughts and crosses, little landings here and there and Turks in between them, I trust the Germans haven't a large force to detach down to this part of the world to coerce the Balkan States into giving them a passage and so effect a junction with the Turk.

Life is rather inactive, but we are comfortable enough, and the only distressing thing is the shaky health of the men. I have kept very well, and have initiated ovens for my people, so that they get roast as well as boiled.

P.S. — I feel that we shall never fight or move, and I shall not know what has happened if I wake up one morning and don't see Achi Baba on the skyline.

Let me here insert a letter to a friend from Mr. F. S. Kelly, of the Hood Battalion, which bears upon the position and the prospect of affairs in Gallipoli at this time. As it also refers to Charles it is not irrelevant. — R.

Charles returned to the Peninsula somewhere about the end of June, when the original battalion was very much reduced in numbers by the heavy losses incurred on May 6th to June 4th.

It was just about this time that every one began to realize that a continuance of the campaign on the lines hitherto laid down was very unlikely to achieve any success, and there was a consequent depression among all the ranks, which, if it had been unchecked, would have undoubtedly had a serious effect on their moral. It was precisely in checking this that Charles's influence was, by universal consent, invaluable.

The heat, the swarm of flies, the horrible stench in the trenches, seemed to have no effect at all on his cheerfulness, and above all he didn't know what fear was. I can well remember the sensation created early one morning in the battalion on our right when they saw some one walking along out in front of their trench apparently quite unconcerned.

It was Charles, to whom much the simplest method of solving a dispute that had been vexing the Staff and other authorities — as to whether there was or wasn't a trench at some particular point in "No Man's Land" — was to go and see. This was just about the time that he was wounded the second time — on the occasion of the rushing of a Turkish sap with some bombers. The last time he was wounded was pure ill-luck.

To Charles's friends no praise would be excessive. I knew him before the war, but have never had an opportunity of cultivating his friendship before we were thrown together in the same battalion. I have certainly never known a more original character, nor one of more sterling worth, nor one either with a more exquisite sense of humour. On his second return from hospital from Imbros, he came laden with fresh fruit, vegetables, wine, and other luxuries, which, in the absence of transport, had to be left on the beach while he came up to camp to arrange for a limber party to be sent down for them.

We all waited its arrival with impatience, and when eventually the party came back to say that there was no gear there, and it became obvious that a stupid servant who had been left in charge had taken his eyes off it, there was a savage outburst of anger from all of us, and imagination ran riot in devising punishment to fit the offence. Charles's suggestion, however, as to what one *could* do with such a man was: "I think we must make him an officer".

> *To Mrs. Graham Smith.*
> *Hood Battalion, R.N.D., M.E.F.,*
> *August 14, 1915*

Ever so many thanks for two charming letters I have had from you. Clare's young man sounds very attractive, and I should think a great riding man, which is what she wants.

The last few days here have been exciting, though we have rather played the rôle of Sister Ann, and waited for the cloud of dust to rise in the distance. The results to date of the new landing have not been brilliant, and the "thrust" at Maidos has not materialized. Our operations have been quite of secondary importance, simply meant to keep the Turks busy here and stop them sending troops away in any great quantities, and the sanguine estimates of a capture of Achi Baba, etc, have been rather beside the mark.

The 29th lost a good many men in the latter fighting; the actual results in capturing trenches, etc., are nil. I think the Turks have also lost prettily heavily, as they did some counter-attacking. We are again supposed to be short of shells. Such is life. It is disappointing, but, of course, no one knows how many troops we have got to play with. Our mess have snaffled a Frenchman to cook for us, of whom we have great hopes. Our only fear is that he may be coveted by some of our generals, etc.

Rumours say that the 2nd Mounted Division (Scats and the rest of them) are

... attack on Achi Baba

fighting on their flat feet on the Anzac front. It is certainly the interesting front just now. I am gloriously well, and have a pleasant mess and plenty of books, so the tedium of always being in the same place is obviated. We always get breezes, so don't suffer much from heat.

To Mrs. Lewis.

Hood Battalion, R.N.D., M.E.F.

Many thanks for your very kind letter. Cigarettes would be most welcome; but send me a nice, damp plum-cake. If made damp and packed in tins they keep splendidly. There will be just time for you to get one cake out to me. We shall be through in six weeks' time I hope.

No home-coming for me till then. We sailors (!) have been here from the first, and will see it out.

It will be a bit sad coming back. … Think of Taplow nowadays. At least out here there is enough to do to stop me dwelling on these things.

I got well from my wound in a week's time. Hospitals give me the pip, and I was very happy to get back to camp among my pals. Great fun we all had at our camp table. We do ourselves very well here, you'll be glad to hear; but there is no Scott [*The hall-porter at the Cavendish Hotel. "Freddy" is Scott's fox-terrier. — R.*] to bring me my boots in the morning. Give him my love, and Freddy.

Be good and look after the family well. Get *The Times* of July 23rd and cut out the Gallipoli news. It is about the Hood Battalion, although they don't give names.

To Lord Ribblesdale.
Hood Battalion, R.N.D., M.E.F.,
August 19, 1915.

We are again in for a spell of work, and have just had Monday to Thursday in the reserve trenches — comfortable lines a good long way back. We shall shortly go up again into the firing-line, which is very nearly as safe, as I don't think we contemplate doing any more attacking on this side till some real progress has been made on the other side. We seem quite jambed on this side, and all efforts to advance which have been recently made have been costly and unsuccessful. Every division tells the same story about its drafts. They come out insufficiently trained, so there is a feeling of stateness about the whole show on this side. We justify our existence by pinning a certain number of Turkish troops here. The Turks, I imagine, hold this line lightly with a few good troops and an enormous number of machine-guns, which are German manned.

Julian and Billy Grenfell with their mother

It is exciting H. being at last in a show and Middlesex having their fling, which they so longed for. I am sure they will do well; they are much better troops than Kitchener's Army, I feel. The 9th Corps have been a disappointment. They neutralized the effects of the expansion of the Anzac position by complete inaction after a virtually unopposed landing at Suvla. As troops they were not thought much of here. One I talked to did not know which hill was Achi Baba, and this after five days in the trenches, for they came here first before going to Suvla.

Is it true, by the way, that Billy Grenfell has been killed? — this would be too cruel news. It is a good

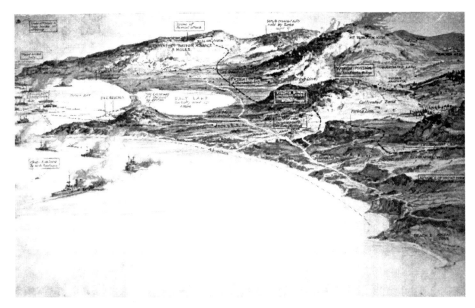

SUVLA BAY
Above: Plan of the bay
Below: The landing

thing Ivo is still too young. We have had rumours of it out here.

I went for a visit to the firing-line yesterday, but saw nothing of any particular interest. At one point an old Turkish communication trench runs right into a sap of ours. We have a huge sandbag barricade with a loophole whence there is always protruding the point of a rifle. I fear the monotonies of trench warfare are still with us, but the discomfort is not serious and shelling is very intermittent. The Turkish shells are bursting very indifferently.

Freyberg, after an absence of twenty-five days, has returned. This must be a record for any one hit in the stomach. He was brilliantly operated on, and the gash is perfectly healed. He saw H. in Egypt, and was probably the source of H.'s information as to me.

I am glad you liked the MS. It is the sort thing to put by, I think, and might be of interest when the events of the last few months have faded into the distance of time.

Look up *The Times* of July 23rd. The last paragraph of the official news from Gallipoli describes the achievements of the Hood in the trenches that led up to my being wounded. I see Sir I. H. says we took the redoubt. Our orders were really on no account to take it. How news is made up. Do get that number. Mrs. Lewis can put the cutting in her scrapbook. Give her my love.

To the Hon. Mrs. Percy Wyndham.

Hood Battalion,
August 23, 1915.

Since last I wrote I fear my worst anticipations as to the Anzac move have been realized, and it was so very nearly a brilliant success. The Turks were surprised, as they thought we were going to land in Asia and in the Gulf of Xeros, and it was only the dilatoriness of the O.C. 9th Corps which prevented us getting right across to Maidos and cutting off the Achi Baba army. If they reinforce heavily *at once* we shall be through by the autumn. If they don't —. My fear is that the Germans may do a push through Serbia, get there before we've done our job, and play old Harry with everything in this part of the world. I only hope Sir Ian will be honest and state his requirements in the most explicit and insistent manner. We have been in the trenches lately — in reserve to the other brigade — and are now going up to hold the sector ourselves, which is fun. We have a jolly little cornfield in front of our old trenches, where was a tree on which a lot of pigeons and doves settled. If only I had had a shot-gun. There were also a lot of jays and little doves.

We have just had a new draft — eight officers and two hundred men. The men impress every one very favourably. ...

How tragic about Billy. I almost dread my home-coming. So many of our old joy-places will be full of ghosts. And here one does not have that feeling of the void and the ghosts which have taken the place of dear living forms. Julian and Billy were very close brothers, so one hopes they will somewhere be united again. Shall write again shortly.

... reinforcements being landed under fire

To Mrs. Hamlyn.

Hood Battalion, R.N.D.,
August 23, 1915.

I must write and thank you very warmly for the Clovelly cake, which was eaten with enthusiasm, and was in pleasing contrast with our normal fare — not that that is so bad, but *toujours perdrix* —.

Since my second wound we have been very quiet till the last few days. The Naval Division are once more in the trenches. We had three pleasant days in a reserve trench — well behind — with any amount to eat and drink, and not too oppressive heat. When one gets away from our dust-heap of a camp the country is very smiling.

The men were pretty happy in the trenches, and pleased me. We have now got a large new draft of men and some new officers. I am for the moment in the giddy position of company commander, with three subordinate officers. I've had a company before, but never so many underlings, and I feel rather embarrassed.

The latest thing in officers in the R.N.D. is no worse than the latest thing in Kitchener's Army, judging from the specimens I saw in the hospitals and rest camps at Imbros — young men of tender age with queasy stomachs, to whom you and I with our Levantine experiences would feel very superior. I met Jones [*Sir Louis Mallet's former butler.*] at Alexandria, where he is with Sir H. McMahon. He is longing to fight, and regrets his age. I hear Francis is Raymond Asquith's senior officer in the Guards.

Raymond Asquith

To Mrs. Graham-Smith.

Hood Battalion, R.N.D.,
August 23, 1915.

We have been pretty quiet lately, and I have had a certain amount of time for reading.

What do you think of Lewes's "Life of Goethe"? He is rather -inclined to moralize and obtrude his own personality, but it is a good biography, I think. Lewes, of course, devoted rather unnecessary space to defending Goethe for actions which need no defence. Why, for example, should Goethe have made an honest woman of Friederike? I should like to have seen Goethe more than almost any other great man, with his ideal beauty and piercing eyes. He is a much greater man than writer, really.

What an odd lapse his writing a treatise on the Gift of Tongues in the Acts and on the real nature of the Ten Commandments. It is curious great men have been seduced into serious discussion of futilities by the spirit of their age.

This is his last letter to me from the hospital ship Gascon. I refer to it in my memoir. At the same time he began a letter to his sister Diana. His nurse advised him not to go on writing it, as he was very restless and ill at ease. He assented, saying there was no hurry, and put the few lines he had written to Diana in one of the books he had been reading. — R.

To Lord Ribblesdale.

Hospital Ship,
August 26, 1915.

Just think, I have been wounded once more, the third time. We were in a trench, observing the Turkish trenches, when suddenly they fired some shells into our trenches. I went along to see what had happened, got my people back into a

HMHS Gascon

bit of a trench they had had to leave, then went down the trench, thinking the show was over, and then got it, being struck in the pelvis and my bladder being deranged, and slight injuries in the legs and calves.

... a hospital ship

I have been operated on, but am sketchy as to what has been done. I am on a hospital ship, comfy enough, but feeling the motion of it a good deal, and I have to be in bed and cannot change my position. The hours go slowly, as one does not feel very much up to reading. However, I got to sleep all right. I feel this will be a longish job, and I don't know where I shall do my cure — perhaps Alexandria.

My doctor is quite happy at the way things are going. The shell that hit me killed one man and wounded the others.

Forgive this scrawl, but it's not easy to write.

In my memoir I spoke of Sir Ian Hamilton's Honours dispatch. A few days ago I wrote and asked whether I might quote its actual words. He has approved of my doing so, and, indeed, seemed to wish it. Here it is.— R.

Copy of Original

"For brilliant deeds of gallantry throughout our operations. On July 16th he was specially brought to notice for heading an assault against an enemy's stronghold. Again, on July 21st, he personally reconnoitred a Turkish communication trench, and, although wounded (for the second time), he returned and led forward a party to the attack. Subsequently he was a third time wounded and has since died, to the sorrow of all ranks who knew him."

One more letter and I have done. Colonel Bernard Freyberg, D.S.O., now commanding the Hood Battalion in France, sent me this letter only the other day. It is dated July 30, 1916, and is written by Lieutenant Ivan Heald, of the Hood Battalion, to Colonel Freyberg. — R.

There is, I learn, some hope that a little memoir will be published by a friend of Charles Lister's. Would it be possible for you to let the author know something of the splendid lead which Lister gave to the junior officers who served with him in the Hood Battalion? Charles Lister was a tower of strength to us, and you, Sir, I am sure, will agree that his wonderful personality was a great aid to you in your task of rebuilding a battalion of fighting men out of the salvage left from the disaster of June 4th.

We had seen our hopes of speedy victory smashed before our eyes; our few men were broken with the endless drudgery of trench digging, and every one was yearning for relief.

Then follows a passage which I've quoted in my memoir, in which Mr. Heald speaks of Charles returning to the battalion — his wounds healed — and assuring them "joyously" that they were having the time of their lives. He goes on:

Henceforward, who were so cheerful as the Hoods? There was no mess in the Peninsula, I'll swear, so merry as ours, with Lister leading such rare wits as Asquith, Kelly, and Patrick Shaw-Stewart — Lister always on the most uncomfortable packing-case, declaiming and denouncing with that dear old stiff gesture of his, which we came to know so well.

But the strongest impression I have of Lister was his eager sense of duty. Throughout the war I have never met a man in whose heart there burned so steadily that first fine flame that sent us all out soldiering. He was ever on the look-out for something useful to be doing. His willingness to sacrifice himself seemed part of some high secret religion of his own; and those who mourn for him must realize that this, coupled with his serene disdain of danger, inevitably meant his fall sooner or later in the campaign.

We were six months in the trenches after he died, but I, for one, know how much his example helped me to carry on through that dreary stretch. The legacy he left us was rich indeed.

... hospital ships collecting the wounded

... burial at sea for those who died en route to hospital

Part II

Recollections

Charles went up for a Foundation Scholarship at Eton in July 1900, and was elected from a private school (St. Aubyn's, Rottingdean) that eschewed all cramming. His master, Mr. T. Stanford, wrote to me that his performance did him great credit, "considering that I have never given him half an hour's more work than any other boy in the school". It was very hot weather at the time, and Charles was not very well. Mr. Stanford goes on to say: "Charles's pluck was to be admired. In the 'General Knowledge' paper his nose bled profusely, but he did not stop working and remained on until he had finished it. His [blood-stained paper has come back to me as a trophy which I shall always keep." Mrs. Warre Cornish thus describes her impression of Charles in these days. — R.

Amongst the contrasts of Charles's life and the several inspirations which swayed him from time to time, it must be remembered that he was born a scholar; that is to say, he not only had linguistic taste and an innate love of Greek and Latin poetry, myth, and history, but that the faculty of grammatical accuracy was thrown in with other gifts. Now, scholarly accuracy, like the blessing of a good verbal memory or the power of early rising, opens an easy school career to not a few; still, great delight was felt at home by the successful result of the examinations for College at Eton. He made light of it himself; the carriage which was to meet him at Gisburne returned without the scholar. It turned out that the train had carried him past his station; the home-comer being occupied at the time under the seats of the compartment trying to recapture some white mice which cared little for junctions or connections.

The question now arose whether Charles should follow his elder brother Tommy's example and enter Eton as an Oppidan or accept the bounty of the Founder. On the one hand was Oppidan Eton, its spacious precedents of school-life, its world-known traditions; on the other hand, College and its vigorous independence; its power to mould and stimulate the natural gifts of a clever boy; its intellectual and individual conservatism. As it happened, there was no immediate vacancy in College, so Charles entered the School in the house of Mr. Bowlby. "From the first", his tutor writes, "things" intellectual attracted him, and by his own preference (after many discussions between his parents and me) and by my advice he chose College. From first to last he loved College, and would cheer like a frenzied thing

Eton College Cloisters

Eton College
Above — the Wall Game
Below - a view of the College from the river

on St. Andrew's Day when Collegers won the match against Oppidans."

Thus in January 1901 he became a Scholar on the Foundation by his own choice. He was placed with a clever and versatile set, all alike in this, that their facility constituted! their chief temptation to taking things easily. One of his greatest friends from 1902 onwards was Julian Grenfell. They were in Mr. Bowlby's pupil-room together. Edward Horner and Rex Benson, also close allies of Charles's, were in Mr. Bowlby's house. Billy Grenfell — a greater scholar than any — was only two years his junior in the school. Contemporary with the two famous Oppidan brothers, Julian and Billy Grenfell were the two Colleger brothers — both also killed in action — Reggie and George Fletcher. In College, too, were Charles's great friends, Patrick Shaw-Stewart and Ronald Knox, Alan Parsons, Robin Laffan and Foss Prior. Of this company six have been killed and two have been wounded in the great war.

At this time Julian Grenfell had raised the level of Eton House debates. And in College, debate rose to quite a high standard. There is an institution called College Pop, a self-elected debating society of twenty of the senior Collegers. College Pop debates were at all times regarded more seriously than those of other Eton societies: and Shaw-Stewart, Fletcher, Knox, Prior, Laffan and Marsden brought something like fame in the School at large to these discussions.

Charles had been three years at Eton and was at the close of his seventeenth year when his elder brother Tommy was killed by some straggling Somali spearman, while carrying dispatches, after the battle of Jidballi in January 1904. Captain Thomas Lister had fought in most of the battles of the cavalry campaign against the Boers with his regiment, the 10th Hussars. He was twice wounded. He won the D.S.O.; in Sir Ian Hamilton's words, "he was a brave leader of men". To soldierly qualities he added no common taste in literature, a power of sustained reading, sterling gifts for friendship and for sport, and every endowment which made him a perfect eldest son. Of his death Lady Ribblesdale wrote: "His only fault was that he was too brave, and when he galloped out of sight and out of hearing into the mists of immortality, he feared no evil".

Charles was at home at Gisburne for his holidays when the first news of his brother being missing, after the victory at Jidballi, reached England. Some days of suspense followed, then the blow fell.

It was not the first time that Charles had been called on to exercise sympathy, perhaps one of the rarest gifts in the school-boy. If we go further back in the annals of Gisburne we find that it had already been his rôle to console. The following letter was written in 1897, when he was ten years old, to his grandmother, Emma

Charles Lister.
Eton, circa 1903-4.

Lady Ribblesdale. As a little boy much of Charles's time had been spent with her, and she possessed the rare gift of turning a child's mind in a perfectly simple way towards high and heavenly things. The death of her second son, Martin Lister, [*My brother was British Resident of Negri Sembilan Malaya. He died on his way home of fever, February 24, 1897, aged 39. — R.*] came as a terrible sorrow to her in the spring of this year. Charles's love of his grandmother and his recognition of her spirituality inspired this letter of his childhood. His relations with her were always intimate and loving: the spell of her beauty and dignity felt by him in these early days remained unbroken to the end.

"Dear Granny, — How unhappy it must have been for you when you heard that dear Martin was dead, for whenever he had the chance of being kind, he was. How unhappy you must have been with us, many unhappinesses at a time, father's, head, [His father had just had a bad fall out hunting.— B. W. C.] *then poor little Charles Tennant's death, alas! God takes away souls and gives back, but think that Uncle Martin is happy up above the sky, where he continually is praising God in the City of gold with the twelve gates of pearl and precious stones; think that he is singing to golden harps, clad in white robes like those holy ones who are continually praising Him at the foot of His throne; think of all the beauties of heaven as described in St. John's Revelation about the golden floor and crystal river. When you feel sad, read overdo yourself that beautiful chapter in Revelation, I forget the number, but I dare say you remember reading it to us in the happy times at Gisburne, when you used to read to me all the beautiful bits of the different books of the Bible. Good-bye from your very affectionate grandson, Charles."*

Childish feeling about death, however fresh, does not touch the reality. With the loss of his elder brother, death entered into the world for Charles. It was about this time that I first knew him at Eton. He was always cheerful, and his gay manner — even reckless gaiety — never failed his friends there. But he felt the event poignantly, and eighteen months afterwards wrote to Lady Ribblesdale at the loss of his friend Merton at Eton: "I was only just beginning to get over the death of Tommy". And it seemed to those who knew him behind the scenes that there was a sense of inadequacy about himself which troubled him that year. Some ideal of a soldier's life on active service might now have floated before him. But he was one of the Collegers who hung the wreath of peace round the neck of the Founder's statue in the school yard on June 2, 1902, at the Peace. And no great European cause appeared likely to draw his country into war. His tutor, Mr. Bowlby, whose perceptive judgment touches the spirit and not the letter of events and character at Eton, has written to me of that time: "Charles was deeply religious by instinct, with rare spiritual depths, not easily revealed, only half understood by himself In fact he was diffident — inclined to be hypersensitive, seeing the ideal more clearly." Here are a few subjects which interested this unusual Eton boy: the teaching of English in South Africa, the problem of our repatriation on Boer soil; Franciscanism in the twentieth century — the great spread and use of its lay Third Order to-day; Mr. Luxmoore's interest in Ruskin's industrial and financial theories.

All this sounds tame, but my impressions are chiefly of backwaters of school-life. The scene of our conversation was sometimes the river. There is a bend in the Thames below the Playing Fields well known to fishermen. Here the great Provost Sir Henry Wotton fished; and here floats the masters' raft, where the boating party starts down-stream with masters and boys and follows the quiet reaches below Romney lock to the Bells of Ouseley. The charm of these expeditions is their remoteness from boisterous school-life — the School only boats up-stream above Windsor Bridge. Charles was not a very hardworking rower, and a "dry bob" by choice, but he pulled with pleasure a leisurely oar. In the Fellows' Library of the Cloisters he was a willing student of its treasures. My husband delighted in showing him mediaeval manuscripts and early printed books. It was noted that his preference was for the chapel-builder's wage -book and Caxton's Piers Plowman. Charles was growing more interested in Socialism every day. But, as I have said, I can but describe backwaters. The great stream of school-life was bearing Charles on, and Mr. Ronald Knox must speak of its wider issues.

One home recollection yet must find its place here: his mother's visit to Charles when he got up a lecture for a Russian reformer. The occasion is described by Mr. Knox. Sufficient to say here that Charles was the subject of much chaff about his mild Revolutionist. The occasion was not merely revolutionary but gently convivial, and he allowed no such trifles to disturb his equanimity.

The tenantry, household, and workpeople on the estate gave Charles a gold watch and chain on his twenty-first birthday. His mother was away from us, trying to recover her health. It is impossible to express through any furniture of words what Charles, his future, and his possibilities meant to her ever since he was a tiny boy; so, though perhaps her letter to our Gisburne people about his coming of age and their present falls outside more recent events, I include it here. — R.

Pendyffryn Hall, Penmaenmawr.

November 15, 1908.

Dear Friends,

I must write you a line from my retreat to tell you how touched I was by your kindness and generosity to my son Charles.

It is the second time you have shown your goodness and generosity to my sons, and I feel most deeply grateful to you all.

Charles will, I am sure, be very delighted with the beautiful watch and chain you were good enough to give him; and the sympathy and interest you have shown him will be an incentive to him to work well at Oxford, and do his best when education is over and real work begins. He will keep the dedication always by him to remind him of all his kind and well-wishing friends. I hope that as he grows older his passionate interest in humanity may be wisely directed and be of use to the world.

It is a sorrow to me to have to be exiled in this sanatorium, away from all I love; but I trust that as I get stronger it may not be so very long before I am allowed to return to you all. It seems such a much quicker process to lose one's health than to regain it; but I am thankful to say I am progressing slowly.

Thanking you all once more and wishing you a prosperous winter,

I am,
Your sincere friend,
C. Ribblesdale.

... the boys working on a potato field during the war

It is hard to say when it was that you first became conscious of Charles at Eton as a public character. There was an early stage at which, as he sat "socking" at Rowland's, he once lamented his own lack of popularity. That certainly did not last long; he had a vogue soon enough, but only in virtue of a reckless, irresponsible manner he carried with (him. He found more serious interests by a process his friends saw nothing of; and by the time it was realized that he had unequalled gifts as a companion it was realized also that he held unusual views. Before the beginning of his last year he was already noted in debate as a champion of the oppressed: it was a political, not an economical, standpoint at first, and took the form of an interest in the fortunes of continental revolutionaries, not always very clearly distinguishable from Anarchists. He collected with marvellous rapidity what seemed an impossible sum from College for the relief of distressed Jews in a foreign capital. He held a meeting in aid of the same object, engaging a hall in Windsor and placarding the town with generous announcements of it. It was not largely attended, but it seemed like an evening in fairyland, especially when solos from "The Tempest" by a well-known singer were interspersed with the speeches (some of them a little tedious) which were the marrow of the occasion. One morning seventy pictures of Father Gapon (then a newspaper hero) arrived for distribution in College, and it was after this that the lecture in hall (already referred to) introduced his friends to a genuine revolutionary — a gentleman who denounced Father Gapon as a renegade, to the mystification of his audience. We lost sight of him when he left England, but his signature remains in the Visitors' Book kept by Charles's "mess", in a mixed company, along with those of three diocesan bishops.

Charles's enthusiasm for the Labour Movement came very little later. He was a Socialist in his utterances before the General Election of 1906, before Labour became a fashion, petted by Society and patted gingerly on the back by dignitaries of the Church. All this was due to width of mind reacting on an intense passion for justice. This passion showed itself in other ways. It was he who inspired a giant protest to the Head Master on a matter affecting the interests of the boys, but not strictly within their province. It is interesting to remember how he had the memorial printed, signed by the three most prominent people in each House, and presented to the Head Master by a trembling Captain of the School, all within two days; interesting, too, to trace in its stately language the love of the democrat for constitutional forms. His sense of justice was even so abstract and detached as to make him feel a slight put upon himself with a quite impersonal indignation; and those who dissuaded him from sending it can still remember the drafting of a letter to one of the masters on some private grievance: "Sir," it began, "this kind of thing will not do".

Such feelings, almost Quixotic in their vehemence, would ordinarily be associated with an angularly minded, unpleasantly precocious boy, whom the schoolboy world would either ignore or make fun of, Eton, probably more than any other public school, is a kindly nurse of eccentricities; but none of her tolerance was needed for acceptance of Charles. For no one was ever more natural, more unlike the morbid, spectacled pariah who leaves and looks back upon his public school with resentment.

At the beginning of his last year (September 1905-6) he was elected, though a Colleger and without athletic distinction, to the rigidly exclusive privileges of "Pop". "Pop", or "Eton Society", is a self-elected athletic and debating society of ancient and intricate traditions. From time to time its debates rise to a high level, for instance when Alfred Lyttelton's genius for games made him a leader and some statesman-like promise was shown in debates in Pop. Mr. Shaw-Stewart

... the interior of Pop

writes in the privately printed Memorials of Julian of "the temporary wave of intellectualism in high places traceable in Pop" in Charles Lister's and Julian Grenfell's time. He speaks of "the *intelligentzya* of Pop, a force stronger then, and more leavening the lump, I distinctly consider, than often of late years". Charles had a freakish spirit of harmless mischief more ordinarily found in less serious characters. To see, for instance, a driverless horse and cart standing in the road was to leap in and drive round the next block of houses with the airs of a charioteer. Authority laughed at such freaks, as it condoned the obtrusion of phrases like "Laodicean prelates and stuffy ecclesiastical laymen" in his "Sunday questions", because it was simply impossible to take amiss, if you knew him, what he did or said. His gaiety was infectious: like the hero of Mr. Chesterton's "Manalive" he "dealt life", and those contemporary Etonians who look back on that year as the happiest they ever spent easily trace the inspiration of it to him. In the Easter holidays of 1906 he was operated on for appendicitis. He and a friend of his who had just had the same operation were consequently interdicted from excessive indulgence (if there was danger of it) either in work or in athletics. The result was a literary venture which had a troubled career, but a sale and a popularity equally undoubted — *The Outsider*, an ephemeral which ran to six numbers in two months. Charles was one of the seven editors, and its columns, dead as their interest is now, show Charles in his happiest vein of fooling. He had an unlimited facility for producing topical nonsense at a moment's notice. His were rough and ready methods. One morning at breakfast one of his mess received a book to review for the *Eton College Chronicle*, and complained of its length — it was a school story. Charles took it out of his hands, opened it exactly in the middle with a bored gesture, and tore it down the back: he returned the first half and dealt with the second himself. The review was sent in the same day, and it would puzzle the most hardened of higher critics now to detect the join in its composition.

As a speaker he often hesitated in the arranging of his ideas, but whether in speaking or writing he was never for a single moment at loss for a word.

To pass from Eton to Oxford, October 1906, was a slight change. He had already the tastes of a man, and he never lost the spirit of a boy. His political activities naturally found freer scope. Old friends of the movement would not dispute him the title of having created Socialism as a practical force in undergraduate Oxford. It was in his second year, autumn 1907 to summer 1908, that the more practical of Charles's departures were made. He was then running closely in harness with the Independent Labour Party and the Fabian Society. He had the great man's power of making others his unwilling or hesitating instruments. You would find yourself entertaining a Labour Member for the evening, or helping to organize an exhibition, or bicycling out with him on a winter's night to Banbury and back to address a nascent trades union. If you shrank from the most trivial of such tasks you might have him striding up and down your bedroom pulverizing you with texts from St. James. It was not that he shone in oratory; he had neither the command of voice nor the self-possession to "go down" at the Union, and even in a private room, though he knew his subject and carried weight, his hands must be nervously busy as he spoke, and you would find the torn fragments of his notes littering the hearthrug when he sat down. But he organized unceasingly and without apparent effort Meetings seemed to spring up at his feet. His political activities hardly seemed to exhaust a tithe of his energies, whether at this time or later. In his first year Charles, however *affairé*, attended the eleven o'clock service at Cowley, in the Church of the Cowley Fathers, on an average of every other Sunday, quite apart from College chapels.

Some of the best meetings which Charles organized were under the auspices of a Committee for Lectures on Social Subjects in Oxford, which he founded and raised subscriptions for and practically controlled. He started two trades unions in the town, and got up a Sweated Industries Exhibition. As we know, he was the animating spirit of the Orthodox Club, one of the liveliest of the mushroom growths of his day. Meanwhile, he never seemed to produce friction with older institutions. He was in constant touch with members of Ruskin College. The University branch of the Fabian Society had a membership of about twenty when he came up, and he left it about a hundred strong; and whatever was thought of his political sympathies by those who have regretted the tendency of them then, or the change in them since, it was due to his magnetic personality that it acquired that strength without incurring the persecution to which new elements in a conservative society are naturally liable.

There is a story that a College authority, estimating the prospects of a friend of Charles, complained that his work suffered from attention to externals, and, when pressed for a definition of these, instanced "Socialism and Christianity". If any such fears were entertained for Charles himself, if anybody supposed that, like other strong partisans, he would gain from Oxford a mere seminarist training, instead of drinking in its intellectual life, they underestimated his infinite variety. Charles justified his exhibition at Balliol by a First in Greats at the end of his third year (June 1909). It was not a mere "scholar's first". Greek history took such hold of him that he went in for a fellowship, declaring his readiness to spend his life in the research of it. He threw himself into everything, if it were merely watching a play or preparing a practical joke, as if that was all he lived for.

Seventeen Etonians came up to Balliol that year, several of them already intimate friends. Naturally there was something of a clique, and it threatened to be an exclusive one. Three, besides Charles, have already died in battle, and if there were any bitter memories, they have been forgotten. But Charles, although he was the life and soul of that society, was never the property of a single set; he seemed to know everyone in a singularly unhomogeneous College, and his friends outside College defied classification. He was quite conscious of his position as a buffer state in these social difficulties. Soon after he went down he expressed the feeling in characteristic language to a friend (Alan Lascelles).

Paris,
March 27, 1910.

Thanks for your Oxford news, confirmed by Sidney to-day, whom I saw on his way to Italy. Edward, I am told on all hands, is immense, living at the rate of thousands a year.

The new "Anna" does not seem to manage the Balliol democracy half as well as in the old days. They have neither Julian to suppress the plebs nor a good fellow like me to keep them in a good temper. Things worked very well when I was there to cover up Julian's tracks, and Julian was there to make fresh tracks, as it were, and overawe the rebellious.

Political Oxford, sporting Oxford, ecclesiastical Oxford, intellectual Oxford, philanthropic Oxford, revolutionary Oxford, all knew him as a familiar. His infectious vitality galvanized everything: no festive occasion was complete without him, no meeting would suffer him to keep silence, and he even contrived to instil a certain heartiness into the cloistered Gregorians of the Cowley Fathers' church. His lighter and his more serious moments were strangely blended. Once when he came into collision with the authorities of Trinity, he was rusticated for the short remnant of a term. Having made arrangements for the entertainment of an expected guest, a Labour M.P., he went off to study poverty at first-hand in an East-End Settlement.

He had none of the inhuman detachment which often makes public characters unknowable in private; while he tolerated widely, he was whole-hearted in his attachments to personal friends. His friendship enriches the past, and the memories you shared with him stand out vividly from a hazier background, whether you picture him shooting on a Scotch moor, or assisting boisterously at a stormy meeting of the Church Congress, or applauding the efforts of M. de Rougemont to ride a turtle in a tank at the Manchester Hippodrome. Though he was at the moment of action regardless of the figure he cut, he could laugh at himself in private and prove his sense of proportion. His richest vein of humour, whether in conversation or in writing, was a running parody of bad journalese; his best serious writing was almost always in this manner. [*I dissent — but perhaps I don't understand. — R.*] But the secrets of personality, especially in a personality so complex, necessarily evade description.

One thing must be added to complete any account of this phase of his career — "phase" it must be called, not in the sense that it was foreign to his true self, or that it left no mark on his character, but because the very conditions of it were transitory. At its conclusion he did not abandon progressive politics; he abandoned politics. If he had been a poor man with his own way to make in the world, he might have betaken himself to journalism or the Bar, with a view to Parliament later on. But he could not tolerate the idea of a political path made easy by the possession of an income and a horizon bounded by the prospect of a seat in the House of Lords. His adventurous spirit found more opportunities promised by a diplomatic career. This is not an inference from what he did, but the substance of a conversation with him before he went down from Oxford — indeed, at a time when his Socialist sympathies were at their height. His friends were not afraid of his being merely absorbed into a machine; they knew that whatever path he took they would hear of him again.

Charles Lister won a Classical Exhibition at Balliol from Eton, and came up in the autumn of 1906 with several of the unusually brilliant group of friends described in the Eton recollections: Ronald Knox and Patrick Shaw-Stewart were among the Classical Scholars of Balliol and Robin Laffan was the Brakenbury Scholar of the year; Julian Grenfell and George Fletcher were contemporaries, too, at Balliol. Charles himself, a Classical Exhibitioner, was not by nature a "pure scholar" or a brilliant composer, and had little of the polish and grace and linguistic wit which makes an Ireland Scholar; his Exhibition had been awarded rather on the promise of a very vigorous mind, which seemed to ride roughshod over minor points and petty difficulties in a fresh and enthusiastic search for the heart of the matter in hand. He decided at once — and rightly — that he would not read for Honours in Moderations, but would take the Greats School at the end of his third year. This meant that there was no immediate pressure of examinations — he had only to take Pass Moderations at the end of his second term — and that he had both time and scope for all his other interests, social and political. "In his first two years", says his Greats tutor, [*Mr. A. D. Lindsay.*] "I have no very clear recollection of his work, except as that of a man who could obviously do very much better if he put more mind into It." But this does not mean that he was idle or inconspicuous: it was impossible for him to be either one or the other.

Charles had already at Eton identified himself fearlessly with the Socialist party, and at Oxford threw himself into work on their lines, both in theory and practice. He had come up as an almost notorious character, and at once assumed the lead. His personality could not escape observation; his rapid movements, his eagerness in discussion, his infectious laugh, and his sudden indignation at anything that seemed to be unjust, were all welded together by a high enthusiasm which made light of details, and by an irresistible charm.

His first start was on the theoretical side; and with a few intimate friends — the more prominent approaching Socialism from the point of view of High Church Christianity — he founded a more or less Socialistic society named the "Orthodox Club".

"It would be difficult", says one who was present at its first meetings, "to find anywhere more concentrated, mixed heresy than in that society, but its members had all in common the gift of 'taking a high line' and insisting that Orthodoxy was *their* doxy, however uncommon that might be."

I think to the outsider the most impressive thing about Charles Lister at that time was just this serene power of taking a high line, and carrying off in the most natural way very different rôles. He had no doubt improved as a speaker since

Eton days, but he would never have made a facile orator: however much he might have prepared his subject, at the time he could not deliver dispassionately what he had thought out, but wrestled again as he spoke, starting new hares and "worrying" afresh: it was his enthusiasm more than his words which carried conviction.

"The Orthodox Club", a Freshman's Club *par excellence*, chiefly represented Socialism at Balliol. Outside Balliol, Charles was soon to ally himself with the Fabian Society, and to spread the same interests in the University. The Fabian Society had hitherto been a small and rather despised group: Charles increased its members fourfold and made it "the thing" to belong to it. This mushroom growth not unnaturally roused scepticism, and it was said superficially that "the only explanation of the apparent sudden conversion of men of the most different lives to the tenets of Socialism was that no one was capable of resisting Charles when he button-holed him for more than two minutes".

From the outside it looked a little unreal, but on closer acquaintance it became clear that so far from Charles being a *poseur*, his extraordinary success came from his being supremely natural and genuine.

He was consumed by a passion to help the poor and weak: that was the driving power of his life, and those of his friends who thought his opinions quite mad were unanimous as to the earnestness with which they were held. His own driving power became a motive to others, and many, to whom a more strictly theoretical Socialism could have made no appeal, were brought to it on the human side with something of Charles's own passion for justice. Charles's practical work was not less noticeable than his theoretic, indeed more so, for it is a most unusual thing for an undergraduate at Oxford to take any prominent part in the affairs of the town. He was soon at home in Ruskin Hall, then newly founded and rather in danger of being "patronized" by the University, and Charles by his perfectly natural manner did much — though quite unconsciously — to bring its students into a real relation with undergraduate life and to lay the foundation for a genuine mutual understanding.

In the same way he formed a natural friendship with the Labour leaders in the town, and won the unswerving love and loyalty of many members of the Oxford Trades' Council and the Oxford Branch of the Independent Labour Party: up to the time of his death they still inquired after him with affection. Indeed, he quickly became their leader, pulling them along into fresh activities and new developments which would have been impossible without him.

Among many other things in the same line, he organized a most successful

Anti-Sweating Exhibition, which undoubtedly aroused many to a serious understanding of industrial evils. "Through all this he displayed the same qualities: a steady working enthusiasm, a power of getting on with everybody and making everybody work, and a great gift of knowing what was practical and what was not". Even more characteristic was the part Charles played in a strike of girls at the Clarendon Press. He brought speakers down from London to encourage the strikers, and night after night arranged concerts and entertainments to keep the girls together. This enterprise got him into some difficulties with the University authorities — for the position of an undergraduate favouring a strike at the chief University institution was, to say the least of it, delicate — and he had several interviews with the Vice-Chancellor. Charles saw the difficulty, and all closed amicably, but he had held his own with the same high-handed frankness as ever.

All this time Charles was in the full swim of the social life of the College. His Eton friends were all around him, and he enjoyed to the full all the irresponsible pleasures of a high-spirited undergraduate's life.

The escapades of a certain dining society, the Annandale, brought him into disfavour with the authorities and its exclusiveness [*see below*] with the rest of the College; but anger was never directed against Charles; not that he was in any sense a conscious peacemaker, but that social distinctions seemed to have no meaning for him, and he ignored quarrels as if they did not exist The combination of this life with his political activities would have been impossible to most men; to Charles it was natural, for he could pass from one set of surroundings to another with complete unconsciousness of inconsistency or even, it sometimes seemed, of change.

"September 13, 1911.
T. and W. have been here lately — Balliol boys, and very good fellows — at least, I think so now. I liked T. only fairly well at Balliol, but I think the Anna cliqueyness warped our judgment — mine less so perhaps than the others'.
The two rival protagonists in the troubles here referred to joined the same battalion in 1914; became (it is said) great friends; and were reported, the one killed, the other missing, in the same casualty list (August 1915)."

In much of the social life he was casual and unguarded, and often really inconsistent with his ideals. He lived too much in the moment, and often was characteristically thoughtless of consequences for others and for himself. In the summer term of 1908 he was suddenly pulled up. There had been a supper and a bonfire in Trinity; Charles was there with his friends of the Annandale, and went too far. There was an unpleasant collision with the Trinity authorities, and, as a consequence, he was sent down for the rest of the term. His undergraduate friends treated the affair frivolously and with no very good taste. Charles carried it off, at the moment, with humour and with his usual high hand; and then with what was almost an inspiration in the "high line", went and worked at the Trinity Mission in West Ham. He said afterwards that he was grateful to the College for what it had done, and that it was "the best thing that ever happened to me". It seems as if, while he thought things over that summer, he must have come to a deliberate conclusion that the real task before him for the moment was to work for "Greats". At any rate, when he came back in the autumn there was no doubt that this was his primary object, and everything else was for the time put in the background. To quote again from his "Greats" tutor; "The next year he was trying to do in one year what was ordinarily done in two. I never saw a man work so hard and so sensibly. He was not by nature a philosopher; he was never sufficiently reflective or abstract, but he 'got up' philosophy with remarkable ability. On the other hand, he showed himself a really good historian. He had a wonderful grasp of detail — the faculty shown in practice in the earlier time was now directed to his work — and a power of seizing the general drift and meaning of detail. The result was that he not only got a First, but a very good First. His History papers won very special commendation from the examiners as being clearly up to the mark of a Fellowship." It was a great effort, carried through with all his enthusiasm, and it was well rewarded. There is no evidence that Charles thought much of his First as such, but he certainly felt that his work had given him a sounder basis to build upon. After he went down, he kept up his devotion to history, and thought seriously of trying for an Ancient History Fellowship.

Charles left Oxford a stronger man than he had come to it. His year of hard work for "Greats" had given him a deeper sense of a problem, and of the value of evidence, and taught him to look for more than one side of a question. He had been, too, amongst many men very different in character, and understood more of the importance of the individual. He became himself less impulsive and reckless of consequences. But the same enthusiasm remained, nor had a stronger judgment weakened his power of throwing himself unstintingly into anything he took in hand or dulled his generosity of mind. He had loved his Oxford life, loved his friends and loved the place; and in later years his mind turned often to Balliol, and he always came back to Oxford with a peculiar pleasure. He had won, too, a peculiar position in the memory of those who knew him there. It was not only that Charles was unique, a wonderful companion through his many interests and his great vitality; but he was the most loyal of friends, and the charm which all acknowledged at first had deepened with many into a sincere affection. They looked for great things from him; yet knew that to them he would be always the same.

When the call came in 1914, Oxford men were not slow to answer. Some were already in the Army and went to France with the first Expeditionary Force, to fight and often to fall in the retreat, on the Marne, and before Ypres; others, the civilians, taking cheerfully to a life they had never contemplated and in many cases loathed, flung up their occupations and professions, and after their period of training were scattered to France and Flanders, to the Dardanelles and Mesopotamia, to Egypt and India. Charles's band of Oxford friends have more than taken their part; they have done good service wherever they have been. Julian and Billy Grenfell have fallen in France, and Charles himself in Gallipoli. With a group of Oxford men of different generations he went out to the East and joined the Hood Battalion, R.N.D. On the voyage he was the life and soul of the party. Like all others, he was filled with the hope of wresting Constantinople from the Turks and finally liberating the Balkans from Turkish tyranny. He met disappointment, hardship, suffering, and danger. Twice hit, he returned again to take his place, and at the last was mortally wounded. Charles's end was, in fact, a crowning expression of himself — the fight for justice and the freeing of the oppressed were again the motives of his inspiration, and with the old high-hearted fearlessness of consequences he gave to the Great Cause his mind his effort, and his life.

As both my boys fell on active service, and as both were Etonians, I include the "In Memoriam" tributes which appeared in the Eton Chronicle. The one about my eldest son was written by his tutor, the Rev. H. T. Bowlby. The English verses to Charles were written by the Rev. Cyril Alington, the new Head Master of Eton; the Latin ones by Mr. Ronald Knox.— R.

In Memoriam.
Captain The Hon. Thomas Lister, D.S.O., 10th Hussars

was killed at Jidballi, Somaliland Expedition, January 10, 1904. "Little wars", fought in little-known lands, demand as useful lives and a greater measure of self-sacrifice than the famous battles of the big campaigns. In the last of these little wars, sought out from pure love of a soldier's duties and a stirring life, Thomas Lister met his death. He was a boy at Miss Evans's in the early 'nineties, where he showed something of the bright and fearless disposition which became so prominent in a character that developed rapidly on his leaving school. After passing through the West York Militia, he joined the loth Hussars in 1897, and rose to be Captain in 1902, at the early age of twenty-four. He took part in the South African War; and, with the late Lord W. Bentinck, was the only officer in his regiment who went through the whole of the campaign, being present at the Relief of Kimberley, the battle of Paardeberg, and many other engagements throughout the Orange Free State, and later the Transvaal. During the critical operations in Cape Colony he was for six months in command of a squadron, and was one of the youngest officers holding such a position in the whole South African force. Luckily fever only claimed him for one fortnight, and a slight wound for another short period of two days. Eventually he was recommended for the V.C. for a gallant action at Vaal Krantz; was twice mentioned in dispatches; and received the medal with six clasps, and the Distinguished Service Order.
He attended the Coronation with a few picked men of his regiment; but found peace life monotonous; and on hearing of the disaster in Somaliland in the early days of the war, volunteered, and was selected out of a long list for special service. On landing he was given command of the Remount Department; and to quote the words of a senior officer, "grappled with a most difficult and far-reaching business in a manner which was absolutely extraordinary for a boy of his age, making a brilliant success of what in most hands would have been a great failure". The news of an impending fight made him impatient of inaction, and he obtained leave to join the main force. At the battle of Jidballi he acted as orderly officer to

Colonel Kenna, V.C., who was in command of the mounted troops; and while riding alone with a message after the engagement, fell in, as it seems, with an unsuspected knot of fugitives, and was shot dead. So ended a career of great promise. His death comes sadly as the result of the repeated energy which took him unsummoned from home to the war, and from the base to the front. But the value of such a spirit is not reckoned by terms of service. If he passed early out of sight, he learnt early how to live. "For honourable age is not that which standeth in length of time, nor that is measured by number of years."

To C. A. L.

To have laughed and talked — wise, witty, fantastic, feckless —
    To have mocked at rules and rulers and learnt to obey,
To have led your men with a daring adored and reckless,
    To have struck your blow for Freedom, the old straight way:

To have hated the world and lived among those who love it,
    To have thought great thoughts, and lived till you knew them true.
To have loved men more than yourself and have died to prove it —
    Yes, Charles, this is to have lived: was there more to do?

C. A. A.

Desipuit sapuitque, dicax, improvidus, audens,
    spreto, quod regeret, recta probare sagax:
dux sibi nil metuit, comites devinxit amore,
    vi servanda tamen civica jura ratus.
Intererat, quibus est curae, nee serviit auro:
    magna puer coepit, nee puditura senem:
non sibi, sed cavisse suis, mors ipsa fatetur.
    Vixerat — baud ultra quod superaret erat.

... action during the Boer War

PART III
ADDITIONAL INFORMATION

EAST MUDROS MILITARY CEMETERY

The Cemetery is on the island of Lemnos in the north-east Aegean. It is situated on rising ground on the north east side of the village of Mudros and is about 1km out of the village next to the Greek Civil Cemetery. Mudros is on the east side of Mudros Bay, on the way to Kaminia village.

Because of its position, the island of Lemnos played an important part in the campaigns against Turkey during the First World War. It was occupied by a force of marines on Tuesday 23rd February 1915 in preparation for the military attack on Gallipoli, and Mudros became a considerable Allied camp. The 1st and 3rd Canadian Stationary Hospitals, the 3rd Australian General Hospital and other medical units were stationed on both sides of Mudros bay and a considerable Egyptian Labour Corps detachment was employed. After the evacuation of Gallipoli, a garrison remained on the island and the 1st Royal Naval Brigade was on Lemnos, Imbros and Tenedos for the first few months of 1916. On Wednesday 30th October 1918, the Armistice between the Entente Powers and Turkey was signed at Mudros. East Mudros Military Cemetery was begun in April 1915 and used until September 1919. It contains eight hundred and eighty-five Commonwealth burials of the First World War, eighty-six of them unidentified, and one Second World War burial. There are also seven non-war naval graves and thirty-two burials of other nationalities in the cemetery, twenty-nine of them Russians who died in the evacuation of Novorossisk in 1921, who are remembered on a memorial plaque set into the boundary wall.

NO OF IDENTIFIED CASUALTIES: 810

The cemetery in the 1920s
(Courtesy of the Commonwealth War Graves Commission)

East Mudros Cemetery

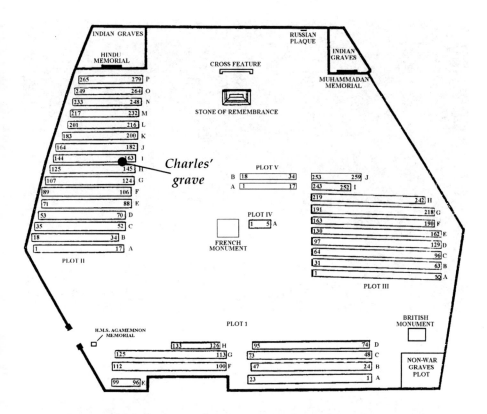

INDIAN GRAVES

HINDU MEMORIAL

RUSSIAN PLAQUE

INDIAN GRAVES

MUHAMMADAN MEMORIAL

CROSS FEATURE

STONE OF REMEMBRANCE

265	279	P
249	264	O
233	248	N
217	232	M
201	216	L
183	200	K
164	182	J
144	163	I
125	145	H
107	124	G
89	106	F
71	88	E
53	70	D
35	52	C
18	34	B
1	17	A

PLOT II

Charles' grave

PLOT V

| B | 18 | 34 |
| A | 1 | 17 |

PLOT IV

| 1 | 5 | A |

FRENCH MONUMENT

253	259	J
243	252	I
219	242	H
191	218	G
163	190	F
130	162	E
97	129	D
64	96	C
31	63	B
1	30	A

PLOT III

BRITISH MONUMENT

H.M.S. AGAMEMNON MEMORIAL

PLOT 1

133	126	H
125	113	G
112	100	F
99	96	E

95	74	D
73	48	C
47	24	B
23	1	A

NON-WAR GRAVES PLOT

(Courtesy of the Commonwealth War Graves Commission)

LIEUTENANT THE HONOURABLE CHARLES ALFRED LISTER

Royal Marines, Hood Battalion Royal Naval Division
Died on Saturday 28th August 1915, aged 27
Grave reference II. J. 179.

Charles was born at 18 Grosvenor Square, London on 26th October 1887, second son of Thomas, 4th Lord Ribblesdale, and Lady Charlotte, of Gisburne Park, near Clitheroe, Lancashire. He attended Eton College as a member of College and went up to Balliol College, Oxford, in 1906. He was awarded a Williams Exhibition in Classics and graduated with a First in Greats. Charles was a 'champagne' socialist from an early age and became involved with the Independent Labour Party. He went to Germany to improve his language skills. He went into the diplomatic service and served in Rome and Constantinople as well as travelling widely including India in 1913. Charles was a keen artist and horseman.

Sir Rennell Rodd (Ambassador to Rome) wrote of him *"Political Oxford, sporting Oxford, ecclesiastical Oxford, intellectual Oxford, philanthropic Oxford, revolutionary Oxford, all knew him as a familiar. His infectious vitality galvanized everything ..."* he also wrote: *"Charles Lister displayed two characteristics which are but rarely found in combination — the spirit of the sportsman and the lover of adventure with the instincts of the scholar gentleman. He was of the type which would have found its right environment in the large-horizoned Elizabethan days, and he would have been of the company of Sidney and Raleigh and the Gilberts and boisterously*

Rennell Rodd

welcomed at the Mermaid Tavern. He would sometimes pretend that he was divided in his mind whether the life of the fox-hunter or that of the college don would have most tempted him if he had only had to follow his instincts. But in reality he was much too deeply imbued with the sense of duty and the higher obligations of life to have devoted himself to the former to the exclusion of graver things. He was, however, seriously drawn towards the student's life, and was a deep and thoughtful reader with a very retentive memory. No doubt he was also a hard and fearless rider, without the graces of the natural horseman, and here in the Roman Campagna, with its long deceptive reaches of grass and its sudden and unexpected obstacles, his impetuosity often alarmed his friends. But there, as in the sea in the bay of Naples, where currents ran strong and seas were high, as afterwards in the deadly battle area of Gallipoli, he was physically the most fearless of men. In the more difficult tests of moral courage I have known no braver soul."

Following the outbreak of war Charles obtained permission from the Foreign

Office to volunteer. He trained at Maudesley and was commissioned to the County of London Yeomanry as an interpreter. In February 1915 he sailed on *SS Franconia* from Avonmouth with the Royal Naval Division, bound for Egypt and commissioned to the Battalion. He served on the Suez Canal and undertook training at Kantara. On Saturday 3rd April the whole Division paraded in Port Said and was inspected by Admiral Pierce. Five days later Charles boarded *SS Grantully Castle* in Alexandria and sailed towards the Gallipoli landing grounds. Various dates were decided upon for their final landing but a number of postponements delayed them. Whilst they were on board ship his great friend, Rupert Brooke, died on Friday 23rd April and Charles was put in charge of the burial party. Shortly after the burial the ships sailed to their final destination, the beaches, arriving on Thursday 29th April. Late on the night of Saturday 1st May Charles went into the support trenches at the Achi Baba Nullah in preparation for an attack. It was a difficult position to mount an attack with casualties mounting by the minute. The attack was not successful, neither was a further counter-attack. Charles was wounded in the rear by a shrapnel bullet and was invalided to Malta. He was contacted by the Foreign Office who requested that he returned to London and retake his post, he refused. Charles soon recovered and sailed back to the battleground. In mid-June Charles took a leading part in an raid on a Turkish barricade but was slightly wounded. Charles was in the front line when he was wounded for third time, this time fatally. He was taken from the Casualty Clearing Station and then to the hospital ship *SS Gascon*. Whilst on board he wrote: *"Just think, I have been wounded once more, the third time. We were in a trench, observing the Turkish trenches, when suddenly they fired some shells into our trenches. I went along to see what had happened, got my people back into a bit of a trench they had had to leave, then went down the trench, thinking the show was over, and then got it, being struck in the pelvis and my bladder being deranged, and slight injuries in the leg and calves."* His condition deteriorated and Charles died on board; his body and was taken off at Mudros then buried in the cemetery.

He was twice Mentioned in Despatches by Sir Ian Hamilton (British Commander-in-Chief in Gallipoli), the second of which reads: *"For brilliant deeds of gallantry throughout our operations. On July 21st he personally reconnoitred a Turkish communication trench, and, although wounded (for a second time) he returned and led forward a party to the attack. Subsequently he was a third time wounded and has since died, to the sorrow of all ranks who knew him."*

After he was wounded for the first time he family and friends tried to persuade him to return to the diplomatic service but he preferred to stay with his Battalion.

His Headmaster, at Eton, wrote of him:

> *"To have laughed and talked — wise, witty, fantastic, feckless —*
> *To have mocked at rules and rulers and learnt to obey,*
> *To have led your men with a daring adored and reckless,*
> *To have struck your blow for Freedom, the old straight way:*
> *To have hated the world and lived among those who love it,*
> *To have thought great thoughts, and lived till you knew them true,*
> *To have loved men more than your and have died to prove it —*
> *Yes, Charles, this is to have lived: was there more to do?"*

He left an estate of £705 3s 6d.

Charles is commemorated on the House of Lords War Memorial and in the Ribblesdale Chapel in St Mary's Church on the Gisburne Estate.

... HM King George V visiting the graves of the fallen after the war

THE GALLIPOLI CAMPAIGN

The war on the Western Front was clearly going to continue into 1915 and not be 'over by Christmas'. Turkey had joined the Central Powers that cut Imperial Russia off via the Black Sea. On Saturday 25th November 1914 Winston Churchill suggested an attack on the Gallipoli Peninsula by use of the Navy supported by the Greek Army. Lord Kitchener was not so keen on the idea but a few weeks later he was actively considering the possibility.

On Saturday 2nd January 1915 HIM Tsar Nicholas II and his government requested assistance as Russia was becoming increasingly isolated and under pressure on all fronts. Members of the War Cabinet considered they that must assist Russia and plans were worked on from Sunday 3rd. On Wednesday 13th Winston Churchill discussed with the War Council a plan *"to bombard and take the Gallipoli peninsula, with Constantinople as its objective"*. By the end of the month Admiral of the Fleet Lord Fisher was doing his best to derail the plans and threatened to resign if the

Left to right:
Field Marshal Lord Kitchener, HIM Tsar Nicholas II,
Winston Churchill, Admiral of the Fleet Lord Fisher

campaign were to go ahead. However, on Thursday 28th it was decided that an attack would take place and Lord Fisher persuaded to remain in post. The essence of the plan was encapsulated by Winston Churchill: *"Beyond those four miles of ridge and scrub on which our soldiers, our French comrades, our gallant Australian and New Zealand fellow-subjects are now battling, lie the downfall of a hostile empire, the destruction of an enemy's fleet and army, the fall of a world-famous capital, and probably the accession of powerful allies. The struggle will be heavy, the risks numerous, the losses cruel; but victory, when it comes, will make amends for all. There never was a great subsidiary operation of war in which a more complete harmony of strategic, political, and economic advantages has combined, or which stood in truer relation to the main decision*

which is in the central theatre. Through the Narrows of the Dardanelles and across the ridges of the Gallipoli peninsula lie some of the shortest paths to a triumphant peace."
The first action was to capture Tenedos Island and agreements were made with the Greeks for Lemnos to be utilised and Mudros as the naval base. In mid-February 1915 the Anglo-French fleet, under the command of Vice-Admiral Sackville Carden and Rear-Admiral Guépratte, had arrived off the Dardanelles where on Friday 19th February they began to bombard the Turkish Forts. Initial reports appeared to confirm that the forts were badly damaged but within twenty-four hours it was clear that this was not the case. The bombardment continued but it did not silence the Turkish guns. On Thursday 18th March a major effort was made and the fleet sailed up the Straits and closed in on the Narrows. The French ship *Bouvet* was hit by shell fire and mines, sinking in three minutes with the majority of her crew. *HMS Irresistible* struck a mine and it soon clear she would not survive. Luckily for the crew sufficient time was allowed to abandon ship before she went down. The *Gaulois* and *HMS Inflexible* were also hit and as the fleet withdrew it was clear that the campaign would not succeed from the sea alone.

HMS Irresistible

Sir Ian Hamilton

During February Lord Kitchener had begun to send troops to Egypt, Salonica and Lemnos. General Sir Ian Hamilton was persuaded by his close and good friend, Field Marshal Lord Kitchener, to take command of the land forces. In early March ANZAC troops sailed from Alexandria to Lemnos and were reinforced by British forces. Here they trained and prepared for the landing on the beaches and the attack on the Turkish forts.

On Sunday 25th April the invasion fleet sailed across the Ægean anchoring off-shore. Troops were loaded into landing boats and they moved to the beaches that included an old collier, *River Clyde*, being towed to the shore carrying two thousand troops.

... a Turkish fort replies to the naval bombardment

The River Clyde

The landings were successful, in the sense troops reached them, but they came under heavy fire from the Turks and considerable losses were taken. The original objectives had not been taken and it was clear that many of the troops were pinned down on the beach.

On Wednesday 28ᵗʰ an attack on the village of Krithia began followed by an attack on the Achi Baba heights. The troops were already shaken and tired from the landing; Krithia and Achi Baba remained in Turkish hands. On Friday 30ᵗʰ

... landing on the beaches

April more troops from the Royal Naval Division arrived and the next day a large number of Indian troops from the 29th Brigade. On Thursday 6th May Krithia was again attacked and the next day the bombardment around Achi Baba heralded a further move forward. Some minor successes were achieved, there was a gain of one thousand yards of front but there it stopped. Liman von Sanders, the German general commanding the Turkish troops, was able to call upon fresh troops from Constantinople. They were able to move into the front without being transported by sea or landing on a beach under heavy fire. A third attempt to take Krithia was mounted on Friday 4th June that advanced the line a few hundred yards but no more — again at a heavy cost.

... attack on Achi Baba

In May the Navy took a number of losses including, *HMS Goliath*, *HMS Triumph* and most significantly *HMS Majestic*.

A large number of Allied reinforcements were now needed. Sir Ian Hamilton wrote of the Dardanelles: *"The country is broken, mountainous, arid, and void of supplies; the water found in the areas occupied by our forces is quite inadequate for their needs; the only practicable beaches are small, cramped breaks in impracticable lines of*

... a view of Mudros harbour from the shore

cliffs; with the wind in certain quarters no sort of landing is possible; the wastage, by bombardment and wreckage, of lighters and small craft has led to crisis after crisis in our carrying capacity; whilst over every single beach plays fitfully throughout each day a devastating shell-fire at medium ranges."

With fresh troops more attacks and counter-attacks were mounted but still no great movement forward could be achieved; the casualties continued to pile up. The wounded could not be adequately dealt with *in situ* they had to be evacuated by sea, taken first to Mudros, then onto Egypt, Malta or England. Supplies of every description came in the opposite direction — drinking water, food, and all forms of military equipment. The troops fighting in the pitiless and constant heat needed specialist supplies, particularly medical, with dysentery a constant problem to all ranks. The main curse for all were flies, they proliferated with so many decomposing bodies blackening in the heat. The danger to both sides of the dead bodies allowed for many informal truces to clear No Man's Land.

Krithia was attacked for the final time on Monday 12th July. The front did move forward some distance but only closer to the village and the heights at Achi Baba remained even more elusive. By the end of the month, like the Western Front, there was stalemate, and as in France and Belgium, a change in strategic planning was made coupled with a further supply of fresh troops.

In August Sir Ian Hamilton planned a series of attacks that he wished to launch before the expected assaults by the Turkish troops could begin. On Friday 6th and attack began from Cape Helles on Achi Baba. This was followed by the Australians against *'Lone Pine'* that was successful but the fight was bitter: a total of seven Victoria Crosses were awarded during the attack on *'Lone Pine'*. The New Zealand forces were pitted against Chunuk Bair where the Wellington Battalion took horrific losses, only fifty three of the seven hundred came through unscathed. Sir Ian Hamilton wrote: *"Every single officer, company sergeant-major, or company quartermaster-sergeant, was either killed or wounded, and the battalion by*

... attack at Lone Pine

midday consisted of small groups of men commanded by junior non-commissioned officers or privates. Chapter and verse may be quoted for the view that the rank and file of an army cannot long endure the strain of close hand-to-hand fighting unless they are given confidence by the example of good officers. " The Turks also took heavy losses, in one attack by five thousand infantry only five hundred survived. A major reinforcement landed in and around Suvla Bay that was followed by an attack at *'Chocolate Hill'*. By the end of Monday 9th August the attacks ran out of steam although the battles continued. Attention was turned to other sectors including Hills 60, 70 and 100 and Lala Baba. By the end of the month Hills 60 and 100 were taken.

The campaign was bogged down and going nowhere. The main battles of the war continued to be planned and waged on the Western Front. The Battle of Loos opened on Saturday 25th September and in the build-up to that and other actions troops were in short supply, no more could be supplied to the Dardanelles. In October, Sir Ian Hamilton was sacrificed and relieved of his command. General Sir Charles Monro was appointed who left France to assume the unenviable post. Now a plan to extricate the troops had to be hatched.

Lord Kitchener arrived to discuss the situation with the commanders and on Monday 22nd November told Prime Minister Asquith evacuation was the only option. The weather in the sector again began to be a major factor. The heat and sun of the summer had changed to freezing temperatures with snow covering the ground: it took a heavy toll on the serving troops, killing hundreds and invaliding thousands.

Sir Charles Monro

On Wednesday 8th December Sir Charles Monro began to issue the orders for evacuation. It was clear that the only way the evacuation could be achieved if the Turks were convinced that the campaign was still being pursued. The first consideration was to get the men away with as few casualties as possible and the second was the removal of as much precious military material as possible, or its destruction. Slowly and surely, but with extreme precision and care the men and materials began to disappear. It must have been a grim prospect for the troops left in the front line who were well aware that they were occupying longer and longer fronts without any prospect of defending them. By early January the Dardanelles was evacuated, quite a remarkable and successful achievement in itself, perhaps the only one of the whole campaign.

It is clear that the Dardanelles Campaign was a total disaster. It achieved nothing, cost tens of thousands of casualties who could have been better employed elsewhere. The colonial troops from Australia and New Zealand left many of their comrades on the battlefield and today ANZAC Day is one of the major public holidays celebrated by them.

... the evacuation, stores and equipment that could not carried are destroyed on the beach

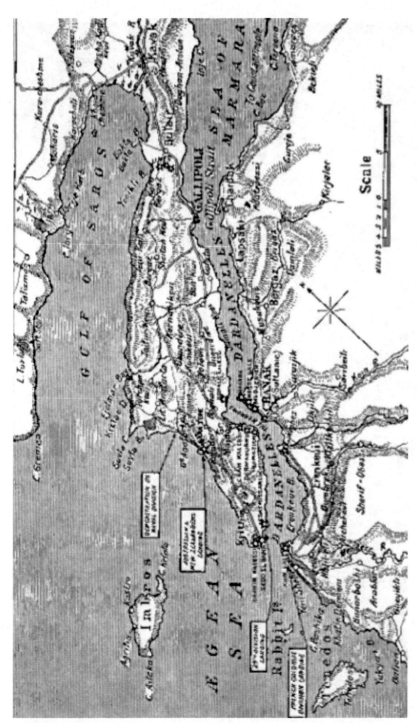

A Selection of Charles' Family

The Lister family coat of arms

Father
Thomas Lister, 4th Baron Ribblesdale

Thomas was born on Sunday 29th October 1854, son of Thomas, 3rd Baron Ribblesdale, and Lady Emma. He succeeded to his titles on Friday 25th August 1876. On Saturday 7th April 1877 Thomas married Charlotte and they had five children.

Thomas was a Liberal Peer, appointed a Lord-in-Waiting to HM Queen Victoria from 1880 to 1885 (under Prime Minister Gladstone) and Master of Her Majesty's Buckhounds from 1892 to 1895. Thomas was a trustee of the National Gallery and of the Nation Portrait Gallery. In 1919 Thomas remarried to Ava Lowle Willing, former wife of John Jacob Astor IV (she died in 1958). Thomas died on Wednesday 21st October 1925 and with him the titles. He left an estate of £42,332 9s 2d.

Mother
Charlotte

Charlotte was the daughter of Sir Charles Tennant, 1st Baronet, and Lady Emma. Charlotte died on Tuesday 2nd May 1911. Her brother Edward became the 1st Baron Glenconner.

SIBLINGS
THOMAS

He was born on Thursday 2nd May 1878. He was gazetted on Wednesday 1st December 1897 and promoted to Lieutenant on Sunday 5th November 1899.

Thomas served through the South African War where he received the Distinguished Service Order on Thursday 26th June 1902: *"For services during the operations in South Africa"*, was twice Mentioned in Despatches and received the Queen's and King's Medals.

In 1903 he was sent to Somaliland and during the Battle of Jidballi he was killed whilst carrying a despatch.

Thomas

See *'In Memoriam'* on pages 239 to 240.

BARBARA

She was born on Sunday 30th May 1880. On Thursday 7th September 1905 she married Major Mathew Richard Henry Wilson (later Lieutenant Colonel and 4th Baronet), eldest son of Sir Mathew Amcotts Wilson, 3rd Baronet, and Lady Georgina Mary. Mathew was created CSI in 1911 following serving as Military Secretary to the Commander in Chief in India. He was elected as a Unionist Member of Parliament for Bethnel Green in 1914. During the First World War Mathew was awarded the Distinguished Service Order in 1918 and was Mentioned in Despatches. They had two children, Mathew Martin born on Monday 2nd July 1906, and Anthony Thomas on Sunday 15th November 1908. Barbara died on Wednesday 22nd December 1943 and Mathew in 1958.

LAURA

She was born on Tuesday 12th January 1892. On Saturday 15th October 1910 she married Simon Joseph, 14th Lord Lovat, KT, GCVO, KCMG, CB, DSO, TD. They had six children: Simon Christopher Joseph 'Shimi', born on Sunday 9th July 1911. He married Rosamund, daughter of Sir Henry Broughton, 11th Baronet. Simon was awarded the Distinguished Service Order and the Military Cross in 1942

Simon Lovat and his coat of arms

and gained great fame for his bravery during the Second World War. He became the 15th Lord Lovat and died on Thursday 16th March 1995;

Magdalen Mary Charlotte, born on Friday 1st August 1913, who married John, 4th Earl of Eldon, GCVO, DL, JP, and died on Saturday 27th September 1969;

Hugh Charles Patrick Joseph, born on Wednesday 23rd January 1918. As Sir Hugh Fraser he was elected a Conservative Member of Parliament in 1945 and served in Parliament until 1884. He married Lady Antonia Fraser in 1956 whom he divorced in 1977. Hugh died in 1894;

Veronica Nell, born in 1920, who married Lieutenant Alan Phipps, RN, who was killed in action on Tuesday 16th November 1943, and secondly to Sir Fitwroy Maclean of Dunconnel, 1st Baronet, KT, CBE, MP;

Mary Diana Rose, born on Thursday 15th April 1926 and died unmarried on Saturday 31st August 1940.

Laura died on Wednesday 24th March 1965 thirty-two years after her husband.

DIANA

Diana dressed as a VAD during the First World War

She was born on Sunday 7th May 1893. She was married to Percy Wyndham by the Bishop of Salisbury on Thursday 17th April 1913 at St Margaret's Westminster; both Herbert Asquith and Arthur Balfour attended the wedding. Percy was killed in the First World War, see below. Diana remarried in 1918 to Captain Arthur Capel, CBE, (who died on Monday 22nd December 1919), and for the third time on Thursday 7th June 1923 to Vere, 14th Earl of Westmorland, and they had three children: David Anthony Thomas, born on Monday 31st March 1924;

Westmorland coat of arms

Julian Charles, born on Wednesday 25th May 1927;

Rose, born on Sunday 4th January 1931.

Diana died on Wednesday 12th May 1948.

LIEUTENANT PERCY LYULPH WYNDHAM
3rd Battalion Coldstream Guards
Died on Monday 14th September 1914
Commemorated on La Ferte-sous-Jouarre Memorial.

Percy was born on Monday 5th December 1887, only son of the late Right Honourable George Wyndham, PC, MP, and Sibell Mary, Dowager Countess Grosvenor, DJStJ, of 35 Park Lane, London W1, daughter of Richard, 9th Earl of

Scarborough. Percy was step-brother of Hugh, 2nd Duke of Westminster.
He was educated at Eton College as a member of Arthur Campbell Ainger then Reginald Saumarez de Havilland's Houses, leaving in 1904.
Percy left with the Battalion from Chelsea Barracks on Wednesday 12th August 1914 and entrained for Southampton as a member of No 3 Company. He received a rapturous welcome in Le Havre as he marched to a camp outside the town for two

days. A long and tiring train journey took the Battalion to Wassigny via Rouen, Arras and Cambrai. After a further period of rest and training Percy marched into Belgium and took position before Mons. He was not actively engaged in the Battle of Mons before orders were received to retire. The Battalion provided rearguard defence to the

... disembarking in France

retreating BEF and came under shell fire and attack. The retirement turned into 'The Retreat' and by Tuesday 1st September they had arrived at the Forêt de Villers-Cotterêts where as they prepared to march on a farm cart that appeared to be carrying refugees, instead it contained a German machine gun that opened fire on them. Thankfully no casualties were taken and the cart was 'seen off'. As they moved south they came under further attack and with the assistance of the 2nd Battalion they were able to beat it off. Shortly afterwards a more serious attack began that pushed the Battalion, and the Guards Division, back towards Villers-Cotterêts. The German line was becoming stretched with the result their attack finally petered out. The men were exhausted and when ordered to rest

... action during The Retreat

at Thury en Valois they fell asleep on and by the roadside. On Thursday 3rd they crossed the main bridge across the Marne at Meaux and as the last man was on the far side the bridge was blown. Two days later the long march south ended,

Percy and his men had marched over two hundred miles in thirteen days.

The BEF was ordered to turn and face the enemy, Sir John French issued a special order: *"After a most trying series of operations, mostly in retirement, which have been rendered necessary by the general strategic plan of the Allied Armies, the British forces stand to-day formed in line with their French comrades, ready to attack the enemy.*

Foiled in their attempt to invest Paris, the Germans have been driven to move in an easterly and south-easterly direction, with the apparent intention of falling in strength on the Fifth French Army. In this operation they are exposing their right flank and their lines of communications to an attack from the combined Sixth French Army and the British forces. I call upon the British Army in France to now show the enemy its power, and to push on vigorously to the attack beside the Sixth French Army. I am sure I shall not call upon them in vain, but that, on the contrary, by another manifestation of the magnificent

Sir John French

spirit which they have shown in the past fortnight, they will fall upon the enemy's flank with all their strength and in unison with their Allies drive them back."

The Battalion, with a renewed spring in their step, turned and marched off, and entrenched at Château de la Fortelle. Trenches at this stage of the war were shallow, slit trenches, dug by the men where they halted. During the Battle of the Marne the Battalion was involved continuously in action that cost them fourteen officers and two hundred and twenty men dead, wounded or missing.

The Aisne was crossed and they took position on the Chemin des Dames near la Cœur de Soupir Farm. They came under heavy and sustained attack. On Monday 14th the battle came to head and Percy was killed. He was buried close by but the grave was subsequently lost. It was claimed that *"... he had been shot by a party of Germans carrying a white flag".*

... early action on the Aisne

He left an estate of £179,003 17s 5d.

Percy is recorded in Debretts Obituary — War Roll of Honour published in the 1921 edition.

Charles was born on Tuesday 4th November 1823, son of John and Robina Tennant. He was married to Emma, daughter of Richard Winsloe, in 1849, she died in 1895. They had six children:

Octavia Laura, born on Saturday 24th April 1886;

Charlotte Monkton, who died on Tuesday 2nd May 1911;

Edward Priaulx, born on Tuesday 31st May 1859 who became 1st Baron Glenconner;

Francis John, born on Sunday 20th October 1861, died on Friday 4th September 1942;

Emma Alice Margaret, born on Tuesday 2nd February 1864, died on Saturday 28th July 1945;

Harold John, born on Saturday 18th November 1865, died on Friday 8th November 1935.

Sir Charles and his coat of arms

Charles remarried to Marguerite Agaranthe, daughter of Charles William Miles, they had three daughters:

Margaret, born on Saturday 4th November 1899;

Katharine, born on Thursday 15th January 1903. She married Baron Elliot of Harwood and died on Monday 3rd January 1944;

Nancy, born on Saturday 20th August 1904 and died on Saturday 17th May 1969.

Charles was Member of Parliament for Glasgow from 1879 to 1880 and for Peebles and Selkirk from 1880 to 1886, being created at Baronet in 1885. He stood unsuccessfully for Partick in 1890. Charles died on Monday 4th June 1906 leaving an estate of £3,151,974 18s 1d.

PATERNAL UNCLES
MARTIN LISTER

He was born on Saturday 25th July 1857, second son of Thomas, 3rd Baron Ribblesdale and Lady Emma. He became the British Resident in the Straits Settlements. He died of fever on Wednesday 24th February 1897 in Suez, Egypt, whilst travelling to England. He left an estate of £2,475 2s.

SIR REGINALD LISTER, KCMG, CVO

Reginald was born on Friday 19th May 1865, third and younger son of Thomas, 3rd Baron Ribblesdale and Lady Emma. He joined the diplomatic service in 1886 and became the Minister Plenipotentiary in Paris from 1906 to 1908, then Consul General in Morocco from 1908 until his death on Sunday 10th November 1912 in Tangiers. He left an estate of £15,471 0s 4d.

PATERNAL AUNT
MRS GRAHAM SMITH

Katherine Lucy was born in 1860. She married Thomas Graham Smith on Wednesday 30th April 1879. They did not have any children and Katherine died in 1942.

Information relating to some of the events and personalities mentioned in Charles Lister's letters

ABDUL HAMID II

Abdul Hamid II

He was born in Constantinople, on Thursday 22nd September 1842, son of Abdul Medjid I. He was considered more enlightened than many of predecessors and prior to succeeding to the throne had travelled widely in Europe. He married officially on seven occasions and also married nine others. His immediate family was extensive! Abdul Hamid was a talented poet and an accomplished carpenter with many of the items of furniture he made on display today in the palaces of Constantinople (Istanbul).

On Thursday 31st August 1876 he deposed his brother, Murad V, and became His Imperial Majesty, The Sultan Abdülhamid, Emperor of the Ottomans, Caliph of the Faithful. He soon found himself involved in a series of wars and international difficulties that reduced the territory of Turkey and shrank its sphere of influence. It also put a great stain on relations with England, Russia and France so Abdul Hamid turned to Germany and Kaiser Wilhelm II. It allowed the Kaiser to further irritate his European neighbours, in particular the British Empire when he was given permission by Abdul Hamid to construct the Berlin to Baghdad railway.

Abdul Hamid in later life

The Balkans remained unstable with smaller states attempting to flex their muscles and break free of the Ottoman Empire. In 1908 Macedonia inflicted a series of defeats on Turkey that brought matters to a head. Abdul Hamid was able to stave off a coup but only for a few months: on Tuesday 13th April 1909 he was deposed by his brother who became Mehmed V.

His last years were spent in secure exile in Salonica then in Constantinople until his death on Sunday 10th February 1918.

Mehmed V

RMS ANDANIA

Built by:	Scotts Shipbuilding and Engineering Co Ltd, Greenock
Launched:	Saturday 22nd March 1913
Length:	520ft
Beam:	64ft
Speed:	15 knots
Capacity:	520 second-class and 1,540 third-class passengers

RMS Andania was first employed on the Atlantic crossing. In August 1914 she was requisitioned as a troop ship. She sailed with a convoy that took the First Canadian Contingent to England in late 1914. She was employed in taking troops to the Gallipoli Campaign during 1915. The next year she returned to normal service running from Liverpool to New York. On Saturday 26th January 1918 she sailed from Liverpool, the next day Captain Leo Hillebrand in U-46 torpedoed her off Ireland. It took some hours for her to go down and of the forty passengers and some two hundred crew only seven crew members were lost.

BRIGADIER GENERAL THE HONOURABLE ARTHUR MELLAND 'OC' ASQUITH, DSO**

Citation for the Distinguished Service Order, London Gazette, Tuesday 17th April 1917:

"For conspicuous gallantry and devotion to duty. He obtained leave to go up to the from when he heard a fight was imminent. Later, although wounded, he returned to Brigade Headquarters and gave a clear account of the situation and of the fighting which had been going on during the nigh. He has previously done fine work.

Citation for the Bar to the Distinguished Service Order, London Gazette, Wednesday 18th July 1917:

"For conspicuous gallantry and determination in the attack and clearance of a village, when he personally captured ten of the enemy and later organized its defence, and, by his contempt of danger under heavy fire, contributed greatly to the success of the operations and to the steadiness of all ranks with him."

Citation for the Second Bar to the Distinguished Service Order, London Gazette, Friday 18th January 1918, details published on Thursday 25th April 1918:

"For conspicuous gallantry and devotion to duty during two days' operations. He went through a heavy barrage and made a successful reconnaissance of an advanced position. Later, in bright moonlight, he reconnoitred some buildings which were reported to be occupied by the enemy. His advance was observed, and the enemy opened fire, but he entered one of the buildings and found it occupied by an exhausted British garrison. He returned, under heavy fire, and brought up three platoons to relieve them. He showed great determination and resource.

Oc Asquith

Oc was born on Tuesday 24th April 1883, third son of the Right Honourable Herbert Henry Asquith, PC, Prime Minister of the United Kingdom 1908 to 1916 (who became 1st Earl of Oxford and Asquith, KG), and Helen, his wife. He was educated at Winchester College from 1896 to 1902 and went up to New College, Oxford, with an exhibition. He was employed by Franklin & Herrera whose main trade was with Argentina. On Tuesday 30th April 1918 he married the Honourable Betty Constance Manners, daughter of John, 3rd Baron Manners. Her brother, Lieutenant The Honourable John Manners was killed in the war, see below. They had four daughters:

April Mary, born on Monday 14th April 1919. She married Keith, 5th Earl of Stradbroke as his second wife;

Jean Constance, born on Sunday 6th November 1921;

Susan Penelope, born on Wednesday 12th July 1922;

Christine, born on Tuesday 23rd March 1926.

The family lived at 22 Upper Berkeley Street, London, and at Clovelly Court, Devon. At the outbreak of war Oc volunteered and joined the Royal Navy and was assigned to the Royal Naval Division. He went out to Belgium to assist with the Defence of Antwerp. In early October the Division was withdrawn and the

... the armoured cars of the Royal Naval Division in action in Gallipoli

city fell, their next deployment was to Gallipoli. *En route* his great friend, Rupert Brooke died (see below). Oc was wounded in action during the campaign and invalided from the Peninsula. Upon recovery he was appointed to the Staff. Oc and the Division were sent to serve on the Western Front following the evacuation of the Gallipoli Peninsula. In December 1917 Oc was badly wounded and when invalided to England had a leg amputated that ended his military career. He retired with the rank of Brigadier General. When he was sufficiently recovered from his injuries he worked in the Ministry of Munitions. Oc was Mentioned in Despatches and awarded the French Croix de Guerre. Following the conclusion of the war Oc returned to 'business', working mainly with South America and was a director of the Westminster Bank. He died at his Devon home on Friday 25th August 1939, leaving an estate of £37,924 10s 5d.

HERBERT HENRY ASQUITH, KG, PC, KC
1ST EARL OF OXFORD AND ASQUITH

Herbert was born on Sunday 12th September 1852, second son of Joseph Dixon and Emily Asquith, of Croft House, Morley. He was educated in Huddersfield, Leeds and the City of London School. He went up to Balliol College, Oxford, with a classical scholarship, and became President of the Oxford Union.

On Thursday 23rd August 1877 he married Helen, daughter of Frederick Melland, and they had five children:

Herbert Asquith and his coat of arms

Margot Asquith

Raymond, see below;

Herbert, born on Friday 11th March 1881, who married Lady Cynthia, daughter of 11th Earl of Wemyss;

Arthur 'Oc' Melland, see above;

Helen Violet born on Friday 15th April 1887; she married Sir Maurice Bonham Carter, KCB, KCVO. Helen was created a life peer as Baroness Asquith of Yarnbury, appointed DBE in 1953 and was the grandmother of Helena Bonham Carter;

Cyril born on Wednesday 5th February 1890, he studied law and became a life peer and Law Lord, he married Anne Stephanie, daughter of Sir Adrian Pollock, KCMG.

Herbert's first wife, Helen, died of typhoid fever in 1891 and three years later he married Margot Tennant, daughter of Sir Charles Tennant, 1st Baronet, and sister of the 1st Baron Glenconner. They had two children:

Elizabeth Charlotte Lucy, born on Friday 30th April 1897, who married Prince Antoine Bibesco;

Anthony, born on Sunday 9th November 1902, and became a famous film director, producing, amongst many other, 'The Winslow Boy', George Archer-Shee (who died on Saturday 31st October 1914 and is commemorated on the Menin Gate).

Herbert studied law and was called to the Bar in 1876 and appointed a QC in 1890. Following his marriage he was known as Henry. He lived at 20 Cavendish Square, London, and held membership of the following Clubs: Athenæum, Brooks's, Reform and National Liberal.

George Archer-Shee

He was elected to Parliament in 1886 as the Liberal Member of East Fife. He was appointed Home Secretary in 1892 under Gladstone and continued under Lord Rosebery. Henry became Chancellor of the Exchequer during Sir Henry Campbell-Bannerman's administration. On Friday 3rd April 1908 Campbell-Bannerman resigned and 'HH' became Prime Minister and travelled to Biarritz to meet HM King Edward, the only a Prime Minister to have been officially appointed

Henry Campbell-Bannerman

outside Great Britain. In 1906 the Liberals had won a landslide in the General Election but following Lloyd George's (see below) budget the January 1910

... *the funeral of Edward VII*

General Election reduced the majority to a mere two. The political controversies were swirling around the Palace of Westminster; the increased workload and pressure on King Edward contributed to his death on Friday 6th May 1910. Herbert was booed by the crowd as he returned to No 10 from Buckingham Palace and was accused by the public as having 'killed the King'. A second General Election took place in December 1910, now he could only govern with the consent of a group of Irish MPs.

Asquith took the country into the First World War on Tuesday 4th August 1914. He continued to serve as Prime Minister until Tuesday 5th December 1916 — following a series of military disasters that had befallen the BEF, including the death of his

son during the Battle of the Somme. In the 1918 General Election he lost his seat, however, he returned to the House of Commons in 1920 at a by-election in Paisley. He lost his seat again in 1924 and the next year he was created a peer,

Asquith, Balfour and Lloyd George at a war conference in Paris

the 1st Earl of Oxford and Asquith. On Wednesday 15th February 1928 he died at his home The Wharf, Sutton Courtenay, Berkshire, leaving an estate of £9,345 9s 2d. He was buried at his local church, All Saints.

... *the Victory Parade passing the Houses of Parliament*

LIEUTENANT RAYMOND ASQUITH
3rd Battalion Grenadier Guards
Died on Friday 15th September 1916, aged 37
Grave reference I. B. 3, Guillemont Road Cemetery, Guillemont.

Raymond Asquith

John Buchan

Rupert Brooke

Raymond was born on Sunday 6th November 1878 the eldest son of the Right Honourable Herbert Henry Asquith, PC, Prime Minister of the United Kingdom 1908 to 1916 (who became 1st Earl of Oxford and Asquith, KG), and Helen his wife. He was educated at Winchester College from 1892 to 1897 as a member of College before going up to Balliol College, Oxford, where he was awarded the Craven, Derby and Ireland Scholarships, and graduated with a First in Classical Moderations and Greats. In 1902 he gained a Fellowship at All Souls College, Oxford. Whilst at Oxford he became the President of the Union with a reputation as an fine speaker and formidable debater. Raymond was a close friend of John Buchan and Rupert Brooke and was, himself, a war poet. His career at Oxford was summed up: *"But the mere record of his academic distinctions give us no picture of his university life. His cleverness was so astonishing that his triumphs seemed lightly won: and indeed they probably cost him as little effort as similar successes have ever cost anyone. It was not that he was a less hard worker than others, but that his brain was amazingly quicker than theirs. His scholarship was unfailing brilliant, his intellectual interests catholic and perpetually alert, but his studies never kept him from the fullest enjoyment of the life of the university and the society of his friends."*

On Thursday 25th July 1907 Raymond married Katharine Frances Horner (daughter of Sir John Francis Fortescue Horner, KCVO, of Mells, Somerset) and lived at of 17 Oxford Square, London W2 (her brother, Edward Horner, died on Wednesday 21st November 1917 and is buried at Rocquigny-Equancourt Road British Cemetery, Manancourt). They had three children, Helen born in 1908, Perdita Rose Mary in 1910 and Julian Edward George, his heir, on Saturday 22nd April 1916, who became the 2nd Earl of Oxford and Asquith.

Raymond was called to the Bar in 1904. He served as a Junior Counsel for the Board of Trade during the inquiry into the sinking of *RMS Titanic*. Later he was appointed Junior Counsel in the Inland Revenue Department. He followed his father into politics and was adopted as the Prospective Parliamentary Candidate for Derby.

At the outbreak of war he volunteered and was commissioned to the Queen's Westminster's before transferring to the Grenadier Guards the following year. Raymond joined No 4 Company, 3rd Battalion in Béthune on Monday 25th October 1915. After two weeks in billets he marched to billets in La Gorgue. Raymond's first experience of the trenches were north of Neuve Chapelle on Sunday 14th opposite the 'Hohenzollern'. He described the conditions in the front line in a

... trenches in front of Neuve Chapelle

letter home: *"I am in the trenches and have been for three or four days now, so far they are more uncomfortable and less dangerous than I had been led to expect. Waders are essential as the mud and water are well above the knee and the cold is intense. An unpleasant feature is the vast number of rats which gnaw the dead bodies and then run about on one's face, making obscene noises and gestures."*

He continued on tours of duty for a week when he returned to La Gorgue. Further tours of duty throughout December were between *'Sion Post Lane'* to the *'Moated Grange'* and spent Christmas Day in the line. On Boxing Day the Battalion was relieved and sent to Merville.

Raymond left the front line to serve on the Staff from January to April 1916 and was stationed at in the picturesque town of Montreuil where Victor Hugo set Les Misérables. Today a statue of Field Marshal Haig stands in the central square, an identical copy of the one placed in Whitehall.

At his own request Raymond returned to his battalion in April in Ypres. In May he undertook tours of duty from *'Duke Street'* to the Roeselare railway line until Sunday 21ˢᵗ when he was relieved to *'Camp N'* close to Poperinghe. After ten days General Lord Cavan and General Geoffrey Feilding inspected them at Volckerinchove where they trained and rehearsed for an attack on German lines. The area had been prepared as an exact replica of the ground they would attack. Training continued until Wednesday 14ᵗʰ June when a fleet of motor buses arrived to take the Battalion to Vlamertinghe. They took the line west of Zillebeke Lake and at *'Sanctuary Wood'*. Raymond continued to serve in the sector and in reserve on the Yser Canal, with period of rest and training in Vlamertinghe until Monday 31ˢᵗ July. The Battalion moved south to Le Souich and spent a week on fatigues. From Sunday 13ᵗʰ August they served in front of Bertrancourt before being sent for training. Whilst training in Morlancourt Raymond met his father, the Prime Minister, only ten days before he was killed. The Battalion moved to a camp at *'Happy Valley'* on Saturday 9ᵗʰ September and three days later marched to Carnoy. The Battalion was held in reserve when on Thursday 14ᵗʰ their surplus kit was sent to Méaulte and all the men were issued with their front-line equipment ready to go into the line. Raymond went with his men to their assembly positions near Ginchy and by 4.00am the next morning they sat and waited for Zero Hour. Some food and a rum ration was issued to the low rumble of slow moving tanks who were coming up to assist in the attack against Les Bœufs. At 6.00am the British barrage began and at 6.15am Raymond ordered his men to fix bayonets. At 6.20am he blew his whistle and led the first half of No 4 Company forward. As they rushed

General Feilding

Lord Cavan

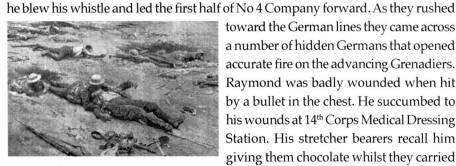

... collecting the wounded

toward the German lines they came across a number of hidden Germans that opened accurate fire on the advancing Grenadiers. Raymond was badly wounded when hit by a bullet in the chest. He succumbed to his wounds at 14ᵗʰ Corps Medical Dressing Station. His stretcher bearers recall him giving them chocolate whilst they carried him back.

It is possible that his body could have been brought home for burial but his father knew that Raymond would have wished to be with his friends and men with whom he died. He is buried next to his great friend, The Honourable Edward Wyndham Tennant. His obituary was published in *The Times* on Tuesday 19th September.

Raymond was Mentioned In Despatches.

He left an estate of £3,189 16s 1d.

His gravestone inscription reads: *"Small time, but in that small, most greatly liv'd, this star of England."*

Edward Tennant

Lord Oliver Chandos wrote *"He should have been spared, but he had shaken off with a shrug a staff appointment which would have made a proper use of his outstanding qualities. He returned to duty and to his brother officers with undisguised satisfaction. In him England lost one of its rarest men. Even a stranger could have see that his good looks and noble profile disclosed a man of the finest character and powers. His astringent but kindly humour many times illuminated our darkness, but with all his brilliance he was simple and unselfish enough to take his chance an make the sacrifice with men who were not his equals."*

Raymond is commemorated on the House of Lords War Memorial.

In St Andrew's Church, Mells, Somerset, a plaque was placed in Raymond's memory designed by Edwin Lutyens together with his original battlefield cross from his grave. The plaque, engraved by Eric Gill, is inscribed: *"In piam memoriam Raymondi Asquith coll wintoniensis et balliolensis scholaris coll omnium animarum co socii qui in ford et republica ad omnia ingenii virtutisque praemuia spe et votis aequalium destinatus medio inflore aetatis armis pro patria sumptis fortiter pugnans cocidiit defunctum terra tenet longinqua et amica desidero in expleto prosequitur siun. VI non MDCCCLXXVIII ob XV Sept MCMXVI."*

Raymond's original grave marker

Raymond's gravestone today

The Celtic cross reads: *"In loving memory Lieut. Raymond Asquith 3rd Battn. Grenadier Guards died of wounds."*

A plaque in his memory was also erected in Amiens Cathedral with the inscription: *"Priez pour l'âime de Raymond Asquith Lieuenant Aux Granadiers de la Gare Royale. Fils ainé de Herbert Henry Asquith premier ministre du Royaume Uni. Né le 6 Nov. 1878. Tombé au champ d'honneur près de Guinchy le 15 Sept. 1916*

O oriens splendor lucis æternæ veni et illumina sedentes in tenebris et umbra motis. Gloriæ memor posuit conjux."

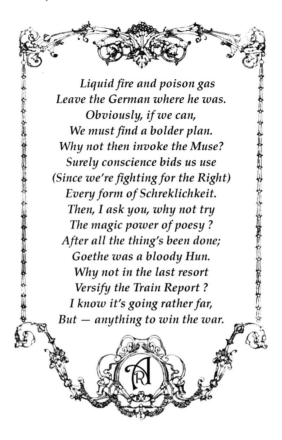

Liquid fire and poison gas
Leave the German where he was.
Obviously, if we can,
We must find a bolder plan.
Why not then invoke the Muse?
Surely conscience bids us use
(Since we're fighting for the Right)
Every form of Schreklichkeit.
Then, I ask you, why not try
The magic power of poesy ?
After all the thing's been done;
Goethe was a bloody Hun.
Why not in the last resort
Versify the Train Report ?
I know it's going rather far,
But — anything to win the war.

MAJOR GENERAL SIR GEORGE GREY ASTON, KCB

George was born on Monday 2nd December, 1861, son of Lieutenant-Colonel and Mrs Henry Aston. He was married to Dorothy Ellen Aston. George was an author of a number military books as well as writing about his passion of fly fishing. He was commissioned to the Royal Marine Artillery in 1879. George served in the Sudan and in the South African War.

He was a member of the embryo Naval Intelligence Department then became Professor of Fortifications at the Royal Naval College from 1896 to 1899. He was Deputy Assistant Adjutant General at the Staff College from 1904 to 1907, and BGGS to Lord Methuen in South Africa from 1908 to 1912. In 1913 George was created KCB.

Above: A view of Ostend
Below: British troops arriving in Ostend, September 1914

At the outbreak of war he was a member of the Admiralty War Staff and was appointed in command of the Royal Marine Brigade. They landed at Ostend and Dunkirk, but George was invalided home on Monday 21st September 1914 with the command taken by General Archibald Paris. From 1918 George served on the War Cabinet secretariat.

He died on his 77th birthday in 1938, leaving an estate of £1,075 1s.

A London bus in Ostend, 1914

Archibald Paris

... a member of the Royal Naval Division in Ostend awaiting evacuation

REVEREND HENRY THOMAS BOWLBY

Henry was born on Wednesday 15th June 1864, son of The Right Reverend Henry Bond and Catherine Bowlby. He was educated at Charterhouse from 1877 as a member of Uskites then Weekites. Henry was a Junior and Senior Scholar and won the Athletic Challenge Cup in 1883. He went up to Balliol College, Oxford, where he continued his athletic career becoming President of Oxford University Athletic Committee and graduated with an MA. He studied for Holy Orders at Cuddesdon Theological College, Oxfordshire. On Thursday 8th August 1889, in St Peter's Church, Malvern, Henry married Annie Margaret Bowlby and they had six children:

Henry Russell, born on Thursday 17th April 1890;

Hugh Savin, born on Monday 11th July 1892;

Cuthbert Francis Bond, born on Friday 23rd August 1895;

Margaret, born on Friday 30th April 1897;

Oliver Gerard, born on Saturday 14th July 1900;

Agatha Frances, born on Wednesday 25th May 1904.

Henry was Assistant Master at Eton College from 1887 to 1909, then appointed Headmaster of Lancing College, a post he held until 1925. Following his retirement he was appointed a Resident Canon in Chichester until 1930.

Henry died on Thursday 8th February 1940, leaving an estate of £14,531 10s 9d.

SUB-LIEUTENANT RUPERT CHAWNER BROOKE
Hood Battalion Royal Naval Division, Royal Naval Volunteer Reserve
Died on Friday 23rd April 1915, aged 27

Rupert was born at Rugby School on Wednesday 3rd August 1887 son of the late William Parker and Mary Ruth Brooke, of 78 Dunchurch Road, Rugby. His father was a housemaster at Rugby School which he attended from 1901 as a member of Brooke. He won the school poetry prize in 1905 and played for the First XI and First XV. He was described as strikingly handsome, with his red-gold hair and being nearly six foot tall.

Rupert Brooke He went up to King's College, Cambridge as a Scholar in 1906. His friends at Cambridge included E M Forster, Virginia Woolf, Maynard and Geoffrey Keynes and Hugh Dalton. He was President of the University Fabian Society. He graduated with a second class in the Cambridge Classical Tripos. After University he travelled through France and Germany. When he returned he was elected to a Fellowship at King's. In 1913 he went to America writing articles for the *Westminster Gazette*. From America he travelled across the Pacific visiting Hawaii, Samoa, Fiji, Tahiti and New Zealand. Rupert Brooke was a published poet as early as 1911.

He was a great patriot and therefore happy to die for his country in battle and was commissioned to the Royal Naval Division. He died of acute blood poisoning after being bitten by a mosquito on the lip before reaching the Gallipoli Front and was buried on the Greek Island of Skyros. Rupert left his royalties to his friends including Lascelles Abercrombie, Wilfrid Gibson and Walter de la Mare. On Saturday 17th April 1915 Rupert disembarked from the *SS Grantully Castle* together with his men onto the island of Skyros *en route* to the Gallipoli Campaign, and one of the other officers on the boat was Arthur 'Oc' Asquith, son of the Prime Minister, and on of Rupert's best friends. The island of Skyros, in Greek legend, is where Achilles was hidden by his mother.

'Oc' Asquith described the island: *"This island is more mountainous than Lemnos and more sparsely inhabited. It is like on great rock-garden of white and pinkish-white marble, with small red poppies and every sort of wild flower; in gorges ilex, dwarf holly and*

HMHS Grantully Castle

occasional groups of olives; and everywhere the smell of thyme (or is it sage? or wild mint?). Our men kill adders and have fun with big tortoises. The water near the shore, where the bottom is white marble, is more beautifully green and blue than I have ever seen anywhere."

For the next couple days all was well, on Wednesday 21st Rupert remained in bed with a swollen lip, feeling ill with a headache and pains in his back. Nothing was thought to be serious but the next morning his temperature was 103° and he was diagnosed with acute blood poisoning. It was decided to move him to the *Duguay-Truin*, a French hospital ship that was anchored in the harbour. On Friday 23rd April, at 4.46pm he died *"with the sun shining all round his cabin, and the cold sea breeze blowing through the door and the shaded windows. No one could have wished a quieter or a calmer end."* Rupert died on St George's Day.

General Hamilton

He left an estate of £923 10s.

General Sir Ian Hamilton, GCB, DSO, wrote on hearing of his illness: *"The wording of the message terrifies me. What a misfortune! I have kept his A.D.C.-ship open for him all the time, and as soon as the Dardanelles affair was over, he was, supposing us both alive, to have come on to my staff but he was bound, he said, to see this first fight through with his own fellows. I have his last poems on my table, and you know how deep was my admiration for his intellect, an admiration which lost nothing, as so many admirations do, by contact with his personality. I pray fervently he may yet pull through."*

His Colonel wrote:— *"I feel his loss immensely, for, since he came to my Battalion, I have had one long opportunity of observing him and getting to know his character and its charm and many fine points. His men were devoted to him and he had all the makings of a first-class officer. His country and his friends could ill spare him."*

Winston Churchill wrote: *"During the last few months of his life, months of preparation in gallant comradeship and open air, the poet soldier told with all the force of genius the sorrow of youth about to die and the sure triumphant consolation of a sincere and valiant spirit.*

He expected to die, he was willing to die for the dear England whose beauty and majesty he knew; and he advanced towards the brink in perfect serenity, with absolute conviction of the righteousness of his country's cause and a heart devoid of hate for fellow men. The thoughts to which he gave expression in the very few in comparable War sonnets, which he has left behind, will be shared by many thousands of young men, moving resolutely and blithely forward into this, the hardest, the cruellest, and the least rewarded of all the wars that men have fought. They are a whole history and revelation of Rupert Brooke himself. Joyous, fearless, versatile, deeply instructed, with classic symmetry of mind and body, ruled by high undoubting purpose, he was all that one would wish England's noblest sons to be in days when no sacrifice but the most precious is acceptable, and the most precious is that which is most freely offered."

Winston Churchill wrote to *'The Times'* on Monday 26th April 1915: "*A voice had become audible, a note had been struck, more true, more thrilling, more able to do justice to the nobility of our youth in arms engaged in this present war, than any other … The voice has been swiftly stilled.*"

Under the direction of Midshipman *'Bertie'* Dickson from *HMS Canopus*, a picket boat took his body ashore and he was buried in the evening in a place he had described to friends as *"one of the loveliest places on this earth"*. The funeral was conducted by the Reverend Bernard Failes.

His brother Officer, Sub-Lieutenant William Denis-Browne, (a close friend and

subsequently killed, see below) wrote of his funeral: "*We found a most lovely place for his grave, about a mile up a valley from the sea, an olive grove above a watercourse, dry now, but torrential in winter. Two mountains flank it on either side, and Mount Khokilas is at its head. We chose a place in the most lovely grove I have ever seen, or imagined, a little glade of about a dozen trees, carpeted with mauve-flowering sage. Over his head droops an olive tree, and round it is a little space clear of all undergrowth.*

William Denis-Browne

About a quarter-past nine the funeral party arrived and made their way up the steep, narrow and rocky path that leads to the grove. The way was so rough and uncertain that we had to have men with lamps every twenty yards to guide the bearers. He was borne by Petty Officers of his own Company, and so slowly did they go that it was not till nearly eleven that they reached the grave.

We buried him by cloudy moonlight. He wore his uniform and on the coffin were his helmet, belt, and pistol (he had no sword). We lined the grave with flowers and olive, and Colonel Quilter laid an olive wreath on the coffin. The Chaplain who saw him in the afternoon read the service very simply. The firing party fired three volleys and the bugles sounded 'Last Post.'

THE WAR SONNETS — RUPERT BROOKE

I. PEACE

Now, God be thanked Who has matched us with His hour,
And caught our youth, and wakened us from sleeping,
With hand made sure, clear eye, and sharpened power,
To turn, as swimmers into cleanness leaping,
Glad from a world grown old and cold and weary,
Leave the sick hearts that honour could not move,
And half-men, and their dirty songs and dreary,
And all the little emptiness of love!

Oh! we, who have known shame, we have found release there,
Where there's no ill, no grief, but sleep has mending,
Naught broken save this body, lost but breath;
Nothing to shake the laughing heart's long peace there
But only agony, and that has ending;
And the worst friend and enemy is but Death.

II. SAFETY

Dear! of all happy in the hour, most blest
He who has found our hid security,
Assured in the dark tides of the world at rest,
And heard our word, "Who is so safe as we?"
We have found safety with all things undying,
The winds, and morning, tears of men and mirth,
The deep night, and birds singing, and clouds flying,
And sleep, and freedom, and the autumnal earth.

We have built a house that is not for Time's throwing.
We have gained a peace unshaken by pain for ever.
War knows no power. Safe shall be my going,
Secretly armed against all death's endeavour;
Safe though all safety's lost; safe where men fall;
And if these poor limbs die, safest of all.

III. THE DEAD

Blow out, you bugles, over the rich Dead!
There's none of these so lonely and poor of old,
But, dying, has made us rarer gifts than gold.
These laid the world away; poured out the red
Sweet wine of youth; gave up the years to be
Of work and joy, and that unhoped serene,
That men call age; and those who would have been,
Their sons, they gave, their immortality.

Blow, bugles, blow! They brought us, for our dearth,
Holiness, lacked so long, and Love, and Pain.
Honour has come back, as a king, to earth,
And paid his subjects with a royal wage;
And nobleness walks in our ways again;
And we have come into our heritage.

IV. THE DEAD

These hearts were woven of human joys and cares,
Washed marvellously with sorrow, swift to mirth.
The years had given them kindness. Dawn was theirs,
And sunset, and the colours of the earth.
These had seen movement, and heard music; known
Slumber and waking; loved; gone proudly friended;
Felt the quick stir of wonder; sat alone;
Touched flowers and furs and cheeks. All this is ended.

There are waters blown by changing winds to laughter
And lit by the rich skies, all day. And after,
Frost, with a gesture, stays the waves that dance
And wandering loveliness. He leaves a white
Unbroken glory, a gathered radiance,
A width, a shining peace, under the night.

V. THE SOLDIER

If I should die, think only this of me:
That there's some corner of a foreign field
That is for ever England. There shall be
In that rich earth a richer dust concealed;
A dust whom England bore, shaped, made aware,
Gave, once, her flowers to love, her ways to road,
A body of England's, breathing English air,
Washed by the rivers, blest by suns of home.

And think, this heart, all evil shed away,
A pulse in the eternal mind, no less
Gives somewhere back the thoughts by England given;
Her sights and sounds; dreams happy as her day;
And laughter, learnt of friends; and gentleness,
In hearts at peace, under an English heaven.

And so we laid him to rest in that lovely valley, his head towards those mountains that he would have loved to know, and his feet towards :he sea. He once said in chance talk that he would like to be buried in a Greek island. He could have no lovelier one than Skyros, and no quieter resting place.

On the grave we heaped great blocks of white marble; the men of his Company made a great wooden cross for his head, with his name upon it, and his Platoon put a smaller one at his feet. On the back of the large cross our interpreter wrote in Greek: 'Here lies the servant of God, Sub Lieutenant in the English Navy, who died for the deliverance of Constantinople from the Turks.'

The next morning we sailed, and had no chance of revisiting his grave."

"The Collected Poems" (Sidgwick & Jackson, London, 1987), "Letters from America" (Sidgwick & Jackson, London, 1987), "The Letters of Rupert Brooke" (Geoffrey Keynes (ed), Faber, London, 1968), "Rupert Brooke, a Biography" (Christopher Hassall, Faber, London 1984).

In 1985 a stone tablet was unveiled in Westminster Abbey on which he is remembered with the inscription, *"My subject is War, and the pity of War. The Poetry is in the pity."*.

His brother, 2nd Lieutenant William Brooke, died on Monday 14th June 1915 and is buried in Fosse 7 Military Cemetery (Quality Street) Mazingarbe.

William Brooke

... Rupert Brooke's original grave

SUB-LIEUTENANT WILLIAM CHARLES DENIS BROWNE

Hood Battalion Royal Naval Division, Royal Naval Volunteer Reserve
Died on Friday 4th June 1915, aged 26
Commemorated on Panels 8 to 15, Helles Memorial.

Denis Browne

Denis was born at home on Saturday 3rd November 1888, the younger son of William and Louisa Denis Browne, of Lynnwood, Leamington Spa, grandson of the Very Reverend Denis Browne, Dean of Emly, Ireland. He was educated at Rugby School from 1903 as a member of Collins; he was awarded a Classical Scholarship, and went up to Clare College, Cambridge, with a Classical Scholarship in 1907. A talented musician Denis was the College organist. He met and became friends with Rupert Brooke, Ralph Vaughan Williams and Arthur Bliss. In 1910 he was appointed Organ Scholar at Clare College and helped run the choir. After leaving Clare College with a MusB Denis was employed as an Assistant Music Master at Repton School. Ill-health compelled him to resign his post, but subsequently he went to London as Organist of Guy's Hospital and conductor of their musical society. William was a musical correspondent and critic for 'The Times', 'The Daily Telegraph' and the 'New Statesman' amongst others.

At the outbreak of war Denis volunteered and, with his friend Rupert Brooke, joined the Royal Naval Division. He left for Belgium and served at Antwerp in September and October 1914 from where he was evacuated and returned to England. He was sent to serve in the Gallipoli Campaign where he was wounded on Saturday 8th May 1915 and invalided to Egypt. Denis recovered to his own satisfaction and returned to join his men at the end of the month and was mortally wounded while leading his men in the attack on the Turkish trenches below Achi Baba. It was not possible to rescue him and he gave some of his personal possessions to one of his NCOs to be sent home to his family.

He left an estate of £79 16s 3d and asked that his musical compositions be destroyed, the majority were. Some did survive and are held by the University Library.

His friend and poet Wilfrid Wilson Gibson dedicated a poem to Denis that was published in 1916 entitled 'Battle, and other Poems'.

... action at Achi Baba

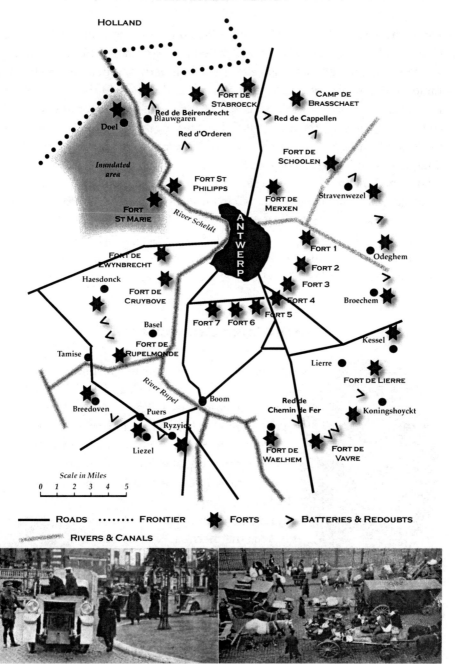

Antwerp 1914

HOLLAND

Fort de Stabroeck

Camp de Brasschaet

Red de Beirendrecht
Blauwgaren

Red de Cappellen

Doel

Red d'Orderen

Fort de Schoolen

Inundated area

Fort St Philipps

Stravenwezel

Fort de Merxen

A N T W E R P

Fort St Marie

River Scheldt

Fort 1

Odeghem

Fort de Zwynbrecht

Fort 2

Haesdonck

Fort 3

Fort de Cruybove

Fort 4

Broechem

Basel

Fort 7   Fort 6   Fort 5

Kessel

Tamise

Fort de Rupelmonde

Lierre

Fort de Lierre

River Rupel

Boom

Red de Chemin de Fer

Koningshoyckt

Breedoven

Puers

Ryzyicz

Fort de Waelhem

Fort de Vavre

Liezel

Scale in Miles

0   1   2   3   4   5

———— ROADS   •••••• FRONTIER   ★ FORTS   > BATTERIES & REDOUBTS

RIVERS & CANALS

Royal Naval Division in Antwerp   *Refugees flee the advancing Germans*

Sir Elliot Graham Colvin, KCSI, KC, JP

Elliot was born on Thursday 18th July 1861, son of Mr and Mrs Bazett Wetenall Colvin, of Lexden, Essex. He was educated at Charterhouse from 1875 to 1878 where he was a member of Pageites then Saunderites. Elliot was elected as a Junior and Senior Scholar, excelled at sport and captained the cricket XI and played in the football XI. He went up to King's College, Cambridge, where he continued to play sports in various College teams. Whilst in England he played for the Old Carthusians. On Thursday 6th December 1888 Elliot married Ethel, daughter of Sir Steuart Bayley, KCSI.

Elliot joined the Indian Civil Service in 1883. He was appointed Secretary to the Lieutenant Governor of Bengal in 1887 followed by Baluchistan in 1889, Postmaster General of Bengal in 1890, the Political Agent of Ulwar in 1896, the Revenue and Judicial Commissioner and Agent to the Governor General of Baluchistan in 1900, Resident of Kashmir in 1903, and Chief Commissioner of Ajmer-Merwara from 1905. He died on Friday 2nd August 1940 leaving an estate of £5,826 16s 1d.

Grand Duke Constantine

Constantine was born in Strelnam on Sunday 22nd August 1858, fourth child of the Grand Duke Konstantin Nikolayevich of Russia and Princess Alexandra of Saxe-Altenburg. He was a grandson of HIM Emperor Nicholas I of Russia. Constantine married in 1884, in St Petersburg, the Princess Elisabeth of Saxe-Altenburg and despite his active homosexuality they had nine children:

Prince Ioann (John), born on Monday 5th July 1886, he married Princess Helen of Serbia on Saturday 2nd September 1911. They had a son, Prince Vsevolod Ivanovich born on Tuesday 20th January 1914 and died on Monday 18th June 1973, and a daughter, Princess Catherine Ivanovna, born on Monday 12th July 1915 who died on Tuesday 13th March 2007, (she was the last member of the Imperial Family to be born before the Revolution). Ioann

HIH Grand Duke Constantine

Prince Ioann

George, Igor, Oleg, Constantine, Tatiana, Gabriel, Ioan,
Elisabeth Mavrikievna, Constantine

was murdered by the Bolsheviks on Thursday 18th July 1918;
Prince Gabriel, born on Friday 15th July 1887 and died on Monday
28th February 1955;

Princess Tatiana, born on Thursday 23rd
January 1890; she married Prince Konstantin
Alexandrovich Bagration-Mukhransky who was
killed in the First World War on Wednesday 19th
May 1915. They had two children: Prince Teymuraz born on
Monday 12th August 1912 who did on Friday 10th April 1992,
and Princess Natalia born on Sunday 6th April 1914 and died
on Sunday 26th August 1984. She remarried in November 1921
to Alexander Korochenzov (ADC of her uncle Grand

Princess Tatiana

Gabriel

Duke Dmitri) who died the next year. Tatiana
became a nun and died on the Mount of Olives
on Tuesday 28th August 1979;

Prince Constantine, born on Sunday 1st January
1891 and was murdered by the Bolsheviks on
Thursday 18th July 1918;

Prince Oleg, born on Sunday 27th November
1892 and was killed on the Eastern Front on

Prince Oleg

Prince Constantine

Monday 12th October 1914;
Prince Igor, born on Sunday 10th June 1894 and was murdered by the Bolsheviks on Thursday 18th July 1918;
Prince George, born on Wednesday 6th May 1903 and died following surgery on Monday 7th November 1938;
Princess Natalia who died aged exactly two months in 1905;

Prince Igor   Princess Vera, born on Tuesday 24th April 1906, she died unmarried on Monday 1st January 2001.

Constantine was devoted to the family and was close to TIM Tsars Alexander III and Nicholas II. He was highly cultured and was a leader of society supporting musical and literary associations.

At the outbreak of war Constantine was in the German spa of Wildungen. He immediately wished to return to Russia but was prevented by the German authorities and temporarily held as a political prisoner. After some negotiation he was released and allowed to continue to St Petersburg. Constantine died of a heart attack on Tuesday 15th June 1915 thus spared the horrors that would befall his family.

MAJOR GENERAL
SIR MICHAEL O'MOORE CREAGH, KBE, MC

Michael was born on Monday 16th May 1892, son of General Sir O'Moore Creagh, VC, GCB, GCSI, and Lady Elizabeth Creagh: his father took command in India from Lord Kitchener. He was Christened Duncan Vandeleur but his name was later changed by Deed Poll. Michael was educated at Wellington College from 1906 and passed into RMC Sandhurst. On Saturday 2nd January 1926 Michael married Jean, daughter of Sir Charles McGrigor, 3rd Baronet, and they lived at Nunton Cottage, Nunton, Salisbury, Wiltshire. He held membership of the United Services and Cox's & King's Clubs.

Michael was commissioned in 1911 to the 7th Hussars.

He served through the First World War and was awarded the Military Cross on Friday 29th December 1916 without citation. By the end of the war he was serving as a Brigade Major.

Michael was promoted Lieutenant Colonel in 1931 and Major General in 1939. During the Second World War he served in Egypt commanding the 7th Armoured Division until September 1941 when he took command of the 3rd Armoured

Group and was knighted. In 1944 Michael retired from the Army. He served with UNRRA from 1944 to 1947.
He died in 1970.

LADY ULRICA DUNCOMBE

Ulrica was the daughter of William, 3rd Earl Feversham, and Countess Mabel. On Thursday 15th September 1904 she married Brigadier General the Honourable Everard Baring, CVO, CBE, son of Edward Charles, 1st Baron Revelstoke and Lady Louisa Emily Charlotte Bulteel. They had three children:

Helen, born on Monday 20th August 1906, died on Wednesday 31st March 1999;

Lady Ulrica Duncombe

Audrey, born on Tuesday 7th September 1909, died in 1997; Elizabeth, born on Saturday 31st July 1915, died unmarried in 1988.

SS EGYPT

Built by:	Caird & Co, Greenock
Class:	India class, single screw
Launched:	Saturday 15th May 1897
Length:	500ft
Beam:	54¼ft
Draft:	24½ft
Speed:	18 knots

The ship first was employed on the England to Australia run before working in the Mediterranean. The *SS Egypt* took The Princess Royal from Alexandria home to England in 1910.

In August 1915 she was

employed as a hospital ship and was able to cater for four hundred and sixty-one wounded, and served until June 1919.

SS *Egypt* returned to normal service. On Friday 19th May 1922 she sailed from Tilbury bound for Bombay. Crossing the Bay of Biscay on Monday 22nd, in thick fog, she was rammed by the cargo steamer *Seine* and the SS *Egypt* went down within twenty minutes, resting four hundred and twenty feet below the surface. The loss of such a ship would have only made headlines for a limited period but SS *Egypt* was carrying over £1,000,000 worth of gold and silver bullion. Not surprisingly the lure of the cargo attracted salvagers within a few years, and after considerable work over 90% of the valuable cargo was recovered between 1932 to 1935. Further expeditions to the wreck were mounted in 1987 and in 2001.

ENVER PASHA

Ismail Enver was born in Constantinople on Tuesday 22nd November 1881 in humble circumstances. He attended various military academies and was commissioned to the army where he immediately excelled. In 1914 in the Ortaköy Palace, Constantinople, he married HIH Princess Emine Naciye Sultan, a member of the Royal Family. The had three children:

HH Princess Dr Mahpeyker Enver Hanımsultan, born in 1917, died in 2000;

HH Princess Turkan Enver Hanımsultan, born in 1919, died in 1989;

HH Prince Sultanzade Captain Ali Enver Beyefend, born in 1921, died in 1971.

Following the military disasters in Salonica in 1908 he became a prominent leader of the Young Turks

Enver Pasha

Movement. As the situation in Turkey settled down Enver Pasha was sent as a Military Attaché to Berlin. In 1911 he left to command Turkish forces in Libya that were defeated and when the Italians took control of the country. In 1913 the Young Turks took control of Turkey and Enver Pasha was appointed War Minister and was responsible for the successes in the Second Balkan War.

Enver Pasha was responsible for the military alliance with Germany. Turkey remained neutral at the outbreak of war until November 1914 when it entered on the German-Austro-Hungarian side. General Liman von Sanders, the German military adviser, sidelined Enver Pasha after his disastrous expedition against the Russians from December 1914 to January 1915. von Sanders and Mustafa Kemel took control of the army as the Dardanelles campaign began. Enver Pasha was dismissed on Friday 4th October 1918 (Turkey sued for peace on Wednesday 30th) and went into exile in Berlin followed by Moscow where he hoped to take advantage of the Russian Revolution to improve his circumstances. He was tried *in absentia* for war crimes against the Armenians and taking Turkey into an unjust war: he was condemned to death. Lenin sent Enver Pasha to stir up problems in the eastern provinces and

Liman von Sanders

help establish a Soviet Republic, however, he changed sides and supported the rebellion. On Friday 4th August 1922 the Red Army attacked and Enver Pasha was killed. He was buried locally until being re-interred in Istanbul in 1966.

FABIAN SOCIETY

The Fabian Society was founded on Friday 4th January 1884, named after the Roman general Fabius Maximus. It became affiliated to the Labour Party and remains an influential pressure group within it.

HM KING FERDINAND OF ROMANIA, KG

Ferdinand of Romania

Ferdinand Viktor Albert Meinrad of Hohenzollern-Sigmaringen was born on Thursday 24th August 1865, son of Prince Leopold of Hohenzollern-Sigmaringen and Infanta Antónia of Portugal. He became the heir to throne of Romania to his childless uncle, HM King Carol I. On Tuesday 10th January 1893 he married Princess Marie of Edinburgh, daughter of HRH Alfred, Duke of Edinburgh, and Grand Duchess Marie Alexandrovna of Russia. They had six children: Prince Carol, Princess Elisabeth (later Queen of Greece),

Princess Maria (later Queen of Yugoslavia), Prince Nicholas, Princess Ileana (later Archduchess of Austria) and Prince Mircea who died in infancy (thought to be fathered by Prince Barbu Stirbey).

Despite his close connections to Germany he took Romania into the First World War as part of the allied cause. The war went badly for the country and in 1918 it was mainly occupied and they were forced to conclude the Treaty of Bucharest but Ferdinand refused to sign it! As the year moved on the Allied forces were able to make advances against the Central Powers and Romania that enabled it to resume the war effort that pushed the Germans from the country. Following the war Romania took considerable territory from Bulgaria who had fought with Germany.

Ferdinand died in Sinaia on Wednesday 20ᵗʰ July 1927.

SECOND LIEUTENANT
REGINALD WILLIAM 'REGGIE' FLETCHER
118ᵗʰ Battery 26ᵗʰ Brigade Royal Field Artillery
Died on Saturday 31ˢᵗ October 1914, aged 22
Commemorated on Panel 5, The Menin Gate.

Reggie Fletcher

Reggie was born in Oxford on Saturday 19ᵗʰ March 1892, the third and youngest son of Charles Robert Leslie, MA, and Katharine Fletcher (née Leslie), of Norham End, Oxford (his father was a Fellow of both All Souls' and Magdalen Colleges and an author). Reggie and his brother, George, were close with their careers mirroring each other. Reggie was described as a *'Viking'* and *'Homeric hero'* with his athletic build, wavy yellow hair and clear-cut features. Reggie educated at The Dragon School from 1900 to 1903 followed by Durnford School, Langton Matravers, Dorset.

He went to Eton College from 1905 to 1910 as a member of College and a scholar, then went up as a Commoner of Balliol College, Oxford, graduating with a BA in 1914. He enjoyed literature and poetry, and often wrote Greek and Latin verse. He rowed for their VIII and IV; Leander IV for Stewards' 1913; stroked Oxford

Reggie as a child

University Boat Club trial eights 1911 to 1913; and received his Oxford Blue 1914 — and could often get upset when things went badly, his Master wrote: *"… however fiercely he had been growling in the barge in the afternoon, there was not a room in College where he would not have been the most welcome guest of all an hour or two afterwards."* Reggie was second in command of the artillery section of the Oxford OTC, becoming Second in Command. Reggie enjoyed the outdoor life and spent holidays in Iceland, Norway, Ireland and Scotland. He was an ardent Freemason.

Reggie was gazetted with a University Commission on the day war was declared. He sailed for France on Thursday 20th August 1914 and served at the Battle of the Aisne with 116th Battery. He was then sent to Belgium with the 118th with his horse *'Playboy'*. He was killed when hit by the bursting of a shell during the First Battle of Ypres at Veldhoek whilst returning from observation duty.

His Major wrote: *"I have lost a very charming and cheery comrade and a very gallant and capable officer. From a military point of view his death is a great loss to the Battery and from a personal point of view it*

has been a great shock and grief to his brother officers."

The *Oxfordian* wrote: "*He had in him the qualities which make a first-class mountaineer, ad the fascination of the rocks caught him during his last two summers when he was with his brother in Skye. What his friends will always remember about him was the whole-heartedness which was in all that he did and felt; the intense enjoyment with which he would wander about the wilds of Iceland or sit by the fireside repeating by heart innumerable lines of poetry. When the boat was not going well he could be depressed almost beyond the limits of tragedy. One who knew him for many years says of him that 'there was something about him which the Ancient Greeks called δαιμονιος, compact of light and fire'. It was a fire that could burn others. He was not tolerant of all opinions, nor yet of all men. He had prejudices which he cherished as precious possessions; but even those who suffered from them often realized that they were only possessions, not part of himself. Given a hard task to do, ad they would fall off him. The task was put upon him; he bore it for some ten weeks (he had only six weeks at the front) in a way which won the admiration and affection of his brother officers; then the end came. What his old friends have lost they would, like all old friends, find it difficult indeed to express.*"

In the Chapel of Eton College a red marble plaque was erected with the inscription: "*Remember with thanksgiving two brothers both scholars of this College, Walter George Fletcher, Captain of the School 1906. Assistant Master 1913-1914. Second Lieutenant Royal Welch Fusiliers. Killed at Bois Grenier, March 20th 1915 aged 27. Reginald William Fletcher, Second Lieutenant Royal Field Artillery, killed at Gheluvelt October 31st 1914 aged 22.*"

His brother, 2nd Lieutenant Walter George Fletcher, is buried in Bois Grenier Communal Cemetery, see below.

SECOND LIEUTENANT WALTER GEORGE FLETCHER
'B' Company 2nd Battalion Royal Welsh Fusiliers
Died on Saturday 20th March 1915, aged 27
Grave reference A. 2, Bois Grenier Communal Cemetery.

George was born on Saturday 7th January 1888, second son of Charles Robert Leslie, MA, and Katharine Fletcher (née Leslie), of Norham End, Oxford (his father was a Fellow of both All Souls' and Magdalen Colleges and an author), grandson of Dr Merry, the Rector of Lincoln College, Oxford. He was educated

George as a young boy at the Dragon

the Dragon School from 1896 to 1900 as a Day Boy. George was academically gifted, winning a number of prizes, also a good sportsman and played in many of the School's teams and was appointed Head of School together with his great friend Robin Laffin (with whom he would attend both Eton and Balliol). He went to Eton College on 1901 as a member of College where he was a scholar. George rowed for the eight, played in the Wall Game, was a member of Pop and Captain of the School. In 1907 he went up to Balliol College, Oxford, where he rowed for their eight and four.

Following Balliol he taught English at the Real-Gymnasium in Schleswig, Germany, then was appointed a Classics Master at Shrewsbury from 1911 to 1913 from where he returned to Eton College to teach classics. He served in the OTC at Eton College as a schoolboy, then at Shrewsbury as a Master in 1911 and again at Eton College as a Master from 1913.

George volunteered on Wednesday 5th August 1914 and went out to France on Thursday 13th and served in the Intelligence Corps as an interpreter seeing action at the Battle of Mons, during the Retreat, and through the Battles of the Marne, Aisne and Ypres.

On Tuesday 16th March 1915 George went across No Man's Land to the German lines and took a French flag that had been captured by the Germans taking it back to his trench. Following George's death the flag was sent to his parents who first had it displayed at the Dragon School before it was presented to Eton College where it hangs to this day.

George shortly after he was commissioned

Robin Laffin remembers both George and Regie: *"The war has taken its cruel toll from a family universally beloved by all who know them. In August last the three sons of Mr. C. R. L. Fletcher flew to arms as a matter of course. To-day Leslie, on board H.M.S. Colossus, is the only one still with us. In November came the tale of Regie's splendid death; and now the blow is renewed with the tidings of George's similar end.*

Thinking of George and Regie, it is hard not to break into the language of David, 'Saul and Jonathan were lovely and pleasant in their lives, and in their death they were not divided; they were swifter than eagles, they were stronger than lions. How are the mighty fallen in the midst of the battle!' But, thank God, we know better than David. The great souls are not lost to us. They are only a stage ahead of us on the way towards the goal of life. In the Litany we pray to be delivered from sudden death. But sudden death is an evil with those alone who are not prepared for the summons and we who know George Fletcher will be thankful that, if he had to die, death came quickly. He was wounded in the head in his trench and never recovered consciousness.

One cannot have known a man at the Dragon School and then mess with him for six years at Eton and the best part of four more years at Balliol without getting to know something of him. For that very reason it is not easy, in speaking of him, to know where to begin. It is like trying to speak of some deep-rooted fact such as Religion, Patriotism, or Civilization, some thing with which we have grown up, and which is so large that it is difficult to set in order what we know and feel about it. But one thing grew ever clearer during a long intimacy with George, and that was that he possessed to a most exceptional degree that elusive thing, the genius for friendship. Others might at certain times be more constantly in one's thoughts, but with George there was a permanent comradeship, the more real for being undemonstrative and taken for granted. He was not one of those men with whom one can strike up a close friendship, only to drop it again when circumstances alter. He was like the hills and rivers and ancient cities of our mother country, so sure and unalterable, that we hardly realize how much they are a part of our own lives. In that comparison we strike what was, perhaps, his most clear characteristic. The traditions of Eton and Oxford and historic England were in his bones. The Englishman, bred in our Preparatory and Public Schools and nourished on field-sports and a literary education, is still generally considered, despite all detractors at home and abroad, the best type of manliness that Europe produces. George was one of the living explanations of this fact. He and his like are the salt of the nation, keeping it frank and vigorous and cultured. Of late years many friendly critics of our country have shared Professor Cramb's fears that the old virile virtues of the English race were in decay. The blood of the patriots like George cannot, we believe, fail to be the seed of national resurrection from a soulless commercialism.

Another trait that leaps at once to the mind was George's humour and that sleepy delivery of his jests, which made the Skipper's choice of him to act Trinculo in As You Like It so happy. And his rendering of Mr. Weller, sen., in the trial scene from Pickwick, at Eton, will ever remain a mirthful memory. He also inherited the gift of vivacious writing. Old letters of his from Italy and Greece are full of amusing reflection and description. His letters from the trenches abound in the fun which kept himself and his men cheery in the midst of their hardships. Knowing his enemies, he had an intense admiration and even affection for them. Like a true patriot, he delighted in the different culture of foreign nations. He had quite exceptional gifts as a linguist, and two months at Tilly's and six months as a school master in Schleswig gave George a considerable knowledge of Germany and the Germans. He used to relieve the tedium of the trenches with friendly sarcasm shouted at the opposite lines. 'It ain't 'alf a joke being in Lieutenant Fletcher's trench,' said his men, "E talks to the b—s in their own b—y language.'

No one will ever forget his delightfully abrupt manner, which some times alarmed those who met him for the first time. Once in Greece, George, who was armed with a stone to keep off dogs, went up to a native of the place, and with his usual snort asked the way to his hotel. His manner of inquiry so terrorized the man that George was woken up later to find the police in his room inquiring why he had threatened an inoffensive citizen.

On the wall of my hut here is hanging a Field Service Post Card from him, bearing the signature 'Hôj'. George himself delighted to explain this name. His version, probably correct, was that in his younger days his directness of speech and a certain lack of urbanity earned him the nick name of Hodge, which was gradually modified, as his manner softened, into the gentler sound of Hôj.

Let us record a few of the facts of George's career. At the Dragon School he showed that he was going to be a classical scholar, and in 1901 he became a colleger at Eton. There his name was adorned in the school-lists with an increasing number of stars and numbers showing distinctions in classical composition, especially verses, and he ended up by being Captain of the School. He was a member of 'Pop', that Olympian Society which governs the internal affairs of the school. But his best achievements were on the river. He was a rowing-man, of course, like his brother, and a member of the Eton VIII in 1906. In January 1907 he joined his many Etonian friends at Balliol. Hearty dubs, like the Annandale and the Brakenbury, and the more serious Canning Club, welcomed him as a kindred spirit. He rowed in the Balliol VIII, got his Leander, developed his classical scholarship, and enjoyed the Elysian life of a deservedly popular leader of College society; 'the greatest unifier of sets among us', said the late Master of Balliol of him. With his classics, his modern languages, and his character he was a most desirable Public School master, and he began his teaching career at Shrewsbury, soon to return, however, to his old school. ...

Of George's courage it is superfluous to say muck Readers of The Times will have seen how an officer described him as 'the bravest man I ever saw'. He was mentioned in dispatches on February 28th, and he was again recommended for distinction after his reckless feat of crawling up to the German lines and recovering from a tree a captured French flag. By such deeds of daring he restored the jaded spirits of his men. But those who were lucky enough to see him in February, when at last he got his leave after six months and a half at the front, realized that the strain had told heavily on him. His light-hearted gallantry was not the result of mere animal vigour, but the triumph of spirit over bodily and mental exhaustion.

George the mountaineer!

A last word as to his convictions. In politics, for the current questions of which he cared little, he was a conservative of the old and honoured type, who believe whole-heartedly in the sacred duty of the educated class paternally to promote the best interests of labour. In ethics, it is enough to say that any wise mother, seeing him, would feel 'That is what I should like my boy to be.' In his religion he had the Englishman's distrust of authority, of system and of 'the specialist'. But he had, what the "typical English man" so often has not, a real desire for worship and prayer and the Sacraments, and a dear perception that religion was something far greater, more beautiful, and more romantic than merely 'keeping straight'. He wrote and spoke of his desire, when in the trenches, to receive the Blessed Sacrament, of which he was able to partake at Christmas. Thinking of him, as he leaves us, we feel the solid truth of the words

  The men who drink the blood of God
  Go gaily in the dark.

R. L., 54 Infantry Brigade."

The *Eton Chronicle* published the following tribute: *"'Yet once more, O ye laurels,' for only the laurel, not any cypress, befits the graves of those who die for Britain in so great a cause, and least of all that of our George Fletcher, tidings of whose fall came early on the 23rd March. An Eton Master killed fighting for his country, and for us; such a thing has never happened before; it crowns our many glories. Now he has joined his splendid brother Regie, whose death on October 31 we mourned last Half.*

The two brothers had much in common; both ardent Collegers, both Balliol men, both rowing men, of course, and, what is more to the point, both conspicuous for strength of will, sound ideals, and indomitable vivacity of spirit, which sometimes overtaxed their fine physical endowment. 'Ama biles et decori in vita sua, in morte quoque non sunt divisi.'

After rowing in the Balliol VIII at Henley, George was hampered by ill-health, and though he might have resumed his oar in his last year, he preferred to work for Greats, in which he was deeply interested; also, his heart being set on a return to Eton, his career seemed to depend on it. Throughout his Oxford life Eton was ever in his mind, and often he referred to this War, which he regarded as inevitable, and vowed that, if it came, he would go out. In 19 he taught in Schleswig Gymnasium, and imbibed an admiration for the Germans which up to the very end he never lost. To remember a phrase of his, referring to the men who held the trench opposite him at Christmas time, 'that it was worth while going across Europe to talk to such fine fellows'. From 1911 to 1913 he made his position as a Master at Shrewsbury under Mr. Alington.

The Michaelmas Half of 1913 launched him in the work at Eton, which had been the ambition of his life. Last summer he said, there never could be another Summer Half like it : he loved every minute of it—pupil-room, coaching on the river, Dufters, Division work, Camp. Then came the War and he was wild with the prospect of it. He joined the Intelligence Corps by invitation with two other Eton Masters, but life there was not full enough for him, and in September he was attached to the Royal Welch Fusiliers, where he struck deep root.

Like his brother he had inherited a knack of vivid writing, which filled his letters with fun and made us see everything as he described it, from his earliest adventures with the service motor-bicycle to the cat that went the round of the trenches snug on his shoulder. 'He was the bravest man I ever saw', wrote an officer. We had heard of his latest exploit, when he crawled at night between the flarelights to climb a tree in the German lines where they had hung a captured French flag. Now it waves in our trench. He ought to have been given the Victoria Cross and a Court-martial; but it was worth doing : nothing delighted and inspirited the Tommies more. For it he was again recommended for distinction. He had already been mentioned in dispatches on February 15, and messages from his C. O., from the Brigadier and Sir John Keir testify to his value.

But though he was full of the humour of his work he felt the strain severely. No leave at all was given him from the beginning till the week which brought him home last month. We thought him worn, though in high spirits, for he saw the serious side of it all the time. "Enjoying myself What do you mean F he said almost angrily to a questioner. One short week at home, largely shared with his Eton friends, has left many memories which we shall always cherish.

In his trench he was wounded in the head and never recovered consciousness.

What Eton loses in his vigour, interest, rightness of aim and devotion, it is better not to dwell on now. What it gains in honour and in his example must help and stimulate all But to the family, which gave him thus to Service, and to his father who has worked for him here, and in that work has taken such hold on our affections, our hearts go out in sympathy and prayer."

George was Mentioned in Despatches on Monday 15th February 1915.

He left an estate of £416 6s 8d.

In the Chapel of Eton College red marble plaque was erected with the inscription: *"Remember with thanksgiving two brothers both scholars of this College, Walter George Fletcher, Captain of the School 1906. Assistant Master 1913 — 1914. Second Lieutenant Royal Welch Fusiliers. Killed at Bois Grenier, March 20th 1915 aged 27. Reginald William Fletcher, Second Lieutenant Royal Field Artillery, killed at Gheluvelt October 31st 1914 aged 22."*

His brother, Reginald William, is commemorated on the Menin Gate, see above. It was said of the two brothers: *"In their death they were not divided: they were swifter than eagles! they were stronger than lions!"*

SS Franconia

Built by:	Swann, Hunter & Wigham
Launched:	Saturday 23rd July 1910
Length:	625ft
Beam:	71ft
Speed:	17 knots
Capacity:	2,850 passengers

The ship served on the North Atlantic run with the Cunard Line. In 1915 she was requisitioned as a troop ship. On Wednesday 4th October 1916 U-47 torpedoed her two hundred miles east of Malta whilst *en route* to Salonica. Thankfully she was not transporting troops and only twelve of the three hundred and fourteen crew were lost.

Lieutenant-General The Right Honourable Bernard Cyril, The Lord Freyberg, VC, GCMG, KCB, KBE, DSO***

Citation for the Victoria Cross, London Gazette, Saturday 16th December 1916:

"For most conspicuous bravery and brilliant leading as a battalion commander. By his splendid personal gallantry he carried the initial attack straight through the enemy's front system of trenches. Owing to mist and heavy fire of all descriptions, Lieutenant Colonel Freyberg's command was much disorganised after the capture of the first objective. He personally rallied and re-formed his men, including men from other units who had become intermixed. He inspired all with his own contempt of danger. At the appointed time he led his men forward to the successful assault of the second objective, many prisoners being captured. During this advance he was twice wounded. He again rallied and re-formed all who were with him, and although unsupported in a very advanced position, he held his ground throughout the day and the following night under heavy artillery and machine-gun fire. When reinforced on the following morning, he organised

the attack on a strongly fortified village and showed a fine example of dash, personally leading the assault, capturing the village and 500 prisoners. In this operation he was again wounded severely but refused to leave the line till he had issued final instructions. The personality, valour and utter contempt of danger on the part of this single officer enabled the furthermost objective of the corps to be permanently held, and on this point d'appui the line was eventually formed."

Citation for the Distinguished Service Order, London Gazette, Thursday 3rd June 1915:
"In recognition of his services with the Mediterranean Expeditionary Force."

Citation for the Bar to the Distinguished Service Order, London Gazette, Saturday 1st February 1919:

"He showed himself a fearless and resourceful commander. The success of the operations of his brigade near Gheluvelt on 28th Sept. and the following days was largely owning to his inspiring example. Whenever the fighting was the hardest he was always to be found encouraging and directing his troops."

Citation for the Second Bar to the Distinguished Service Order, London Gazette, Saturday 8th March 1915:

"His Majesty the King has been graciously pleased to approve of the following awards to the undermentioned Officers, in recognition of their gallantry and devotion to duty in the field." His name is listed below.

Bernard was born in Richmond, Surrey, on Thursday 21st March 1889. Two years later he was taken by his parents to live in New Zealand and was educated at Wellington College from 1897 to 1904. He studied medicine, qualifying as a dentist in 1911. Bernard joined the Militia whilst living in Morrinsville. Bernard was a passionate and successful swimmer which was to prove

Bernard and his coat of arms

useful in later life.

In 1914 he left for America and participated in the civil war in Mexico. At the outbreak of war Bernard sailed to England and volunteered. He was commissioned to the Royal Naval Division, Hood Battalion, and after training left with them for the Dardanelles. *En route* from Egypt to the beaches of the Gallipoli Peninsula, Rupert Brooke died (see above) and Bernard was a member of the burial party. When the Battalion was preparing to land at Gallipoli Bernard, a Lieutenant Commander, volunteered to swim ashore to light flares and guide them in. In the still, cold, dark night, the naked Bernard was greased and painted black. At 10.00pm he began the swim ashore towing a small raft behind him upon which were the flares. He was only armed with a revolver and a knife, two hours of swimming took him to the beach. After a short period of time he was able to light the flares which drew the attention of the Turks who opened fire on him, then the troops. Bernard rushed back into the shallows as to stay on the beach would have meant certain death. For his swimming feat he was awarded the Distinguished Service Order. Bernard was wounded in July whilst in temporary command of the Battalion and shortly afterwards was given full command of both the Hood and Drake Battalions. He successfully organised the evacuation of his men from the Peninsula from where he eventually transferred to the Western Front.

Bernard was attached to the Queen's (Royal West Surrey) Regiment then promoted to Lieutenant Colonel commanding the Hood Battalion. He began his service on the Western Front on the Somme where during an assault on Beaucourt for his bravery he was awarded the Victoria Cross. In April 1917 he was appointed Temporary Brigadier General. In September 1917 a shell burst close to him causing further wounds, the most severe of his nine wounds sustained during the war. Bernard was created CMG in 1917, was awarded the Bar to his Distinguished Service Order in September 1918 and a second Bar at Lessines for his work only minutes before the Armistice. Bernard was Mentioned in Despatches six times and awarded the French Croix de Guerre.

Bernard continued serving in the army following the conclusion of the war and served in the Grenadier Guards followed by the command of the Manchester Regiment. In 1922 he stood unsuccessfully for the Liberal Party in Cardiff South. He continued to serve in the army was promoted Major General in July 1934 but due to heart problems was forced to retire in October 1937.

Following the outbreak of the Second World War Bernard was given the command of the 2nd New Zealand Expeditionary Force. He commanded Allied forces during the Battle of Crete. He was promoted to Lieutenant General and created KBE then KCB following El Alamein. Bernard was badly hurt in an aeroplane crash in September 1944 but was able to return to duty to witness the end of the war where he won the third bar to the Distinguished Service Order. Bernard was severely criticised by many for his decision to bomb the monastery at Monte Cassino. In 1946 he returned to New Zealand as Governor General and created KCMG.

In 1951 he was raised to the peerage, retiring as Governor the next year. In 1953 Bernard was appointed Deputy Constable and Lieutenant Governor of Windsor Castle. On Wednesday 14th June 1922 Bernard married Barbara McLaren, the widow of Francis McLaren (see below), they had a son, Paul Richard, born on Sunday 27th May 1923. On Thursday 4th July 1963 one of his First World War wounds ruptured and he died in Windsor, leaving an estate of £34,620.

HMHS Gascon

Built by:	Harland & Wolff, Belfast
Length:	430ft
Beam:	52ft 2in
Speed:	12.5 knots

In March 1900 the *Gascon* was acquired by Union Castle.
In November 1914 she was requisitioned as a hospital ship able to accommodate four hundred and thirty-four patients.

She served through the war and then returned 'normal service' until scrapped in 1928.

G. B. S.
George Bernard Shaw

GBS

GBS was born in Dublin on Saturday 26th July 1856, son of George Carr and Lucinda Elizabeth Shaw. He became a prolific popular novelist and playwright. He was a committed socialist helping to found the Fabian Society. In 1898 GBS married the heiress Charlotte Payne-Townshend, a fellow Fabian and champagne socialist. They lived at Ayot St Lawrence, Hertfordshire, and at 29 Fitzroy Square, London.

His vocal opposition to the British involvement in the First World War severely dented his popularity. He visited Russia in the 1930s and after meeting Stalin extolled the virtues of Bolshevik Russia.

GBS was a founder of the London School of Economics in 1895. He was awarded the Nobel Prize for Literature and an Oscar in 1938.

He died at home on Saturday 2nd November 1950, he left an estate of £367,233 13s.

GISBURNE PARK

Gisburne Park was created with its mansion in the 18th century. The park was developed and vast quantities of oak trees were planted. The deer park was a popular hunting ground and Charles' father was never happier than when in the saddle. Following Lord Ribblesdale's death part of the estate had to be sold to pay for crippling death duties with the residue disposed of in 1944.

Thankfully the house survived and was not pulled down to build a modern housing estate, but was sold in 1985 and converted into a private hospital. Unlike to so many properties the appearance of the original splendour of the house has been maintained.

SMS GOEBEN AND BRESLAU

	Goeben	*Breslau*
Built by:	Blohm & Voss, Hamburg	A. G. Vulcan
Class:	Moltke-class battle cruiser	Magdeburg-class light cruiser
Launched:	Tuesday 28th March 1911	Tuesday 16th May 1911
Renamed:	*Yavuz Sultan Selim*	*Midilli*
Length:	186.6m	136.6m
Beam:	30m	14m
Draft:	9.2m	5.48m
Speed:	25.5 to 28.4 knots	25 knots
Range:	7,630kms	
Complement:	43 officers and 1,010 men	370 officers and men

SMS Goeben and *Breslau* were on patrol in the Mediterranean at the outbreak of war. Under the command of Admiral Wilhelm Souchon the ships were ordered to bombard the French-Algerian ports of Bone and Philippeville on Tuesday 4th August 1914. Orders were received to sail to Turkey which they did after refuelling in Italy *en route*. They became targets for the British and French navies but successfully evaded them and arrived safely in Constantinople. The German Government presented the Turkish Government with the two ships on Sunday 16th August who renamed them. Admiral Souchon then accepted the position of head of the Turkish Navy, serving until September 1917.

SMS Goeben arriving in Constantinople

Admiral Souchon took his Turkish Navy into the Black Sea and on Thursday 29th October 1914 bombarded Sebastapol despite there not being any declaration of war between Turkey and Russia. On Sunday 1st November Russia declared was on Turkey in response to the unprovoked attack.

SMS Breslau

The ships participated in defending the Dardanelles when the peninsula was attacked and invaded in 1915. The ships continued in service until Monday 28th January 1918 when Vice Admiral Rebeur-Paschwitz ordered them to attack allied ships in Mudros. *En route* both ships sailed into a well-constructed minefield and hit a number of mines. The *Breslau* (*Midilli*) went down with the loss of three hundred and thirty men but the *Goeben* (*Yavuz*) limped back towards Turkey. The *Goeben* was beached on the Gallipoli Peninsula where she came under attack that caused further damage. The ship was eventually 'made good' but a total refit was not undertaken until 1927 that took three

... Mudros Harbour

years to complete. In 1938 she carried the body of Kemel Ataturk from Istanbul to Izmit. The *Goeben* served through the Second World War and remained in service until scrapped in the early 1970s.

GENERAL HENRI JOSEPH EUGÈNE GOURAUD

Henri was born in Paris on Sunday 17th November 1867, eldest child of Doctor Xavier and Mary Gouraud. Following his formal education he passed into Saint Cyr Military Academy in 1888, passing out two years later. In 1894 he left to serve in Africa, initially in the Sudan. In 1898 Henri became a national figure for his action in capturing the rebel leader Samori. He continued to serve in the main French colonial possessions in Africa and was promoted to command the forces in Western Morocco in 1914.

Henri commanded the French forces at Gallipoli until he was badly wounded when a shell burst close to him, breaking both legs he later had an arm amputated. He commanded the French Fourth Army from July 1917 and 'liberated' Strasbourg in late November 1918.

General Gouraud at the front

From 1919 Henri was sent to the Middle East where he commanded the troops in the continuing war against Turkey and where he established French control of Syria and Lebanon.

From 1923 to 1937 Henri was the Military Governor of Paris and a member of the Supreme Allied War Council.

He died in Paris on Monday 16th September 1946.

GRAND VIZIER

The Grand Vizier was the senior minister of the Turkish government, equivalent to Prime Minister. Many of them were replaced after only a short period of service but often returned to the post several times. The appointment was held by the following covering the period of Charles' letters and during the First World War:

Halil Rifat Pasha	*November 1895 to Saturday 9th November 1901*
Küçük Mehmed Said Pasha	*Wednesday 13th November 1901 to Thursday 15th January 1903*
Avlonyalı Mehmed Ferid Pasha	*Thursday 15th January 1903 to Thursday 6th July 1908*
Küçük Mehmed Said Pasha	*Wednesday 22nd July 1908 to Thursday 6th August 1908*
Kıbrıslı Mehmed Kamil Pasha	*Friday 7th August 1908 to Sunday 14th February 1909*

Hüseyin Hilmi Pasha	Sunday 14th February to Wednesday 14th April 1909
Ahmed Tevfik Pasha	Wednesday 14th April 1909 to Wednesday 5th May 1909
Hüseyin Hilmi Pasha	Wednesday 5th May 1909 to Wednesday 12th January 1910
İbrahim Hakkı Pasha	Wednesday 12th January 1910 to Saturday 30th September 1911
Küçük Mehmed Said Pasha	Saturday 30th September 1911 to Monday 22nd July 1912
Ahmed Muhtar Pasha	Monday 22nd July to Tuesday 29th October 1912
Kıbrıslı Mehmed Kamil Pasha	Tuesday 29th October 1912 to Thursday 23rd January 1913
Mahmud Şevket Pasha	Thursday 23rd January to Wednesday 11th June 1913
Said Halim Pasha	Thursday 12th June 1913 to Sunday 4th February 1917
Mehmed Talat Pasha	Sunday 4th February 1917 to Monday 14th October 1918
Ahmed İzzet Pasha	Monday 14th October 1918 to Monday 11th November 1918
Ahmed Tevfik Pasha	Monday 11th November 1918 to Tuesday 4th March 1919
Damat Ferid Pasha	Tuesday 4th March 1919 to Thursday 2nd October 1919

CAPTAIN
FRANCIS OCTAVIUS GRENFELL, VC
9th (Queen's Royal) Lancers
Died on Monday 24th May 1915, aged 35
Grave reference II. B. 14, Vlamertinghe Military Cemetery.

An extract taken from the London Gazette dated 16th November, 1914 records the following:

"For gallantry in action against unbroken Infantry at Andregnies, Belgium, on 24th August, 1914, and for gallant conduct in assisting to save the guns of 119th Battery, Royal Field Artillery, near Doubon the same day."

Francis Grenfell

Francis was born at Hatchlands, Guildford, on Saturday 4th September 1880, twin son of Pascoe Du Pre Grenfell and Sophia, his wife of 69 Eaton Place, London and Wilton Park, Beaconsfield, nephew of Field Marshal Lord Grenfell. Francis went to Eton College aged 14 as a member of Sir Walter Durnford's House, and was a keen sportsman, scoring eighty runs at Lords in the match against Harrow in 1899 as a member of the First XI. Francis became Master of the Beagles and his brother Whip, raising considerable sums of money that assisted in the building of new kennels. A keen polo player he formed the Old Etonian Polo Team, again with his brother. Francis was a keen horseman winning many inter-regimental races, and Point-to-Point races. He was a member of the Bath Club, Piccadilly.

In May 1901 Francis was gazetted to the Seaforth Highlanders, serving in Egypt, and then gained a commission in the King's Royal Rifle Corps fighting in the Boer War being awarded the Queen's Medal with five clasps. Finally he joined the prestigious cavalry regiment, the 9th Lancers. He was promoted Lieutenant in January 1905 and Captain in September 1912.

In August 1914 Francis went to France with the 9th Lancers and during the Battle of Mons he was ordered to charge the German guns and suffered heavy losses. Later in the day Francis Grenfell and his men volunteered to attempt to rescue the 119th Field Battery who were about to be over-run by the Germans. During this action he was badly wounded and was awarded the Victoria Cross. He was taken by Rolls-Royce to hospital in Bavai, driven by his friend, the Duke of Westminster. He recovered from his wounds and returned to France, and the front, in October 1914 but was again badly wounded, returned to England to recover. By April 1915 he had recovered sufficiently to return to the front, on the evening of

... Francis' action that won him the VC

Wednesday 7th he held a farewell dinner which included notables such as John Buchan and Winston Churchill. Francis was in the Ypres Salient when the first German gas attack took place and the next day, Monday 24th May, he was shot and killed on the Menin Road at Hooge.

He was Mentioned in Despatches on Thursday 8th October 1914.

He left an estate of £40,569 12s 6d.

His gravestone inscription reads: *"Also to the memory of his twin brother Riversdale. Born in 1880. Sons of Pascoe & Sofia Grenfell."*.

His Victoria Cross is displayed at Regimental Headquarters 9th/12th Lancers, Derby. Francis and Riversdale are commemorated in the vestry window of St George's Memorial Church, Ypres. His twin brother, Captain Riversdale Grenfell, died on Friday 4th September 1914 and is buried in Vendresse Churchyard. He was cousin of both 2nd Lieutenant The Honourable Gerald 'Billy' Grenfell who is commemorated on the Menin Gate, and Captain Julian Grenfell who is buried in Boulogne Eastern Cemetery (see below).

Captain Julian Henry Francis Grenfell, DSO
1st (Royal) Dragoons
Died on Wednesday 26th May 1915, aged 27
Grave reference II.A.18, Boulogne Eastern Cemetery.

Citation for the Distinguished Service Order, London Gazette, Friday 1st January 1915:

"On the 15th of Nov. he succeeded in reaching a point behind the enemy's trenches and make an excellent reconnaissance, furnishing early information of an impending attack by the enemy."

Julian Grenfell

Julian was born Friday 30th March 1888, eldest son of Lord and Lady Desborough of Taplow Court, Taplow, Buckinghamshire, Panshanger, Hertford, and 4 St James's Square, London, a grandson of 11th Earl of Westmorland. After attending Summerfields, he went to Eton College at 14 and was a keen sportsman. He went up to Balliol College Oxford, in 1906 where he rowed for their eight and four; owed for Ladies' 1907 and 1908; won Wyfold 1909 in addition he was a good shot and athlete as well as an excellent boxer knocking out two professionals in the same week as he wrote *"Into Battle"*.

Julian joined the Army with the Seaforth Highlanders in Egypt. He gained a commission in the King's Royal Rifle Corps and served in South Africa where he was promoted Lieutenant on 6th October 1911. Whilst in South Africa he set the regimental high jump record at 6' 5". Finally he joined a prestigious cavalry regiment, the 1st (Royal) Dragoons.

On 5th October he went out to France with his regiment. He wrote home *"We have been fighting night and day; first real rest today for four days. The worst of it is, no sleep practically. I cannot tell you how wonderful our men were, going straight for the first time into a fierce fire. They surpassed my utmost expectations. I have never been so fit or nearly so happy in my life before. I adore the fighting, and the continual interest which compensates for every disadvantage. I have longed to be able to say that I liked it, after all one has heard of being under fire for the first time. But it is beastly. I pretended a bit that I liked it, but it was no good, it only made one careless and unwatchful and self-absorbed; but when one acknowledged to oneself that it was beastly, one became all right again, and cool." "We took a German officer and some men prisoners in a wood the other day. One felt hatred for them as one thought of our dead; and as the officer came by me I scowled at him, and the men were cursing him. The officer looked at me in the face and saluted me as he passed, and I have never seen a man look so proud and resolute and smart and confident in his hour of bitterness. It made me terribly ashamed of myself."*

Julian was awarded his Distinguished Service Order for reconnaissance on Saturday 7th November 1914 and on Friday 20th he was Mentioned in Despatches by Field Marshal Sir John French. He wrote home from the front: *"I adore war. It's like a big picnic without the objectlessness of a picnic. ... Here we are in the burning centre of it all, and I would not be anywhere else for a million pounds and the Queen of Sheba."*

He was promoted Captain on Thursday 10th December 1914. He was Mentioned in Despatches on Thursday 14th January 1915.

On 12th May Julian was five hundred yards behind the front line along the Ypres

... tending to the wounded

to Menin Road waiting to attack Hooge. On 13th May he was in front of Hooge Lake, on top of a small hill, *'Railway Hill'*, which gave a vantage point towards the Germans, he was accompanying General Campbell. He was blasted by a shell which ripped his coat open. He continued on with the tour with Colonel Steele who was then badly wounded in the head and a shell splinter struck him on the head. Julian felt his feet go suddenly cold and told the General *"Go down, sir, don't bother about me, I'm done."* General Campbell helped carry him back but was also wounded *en route.*

Back at the rear he said *"Do you know, I think I shall die"* which was contradicted to which he replied *"Well, you see if I don't."*

Julian went to a Field Dressing Station before being transported to Boulogne where his sister was a nurse in the same hospital and he was operated upon by Sir Anthony Bowlby to remove the one inch splinter. His parents were advised by telegram and were given permission to come to Boulogne on an ammunition ship. The wound

... transporting the wounded by train

turned septic, and a second operation had to be performed. Mrs Meynell stated *"His strength and youth were fighting against the deadly poison of his wound. During all those eleven days when he lay there he prayed, probably unaware that he spoke aloud. Sometime he preyed that he might be able to bear the pain. The psalms and the hymns of his childhood were said to him aloud; that was what he liked, also George Herbert's poems."* With his parents by his side, he said to his mother *"Hold my hand before I go"* and kissed his mother's hand. Julian succumbed to his injuries during the afternoon. Lieutenant Colonel Maclachlan wrote *"Julian set an example of light-hearted courage which is famous all through the Army in France, and has stood out even above the lost lion-hearted."*

His younger brother wrote *"I love to think that he had attained that perfection for which he sought so untiringly. I seem to hear him cheering me on in the moments of stress here with even more vivid power. There is no one whose victory over the grave can be more complete."*

Raymond Asquith wrote of him: *"There was something primitive in Julian, a simplicity, force, and directness which were almost savage, but tempered with a natural courtesy and grace which gave him the finest manners and a smile which was indescribably charming and intimate."*

A poem was dedicated to him:

JULIAN GRENFELL
Because of you we will be glad and gay;
Remembering you we will be brave and strong;
And hail the advent of each dangerous day,
And meet the great adventure with a song.
And as you proudly gave your jewelled gift,
We'll give our lesser offering with a smile,
Nor falter on that path where, all too swift,
You led the way and leapt the golden stile.
Whether new seas, new heights to climb you find,
Or gallop through the unfooted asphodel,
We know you know we shall not lag behind,
Nor halt to waste a moment on a tear.
And you will speed us onward with a cheer,
And know beyond the stars that all is well.

At Taplow Court a sculpture of Apollo in his chariot of the sun, placed on a boulder, on the boulder an inscription reads: *"In memory of the happy lives of Julian Henry Francis Grenfell Captain Royal Dragoons, died of wounds at Boulogne May 26th 1915 aged 27, and of Gerald William Grenfell, Second Lieutenant Rifle Brigade killed leading a charge near Hooge July 30th 1915, aged 25. "*

The associated plaque has *'Into Battle'*, composed by Julian Grenfell, inscribed:

"The naked earth is warm with spring,
And with green grass and bursting trees
Leans to the sun's gaze glorying,
And quivers in the sunny breeze;
And Life is Colour and Warmth and Light,
And a striving evermore for these;
And he is dead who will not fight;
And who dies fighting has increase.

The fighting man shall from the sun
Take warmth, and life from the glowing earth;
Speed with the light-foot winds to run,
And with the trees to newer birth;
And find when fighting shall be done,
Great rest and fulness after death.

All the bright company of Heaven
Hold him in their high comradeship,
The Dog Star, and the Sisters Seven,
Orion's Belt and Sworded Hip.

The woodland trees that stand together,
They stand to him each one a friend,
They gently speak in the windy weather,
They guide to valley and ridges' end.

The kestrel hovering by day
And the little owls that call by night,
Bid him be swift and keen as they,
As keen of ear, as swift of sight.

The blackbird sings to him, 'Brother, brother,
If this be the last song you shall sing,
Sing well, for you may not sing another;
Brother, sing.'

In dreary, doubtful, wiling hours,
Before the brazen frenzy starts,
The horses show him nobler powers;
O! patient eyes, courageous hearts

And when the burning moment breaks,
And all things else are out of mind,
And only Joy of Battle takes
Him by the throat, and makes him blind

Through joy and blindness he shall know,
Not caring much to know, that still
Nor lead nor steel shall reach him, so
That it be not the Destined Will.

The thundering lines of battle stands,
And in the air Death moans and sings;
But Day shall clasp him with strong hands,
And Night shall fold him in soft wings."

Julian is commemorated on the House of Lords War Memorial.

In Eton College, Eton, a plaque was placed in the Cloisters with the inscription: *"In memory of the Hon. Julian Henry Francis Grenfell, D.S.O., Captain 1st Royal Dragoons, died of wounds received in action at Ypres 13th May 1915. A.A. Somerville 1901-1906, The Hon. Gerald William Grenfell Lieut. 8th Battalion Rifle Brigade, killed in action at Ypres 30th July 1915. A.M. Goodhart 1903-1909, sons of 1st Baron Desborough of Taplow Court Buckinghamshire. Francis Octavus Grenfell VC, Captain, 9th Lancers killed in action at Ypres 24th May 1915. Walter Durnford 1894-1899. Riversdale Nonus Grenfell, Captain, Bucks Hussars (Attached) 9th Lancers killed in action at the Aisne Friday 4th September 1914. Walter Durnford 1889-1893 also of Robert Septimus Grenfell, Lieut. 12th Lancers killed in action at Omdurman 2nd September 1898. Walter Durnford 1889-1893. Pascoe St Leger Grenfell, killed in the Matabele War March 1896. Jane Evans 1875-1880. Reginald Du Pre Grenfell Lieut. 17th Lancers died of fever contracted on service in India March 1888. Jane Evans 1880-1883 sons of Pascoe Du Pre Grenfell of Wilton Park, Bucks, W. Evans 1841-1846."*

Another memorial to the Grenfell Family and others, was erected at Mostyn House School, Parkgate, Cheshire and they read:

(Plaque 1): *"Captain Francis Octavius Grenfell, VC, The 9th Lancers. Killed at Ypres, May 24th 1915. Saved the guns in retreat from Mons. Aged 34. (Twin Brother)"*

(Plaque 2): *"Lieut. Riversdale Nonus Grenfell, attached to 9th Lancers. Killed at Battle of the Aisne, Sept. 14th 1914. Aged 34."* (Twin Brother.)

(Plaque 3): *"Captain The Hon. Julian H.F. Grenfell, DSO: The Royal Dragoons. Wounded at Ypres, May 13, & died at Boulogne, May 26th. 1915, aged 27. Author of 'Into Battle'."*

(Plaque 4): *"2nd Lieut. The Hon. G.W. Grenfell 8th Batt. The Rifle Brigade. Killed at

Hooge, July 29th 1915, aged 25. Scholar of Eton & of Balliol Coll., Newcastle Scholar of Eton, Craven Scholar of Oxford."

His brother 2nd Lieutenant The Honourable Gerald 'Billy' Grenfell who is commemorated on the Menin Gate, and his cousin of Captain Francis Grenfell, VC is buried in Vlamertinghe Cemetery.

SECOND LIEUTENANT THE HONOURABLE
GERALD WILLIAM GRENFELL
(KNOWN AS 'BILLY')
8th Battalion Rifle Brigade
Died on Friday 30th July 1915, aged 25
Commemorated on Panel 46, The Menin Gate.

Billy Grenfell

Billy was born on Saturday 29th March 1890, son of William Henry, 1st Baron Desborough, KG, GCVO, and Ethel Anne Priscilla, Lady Desborough (Lady of the Bedchamber to HM the Queen), of Taplow Court, Clivedon Road, Taplow, Buckinghamshire, grandson of John, 11th Earl of Westmorland.

He was educated at Summer Fields from 1899 where he was a good athlete and held four School records. He then attended Eton College from 1903 to 1909 where he won an entrance Scholarship and the Newcastle Scholarship (one of the few Oppidans to be so awarded) as a member of Mr Arthur Christopher Benson's and Mr Arthur Murray Goodhart's Houses. He was one the editors of the *'Eton College Chronicle'* from 1907 to 1909. Billy went up to Balliol College, Oxford, in 1909, and was awarded the Craven Scholarship in 1911. He won a Real Tennis Blue and boxed for the College. Billy had intended to read for the Bar but the war intervened.

Lord Desborough and his coat of arms

Billy volunteered at the outbreak of war and was gazetted on Saturday 12th September 1914. He was sent for training until Saturday 22nd May 1915 when he sailed for France. He entrained for Watten in northern France to continue training; from Friday 28th he was attached to the North and South Staffordshires for training in the front line on the French-Belgian border. On Saturday 29th Major Billy Congreve, VC, DSO, MC, wrote: *"I rode off to look for Ronnie who is now out here commanding the 8th Battalion which is in the 14th Division. Eventually found him in a farm between Neuve Eglise and Bailleul. I much admired the general appearance of the good riflemen. They may be new but they look splendid and have such a fine lot of officers."* (Major Congreve was killed on Thursday 27th July 1916 and is buried in Corbie Communal Cemetery Extension.)

Billy Congreve

On Monday 7th June Billy went into the line for the first time at St Eloi for a three day tour of duty after which they were relieved by the 7th Battalion. On Monday 5th July the Germans bombarded their lines and twenty of them managed to enter the trenches. The North Staffordshire's Bombing Officer rushed in and helped mount the counter-attack which cleared them out. On Friday 30th July Billy was leading his troops from a trench in *'Zouave Wood'*, near Hooge, at 3.00pm when he was killed by machine-gun fire. He spoke to the men of his platoon and urged them: *"Remember, you are Englishmen. Do nothing to dishonour that name."* Due to the fierce battle that raged, Billy's body was not recovered until Sunday 15th August when it was buried but the grave was subsequently lost. He had written: *"Death is such a frail barrier out here that men cross it smilingly and gallantly every day."*

Lieutenant Carey (later Lieutenant Colonel Carey, DSO) wrote a comprehensive account of the action:

"The 8th Battalion left Ypres by the Lille Gate something after 10 p.m. on July 29. 'A' Company was commanded by Lieutenant L. A. McAfee, an old Cambridge Rugger Blue, beloved of both officers and men; he was also in charge of No. 1 Platoon (we lost our original company commander a week or so earlier at Railway Wood — the first officer of the Battalion killed). I commanded No. 2 Platoon, Lieutenant M. Scrimgeour No. 3 and 2nd Lieutenant S. C. Woodroffe No. 4. 'A' Company was to hold the line on the left of the crater, with my platoon on the right of our sector holding up to the left edge of the crater. No. 4 Platoon was on my left, and Nos. 1 and 3 in a trench running parallel to No. 4's bit, a few yards in rear of it. 'C' Company (Captain E. F. Prior) was to hold the line on the right of the crater; Keith Rae commanded a platoon in this company and I'm pretty sure his platoon's sector was that nearest the right-hand edge of the crater. 'B' Company (Captain A. L. C. Cavendish) and 'D' Company (Captain A. C. Sheepshanks) were in support, in trenches at the near edge of the wood.

I remember having a strong presentiment as I plodded up to the line that night that I should never come back from it alive; in the event I was the only officer in my company to survive the next twenty-four hours.

The relief was complete shortly after midnight. It has been rather a tiring business, for we had two miles to cover before the line was reached, with the delays inevitable to troops moving over strange ground in the dark; and the difficulty of getting our men into the broken-down trenches while the 7th Battalion were getting out of them was even greater here than we had found elsewhere. I had warned my men of the need for silence, owing to the nearness of the Boche, and I remember when the time came feeling certain that the tramp of feet and the clatter of rifles must have given the show away (I need not have worried — we knew afterwards that the Boche learned from more reliable sources when a relief was to take place). Indeed, the night was ominously quiet. There had been very little shelling on the way up — for which we were duly thankful; but the absence of the sniper's bullet as we filed up the communication trench from Zouave Wood was something more surprising. The continued silence after we got into the line became uncanny. About an hour after we were settled in and the last of the 7th Battalion had disappeared into the darkness, I decided that a bomb or two lobbed over into the Boche trench running close to mine near the crater might disturb him if he were up to mischief there. (It should be mentioned here that in these early days of bombs there was only a limited number of men in each battalion who could use them, and these were organized as a squad under

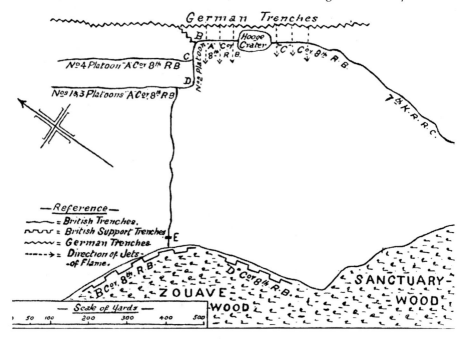

... bombing their way forward

a single officer. Their disposition over the battalion sector and their supply of bombs was under the supervision of the Battalion bombing officer, who on this night had begun his rounds on the 'C' Company sector and had not yet reached mine. I had in the meanwhile posted a few bombers attached to my platoon at what I considered the vital spots, the point where my trench joined the crater, and Point B. Our supply of bombs was small, though more were expected to be up before daylight.) Accordingly I got one of the bombers to throw over a hand grenade; it looked to carry about the right length and it exploded well. We waited; no reply. At short intervals he sent over two more. 'This ought to rouse them,' we said; again no reply. There was something sinister about this.

It was now about half an hour before dawn, and just then the order for the usual morning 'stand-to' came through from the Company Commander. I started on the extreme right of my bit of the line, to ensure that all my men were lining the trench, with their swords fixed. Working down gradually to the Point B, I decided to go on along the stretch of trench which bent back from the German line almost in the form of a communication trench; there were servants and some odd men from my platoon in so-called shelters along here, and I wanted to make sure that these people, who are apt to be forgotten at 'stand-to,' were all on the alert. Just as I was getting to the last of these (Point D in plan), there was a sudden hissing sound, and a bright crimson glare over the crater turned the whole scene red. As I looked I saw three or four distinct jets of flame—like a line of powerful fire-hoses spraying fire instead of water—shoot across my fire-trench (see dotted lines in plan). How long this lasted it is impossible to say— probably not more than a minute; but the effect was so stupefying that, for my own part, I was

... liquid fire

utterly unable for some moments to think — collectedly. I remember catching hold of a rifle with fixed sword of a man standing next to me and making for Point B, when there was a terrific explosion, and almost immediately afterwards one of my men, with blood running down his face, stumbled into me, coming from the direction of the crater. He was followed by one or two others, most of them wounded. The minenwerfer had started, and such men as had survived the liquid fire were, in accordance with orders, giving the crater a wide berth. Then broke out every noise under Heaven! 'Minnie' and bombs in our front trench, machine-guns from places unseen, shrapnel over the communication trenches and the open ground between us and the support line in Zouave Wood, and high-explosive on the wood and its vicinity. It was impossible to get up the trench towards the crater while men were coming down in driblets, so I got out of the trench to the right of Point C to try and get a better idea of the situation. I was immediately hit in the right shoulder by a shrapnel bullet, but I didn't have time to think much about it; still less did I realize that it was to prove my salvation. The first thing I saw was men jumping over the edge of the crater into 'C' Company's trench. It was still the grey light of dawn and for some moments I could not distinguish whether they were Boche or British; but, deciding soon that they must be Boche, I told the few survivors of my platoon, who by that time had joined me, to open fire on them, which they promptly did. At this point McAfee came up, followed by Michael Scrimgeour, and we had a hurried consultation. By this time the Boches were in my bit of trench as well, and we saw that my handful couldn't get back into it. It was a death-trap to stay where we were, under a shrapnel barrage; so Mac, after weighing the possibility of going for the Boche across the open with the bayonet, reluctantly gave the order for me to get the remnant of my platoon back to the support line, and said that he and Michael would follow with the rest of the company. About a dozen men of No. 2 Platoon were all that I could find — those who had faced the flame attack were never seen again — and we started back over the open. I doubt if we could have found the communication trench if we had wanted to, but for the moment there was open fighting to be done (we had no reason to suppose that the Germans were coming no farther than our front line). A retirement is a miserable business, but there can be nothing but praise for the conduct of the men in this one; there was nothing approaching a 'run,' and at every few yards they lay down and fired with the coolness of an Aldershot field day at any Bosches who could be seen coming over into our line. There was a matter of four hundred yards of open ground to be covered under a regular hail of machine-gun and shrapnel fire, and I have always marvelled how anyone got over it alive; as it was, most of my fellows were wounded during that half-hour's retirement, if not before, and one was shot dead within a yard of me while in the act of firing. Eventually, I (literally) fell into the main communication trench about twenty yards ahead of the support line (at Point E); it must have been then about 4.30 a.m. Here I was joined almost at once by Cavendish (O.C. 'B' Coy.), who, on learning that our front line was lost, suggested that we should there and then build a barricade in the communication trench—it was still expected that the Boche would come on. My small party set to, using sandbags from the side of the trench, and a supply of bombs came up while we were working. It was rather ticklish work when it came to the upper part of the barricade, as the Boche was using shrapnel very accurately, and there were a lot of rifle and machine-gun bullets flying about. But the men in the support trenches behind us were having a worse time, for Zouave Wood was being heavily bombarded and 'B' and 'D' Companies were 'suffering a

... close fighting at the German line

lot of casualties. During this time, Mac, having got his survivors back to the supports, came up to see how I had fared. He was very cool, but terribly unhappy at our losses of men and ground; and especially at having been unable to get into touch with Woodroffe. I was thankful at finding him safe, and still more so to learn that Michael also was all right. He went off almost at once to reorganize the remainder of the company. We continued to stand by our barricade, and I borrowed a rifle and tried to do a bit of sniping; the Boche could be seen throwing up the earth in our front line, and it now looked as if he were going to stay there. About this time came our first bit of consolation. Our artillery had begun to retaliate, and we could see shells bursting in our old front line; but the effort was feeble as compared with the German bombardment. Some hour and a half later Mac came back with the grievous news that Michael Scrimgeour had been killed while reorganizing his men in the wood. He also began to fuss about my wound, and eventually gave me a direct order to go back to the dressing-station. I had to go, and that was the last I saw of poor McAfee, who was killed that afternoon leading his men in a counter-attack."

Of the officers mentioned in the narrative above, Captain Edward Prior died on Friday 15th September 1916 and is buried in Bernafay Wood British Cemetery, Montauban, 2nd Lieutenant Sidney Woodroffe won his Victoria Cross in this action and together with Lieutenant Michael Scrimgeour, 2nd Lieutenant Keith Rae and Lieutenant Lewis McAfee they died in the action and are commemorated on the Menin Gate.

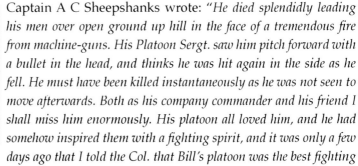

Captain A C Sheepshanks wrote: *"He died splendidly leading his men over open ground up hill in the face of a tremendous fire from machine-guns. His Platoon Sergt. saw him pitch forward with a bullet in the head, and thinks he was hit again in the side as he fell. He must have been killed instantaneously as he was not seen to move afterwards. Both as his company commander and his friend I shall miss him enormously. His platoon all loved him, and he had somehow inspired them with a fighting spirit, and it was only a few days ago that I told the Col. that Bill's platoon was the best fighting platoon I had."*

Keith Rae and the private memorial erected by his parents and now outside Sanctuary Wood Cemetery

On Saturday 31st July, Lieutenant Colonel Alexander Maclachlan*, Commander of the 8th Battalion, wrote to Lord Desborough: *"Billy was killed yesterday afternoon about 3.00pm when gallantly charging over the open at the head of his men. It is all too tragic and I dare not think what this double shock can mean to you."* (* Lieutenant Colonel Maclachlan was killed and is buried in Savy British Cemetery.)

Billy had been killed less than a mile away from where his brother, Julian, had been fatally injured. Billy was one of the war poets.

At Taplow Court a sculpture of Apollo in his chariot of the sun, placed on a boulder, with an inscription that reads: *"In memory of the happy lives of Julian Henry Francis Grenfell Captain Royal Dragoons, died of wounds at Boulogne May 26th 1915 aged 27, and of Gerald William Grenfell, Second*

Taplow Court

Lieutenant Rifle Brigade killed leading a charge near Hooge July 30th 1915, aged 25."

The associated plaque has *'Into Battle'*, composed by Julian Grenfell inscribed on it, in Eton College, Eton, a plaque was placed in the Cloisters and another memorial to the Grenfell Family and others, was erected at Mostyn House School, Parkgate, Cheshire. For the inscriptions see Julian above.

The grave of an unknown officer in a cemetery close to where Billy was killed

Billy is commemorated on the House of Lords War Memorial.

The Right Honourable Sir Edward Grey, KG, PC, JP, DL
3rd Baronet and 1st Viscount Grey of Fallodon

Edward Grey and his coat of arms

Edward was born in London on Friday 25th April 1862, the eldest son of Colonel George Henry and Mrs Harriet Jane Grey, grandson of Sir George Grey, 2nd Baronet. He was educated at Winchester College from 1876 before going up to Balliol College, Oxford, in 1880. His father died in 1874 so his grandfather took control of his education and well-being. Edward succeeded to the Baronetcy on the death of his grandfather on Saturday 9th September 1882. On Tuesday 20th October 1885 Edward married Dorothy (née Widdrington) who died on Sunday 4th February 1906, he married again on Sunday 4th June 1922 to Lady Pamela, widow of the 1st Baron Glenconner. Edward lived at Fallodon, Lesbury, Northumberland, he did not have children from either marriage.

Edward speaking in the House of Commons

He was first elected as a Member of Parliament for Berwick in 1885 aged 23 and rose through the Liberal Party to be appointed Foreign Secretary on Sunday 10th December 1905 and served in post for ten years.

Franz Ferdinand

Following the assassination of Archduke Franz-Ferdinand and the crisis that followed Edward strove to avert war. It ended in failure with the outbreak of the First World War. Edward famously said on the evening of Monday 3rd August 1914, the night before war was declared: *"The lamps are going out all over Europe; we shall not see them lit again in our lifetime"*. (A full copy of the speech is reproduced below.) Edward was elevated to the Lords on Thursday 27th July 1916 and remained active in mainstream politics until he retired in 1923. He died on Thursday 7th September 1933, leaving an estate of £123,791 0s 1d.

LIEUTENANT GENERAL MAHARAJA OF GWALIOR, GCSI, GCVO, GBE, KIH, GCStJ

Madho Rao Scindia was born on Friday 20th October 1876 was the 5th Maharaja Scindia of Gwalior. He acceded to the throne in 1886. He was awarded the Coronation Medals for HM King Edward VII and George V. He took a leading part in the Indian Durbar in 1911 and awarded the medal.

He was married twice and had a son, Sir George Jivaji Rao Scindia, who became the 6th Maharaja, and a daughter by his second wife. King George V and HM Queen Mary stood sponsor to both children.

The Maharaja of Gwalior

He died on Friday 5th June 1925.

GENERAL SIR IAN STANDISH MONTEITH HAMILTON, GCB, GCMG, DSO, TD

Ian was born in Corfu on Sunday 16th January 1853, son of Colonel Christian Monteith Hamilton and Maria Corinna, daughter of John, 3rd Viscount Gort. His father died in January 1855 and his mother in July 1856. He was educated at Cheam Preparatory School followed by Wellington College from 1867. William studied in Germany before he passed into RMC Sandhurst where he played in the XV. In 1887 Ian married Jean, daughter of Sir John Muit, 1st Baronet.

Sir Ian Hamilton

He was gazetted Lieutenant on Wednesday 24th April 1872 and a year later he transferred to the Gordon Highlanders and was sent out to India. He was promoted to Lieutenant on Wednesday 24th September 1873, Captain on Saturday 25th February 1882, Major on Saturday 7th November 1885, Lieutenant Colonel on Friday 1st July 1887, Colonel in 1891, Major General on Thursday 12th October 1899, Lieutenant General in 1902, and General in 1907.

He served in the Afghan War (1878 to 1880) being Mentioned in Despatches twice and receiving the Medal with two clasps. In the Boer War, 1881, he was Mentioned in Despatches. Ian was badly wounded in his wrist, hand an knee and was taken prisoner. The Dutch doctor told him that he would probably die

and was released, then was recovered by a search party. His next main action was the Nile Expedition where he was Mentioned in Despatches, received the Medal with two clasps and the Khedive's Star. Ian went back to India and appointed ADC to Lord Roberts, was his Persian Interpreter and went with him to take part in the Burma Campaign. He was awarded the Distinguished Service Order gazetted on Saturday 30th May 1891. From April 1893 to October 1895 he served as Military Secretary to General Sir George White. He took part in the Chitral and was again Mentioned in Despatches and awarded the Medal with clasp. In 1896 he commanded a Brigade during the Tirah Expedition but was hospitalised when his horse fell on top of him breaking his leg. Ian left India to take command of the School of Musketry, Hythe, from May 1898 to September 1899. He rejoined Sir George White as Assistant Adjutant General in Natal and whilst in action at Elandslaagte was recommended for the Victoria

Cross by Sir John French but was considered to be of too higher rank to deserve it, bravery such as his was 'expected'. He saw considerable service until another accident when falling from his horse he broke his collar bone. He served in the War Office from December 1900 to November 1901, then appointed Chief of Staff to Lord Kitchener until April 1902. Ian returned to the front to command in the Transvaal. For his services in the South African War he was Mentioned in Despatches three times, awarded the Queen's Medal with six clasps, the

Lord Kitchener

King's Medal with two clasps and created KCB. Ian returned to the War Office and was Quartermaster General to the Forces until February 1904. From March 1904 to April 1905 he served in Manchuria as the Military Representative of India. Ian returned to England to be appointed General Officer Commanding, Southern Command, from June 1905 to May 1909, then Adjutant General of the Forces from

June 1909 to May 1909. He took command of the Mediterranean Expeditionary Force from August 1910 to August 1914.

At the outbreak of war he was Commander in Chief, Central Striking Force, and based in London until Saturday 13th March 1915. Lord Kitchener persuaded his friend Ian to take command of the Mediterranean Expeditionary Force for the ill-fated Gallipoli Campaign that ended for him on Saturday 16th October

Charles Monro 1915 when he was replaced by General Sir Charles Monro and recalled to London, 'the kindness' done to Lord Kitchener was forgotten. In addition to his British honours Ian was awarded the Grand Cross of the Japanese Order of the Sacred Treasure, Prussian Orders of the Royal Crown and of the Red Eagle, Spanish Order of Military Merit, and Grand Officer of the French Foreign Legion.

Ian was appointed Lieutenant of the Tower of London from 1918 to 1920. He was active in supporting veterans of the First World War in the 1920s and helped found the Anglo-German Association and was an admirer of Adolf Hitler.

Ian wrote a number of military books and died on Wednesday 12th October 1947, leaving an estate of £98,055 12s 11d.

JAMES KEIR HARDIE

Keir Hardie

Keir Hardie was born in Scotland on Friday 15th August 1856, son of David Hardie and Mary Keir. He began work as a small boy, first as a messenger, then in the mines. By the end of the 1870s Keir Hardie was heavily involved in the Trade Union Movement and began to dabble in journalism. In 1887 he published 'The Miner' and the next year stood as an Independent Labour candidate in Mid-Lanarkshire but came last. In August 1888 he was elected as Secretary of the Scottish Labour Party. Keir Hardie was elected as a Member of Parliament for West Ham South in 1892. The following year he helped establish the Independent Labour Party (see below). In 1895 he lost his seat but continued to agitate and work for the Labour movement. In 1900 he returned to the Commons as member for Merthyr Tydfil and Aberdare.

Keir Hardie supported the campaign for women's votes, self-rule in India and was a pacifist. He opposed the British entry in the First World War which cost him considerable popularity in the country. He continued to speak against the war until he died on Sunday 26th September 1915.

LIEUTENANT EDWARD WILLIAM HORNER

18th (Queen Mary's Own) Hussars
Died on Wednesday 21st November 1917, aged 28
Grave reference I. E. 23,
Rocquigny-Equancourt Road British Cemetery, Manancourt.

Edward Horner

Edward was born on Thursday 3rd May 1888, son of Sir John Francis Fortescue and Frances Horner, KCVO, of Mells Park, Frome, Somerset. He was educated at Summerfields from 1898 followed by Eton College in 1901 as a member of Edward Imprey House where he was an Oppidan Scholar. He went up to Balliol College, Oxford, in 1906, rowed in the College eight and four and was a member of the Dervorguilla Society. He graduated in 1910 in Literæ Humaniores and subsequently called to the Bar. He was closely associated with Lady Diana Manners but they did not marry instead she married one of his best friends, Duff Cooper. Edward was a close friend of Julian Grenfell, Patrick Shaw-Stewart and Charles Lister.

Edward joined North Somerset Yeomanry in 1914 and was transferred to the 18th Hussars, 1915. In early May, 1915, whilst fighting at the Ypres Salient along the Yser Canal, he was severely wounded by shell fire that damaged his liver

Diana Manners

... fighting around Cambrai

and kidneys, one of which was removed. He was initially hospitalised in Boulogne at the same time as Julian Grenfell who was in the next room and Lady Diana Manners helped nurse him. He was invalided back to England and after he recovered he went out to Egypt in February 1916.

Edward wished to return to the Western Front and he rejoined his regiment in France in March 1917. Near the village of Noyelles near Cambrai he was shot by a sniper and died of his wounds.

He left an estate of £80,771 5s.

In the St Andrew's Chapel at Mells Park there is full-sized bronze statue of Edward Horner on horseback by Sir Alfred Munnings on a plinth designed by their family friend, Edwin Lutyens, with the inscription:

South side: *"Edward dear son of John Horner and Frances his wife who fell in action at Noyelles Nov. 21 1917. Aged twenty-eight."*

West side: *"Sacred to the memory of Lieut. E. W. Horner 18th W.Q.M.O. Hussars died of wounds received in action Nov. 21st 1917."*

North side: *"He hath outsoared the shadow of our night."*

In addition his battlefield cross is also displayed with an associated wooden memorial plaque that reads: *"Edward William Horner Lieutenant in the Eighteenth Hussars who was born on the 3rd of May 1888 and died on 21 Nov. 1917. He was greatly loved in his home at Mells but with eager valour he left his heritage at the outbreak of war to fight in France. Seriously wounded at Ypres he recovered and returned to his regiment and fell at last in Picardy whilst defending the village of Noyelles against the German Army in The Battle Of Cambrai. Thus in the morning of his youth he hastened to rejoin his friends and comrades by a swift and noble death his grave is at Fins near Etrecourt and his only brother Mark is buried in this churchyard in their lives they were the love of many and having died are not dead".*

He was recorded in Debretts Obituary — War Roll of Honour published in the 1921 edition.

His brother-in-law, Lieutenant Raymond Asquith, died on Friday 15th September 1916 and is buried in Guillemont Road Cemetery, Guillemont (see above).

INDEPENDENT LABOUR PARTY (ILP)

It was established in 1893 and dissolved in 1975. Keir Hardy, MP, became its first Chairman (see above). Prominent members of the Party included Ramsay Macdonald and Phillip Snowden. When the 'real' Labour Party was formed in 1906 the ILP affiliated to it. It attracted many well-connected and rich members who seemed oblivious to their own privileged backgrounds conflicting with the diatribe they supported. As with all 'champagne socialists' they could 'talk the talk' but could never 'walk the walk'. At the outbreak of war the ILP voted to oppose Britain's involvement although some of its Members of Parliament left the movement as a result. The decision of the ILP was not popular amongst the electorate. The Party moved ever more to the left and towards communism. In 1975 the ILP became a pressure group within the Labour Party.

MARSHAL JOSEPH JOFFRE, GCB, OM

Joseph was born in Rivesaltes, on Monday 12th January 1852. He first served in the Franco-Prussian War, 1870, then spent considerable time serving with the French Armies in their colonies. In 1911 he was made Commander in Chief, leading the French at the outbreak of war, a post he held until December 1916 when replaced by General Robert Nivelle. In 1917 he was sent to help the situation in Romania and organise the Romanian Army. In June 1917 he *Joseph Joffre* was sent as Head of the Military Mission in America. Joseph retired from the army in 1919 and died in Paris on Saturday 3rd January 1931.

BRIGADIER GENERAL PAUL ALOYSIUS KENNA, VC, DSO
General Staff, Commanding 3rd Mounted Brigade
and ADC 21st (Empress of India's) Lancers
Died on Monday 30th August 1915, aged 53
Grave reference II. A. 1, La Baba Cemetery, Turkey.

An extract from the London Gazette dated Tuesday 15th November 1898:

"At the Battle of Khartoum, on 2nd September 1898, Captain P.A. Kenna assisted Major Crole Wyndham, of the same regiment, by taking him on his horse, behind the saddle (Major Wyndham's horse having been killed in the charge), thus enabling him to reach a place of safety; and after the charge of the 21st Lancers, Captain Kenna returned to assist Lieutenant de Montmorency, who was endeavouring to recover the body of second Lieutenant R. G. Grenfell."

Paul was born in Everton, Liverpool, on Saturday 16th August 1862, second son of Thomas and Julia Kenna, of Ballinakill House, County Meath, and Oakfield House, Lancaster. He was educated at Stonyhurst College and at the St Francis Xavier College, Liverpool followed by RMC Sandhurst. On Thursday 18th July 1895 Paul married Cecil Josephine Kenna, daughter of Montagu, 7th Earl of Abingdon, JP, DL, who died a few months later on Thursday 3rd October. On Thursday 2nd March 1905 he married for the second time to Angela Mary

Paul Kenna

Kenna (daughter of Herbert Aloysius and Mary Hibbert), of Trowle House, Trowbridge, Wiltshire, they had a daughter, Kathleen Mary Pauline.

After passing out of Sandhurst Paul joined the 2nd West India Regiment and was gazetted to the 21st Lancers in 1889. He served during the Nile Expedition in 1898 and won the Victoria Cross at the Battle of Omdurman. In the South African War he commanded a column and won the Distinguished Service Order, gazetted on Thursday 26th June 1902: *"In recognition of services during the operations in South Africa"*. He was Mentioned in Despatches twice. Paul then commanded mounted troops in the Somaliland Expedition from 1902 to 1904 where he was again Mentioned in Despatches. From 1905 to 1907 he was a Brigade Major in the 1st Cavalry Brigade. On Saturday

... capturing the Black Flag at Omdurman

1st December 1906 he was promoted to Brevet of Colonel and appointed ADC.

The opening ceremony 1912 Olympics

Paul rode in the 1912 Olympics but did not make much impression as an individual competitor or in the team event.

At the outbreak of war he was recalled to the colours with the rank of Brigadier General. He was initially based in Dover commanding the Territorial Force until July 1915 when he was sent to command the Notts and Derbys. Whilst visiting the advanced trenches he was shot by a sniper and mortally wounded. He was carried to a Dressing Station on the beach where he received the Last Rites from Father Farrel and Father Henry Day was with him when he died.

... dressing stations on the beach

2nd Lieutenant Alan Brodrick wrote from his dugout: *"He was shot by a sniper last night in the trench on our right. The bullet passed through his arm, smashing it, and then through his stomach, making a terrible wound. He died in hospital a few hours later. Had it not been for his desire of going right up to the forward trench, to cheer up everyone and have a yarn with the men, he would be alive now."*

Corporal John Forsyth wrote: *"I was there when he was hit, and help to ease him by bathing his head. I heard him say something about Agnus Dei, so I asked him if he wished for one. He said he had one, but would like to have a crucifix. At the moment I forgot about my rosary, so I gave him the medal, which he eagerly took. I took them back before I left, as my identity disc was on the string. He died about four hours later. The two hours I spent with him I shall always remember, and it was grand to see the comfort and relief these simple objects of piety gave his mind."*

He was Mentioned in Despatches on Friday 28th January 1916.

Paul left an estate of £950.

He is commemorated in St Andrew's Church, North Kilworth, Leicestershire, as well as in both *alma mater*.

Paul's Victoria Cross and medals are displayed in The Queen's Royal Lancers Museum in Belvoir Castle.

MARY HENRIETTA KINGSLEY

Mary was born in Highbury, London, in 1862, daughter of Dr and Mrs George Kingsley. Following the death of her parents within weeks of each other in 1892 Mary began travelling. She sailed via Las Palmas to West Africa (Sierra Leone) from where she travelled along the coastline carefully detailing her travels and collecting specimens for the British Museum. It was to be the first of her visits to the *'Dark Continent'* and she championed the native African cause.

Mary Kingsley

Mary was not the marrying kind, however she was not the monocle wearing, tweed suit and brogues type, but insisted on wearing female clothing at all times. In 1899 she left England as a nurse to assist the war effort in South Africa where she contracted enteric fever and died on Sunday 3rd June 1900, leaving an estate of £3,439 12s.

Her publications include: *Travels in West Africa, Congo Français, Corisco and Cameroons.* Macmillan. London, 1897; *West African Studies*. Macmillan & Co Ltd, London, 1899; *The Story of West Africa*. (The Story of the Empire Series) Horace Marshall, London, 1900. A number of books were written about her exploits and her dream of an African Society came to fruition, eventually to become the Royal African Society.

THE RIGHT REVEREND RONALD ARBUTHNOT KNOX

Ronald was born on Friday 17th February 1888, fourth son of the Right Reverend Edmund Arbuthnot Knox, the Bishop of Manchester, and Mrs Ellen Penelope Knox. He was educated at Eton College from 1900 to 1906 as a member of College. He was a Newcastle Medallist in 1905, an editor of the Eton College *Chronicle* and Head of School. He went up to Balliol College, Oxford, with a number of scholarships and became President of the Oxford Union. Ronald was elected a Fellow of Trinity College, Oxford, and following studies at St Edmund's College he became a Roman Catholic priest. He became the Catholic Chaplain at Oxford University from 1926. He was a prolific author. He died in 1957 and left his estate of £7,049 to Evelyn Waugh. Ronald is buried in Mells Churchyard where Edward Horner is commemorated in the church.

THE RIGHT HONOURABLE
SIR ALAN FREDERICK 'TOMMY' LASCELLES, GCB, GCVO, CMG, MC

Tommy was born on Monday 11th April 1887, son of Commander The Honourable Frederick Canning and Frederica Maria Lascelles, and grandson of Henry, 4th Earl of Harewood. His cousin, the 6th Earl married Mary, The Princess Royal. Tommy was educated at Marlborough College from 1900 to 1905 where he was a Junior and Senior Scholar and went up to Trinity College, Oxford.
In 1913 Tommy was commissioned to the Bedfordshire Yeomanry. He served in the First World War, awarded the Military Cross in 1919 and Mentioned in Despatches.

The Princess Royal

From 1919 to 1920 he was appointed ADC to the Governor of Bombay and then Assistant Private Secretary to HRH The Prince of Wales until 1931. Tommy served as Secretary to the Governor of Canada before returning to royal duties as Assistant Private Secretary to HM King George V in 1935. He served HM King Edward VIII, George VI and Queen Elizabeth II, before retiring in 1953. From 1943 to 1953 he was Keeper of the Royal Archives. Upon retirement he was appointed a Director of the Midland Bank.
On Tuesday 16th March 1920 he married the Honourable Joan Frances Vere

Thesiger, daughter of Frederick, 1st Viscount Chelmsford. They had three children: John Frederick born on Sunday 11th June 1922; Lavinia Joan on Wednesday 27th June 1923 and Caroline Mary on Thursday 15th February 1928. They lived at Sutton Waldron House, Blandford, Dorset. Tommy died aged 94 in 1981.

THE HONOURABLE IRENE CONSTANCE LAWLEY

Irene Lawley

Irene was born on Tuesday 7th May 1889. She was the only child of Beilby, 3rd Baron Wenlock, GCSI, GCIE, KCB, PC, and Lady Constance Mary, granddaughter of Henry, 4th Earl of Harewood. On Friday 3rd December 1920 she married Colin Gurden Forbes Adam, CSI, DL, JP, son of Sir Frank Forbes Adam, 1st Baronet and Lady Rose Frances Kemball. They had four children: Stephen Timothy, born on Monday 19th November 1923;
Desmond Francis, born on Wednesday 27th January 1926. He married the Honourable Vivien Elizabeth, only daughter of Sir Oswald Moseley, and died on Friday 3rd January 1958;
Nigel Colin, born on Sunday 7th December 1930.
Irene who died in 1976.

Baron Wenlock and his coat of arms

PRINCE KARL MAX LICHNOWSKY

Prince Karl

Karl was born in Kreuzenort, Upper Silesia, on Thursday 8th March 1860 into a well-established and rich family that also had estates in Austria. He succeeded to his titles in 1901 and took his seat in the Prussian equivalent of the English House of Lords. He served in the diplomatic corps, with his first post in London, followed by Bucharest and then Ambassador in Vienna, a senior post. He was forced to retire in 1904 as he was considered to be a 'loose cannon'.

In 1912 he was recalled to service and appointed Ambassador to London and was considered to be a great Anglophile. As the situation in Europe deteriorated following the assassination of Archduke Franz-Ferdinand and his wife Sophie in June 1914 Karl did his best to avoid war between Germany and Great Britain. His efforts failed and a deeply upset Karl left England following the declaration of war in August 1914.

He published a number of books defending and promoting his opinions relating to the outbreak and conduct of the First World War. Karl died on Monday 27th February 1928.

DAVID LLOYD GEORGE
1ST EARL LLOYD-GEORGE OF DWYFOR

Lloyd George was born in Chortlon-on-Medlock on Saturday 17th January 1863, son of William and Elizabeth. After school he studied the law and became a solicitor in 1885. He married Margaret Owen on Tuesday 24th January 1888 and the next year was appointed an Alderman on Caenarfonshire County Council. He was elected as a Liberal Member of Parliament for Caernarfon Borough at a by-election on Monday 13th April 1890, remaining in the House until 1945. He joined Sir Henry Campbell-Bannerman's Government in 1906 as President of the Board of Trade.

Lloyd George and his coat of arms

From 1908 to 1915 he was the Chancellor of the Exchequer. He was appointed Minister of Munitions in 1915, followed by the Secretary State for War in 1916 before he became Prime Minister. He continued to serve as Prime Minister until 1922 and finally fell when it became clear that he was selling honours. From 1929 to 1945 he was the Father of the House. In March 1936 he met Adolf Hitler at Berchtesgarten whom he described as "the greatest living German".

Lloyd George speaking in the House of Commons

His wife died on Monday 20th January 1941 and he married his long-time mistress, Frances Louise Stevenson. Lloyd George was elevated to the peerage as the 1st Earl on Monday 1st January 1945, however, he died on Monday 26th March without ever taking his seat in the House. He left an estate of £139,855 8s 2d.

Sir Edwin Landseer Lutyens, OM, KCIE, PRA, FRIBA

Edwin Lutyens

Edwin, or Ned as he was known by the family, was born on Monday 29th March 1869, tenth child of Charles and Mary Lutyens, of London and Thursley in Surrey. Due to childhood illness he was educated at home. In 1885 he attended the Kensington School of Art for two years when he was apprenticed to the firm of Ernest George and Peto. He began his own practice the following year and his reputation was soon established. Edwin worked on a range of country houses with his work being published in the influential papers and magazines of the time. In 1897 he married Emily, daughter of Edward, 1st Earl of Lytton, GCB, GCSI, GCIE, who had been Viceroy of India. They five children: Barbara, born in 1898; Robert, in 1901; Ursula in 1904; Agnes in 1906; and Edith in 1908.

Edwin worked on numerous projects in India including the Viceroy's House in Delhi from 1912, now the home of the Indian President, and a new home for the Nizam of Hyderabad. Following the First World War Edwin's fame was complete with his design of the Cenotaph in Whitehall, Thiepval Memorial, Tower Hill Memorial to the Merchant Navy and numerous other war memorials throughout the Empire. He designed Queen Mary's dollhouse which is displayed at Windsor Castle.

Edwin was knighted and awarded the prestigious Order of Merit. He died on New Year's Day 1944, leaving an estate of £42,271 0s 8d.

His legacy is a great one that today is much admired and copied.

SECOND LIEUTENANT THE HONOURABLE FRANCIS WALTER STAFFORD MCLAREN, MP

Royal Flying Corps and General List
Died on Thursday 30th August 1917, aged 31
Grave reference east of Busbridge (St John The Baptist) Churchyard, Surrey

Francis McLaren and his family coat of arms

Francis was born on Sunday 6th June 1886, the second and younger son of Charles, 1st Baron and Lady Aberconway of Bodnant, Tal-y-Cafn, Denbighshire. He was educated at Eton College as a member of Henry Elford Luxmoore's and Richard Stephen Kindersley's houses where he excelled at sport receiving his colours for football. He went up to Balliol College, Oxford, in 1905 where he graduated in History. Francis was a prominent member of the Oxford Union and played for the College Tennis VI. He was called to the bar, Inner Temple, and was Justice of the Peace for Denbighshire. On Thursday 20th July 1911 Francis married Barbara, daughter of Colonel Sir Herbert Jekyll, and they had two children, Martin John born on Sunday 11th January 1914 and Guy Lewis Ian on Monday 8th November 1915. Following the war Francis' widow married Bernard Freyberg (see above). Francis was a member of the Bachelors' Club.

In 1910 he was elected as Member of Parliament for Spalding and was one of the youngest Members. Francis was appointed Parliamentary Private Secretary to the Right Honourable Lewis Harcourt (later Lord Harcourt) who was Commissioner of Works then Colonial Secretary. He seconded the Gracious Speech after the Opening of Parliament in February 1913 at the same time his father was moving the same in the House of Lords. Francis had been a member of the Inns of Court OTC for a number of years prior to the outbreak of war. In September 1914 he joined the RNVR and served with the armoured car section at the abortive expedition to Antwerp. He then was sent to Gallipoli and when his car was hit Francis carried the driver on his back to the dressing station —the next day he went back to retrieve the vehicle! He continued to serve in the campaign until he was hospitalised with dysentery and sent to Egypt to recover. He returned to England with the armoured cars and joined the Royal Flying Corps, training at Brooklands. Following a period of illness he returned to the Royal Flying Corps. In July 1917 Francis was sent

to Montrose to complete his training. On his final training flight his aeroplane crashed into the sea. It was recorded: *"He was about a mile out at sea in fine weather at a considerable height when his machine was seen to descend rapidly, almost perpendicularly, and the to right itself again, move along on the level, and circle once, or twice. When about 60ft. from the water it suddenly dived straight down into the sea. Before a rowing boat from the beach reached the spot, two motor fishing boats had arrived, and after some difficulty Mr. McLaren, who was unconscious, was removed from the aeroplane. He had received severe internal injuries and was badly hurt in the face, and his death took place just before the boats landed at the harbour."*

Herbert Asquith paid tribute to him in the House of Commons on Monday 29th October 1917: *"We have lost one of the youngest and most loved our Members, Francis McLaren, cut off in his youth of radiant promise, still untarnished by disappointment, with clear and firm conviction, a faithful and loyal friend, and those who knew him best knew how much there was in the coming years to be hoped for."*

He left an estate of £9,000 19s 10d.

Francis is commemorated on the House of Lords and House of Commons War Memorials and recorded in Debretts Obituary — War Roll of Honour published in the 1921 edition.

House of Commons Memorial

HMS MAJESTIC

Built by:	HM Dockyard Portsmouth
Launched:	Thursday 31st January 1895
Length:	413ft
Beam:	75ft
Draft:	28ft
Speed:	17 knots
Range:	4,700 nautical miles
Crew:	757

She first served with the Channel Squadron until transferring to the Atlantic Fleet. In late 1906 she was sent to Portsmouth until February 1907 when she was recommissioned and received a refit. After serving in the Nore Division HMS Majestic transferred to the Devonport Division. At the outbreak of war the Majestic underwent a further refit and in late September was escorting troop ships across the English Channel. She was sent across the Atlantic to be part of the convoy that escorted the First Canadian Contingent in October. In February 1915, under the command of Captain Talbot, she sailed to the Gallipoli Peninsula and bombarded the Turkish forts. During the period when the Royal Navy was hoping to shell the Turks into submission the Majestic was hit on Saturday 27th February then more seriously on Thursday 18th March. After only four days the repairs had been completed and further tours continued. She helped cover the landings on the beaches and taking some of those wounded in the first wave. Admiral Nicholson made HMS Majestic his flagship on Tuesday 25th May. Two days later, whilst off 'W' Beach, Commander Otto Hersing in U-21 fired a torpedo that struck the Majestic. A huge explosion followed and within ten minutes she was resting on the bottom, of her crew, forty-nine were killed.

The hull above the water

SIR LOUIS DU PAN MALLET, KCMG, CB, PC

Sir Louis Mallet

Louis was born on Sunday 10th July 1864, son of the Right Honourable Sir Louis Mallet, CB, PC. He first served in Rio de Janeiro in 1893, followed by an appointment to Rome as Acting Third Secretary from 1896 to 1897. He transferred to Egypt for two years in 1898 before returning to work in the Foreign Office in London. He was appointed as a secretary to the Marquess of Lansdown then as Private Secretary to Sir Edward Grey when both men were Secretary of State for Foreign Affairs. From 1907 to 1913 he was appointed Assistant Under Secretary of State then was sent to Constantinople as Ambassador.

LIEUTENANT THE HONOURABLE JOHN NEVILLE MANNERS
2nd Battalion Grenadier Guards
Died on Tuesday 1st September 1914, aged 22
Commemorated on La Ferté-sous-Jouarre Memorial.

John Manners and his family coat of arms

John was born on Wednesday 6th January 1892, eldest son of John Thomas Manners, 3rd Baron Manners, and Baroness Constance Edwina Adeline Manners, of Avon Tyrrell, Christchurch, Hampshire. He was educated at Eton College as a member of Mr Hubert Brinton's House where he excelled at cricket and was described as a 'star' of the House Dramatic Society. He went up to Balliol College, Oxford, in 1910, graduating in History, and played for the University at both tennis and polo.

He was gazetted in the Grenadier Guards in 1912 being promoted to Lieutenant in 1913.

On Wednesday 12th August 1914 HM Queen Alexandra, with TRH Princesses Victoria and Beatrice, arrived at Chelsea Barracks to wave off the Battalion as it left for France. They entrained for Southampton and sailed from Southampton for Le Havre on board *SS Cawdor Castle*, arriving the next day. The port was filled with an

Route of the
Second Battalion
1914

English Miles
0 10 20 30 40 50

FLANDERS

Calais
Ypres
BELGIUM
Hazebrouck
Tournai
Étaples
Mons
Condé
La Longueville
Arras
Cambrai
Maubeuge
Busigny
Landrecie
Grougis
Vadencourt
Flavigni
Amiens
La Fère
Havre
R. Oise
Pont-Arcy
R. Aisne
Rouen
Beauvais
Soissons
Fismes
VillersCotterêts
Betz
Oulchy
Neuilly
R. Marne
Meaux
Charly
Coulommiers

Route to Mons:—
by train......
by road.......
Retreat from Mons & ad-
vance to the Aisne..
Route from the Aisne
to Flanders....

PARIS

Condé
Mons
St. Symphorien
Spiennes
Binche
Genly
Harveng
Blaregnies
Quevy-le-Petit
Malplaquet
Quevy-le-Grand
La Longueville
R. Sambre
Maubeuge
Pont-sur-Sambre
Cambrai
Caudry
Leval
Noyelles
Landrecies
Maroilles
Le Cateau
Busigny
Vaux-Andigny
Oisy
Le Nouvion
Wassigny
Etreux
Vénérolles
The Mons Area
Grougis
Tupigny
1914
Vadencourt
English Miles
0 5 10
Flavigny

— 340 —

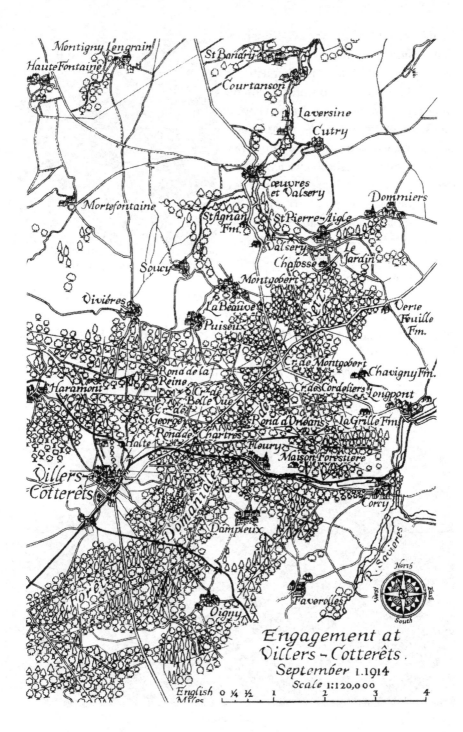

Engagement at
Villers - Cotterêts.
September 1.1914
Scale 1:120,000

English Miles 0 ¼ ½ 1 2 3 4

excited crowd of French well-wishers that provided a great welcome. A five mile march took John and his men to a camp where they rested until 2.00am on Saturday 15th when they entrained bound for 'somewhere in France'. A long and slow journey took them via Rouen, Arras, to Flavigny in northern France where they detrained and were billeted. They moved towards Belgium arriving to the sound of battle at Mons on Sunday 23rd August. Orders were received for them to take position at Spiennes via Harveng. Before they could engage the enemy

... a generous welcome to Le Havre

orders were received to retire in the early hours of the next morning, and the long march south began. They arrived at Landrecies on Tuesday 25th where a fierce, close quarter fight, ensued. Sir John French wrote in his despatch: *"The 4th Guards Brigade was heavily attacked by troops of the Ninth German Army Corps, who were coming through the forest on the north of the town. This brigade fought most gallantly and caused the enemy to suffer tremendous loss in issuing from the forest into the narrow streets of the town. This loss has been estimated from reliable sources at from 700 to 1,000."* Following the action John marched with his men via Etreux and reached Villers-

Landrecies

... *onward march of the German army*

Cotterêts on Tuesday 1st September. A heavy mist hung over the forest and the Germans were being engaged. He was fighting with the Honourable George Gascoyne-Cecil and they were both killed at the head of their men at the cross roads at Ronde le la Reine. John's body was never recovered but George was found and buried in Guards Grave, Villers-Cotterêts Forest British Cemetery.

John was the first from Balliol to be killed in the war and his good friend, Billy Grenfell (see above), wrote the following poem in his memory:

O heart-and-soul and careless played
Our little band of brothers,
And never recked the time would come
To change our games for others.
It's joy for those who played with you
To picture now what grace
Was in your mind and single heart
And in your radiant face.
Your light-foot strength by flood and field
For England keener glowed;
To whatsoever thing are fair
We know, through you, the road.
Nor is our grief the less thereby;
O swift and strong and dear, good-bye.

John is commemorated on the House of Lords War Memorial and was recorded in Debretts Obituary — War Roll of Honour published in the 1921 edition.

In the Visitor Centre in Mount Pleasant Park, Clovelly, Devon, a stone cross, is displayed with the inscription: *"To the memory of John Manners, Lieutenant in the Grenadier Guards. The dearly loved son of a dearly loved sister. This cross is dedicated by Christine Hamlyn. He fell in combat with the Germans in the woodland of Villers Cotterets, France on the first of September 1914 and lies with his comrades of a devoted rearguard at peace in the silence of the forest."*

Marie Sophie Fredrica Dagmar, or Minnie as she was known within the family, was born in the Yellow Palace, Copenhagen, on Friday 26th November 1847, the second daughter of Christian and Louise of Denmark. Her father became Christian IX of Denmark, the 'father-in-law' of Europe. Her elder sister, Alexandra, married Bertie, Prince of Wales, who became King Edward VII. In 1864 she became engaged to the Tsarevitch Nicholas of Russia but he died the next year so she returned to Denmark. In 1866

Empress Marie

Nicholas' brother, Alexander (now Tsarevitch) visited Copenhagen and proposed to her, they were married in the Winter Palace, St Petersburg, on Wednesday 9th November. She had six children:

Alexander and Marie's marriage

Nicholas and his family

Tsar Nicholas II, born on Wednesday 6th May 1868, murdered by the Bolsheviks on Wednesday 17th July 1918 together with his family and a number of his retinue;

Grand Duke Alexander Alexandrovich of Russia, born on Monday 7th June 1869 and died of meningitis on Monday 2nd May 1870;

Alexander

Grand Duke George Alexandrovich of Russia, born on Saturday 6th May 1871. When his brother ascended to the throne he became Tsarevitch. He suffered with ill-health and died on Wednesday 9th August 1899;

Grand Duchess Xenia Alexandrovna of Russia, born on Tuesday 6th April

George

Xenia and her family

1875. She married her cousin Grand Duke Alexander Mikailovich of Russia, with whom she had seven children. She escaped from Russia with her mother. HM King George V provided her with a home at Frogmore House then at Hampton Court Palace where she died on Wednesday 20th April 1960;

Michael

Grand Duke Michael Alexandrovich, born on Friday 22nd November 1878. On the death of his brother, George, he became Tsarevitch until the birth of his nephew Alexei. He had a series of romances and in September 1912 he married Natalia Brosova in Vienna in secret. His brother, Tsar Nicholas, was furious and Michael was banished from Russia and removed from the succession. He came to England and rented the Knebworth estate where he lived until the outbreak of the First World War. He returned with his family, including his young son George, to St Petersburg (renamed Petrograd) and served Russia until the revolution. When Nicholas was forced to abdicate he stated in the document: *"We have judged it right to abdicate the Throne of the Russian State and to lay down the Supreme Power. Not wishing to be parted from Our Beloved Son, We hand over Our Succession to Our Brother the Grand Duke Michael Aleksandrovich and Bless Him on his accession to the Throne."* He thus became by same instrument Tsar Michael II. Just before Nicholas and the Imperial Family were transferred from the Alexander Palace to Tobolsk Michael was allowed to visit him, it would be the last time they would meet. In March 1918 the Bolsheviks arrested Michael and he was exiled to Perm. His wife was able to visit him for a week at Easter, it would be the last time they would meet. Late on Wednesday 12th June Michael, together with his English secretary Nicholas Johnson, were taken to a remote spot and murdered in cold blood, shot in the head. Neither body has ever been recovered;

Olga

Grand Duchess Olga Alexandrovna of Russia, born on Tuesday 13th June 1882. She first married in 1901 to Duke Peter Alexandrovich of Oldenburg, however the marriage was annulled in 1916. Shortly afterwards she married Colonel Kulikovsky and they had a son, Tikhon Nikolaevich, who was born whilst she was imprisoned after the Revolution on Sunday 12th August 1917, and Guri Nikolaevich, on Wednesday 23rd April 1919. She finally escaped from Russia in November 1919 and five months later was able to join her mother in Copenhagen. Olga met Anna Anderson who claimed to be HIH Grand Duchess Anastasia but did not recognise her as her niece. In 1948 Olga

Alexander, Marie and family

moved with her family to Hampton Court Palace before emigrating to Canada. She was living in a small apartment in Toronto when HM Queen Elizabeth visited Canada in 1959 and invited Olga for lunch on *The Britannia*. She died a few months after her sister on Thursday 24th November 1960.

On Sunday 13th March 1881, HIM Tsar Alexander II, was assassinated in St Petersburg, and Minnie became Empress Consort to her husband HIM Tsar Alexander III. On Thursday 1st November 1894 Alexander died aged only 49 and her eldest son became HIM Tsar Nicholas II.

Following the Russian Revolution in March 1917 Minnie left her palace in Kiev for the Crimea with other members of the family. In 1919 HM King George V sent *HMS Marlborough* to rescue his aunt and other relations. Minnie lived for a short period of time with her sister, HM Queen Alexandra, in London and at Sandringham.

Tsar Nicholas II with Marie

Minnie's last years were spent at the home she had bought with Alexandra in Villa Hvidøre, near Copenhagen, which became the epicentre of monarchist Russia. She continued to live with the slim hope that her murdered children, grandchildren and family would be found alive. On

Saturday 13th October 1928 she died at her home and was buried in the Royal vaults in Roskilde Cathedral. Minnie finally returned to St Petersburg and Russia in September 2006 and was buried next to her husband in the Cathedral of St Peter and St Paul, near to the grave of her son, Nicholas II, and his family.

Marie's grave in St Petersburg

MEHMED V

Medhed V

Mehmed was born in the Topkapi Palace, Constantinople, on Saturday 2nd November 1844, son of Sultan Abdülmecid. He married five times and had three sons and a daughter. On Tuesday 27th April 1909 he deposed his brother Sultan Abdul Hamid. Turkey kept out of the war in August 1914 but with the encouragement of the German authorities took their position supporting the Central Powers in November. He was a keen supporter of Kaiser Wilhelm II who created him a German

Kaiser Wilhelm, Sultan Mehmed and Emperor Franz Joseph

Field Marshal in 1916. Mehmed died on Wednesday 3rd July 1918 shortly before the end of the war and the fall of the Ottoman Empire.

A depiction of Mehmed following the outbreak of war

... a Turkish fort defending the Dardanelles and the route to Constantinople

FIELD MARSHAL LORD PAUL SANFORD METHUEN, GCB, GCMG, GCVO, LLD, 3ʳᴰ BARON METHUEN

Paul Methuen and his coat of arms

Paul was born at Corsham Court, Wiltshire, on Monday 1ˢᵗ September 1845, eldest son of Frederick Henry Paul, 2ⁿᵈ Baron Methuen, and Lady Anna Horatia Caroline. He was christened Paul Sanford Methuen and was educated at Eton College from 1858 to 1860 as a member of the Reverend Russel Day's House. On Saturday 1ˢᵗ June 1878 Paul married Evelyn (daughter of Sir Frederick Hutchinson Hervey-Bathurst, 3ʳᵈ Baronet), she died on Monday 2ⁿᵈ June 1879. He married for the second time on Wednesday 9ᵗʰ January 1884 to Mary Ethel (daughter of William Ayshford Sanford) and they had three sons and two daughters: Paul Ayshford, born on Wednesday 29ᵗʰ September 1886 (4ᵗʰ Baron, see below), Ethel Christian on Thursday 7ᵗʰ March 1889, Anthony Paul on Friday 26ᵗʰ June 1891 (5ᵗʰ Baron), Ellen Seymour on Thursday 23ʳᵈ November 1893, and Laurence Paul on Sunday 18ᵗʰ September 1898.

Paul was a keen sportsman that included skating, cycling and lacrosse. He was an accomplished horseman and rode in the Grand National five times.

Paul became a professional army officer and was commissioned on Tuesday 22ⁿᵈ November 1864. He rose to Lieutenant Colonel of the Scots Guards in 1876, promoted to Colonel on Thursday 29ᵗʰ November 1888, Major General on

South Africa — surrendering to General de la Rey

Wednesday 21ˢᵗ May 1890, Lieutenant General on Friday 1ˢᵗ April 1898, General on Thursday 26ᵗʰ May 1904, and Field Marshal on Monday 19ᵗʰ June 1911.

He served in the Ashanti War, in the Egyptian Expeditions, in Bechuanaland, and the Tirah. Paul held a wide range of senior military appointments in England and Ireland, military attaché in Berlin, and in South Africa. During the South African War Paul was badly wounded, his force defeated and he was captured by General Koos de la Rey who almost immediately released Paul, due to his injuries, and had him transported to hospital. He was Mentioned in Despatches on Friday 8th February, Tuesday 16th April 1901 and on Tuesday 29th July 1902, awarded the Queen's Medal with four clasps and the King's Medal with two clasps.

From June 1904 to May 1905 Paul was General Officer Commanding Eastern Command, he was then appointed commander of South African Forces and two years later the Governor of Natal.

In 1915 Paul was appointed Governor of Malta, retiring in 1919. Upon his return to England he was appointed Constable of the Tower of London from Wednesday 3rd December 1919 until his death. Paul died at his home on Sunday 30th October 1932 and was buried in the family vault three days later, leaving an estate of £165,911 17s 7d.

THE HONOURABLE PAUL METHUEN
4TH BARON METHUEN OF CORSHAM

Paul was born at home on Wednesday 29th September 1886, son of Field Marshal Paul Methuen, GCB, GCMG, GCVO, JP, DL, 3rd Baron, and Lady Mary Ethel (see above). He was educated at Eton College from 1899 to 1905 as a member of the Reverend Stuart Alexander Donaldson's and Philip Vere Broke's Houses where he played in the XI. He went up to New College, Oxford, where he graduated with a BA in 1910 and an MA in 1914. On Tuesday 6th July 1915 he married Eleanor (Norah), they did not have any children, and they lived at Corsham Court, Corsham, Wiltshire. He was a member of Travellers' and an ardent Freemason, a member of Chaloner Lodge. Paul was a painter and zoologist working in the Transvaal Museum, Pretoria, from 1910 to 1914. He undertook expeditions to Madagascar and South West Africa. During the First and Second World Wars he served in the Scots Guards and appointed an ADC on General Rawlinson's staff.

In 1925 he was appointed to the Ministry of Agriculture. Paul wrote a large number of papers and articles relating to scientific matters. He was an accomplished painters and in 1952 he published 'Normandy Diary'. Paul was a Trustee of the National Gallery and Tate Gallery.

Paul died on Monday 7th January 1974.

General Rawlinson at the Querrieu Château where Paul served on his staff in the First World War

The Honourable Sir Harold George Nicolson, KCVO, CMG

Harold Nicholson and his family coat of arms

Harold was born in Tehran, Persia, on Sunday 21ˢᵗ November 1886, the younger son of diplomat Arthur, 1ˢᵗ Baron Carnock, GCB, GCMG, GCVO, KCIE, PC, and Lady Mary Catherine. He was educated at Wellington College from 1900 to 1903 and went up to Balliol College, Oxford, graduating with an MA. In 1913 he married the Honourable Victoria Mary 'Vita' Sackville-West, daughter of Lionel, 3ʳᵈ Baron Sackville. Despite both parties were homosexual and had numerous same-sex affairs, the marriage lasted and they had two sons: Lionel Benedict born on Thursday 6ᵗʰ August 1914 and Nigel Nicolson on Friday 19ᵗʰ January 1917. In the 1930s Harold and Vita bought Sissinghurst Castle, Kent, and they also lived at Ebury Street, London SW1.

Following university he joined the Diplomatic Corps with his first posting in Madrid before transferring to Constantinople from January 1912. In October 1914 and the declaration of war between Great Britain and Turkey Harold returned to work in the Foreign Office where he remained throughout the war. He was sent to France after the war and participated in the Peace Conference, Versailles. He was created CMG in 1920.

Harold served at the League of Nations, in Tehran and in Berlin before retiring in 1929. He decided to become a politician, first standing as a candidate for Sir Oswald Moseley's New Party but did not join him in the British Union of Fascists. In 1935 he was elected as a National Labour Member of Parliament for Leicester West.

During the Second World War he served under Duff Cooper in the Ministry of Information. At the General Election that followed the war he lost his seat so joined the Labour Party and stood unsuccessfully in a by-election in 1948 in Croydon North, ending his Parliamentary career.

Harold wrote the official biography of HM King George V in 1952 and was knighted the following year. He wrote numerous well-written and received books and kept a diary throughout his life recording a fascinating life that recorded his friendships with the majority of the 'great and the good' throughout the 20ᵗʰ Century until his death on Wednesday 1ˢᵗ May 1968.

SS Osiris

Built by: Caird & Co
Launched: Monday 6th June 1898
Length: 300ft
Beam: 37ft
Draft: 16ft
Speed: 20 knots
Crew: 115

She first served on the Port Said to Brindisi ferry service and was sister ship to the 'Isis'. She carried seventy-eight first class passenger taking just over twenty-four hours to complete the journey. On Wednesday 5th August 1914 she was put to military service as an armed merchant cruiser and became a submarine depôt ship. In 1916 she was renamed 'Osiris II' and was finally released in 1920.

General Sir Archibald Paris, KBE

Archibald Paris

Archibald joined the Royal Marine Artillery 1879. He joined the Naval Intelligence Department in 1899 and after a year was sent to join the Rhodesian Field Force during the South African War. From 1903 to 1904 he was appointed Professor of Royal Marine Artillery 1903-1904 then Chief Instructor until 1905 and served as Inspector of Marine Recruiting from 1913 to 1914. He served from the outbreak of the First World War and was appointed as Commander of the Royal Marine to replace General Sir George Grey Aston (see above). Archibald commanded the Royal Naval Division at Antwerp and took them out to Gallipoli. Following the evacuation he served on the Western Front where he was wounded in 1916. Archibald retired in 1917. He died on 30th October 1937, leaving an estate of £12,925 15s 9d.

LIEUTENANT COLONEL
JOHN ARNOLD CUTHBERT QUILTER
Grenadier Guards, Commanding Hood Battalion Royal Naval Division
Died on Thursday 6th May 1915, aged 40
Grave reference II. B. 4, Skew Bridge Cemetery.

John Quilter and his family coat of arms

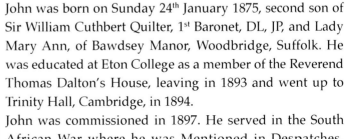

John was born on Sunday 24th January 1875, second son of Sir William Cuthbert Quilter, 1st Baronet, DL, JP, and Lady Mary Ann, of Bawdsey Manor, Woodbridge, Suffolk. He was educated at Eton College as a member of the Reverend Thomas Dalton's House, leaving in 1893 and went up to Trinity Hall, Cambridge, in 1894.

John was commissioned in 1897. He served in the South African War where he was Mentioned in Despatches. Following the War John was appointed Military Secretary of the Governor General of Australia.

In September 1914 John was appointed Lieutenant Colonel of the Hood Battalion and took them to serve in Antwerp. They were evacuated in October 1914 and returned to England. Training continued until being sent to serve in the Gallipoli Campaign. He was killed near Achi Baba Nullah during the Second Battle Krithia. He was Mentioned In Despatches.

Commodore Backhouse wrote *"… Quilter was killed leading his men into battle carrying an oversized walking stick. He was buried near Backhouse Post in a gully behind the trenches at position 169 L3. The Reverend Henry Foster conducted the burial service …"*

Reverend Henry Foster *"This brave officer was laid to rest at about 8 o'clock in the morning, in the presence of Commodore Backhouse and the staff of 2nd Naval Brigade. A firing party from his battalion fired three volleys over the grave as their last token of respect, and the buglers sounded the Last Post."*

He left an estate of £50,568 7s 8d.

In Bawdsley Parish Church, Suffolk, an alabaster and marble tablet was placed in his memory with the inscription: *"Sacred to the memory of John Arnold Cuthbert Quilter second son Sir W. Cuthbert Quilter Bart. of Bawdsey Manor in the county of Suffolk. Born January 29 1875. He joined the Grenadier Guards in 1897 and served with distinction in the South African Campaign being mentioned for conspicuous bravery at the Battle of Biddulphsberg. He was gazetted Lieut. Colonel to the Hood Battalion of the*

Royal Naval Division in September 1914 which battalion he commanded at Antwerp (October 4th 1914) and later in Gallipoli in which place (on May 6th 1915) while leading his men he laid down his life for his country. Greater love hath no man than this that a man lay down his life for his friends."

John is commemorated on the Shottisham, Sutton, Bawdsey Recreation Ground and Ramsholt War Memorials. He was recorded in Debretts Obituary — War Roll of Honour published in the 1921 edition.

JAMES RENNELL RODD, 1ST BARON RENNELL, GCB, GCMG, GCVO, PC

James Rennell Rodd

Rennell was born on Tuesday 9th November 1858, son of Major James Rennell and Elizabeth Rodd. He was educated at Haileybury and went up to Balliol College, Oxford, where he won the Newdigate Prize in 1880. On Saturday 27th October 1894 Rennell married Georgina Lillias Rodd (née Guthrie), of 39 Bryanston Square, London W1, they had six children:

Francis James, born on Friday 25th October 1895. He married the Honourable Mary Constance Vivian Smith, daughter of 1st Baron Bicester. Francis became the 2nd Baron Rennell and was created KBE and CB. He died on Wednesday 15th March 1978;

Christopher John, born and died 1896;

Evelyn Violet Elizabeth, born on Saturday 18th March 1899. She was created Baroness Emmet of Amberley in 1964 and died on Friday 10th October 1980;

Peter Murray Rennell, born on Saturday 16th April 1904. He was married to the Honourable Nancy Mitford from 1933 until their divorce in 1958. He died on Wednesday 17th July 1968;

Gustaf Guthrie Rennell, born on Thursday 13th July 1905 and died on Wednesday 26th June 1974;

Gloria Elinor who died on Wednesday 8th October 1975.

Rennell joined the Diplomatic Service in 1883 and served Berlin, Rome, Athens and Paris. Rennell left for Egypt to work with Lord Cromer in 1894 from where he returned to Rome followed by Stockholm. Late in 1908 he was appointed Ambassador in Rome a post he held until 1919 when he retired.

Rennell was elected as Member of Parliament for St Marylebone from 1928 to 1932. The next year he was elevated to the House of Lords. He died on Saturday 26th July 1941, leaving an estate of £16,810 4s 3d.

Rennell wrote of Charles Lister in his book *'Social And Diplomatic Memories'*:

"... we were profoundly saddened by the announcement of the death of Charles Lister after he had been for the third time wounded at Gallipoli. Rome had been his first diplomatic post, and in the intimate summer life of Posillipo he had become like a member of the family. He was moreover the son of some of my oldest friends. Charles Lister struck me as probably the most remarkable of the younger generation with whom I had been in contact, and of the many who served on my staff

... as a young man

none established stronger claim to my affection and regard. At Balliol his humanitarian instincts and a "passion for reforming the world" had made him a convinced Socialist. But he became before long equally convinced that the Socialists with whom he had had to do were moving on wrong lines. He was a keen scholar with a natural disposition to research, but at the same time an original thinker, conscientious in the performance of all duties and generous in every fibre. With a clumsy seat on a horse he was a fearless rider, who confessed to a divided mind as to whether the life of a fox-hunting squire or that of a college don attracted him most. Putting neither to the test, he became a diplomatist. I never quite understood how he had succeeded on the outbreak of war in cutting himself free from the liens of the public service when the spirit of the crusader moved him, like Rupert Brook, Patrick Shaw Stewart, and other brilliant contemporaries, to devote, their lives to the great adventure which cut them off in the flower of their youth. His elder brother, Tommy, less gifted no doubt but equally attractive in a different way, had fallen some ten years earlier, intercepted when carrying dispatches by the Mad Mullah's tribesmen in the Somali bush."

LIEUTENANT COMMANDER
PATRICK HOUSTON SHAW-STEWART

Royal Naval Volunteer Reserve, Hood Battalion Royal Naval Division

Died on Sunday 30th December 1917, aged 29

Grave reference II. E. 1,

Metz-en-Couture Communal Cemetery British Extension.

Patrick Shaw-Stewart

Patrick was born at Aberartro Llanenddwyn on Friday 17th August 1888, second and youngest son of Major General John Heron Maxwell Shaw Stewart and Mary Catherine Bedingfeld Shaw Stewart. He was educated at Eton College from 1901 to 1906 as a member of College where he was a Scholar. He went up to Balliol College, Oxford, in 1907 with Julian Grenfell, and was awarded the Hertford and Ireland Scholarships. Patrick was President of the Annadale, Secretary of the Dervorguilla and the Arnold, and he rowed in the second Torpid. He graduated with a Double First and was considered by his peers to be brilliant, in fact *'the most brilliant of all the Balliol men killed in the war'*. Patrick was awarded the Eldon Law Scholarship and studied at Inner Temple. He was elected a Fellow of All Souls then was employed by Baring's Bank and became managing director.

... a moment of relaxation, bathing in the sea

In September 1914 he volunteered and was commissioned. After training at Crystal Palace and at Blandford he sailed with the Hood Battalion for the Dardanelles. Amongst the fellow officers was his great friend, Rupert Brooke, who wrote shortly before he died that Patrick was *"the most brilliant man they've had in Oxford for ten years".*

Whilst in action in Gallipoli he wrote:

ACHILLES IN THE TRENCH

I saw a man this morning
Who did not wish to die
I ask, and cannot answer,
If otherwise wish I.

Fair broke the day this morning
Against the Dardanelles;
The breeze blew soft, the morn's cheeks
Were cold as cold sea-shells.

But other shells are waiting
Across the Aegean sea,
Shrapnel and high explosive,
Shells and hells for me.

O hell of ships and cities,
Hell of men like me,
Fatal second Helen,
Why must I follow thee?

Achilles came to Troyland
And I to Chersonese:
He turned from wrath to battle,
And I from three days' peace.

Was it so hard, Achilles,
So very hard to die?
Thou knewest and I know not -
So much the happier I.

I will go back this morning
From Imbros over the sea;
Stand in the trench, Achilles,
Flame-capped, and shout for me.

Following the evacuation from Gallipoli in March 1916 Patrick was appointed Liaison Officer attached to the French in Salonica.

... watering horses in Salonica

In early 1917 he returned to England on home leave then left to join the Hood Battalion on the Western Front. By December he was in temporary command when on Sunday 30th he was visiting his men just as the Germans laid down a barrage. He was hit in the ear but refused treatment and shortly afterwards a shell burst that killed him.

Patrick was awarded the Chevalier of the Legion of Honour and the French Croix de Guerre.

His great friend, Ronald Knox, published a selection of letters with some verses in *"Patrick Shaw-Stewart"*, London 1920.

ST JAMES'S CLUB

The St James's Club was founded in 1857 by the Earl Granville (former Foreign Secretary) and Marchese d'Azeglio (a Sardinian Minister) to provide a comfortable and hospitable Club for diplomats. Originally sited in St James's Street it later moved to Grafton Street then to Coventry House, 106 Piccadilly in 1868. The Club was popular with the aristocracy (most of the Dukes of the land being members) and in particular with Lord Randolph Churchill then his son, Sir Winston.

In 1975 the Club closed but has reopened as part of the St James's Hotel and Club in Park Place. (I am grateful to Mrs Pam Carter for the historical information supplied.) The Club can now be viewed at www.stjamesclubandhotel.co.uk/en/club

VICEROYS OF INDIA

The title of Viceroy was created in 1858 and added to that of Governor-General of India. It was expected that the holder would serve a fixed period of five years. India was the 'jewel in the crown' of the British Empire with the Viceroy and Vicereine living in sumptuous luxury at a standard that often outstripped the crowned heads of Europe. The Empire's two orders of chivalry relating to India were Order of the Star of India and the Order of the Indian Empire, each having the Viceroy as their Grand Master.

In 1912 a new residence began construction in Delhi, designed by Sir Edwin Lutyens that was not completed until 1929, that cost a small fortune. Following independence it became the official home of the President of India.

The Viceroys of India that cover the period of this book and the First World War were:

Lord Curzon: Friday 6th January 1899 to Saturday 18th November 1905;

Lord Minto: Saturday 18th November 1905 to Wednesday 23rd November 1910;

Lord Hardinge: Wednesday 23rd November 1910 to Tuesday 4th April 1916;

Lord Chelmsford: Tuesday 4th April 1916 to Saturday 2nd April 1921.

VILLA ROSEBERY

The property was begun in the early nineteenth century on Cape Posillipo. In 1897 the Earl of Rosebery (who had been Prime Minister) purchased the property but did not make much use of it. He was able to arrange, via the Foreign Office, to lease it for the use of the British Ambassador to Italy. In 1932 the ownership was taken by the Italian Government and used by its royal family. Crown Prince Umberto's eldest daughter was born there and the house was renamed Villa Maria Pia. TM King Victor Emmanuel III and Queen Elena lived there following his abdication until they left Italy for Egypt and exile in 1946.

Victor Emmanuel

General Otto Liman von Sanders

Liman von Sanders

Otto was born in East Prussia on Saturday 17th February 1855, son of Jewish parents. Despite his Jewish heritage he was able to advance through the ranks of the army.

In 1913 Otto was appointed as head of the German Military Mission in Constantinople. He thought little of Enver Pasha and did his best to sideline him to allow the German influence to take pre-eminence. Otto took a leading rôle in the Gallipoli Campaign together with his preferred senior Turkish officer Mustafa Kemmel. In 1918 he replaced General Erich von Falkenhayn in Palestine where he remained until the end of the war. Otto was arrested and charged with war crimes but was soon released.

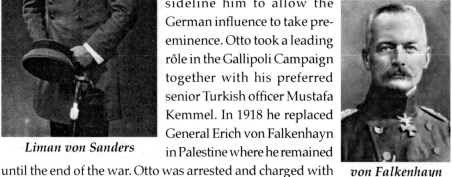

von Falkenhayn

In 1927 he published a book of his experiences during the war. He died in 1929.

Liman von Sanders and his staff officers

Hans, Freiherr von Wangenheim

Hans was born in 1859 and became a career diplomat. He was appointed Ambassador to Mexico before being sent as Ambassador to Greece from 1909 to 1912 from where he went to Turkey and Constantinople. He was devoted to the Kaiser and helped enormously in developing the relationship between Germany and the Ottoman Empire.

The Turkish Government began a series of actions against the Armenians that in 1915 came to the attention of the international press. To ensure that no blame could be attached to the German Government Hans issued a statement that included: *"On the other hand, the German Government cannot disguise the dangers created by these rigorous measures and notably by the mass expatriations which include the guilty and the innocent indiscriminately, especially when these measures are accompanied by acts of violence, such as massacre and pillage."* Has died in office on Monday 25th October 1915.

Beilby, 3ʳᴰ Baron Wenlock, GCSI, GCIE, KCB, VD, PC

Beilby was born on Saturday 12ᵗʰ May 1849, eldest son of Beilby, 2ⁿᵈ Baron Wenlock and Lady Elizabeth Grosvenor, daughter of Richard Grosvenor, 2ⁿᵈ Marquess of Westminster, KG. He was educated at Eton College and went up to Trinity College, Cambridge. On Tuesday 14ᵗʰ May 1872 Beilby married Lady Constance Mary Lascelles, CI, daughter of Henry, 4ᵗʰ Earl of Harewood. They had one daughter, Irene Constance Lawley (see above).

He was commissioned into the Yorkshire Hussars in 1869. In 1880 he was elected member of Parliament for Chester but shortly afterwards his father died and Beilby went to the House of Lords. From Friday 23ʳᵈ January 1891 to Wednesday 18ᵗʰ March 1896 he served as Governor of Madras. From 1901 to 1910 Beilby was Lord of

Beilby and his coat of arms

the Bedchamber to HRH The Prince of Wales (later HM George V), and Vice-Chamberlain to HM Queen Mary from 1910. He served as High Steward of Hull from 1909 to 1912 and was Honorary Colonel of the Yorkshire Yeomanry and the Northumberland Brigade.

He died on Monday 15ᵗʰ January 1912 and was succeeded by his brother Richard. He left an estate of £519,487 18s 7d.

His Grace, Hugh, 2ND Duke of Westminster, GCVO, DSO

Hugh and his coat of arms

Hugh was born on Wednesday 19th March 1879, son of Victor, Earl Grosvenor and Lady Sibell, the daughter of 9th Earl of Scarborough. He was grandson of Hugh, 1st Duke of Westminster, and following the death of his father on Tuesday 22nd January 1884 became the heir to the Dukedom. He was nicknamed 'Bend Or' by the family. Hugh was educated at Eton College. He inherited his titles on Friday 22nd December 1899. Hugh married four times:

Firstly to Constance Edwina, daughter of Colonel William and Mary Cornwallis Cornwallis-West. They married on Saturday 16th February 1901 and had three children:

Ursula Mary Olivia, born on Friday 21st February 1902 who died on Monday 5th June 1978;

Edward George Hugh, the Earl Grosvenor, born on Wednesday 16th November 1904 who died on Wednesday 13th February 1909 (HM King Edward VII stood sponsor);

Constance

Mary Constance born on Monday 27th June 1910 who died on Wednesday 7th June 2000;

Constance was created CBE in 1918 for he war work. She divorced Hugh in 1919;

Secondly to Violet Mary Rowley, daughter of Sir William Nelson, 1st Baronet, and former wife of George Rowley. They married on Monday 26th November 1920 and divorced in 1926;

Thirdly to The Honourable Loelia Mary Ponsonby, daughter of Frederick, 1st Baron Sysonby. They married on Thursday 20th February 1930 and divorced in 1947;

Fourthly to Anne Winifred Sullivan whom he married on Friday 7th February 1947, she was the owner of the famous racehorse, *Arkle*.

Hugh was commissioned to the Royal Horse Guards and served in the South Africa War and was ADC to Lords Roberts and Milner, and was Mentioned in Despatches and awarded the Queen's Medal with five clasps.

... Hugh's armoured cars in action

During the First World War Hugh assisted the war effort considerably providing cars and materials from the outbreak and in addition he served with the Cheshire Yeomanry. He helped to develop armoured cars and other useful vehicles. Following action on the Western Front he went to serve in Egypt where he was awarded the Distinguished Service Order on Tuesday 28th March 1916 for action at Sollum, Egypt, between Tuesday 14th to Friday 17th March.

Hugh was involved in various right-wing causes during the 1920s and 1930s. He died on Sunday 19th July 1953, his titles being inherited by his cousin William.

KAISER WILHELM II

Wilhelm II

Friedrich Wilhelm Viktor Albrecht was born in Berlin on Thursday 27th January 1859, eldest son HRH Prince Friedrich Wilhelm of Prussia (later Friedrich Wilhelm III) and HRH Princess Victoria (Princess Royal of Great Britain). He was the first grandchild of Queen Victoria and HRH Prince Albert and remained the Queen's favourite particularly as HRH Prince Albert had known him. Wilhelm's birth was a difficult one that resulted in his left arm being permanently damaged. It did not develop properly and was shorter than his right arm and was useless, a fact that Wilhelm always tried to conceal and ignore.

Friedrich Wilhelm III and Empress Viktoria

Wilhelm, Dona and their family

On Sunday 27th February 1881 Wilhelm married Princess Augusta Viktoria of Schleswig-Holstein, known as 'Dona' within the family. They had seven children:

Crown Prince Wilhelm

Crown Prince Wilhelm, born on Saturday 6th May 1882. He married Duchess Cecilie of Mecklenburg-Schwerin, daughter of Frederick Francis III, Grand Duke of Mecklenburg-Schwerin and Grand Duchess Anastasia Mikhailovna of Russia They had six children. Their eldest son Prince Wilhelm of Prussia was killed in World War II and given a state funeral in Berlin that was so popular Adolf Hitler banned all further public royal funerals. Their family home, the Ceciliehof, was where the Potsdam Conference was held and is now a museum. Wilhelm died on Friday 20th July 1951;

Prince Wilhelm Eitel Friedrich Christian Karl, born on Saturday 7th July 1883, he died on Tuesday 8th December 1942;

Prince Adalbert Ferdinand Berengar Viktor, born on Monday 14th July 1884 and died on Wednesday 22nd September 1948;

Prince August Wilhelm Heinrich Günther Viktor,

Adalbert

Eitel

Auwi

known as 'Auwi', born on Saturday 29th January 1887. He joined the Nazi Party and became a leading member of the SA with the rank of Obergruppenführer and was a member of the Reichstag. He died in Stuttgart on Friday 25th March 1949;

Prince Oskar Karl Gustav Adolf, born on Friday 27th July 1888 and died on Monday 27th January 1958, his eldest son, Prince Oskar Wilhelm Karl Hans Kuno of Prussia, was killed in action in 1939;

Prince Joachim Franz Humbert, born on Wednesday 17th December 1890. He was unable to adjust to republican Germany and shortly after he divorced his wife, Princess Marie-Auguste of Anhalt, he committed suicide by shooting himself on Sunday 18th July 1920, leaving a young son, Prince Karl Franz Josef Wilhelm Friedrich Eduard Paul;

Joachim

Viktoria Luise

Princess Viktoria Luise Adelheid Mathilde Charlotte, born on Tuesday 13th September 1892. She married Ernest Augustus, Duke of Brunswick, the head of the House of Hanover. Her grandchildren are the King of Spain and the Queen of Greece. Viktoria Luise died on Thursday 11th December 1980.

On Monday 11th April 1921 Dona died which was a severe blow to Wilhelm who adored her and was now left alone. However, in November 1922 he married Princess Hermine Reuss of Greiz much to the dismay of his immediate family who never accepted her. She used the titles of German Empress and Queen of Prussia. Princess Hermine's daughter Henriette married Prince Karl Franz Josef, son the late

Hermine, Wilhelm and Henriette

Prince Joachim. Following the death of Wilhelm the family ensured that Hermine left Huis Doorn and she went to live at her old home in Silesia. She died in appalling conditions following the end of the Second World War on Thursday 7th August 1947.

Wilhelm was close to his grandfather, Wilhelm I, who had unified Germany

following the Battle of Sedan in 1870 and was proclaimed German Emperor in the Hall of Mirrors, Palace of Versailles. In turn he came under the influence of Prince Otto von Bismarck whose policies and attitudes ran in the opposite direction to that of Wilhelm's parents.

Kaiser Wilhelm I lived to be an old man, dying on Friday 9th March 1888 only two weeks short of his 91st birthday. His son, Friedrich Wilhelm III, ascended the throne but his reign only lasted ninety-nine days as he was dying of throat cancer. On Friday 15th June Wilhelm became King of Prussia and German Emperor aged 29. Bismarck had flexed his muscles with his previous monarchs, particularly Wilhelm I, using a threat of resignation to get his own way. Wilhelm II did not take long to break with the old politician and in 1890 Bismarck was dismissed — famously described as *'Dropping the Pilot'* by Punch magazine.

1870 — The Pilots — 1914

Wilhelm enjoyed involving himself in both military and foreign affairs. Many of his foreign exploits caused more damage than good but he did build up the German army and develop the German navy to rival that of Great Britain.

Despite his oft notable gaffes and famed anti-British feelings he was very popular in Great Britain. HM Queen Victoria had died in his arms and he remained in London for her funeral. On subsequent visits to England he was cheered and fêted.

Sophie, Ferdinand and their children

Wilhelm was closely related to all the royal houses of Europe and was a confidant of many, including Archduke Franz Ferdinand of Austria-Hungary. He was appalled and deeply upset by his assassination, despite giving Emperor Franz Josef and the Government of Austria-Hungary his total support against the Serbs he left for a cruise not assuming a European war would ensue.

Manipulating politicians in the courts of Vienna and Berlin ensured that Russia mobilised and from that point it became impossible to stop the onward march to the First World War.

The conduct of the war was played out by the Imperial General Staff with Wilhelm's influence reducing all the time particularly when it was commanded by von Hindenburg and Ludendorff. On Saturday 9th November 1918 Wilhelm's effective reign came to an end and he left Spa by train then took a car that conveyed him across the Dutch border and into exile. He requested the Queen of Holland to grant him refuge as a Prince of Orange which was granted.

Wilhelm eventually purchased Huis Doorn near Utrecht (now a wonderful museum) where he lived until his death on Tuesday 3rd June 1941. When the Netherlands were invaded in 1940 Winston Churchill (who had known the Kaiser well prior to the First World War) offered Wilhelm sanctuary in England. Wilhelm politely declined the offer preferring to remain in his exile home. He never gave up hope that he and his family would be restored to the thrones of Prussia and Germany. He reposes in a coffin in the mausoleum at Huis Doorn waiting to be buried in Germany upon the restoration of the House of Hohenzollern.

Wilhelm visiting Turkey

Kaiser Wilhelm and his generals

... with Albert of Belgium

... at his house in Spa

... with Nicholas II

... with Ferdinand of Bulgaria

... with Franz Joseph

... with von Hindenburg and Ludendorff

... in Flanders fields

HIH Crown Prince Wilhelm

Crown Prince Wilhelm and his coat of arms

Wilhelm was born in the Marble Palace, Potsdam, the eldest son of HIM Wilhelm II and HIM Queen Augusta Viktoria, on Saturday 6th May 1882. He was named Friedrich Wilhelm Victor August Ernst and when born was third in line, following his grandfather (Friedrich Wilhelm III) and his father. Wilhelm married Cecilie, daughter of Grand Duke Frederick Francis III of Mecklenburg-Schwerin, and his wife HIH Grand Duchess Anastasia Mikhailovna of Russia, on Tuesday 6th June 1905. They had four sons and two daughters. His eldest son, HIH Prince Wilhelm, was killed during the invasion of France in 1940; his funeral was so well supported in Germany no other senior royal was allowed a public funeral again during the Second World War.

Wilhelm was appointed a Field Marshal and played an important part during the war. His favourite Regiment was the Death Head Hussars and if often pictured in its uniform (see left).

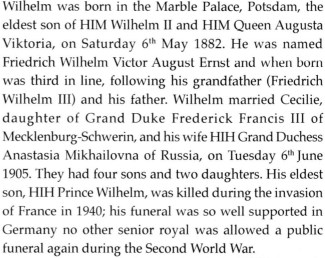

... with his staff in France

In November 1918 he went into exile in Wieringen, Holland, until being allowed to return to Germany in 1923. He had ambitions to become President of the Weimar Republic on the death of Field Marshal von Hindenburg, but his father was against the idea. Hitler, in any event, succeeded and combined the posts of Chancellor and President in his name.

Wilhelm became head of the House of Hohenzollern on the death of Kaiser Wilhelm II in May 1941. He lived for a further ten years until he died of a heart-attack. Wilhelm was buried in his favourite Death Head's Hussars uniform at Hohenzollern Castle.

His family home in Berlin, the Ceciliehof named after his wife, was where the Potsdam Conference was held following the Second World War, and is now museum.

IVOR MILES WINDSOR-CLIVE
2ND EARL OF PLYMOUTH

Ivor Windsor-Clive and his coat of arms

Ivor was born on at Hewell Grange, Redditch, Worcestershire, on Monday 4th February 1889, eldest son of Robert, 1st Earl of Plymouth, GBE, CB, TD, LLD, and Countess Alberta Victoria Sarah Caroline. He was educated at Eton College from 1902 to 1907 as a member of the Reverend Stuart Alexander Donaldson and Philip Vere Broke's Houses. He went up to Trinity College, Cambridge, where he played tennis for the College. On Thursday 14th July 1921 he married Lady Irene Corona, daughter of Hugo, 11th Earl of Wemyss. They had six children:

Other Robert Ivor, born on Tuesday 9th October 1923;
Richard Archer Alan, born on Sunday 5th February 1928;
Gillian Mary, who was killed in a car crash on Sunday 10th December 1961;
Clarissa, born on Thursday 15th January 1931;
Rosula Caroline, born on Tuesday 30th April 1935;
Rowland David Owain, born on Tuesday 30th August 1938;

During the First World War Ivor was commissioned and served with the Worcestershire Yeomanry then the Intelligence Corps on the Western Front, rising to the rank of Captain. He was Mentioned in Despatches. Ivor was elected as Conservative Member of Parliament for West Pancras from 1913 to 1919 and for Ludlow from January 1922 but when his father died on Tuesday 6th March 1923 he entered the House of Lords where he continued his Parliamentary career. From Friday 26th June 1925 to Monday 31st December 1928 he was Captain of the Honourable Corps of Gentlemen-at-Arms, Parliamentary Under-Secretary of State for Dominion Affairs from Tuesday 1st January to Friday 7th June 1929 and made a Privy Councillor on Friday 5th July 1929, Parliamentary Secretary to the Ministry of Transport November 1931 to September 1932, and Parliamentary Under-Secretary of State for the Colonies from Friday 30th September 1932.

Ivor was a member of the Carlton and Bachelors' Clubs and died in 1943.

Speech to the House of Commons on Monday 3rd August 1914 by Sir Edward Grey, The Secretary of State for Foreign Affairs

L
ast week I stated that we were working for peace not only for this country, but to preserve the peace of Europe. To-day events move so rapidly that it is exceedingly difficult to state with technical accuracy the actual state of affairs, but it is clear that the peace of Europe cannot be preserved. Russia and Germany, at any rate, have declared war upon each other.

Before I proceed to state the position of His Majesty's Government, I would like to clear the ground so that, before I come to state to the House what our attitude is with regard to the present crisis, the House may know exactly under what obligations the Government is, or the House can be said to be, in coming to a decision on the matter. First of all let me say, very shortly, that we have consistently worked with a single mind, with all the earnestness in our power, to preserve peace. The House may be satisfied on that point. We have always done it. During these last years, as far as His Majesty's Government are concerned, we would have no difficulty in proving that we have done so. Throughout the Balkan crisis, by general admission, we worked for peace. The co-operation of the Great Powers of Europe was successful in working for peace in the Balkan crisis. It is true that some of the Powers had great difficulty in adjusting their points of view. It took

much time and labour and discussion before they could settle their differences, but peace was secured, because peace was their main object, and they were willing to give time and trouble rather than accentuate differences rapidly.

In the present crisis, it has not been possible to secure the peace of Europe; because there has been little time, and there has been a disposition — at any rate in some quarters on which I will not dwell — to force things rapidly to an issue, at any rate, to the great risk of peace, and, as we now know, the result of that is that the policy of peace, as far as the Great Powers generally are concerned, is in danger. I do not want to dwell on that, and to comment on it, and to say where the blame seems to us to lie, which Powers were most in favour of peace, which were most disposed to risk or endanger peace, because I would like the House to approach this crisis in which we are now, from the point of view of British interests, British honour, and British' obligations, free from all passion as to why peace has not been preserved.

We shall publish Papers as soon as we can regarding what took place last week when we were working for peace; and when those Papers are published, I have no doubt that to every human being they will make it clear how strenuous and genuine and whole-hearted our efforts for peace were, and that they will enable people to form their own judgment as to what forces were at work which operated against peace.

I come first, now, to the question of British obligations. I have assured the House — and the Prime Minister has assured the House more than once — that if any crisis such as this arose, we should come before the House of Commons and be able to say to the House that it was free to decide what the British attitude should be, that we would have no secret engagement which we should spring upon the House, and tell the House that, because we had entered into that engagement, there was an obligation of honour upon the country. I will deal with that point to clear the ground first.

There has been in Europe two diplomatic groups, the Triple Alliance and what came to be called the 'Triple Entente', for some years past. The Triple Entente was not an Alliance — it was a Diplomatic group. The House will remember that in 1908 there was a crisis, also a Balkan crisis, originating in the annexation of Bosnia and Herzegovina. The Russian Minister, M. Isvolsky, came to London, or happened to come to London, because his visit was planned before the crisis broke out. I told him definitely then, this being a Balkan crisis, a Balkan affair, I did not consider that public opinion in this country would justify us in promising to give anything more than diplomatic support. More was never asked from us, more was never given, and more was never promised.

In this present crisis, up till yesterday, we have also given no promise of anything more than diplomatic support — up till yesterday no promise of more than diplomatic support. Now I must make this question of obligation clear to the House. I must go back to the first Moroccan crisis of 1906. That was the time of the Algeciras Conference, and it came at a time of very great difficulty to His Majesty's Government when a General Election was in progress, and Ministers were scattered over the country, and I — spending three days a week in my constituency and three days at the Foreign Office — was asked the question whether if that crisis developed into war between France and Germany we would give armed support. I said then that I could promise nothing to any foreign Power unless it was subsequently to receive the whole-hearted support of public opinion here if the occasion arose. I said, in my opinion, if war was forced upon France then on the question of Morocco — a question which had just been the subject of agreement between this country and France, an agreement exceedingly popular on both sides — that if out of that agreement war was forced on France at that time, in my view public opinion in this country would have rallied to the material support of France.

I gave no promise, but I expressed that opinion during the crisis, as far as I remember, almost in the same words, to the French Ambassador and the German Ambassador at the time. I made no promise, and I used no threats; but I expressed 1812 that opinion. That position was accepted by the French Government, but they said to me at the time — and I think very reasonably — *"If you think it possible that the public opinion of Great Britain might, should a sudden crisis arise, justify you in giving to France the armed support which you cannot promise in advance, you will not be able to give that support, even if you wish to give it, when the time comes, unless some conversations have already taken place between naval and military experts"*. There was force in that. I agreed to it, and authorised those conversations to take place, but on the distinct understanding that nothing which passed between military or naval experts should bind either Government or restrict in any way their freedom to make a decision as to whether or not they would give that support when the time arose.

As I have told the House, upon that occasion a General Election was in prospect. I had to take the responsibility of doing that without the Cabinet. It could not be summoned. An answer had to be given. I consulted Sir Henry Campbell-Bannerman, the Prime Minister; I consulted, I remember, Lord Haldane, who was then Secretary of State for War, and the present Prime Minister, who was then

Chancellor of the Exchequer. That was the most I could do, and they authorised that on the distinct understanding that it left the hands of the Government free whenever the crisis arose. The fact that conversations between military and naval experts took place was later on — I think much later on, because that crisis passed, and the thing ceased to be of importance — but later on it was brought to the knowledge of the Cabinet.

The Agadir crisis came — another Morocco crisis — and throughout that I took precisely the same line that had been taken in 1906. But subsequently, in 1912, after discussion and consideration in the Cabinet it was decided that we ought to have a definite understanding in writing, which was to be only in the form of an unofficial letter, that these conversations which took place were not binding upon the freedom of either Government; and on the 22nd of November, 1912, I wrote to the French Ambassador the letter which I will now read to the House, and I received from him a letter in similar terms in reply. The letter which I have to read to the House is this, and it will be known to the public now as the record that, whatever took place between military and naval experts, they were not binding engagements upon the Government:—

"My dear Ambassador, — From time to time in recent years the French and British naval and military experts have consulted together. It has always been understood that such consultation does not restrict the freedom of either Government to decide at any future time whether or not to assist the other by armed force. We have agreed that consultation between experts is not and ought not to be regarded as an engagement that commits either Government to action in a contingency that has not yet arisen and may never arise. The disposition, for instance, of the French and British Fleets respectively at the present moment is not based upon an engagement to co-operate in war.

You have, however, pointed out that, if either Government had grave reason to expect an unprovoked attack by a third Power, it might become essential to know whether it could in that event depend upon the armed assistance of the other.

I agree that, if either Government had grave reason to expect an unprovoked attack by a third Power, or something that threatened the general peace, it should immediately discuss with the other whether both Governments should act together to prevent aggression and to preserve peace, and, if so, what measures they would be prepared to take in common."

[The 22nd November, 1912.] That is the starting point for the Government with regard to the present crisis. I think it makes it clear that what the Prime Minister and I said to the House of Commons was perfectly justified, and that, as regards our freedom to decide in a crisis what our line should be, whether we should intervene or whether we should abstain, the Government remained perfectly free and, a fortiori, the House of Commons remains perfectly free. That I say to clear the ground from the point of view of obligation. I think it was due to prove our good faith to the House of Commons that I should give that full information to the House now, and say what I think is obvious from the letter I have just read, that we do not construe anything which has previously taken place in our diplomatic relations with other Powers in this matter as restricting the freedom of the Government to decide what attitude they should take now, or restrict the freedom of the House of Commons to decide what their attitude should be.

Well, Sir, I will go further, and I will say this: The situation in the present crisis is not precisely the same as it was in the Morocco question. In the Morocco question it was primarily a dispute which concerned France — a dispute which concerned France and France primarily — a dispute, as it seemed to us, affecting France, out of an agreement subsisting between us and France, and published to the whole world, in which we engaged to give France diplomatic support. No doubt we were pledged to give nothing but diplomatic support; we were, at any rate, pledged by a definite public agreement to stand with France diplomatically in that question.

The present crisis has originated differently. It has not originated with regard to Morocco. It has not originated as regards anything with which we had a special agreement with France; it has not originated with anything which primarily concerned France. It has originated in a dispute between Austria and Servia. I can say this with the most absolute confidence — no Government and no country has less desire to be involved in war over a dispute with Austria and Servia than tl.e Government and the country of France. They are involved in it because of their obligation of honour under a definite alliance with Russia. Well, it is only fair to say to the House that that obligation of honour cannot apply in the same way to us. We are not parties to the Franco-Russian Alliance. We do not even know the terms of that Alliance. So far I have, I think, faithfully and completely cleared the ground with regard to the question of obligation.

I now come to what we think the situation requires of us. For many years we have had a long-standing friendship with France. I remember well the feeling in the House — and my own feeling — for I spoke on the subject, I think, when the late Government made their agreement with France — the warm and cordial feeling resulting from the fact that these two nations, who had had perpetual differences in the past, had cleared these differences away. I remember saying, I think, that it seemed to me that some benign influence had been at work to produce the cordial atmosphere that had made that possible. But how far that friendship entails obligation — it has been a friendship between the nations and ratified by the nations — how far that entails an obligation let every man look into his own heart, and his own feelings, and construe the extent of the obligation for himself. I construe it myself as I feel it, but I do not wish to urge upon anyone else more than their feelings dictate as to what they should feel about the obligation. The House, individually and collectively may judge for itself. I speak my personal view, and I have given the House my own feeling in the matter.

The French fleet is now in the Mediterranean, and the Northern and Western coasts of France are absolutely undefended. The French fleet being concentrated in the Mediterranean the situation is very different from what it used to be, because the friendship which has grown up between the two countries has given them a sense of security that there was nothing to be feared from us. The French coasts are absolutely undefended. The French fleet is in the Mediterranean, and has for some years been concentrated there because of the feeling of confidence and friendship which has existed between the two countries. My own feeling is that if a foreign fleet engaged in a war which France had not sought, and in which she had not been the aggressor, came down the English Channel and bombarded and battered the undefended coasts of France, we could not stand aside and see this going on practically within sight of our eyes, with our arms folded, looking on dispassionately, doing nothing! I believe that would be the feeling of this country. There are times when one feels that if these circumstances actually did arise, it would be a feeling which would spread with irresistible force throughout the land.

But I also want to look at the matter without sentiment, and from the point of view of British interests, and it is on that that I am going to base and justify what I am presently going to say to the House. If we say nothing at this moment, what is France to do with her Fleet in the Mediterranean? If she leaves it there, with no statement from us as to what we will do, she leaves her Northern and Western coasts absolutely undefended, at the mercy of a German fleet coming down the Channel, to do as it pleases in a war which is a war of life and death between them. If we say nothing, it may be that the French fleet is withdrawn from the Mediterranean. We are in the presence of a European conflagration; can anybody set limits to the consequences that may arise out of it. Let us assume that to-day we stand aside in an attitude of neutrality, saying, *"No, we cannot undertake and engage to help either party in this conflict"*. Let us suppose the French fleet is withdrawn from the Mediterranean; and let us assume that the consequences — which are already tremendous in what has happened in Europe even to countries which are at peace — in fact, equally whether countries are at peace or at war — let us assume that out of that come consequences unforeseen, which make it necessary at a sudden moment that, in defence of vital British interests, we should go to war and let us assume — which is quite possible — that Italy, who is now neutral — because, as I understand, she considers that this war is an aggressive war, and the Triple Alliance being a defensive alliance her obligation did not arise — let us assume that consequences which are not yet foreseen — and which perfectly legitimately consulting her own interests — make Italy depart from her attitude of neutrality at a time when we are forced in defence of vital British interests ourselves to fight, what then will be the position in the Mediterranean? It might be that at some critical moment those consequences would be forced upon us because our trade routes in the Mediterranean might be vital to this country?

Nobody can say that in the course of the next few weeks there is any particular trade route the keeping open of which may not be vital to this country. What will be our position then? We have not kept a Fleet in the Mediterranean which is equal to dealing alone with a combination of other fleets in the Mediterranean. It would be the very moment when we could not detach more ships to the Mediterranean, and we might have exposed this country from our negative attitude at the present moment to the most appalling risk, I say that from the point of view of British interests. We feel strongly that France was entitled to know — and to know at once! — whether or not in the event of attack upon her unprotected Northern and Western Coasts she could depend upon British support. In that emergency, and in these compelling circumstances, yesterday afternoon I gave to the French Ambassador the following statement:—

"I am authorised to give an assurance that if the German Fleet comes into the Channel or through the North Sea to undertake hostile operations against the French coasts or shipping, the British Fleet will give all the protection in its power. This assurance is, of course, subject to the policy of His Majesty's Government receiving the support of Parliament, and must not be taken as binding His Majesty's Government to take any action until the above contingency of action by the German Fleet takes place."

I read that to the House, not as a declaration of war on our part, not as entailing immediate aggressive action on our part, but as binding us to take aggressive action should that contingency arise. Things move very hurriedly from hour to hour. Fresh news comes in, and I cannot give this in any very formal way; but I understand that the German Government would be prepared, if we would pledge ourselves to neutrality, to agree that its fleet would cot attack the Northern coast of France. I have only heard that shortly before I came to the House, but it is far too narrow an engagement for us. And, Sir, there is the more serious consideration — becoming more serious every hour — there is the question of the neutrality of Belgium.

I shall have to put before the House at some length what is our position in regard to Belgium. The governing factor is the Treaty of 1839, but this is a Treaty with a history — a history accumulated since. In 1870, when there was war between France and Germany, the question of the neutrality of Belgium arose, and various things were said. Amongst other things, Prince Bismarck gave an assurance to Belgium that, confirming his verbal assurance, he gave in writing a declaration which he said was superfluous in reference to the Treaty in existence — that the German Confederation and its allies would respect the neutrality of Belgium, it being always understood that that neutrality would be respected by the other belligerent Powers. That is valuable as a recognition in 1870 on the part of Germany of the sacredness of these Treaty rights.

What was our own attitude? The people who laid down the attitude of the British Government were Lord Granville in the House of Lords, and Mr. Gladstone in the House of Commons. Lord Granville, on the 8th of August, 1870, used these words. He said:—

"We might have explained to the country and to foreign nations that we did not think this country was bound 1819 either morally or internationally or that its interests were concerned in the maintenance of the neutrality of Belgium, though this course might have had some conveniences, though it might have been easy to adhere to it, though it might have saved us from some immediate danger, it is a course which Her Majesty's Government thought it impossible to adopt in the name of the country with any due regard to the country's honour or to the country's interests."

Mr. Gladstone spoke as follows two days later:—

"There is, I admit, the obligation of the Treaty. It is not necessary, nor would time permit me, to enter into the complicated question of the nature of the obligations of that Treaty; but I am not able to subscribe to the doctrine of those who have held in this House what plainly amounts to an assertion, that the simple fact of the existence of a guarantee is binding on every party to it, irrespectively altogether of the particular position in which it may find itself at the time when the occasion for acting on the guarantee arises. The great authorities upon foreign policy to whom I have been accustomed to listen, such as Lord Aberdeen and Lord Palmerston, never to my knowledge took that rigid and, if I may venture to say so, that impracticable view of the guarantee. The circumstance that there is already an existing guarantee in force is of necessity an important fact, and a weighty element in the case to which we are bound to give full and ample consideration. There is

also this further consideration, the force of which we must all feel most deeply, and that is, the common interests against the unmeasured aggrandisement of any Power whatever." The Treaty is an old Treaty — 1839 — and that was the view taken of it in 1870. It is one of those Treaties which are founded, not only on consideration for Belgium, which benefits under the Treaty, but in the interests of those who guarantee the neutrality of Belgium. The honour and interests are, at least, as strong to-day as in 1870, and we cannot take a more narrow view or a less serious view of our obligations, and of the importance of those obligations than was taken by Mr. Gladstone's Government in 1870.

I will read to the House what took place last week on this subject. When mobilisation was beginning, I knew that this question must be a most important element in our policy — a most important subject for the House of Commons. I telegraphed at the same time in similar terms to both Paris and Berlin to say that it was essential for us to know whether the French and German Governments respectively were prepared to undertake an engagement to respect the neutrality of Belgium. These are the replies. I got from the French Government this reply:—

"The French Government are resolved to respect the neutrality of Belgium, and it would only be in the event of some other Power violating that neutrality that France might find herself under the necessity, in order to assure the defence of her security, to act otherwise. This assurance has been given several times. The President of the Republic spoke of it to the King of the Belgians, and the French Minister at Brussels has spontaneously renewed the assurance to the Belgian Minister of Foreign Affairs to-day."

From the German Government the reply was:—

"The Secretary of State for Foreign Affairs could not possibly give an answer before consulting the Emperor and the Imperial Chancellor." Sir Edward Goschen, to whom I had said it was important to have an answer soon, said he hoped the answer would not be-too long delayed. The German Minister for Foreign Affairs then gave Sir Edward Goschen to understand that he rather doubted whether they could answer at all, as any reply they might give could not fail, in the event of war, to have the undesirable effect of disclosing, to a certain extent, part of then-plan of campaign. I telegraphed at the same time to Brussels to the Belgian Government, and I got the following reply from Sir Francis Villiers:—

"The Minister for Foreign Affairs thanks me for the communication, and replies that Belgium will, to the utmost of her power, maintain neutrality, and expects and desires other Powers to observe and uphold it. He begged me to add that the relations between Belgium and the neighbouring Powers were excellent, and there was no reason to suspect their intentions, but that the Belgian Government believe, in the case of violation, they

were in a position to defend the neutrality of their country."

It now appears from the news I have received to-day — which has come quite recently, and I am not yet quite sure how far it has reached me in an accurate form — that an ultimatum has been given to Belgium by Germany, the object of which was to offer Belgium friendly relations with Germany on condition that she would facilitate the passage of German troops through Belgium. Well, Sir, until one has these things absolutely definitely, up to the last moment, I do not wish to say all that one would say if one were in a position to give the House full, complete, and absolute information upon the point. We were sounded in the course of last week as to whether if a guarantee were given that, after the war, Belgium integrity would be preserved that would content us. We replied that we could not bargain away whatever interests or obligations we had in Belgian neutrality.

Shortly before I reached the House I was informed that the following telegram had been received from the King of the Belgians by our King — King George:—

"Remembering the numerous proofs of your Majesty's friendship and that of your predecessors, and the friendly attitude of England in 1870, and the proof of friendship she has just given us again, I make a supreme appeal to the Diplomatic intervention of your Majesty's Government to safeguard the integrity of Belgium."

Diplomatic intervention took place last week on our part. What can diplomatic intervention do now? We have great and vital interests in the independence — and integrity is the least part — of Belgium. If Belgium is compelled to submit to allow her neutrality to be violated, of course the situation is clear. Even if by agreement she admitted the violation of her neutrality, it is clear she could only do sounder duress. The smaller States in that region of Europe ask but one thing. Their one desire is that they should be left alone and independent. The one thing they fear is, I think, not so much that their integrity but that their independence should be interfered with. If in this war which is before Europe the neutrality of one of those countries is violated, if the troops of one of the combatants violate its neutrality and no action be taken to resent it, at the end of the war, whatever the integrity may be the independence will be gone.

I have one further quotation from Mr. Gladstone as to what he thought about the independence of Belgium. It will be found in "Hansard," Volume 203, Page 1787. I have not had time to read the whole speech and verify the context, but the thing seems to me so clear that no-context could make any difference to the meaning of it. Mr. Gladstone said:—

"We have an interest in the independence of Belgium which is wider than that which

we may have in the literal operation of the guarantee. It is found in the answer to the question whether under the circumstances of the case, this country, endowed as it is with influence and power, would quietly stand by and witness the perpetration of the direst crime that ever stained the pages of history, and thus become participators in the sin."

No, Sir, if it be the case that there has been anything in the nature of an ultimatum to Belgium, asking her to compromise or violate her neutrality, whatever may have been offered to her in return, her independence is gone if that holds. If her independence goes, the independence of Holland will follow. I ask the House from the point of view of British interests, to consider what may be at stake. If France is beaten in a struggle of life and death, beaten to her knees, loses her position as a great Power, becomes subordinate to the will and power of one greater than herself — consequences which I do not anticipate, because I am sure that France has the power to defend herself with all the energy and ability and patriotism which she has shown so often — still, if that were to happen, and if Belgium fell under the same dominating influence, and then Holland, and then Denmark, then would not Mr. Gladstone's words come true, that just opposite to us there would be a common interest against the unmeasured aggrandisement of any Power?

It may be said, I suppose, that we might stand aside, husband our strength, and that whatever happened in the course of this war at the end of it intervene with effect to put things right, and to adjust them to our own point of view. If, in a crisis like this, we run away from those obligations of honour and interest as regards the Belgian Treaty, I doubt whether, whatever material force we might have at the end, it would be of very much value in face of the respect that we should have lost. And do not believe, whether a great Power stands outside this war or not, it is going to be in a position at the end of it to exert its superior strength. For us, with a powerful Fleet, which we believe able to protect our commerce, to protect our shores, and to protect our interests, if we are engaged in war, we shall suffer but little more than we shall suffer even if we stand aside.

We are going to suffer, I am afraid, terribly in this war whether we are in it or whether we stand aside. Foreign trade is going to stop, not because the trade routes are closed, but because there is no trade at the other end. Continental nations engaged in war — all their populations, all their energies, all their wealth, engaged in a desperate struggle — they cannot carry on the trade with us that they are carrying on in times of peace, whether we are parties to the war or whether we are not. I do not believe for a moment, that at the end of this war, even if we stood aside and remained aside, we should be in a position, a material position, to use our force decisively to undo what had happened in the course of the war, to prevent the whole of the West of Europe opposite to us — if that had been the result of the war — falling under the domination of a single Power, and I am quite sure that our moral position would be such as to have lost us all respect. I can only say that I have put the question of Belgium somewhat hypothetically, because I am not yet sure of all the facts, but, if the facts turn out to be as they have reached us at present, it is quite clear that there is an obligation on this country to do its utmost to prevent the consequences to which those facts will lead if they are undisputed.

I have read to the House the only engagements that we have yet taken definitely with regard to the use of force. I think it is due to the House to say that we have taken no engagement yet with regard to sending an Expeditionary armed force out of the country. Mobilisation of the Fleet has taken place; mobilisation of the Army is taking place; but we have as yet taken no engagement, because I do feel that in the case of a European conflagration such as this, unprecedented, with our enormous responsibilities in India and other parts of the Empire, or in countries in British occupation, with all the unknown factors, we must take very carefully into consideration the use which we make of sending an Expeditionary Force out of the country until we know how we stand. One thing I would say.

The one bright spot in the whole of this terrible situation is Ireland. The general feeling throughout Ireland — and I would like this to be clearly understood abroad — does not make the Irish question a consideration which we feel we have now to take into account. I have told the House how far we have at present gone in commitments and the conditions which influence our policy, and I have put to the House and dwelt at length upon how vital is the condition of the neutrality of Belgium.

What other policy is there before the House? There is but one way in which the Government could make certain at the present moment of keeping outside this war, and that would be that it should immediately issue a proclamation of unconditional neutrality. We cannot do that. We have made the commitment to France that I have read to the House which prevents us from doing that. We have got the consideration of Belgium which prevents us also from any unconditional neutrality, and, without those conditions absolutely satisfied and satisfactory, we are bound not to shrink from proceeding to the use of all the forces in our power. If we did take that line by saying, *"We will have nothing whatever to do with this matter"* under no conditions — the Belgian Treaty obligations, the possible position in the Mediterranean, with damage to British interests, and what may happen to France from our failure to support France — if we were to say that all those things mattered nothing, were as nothing, and to say we would stand aside, we should, I believe, sacrifice our respect and good name and reputation before the world, and should not escape the most serious and grave economic consequences.

My object has been to explain the view of the Government, and to place before the House the issue and the choice. I do not for a moment conceal, after what I have said, and after the information, incomplete as it is, that I have given to the House with regard to Belgium, that we must be prepared, and we are prepared, for the consequences of having to use all the strength we have at any moment — we know not how soon — to defend ourselves and to take our part. We know, if the facts all be as I have stated them, though I have announced no intending aggressive action on our part, no final decision to resort to force at a moment's notice, until we know the whole of the case, that the use of it may be forced upon us. As far as the forces of the Crown are concerned, we are ready. I believe the Prime Minister and my Right Hon. Friend the First Lord of the Admiralty have no doubt whatever that the readiness and the efficiency of those Forces were never at a higher mark than they are to-day, and never was there a time when confidence was more justified in the power of the Navy to protect our commerce and to protect our shores. The thought is with us always of the suffering and misery entailed from which no country in Europe will escape and from which no abdication or neutrality will save us. The amount of harm that can be done by an enemy ship to our trade is infinitesimal, compared with the amount of harm that must be done by the economic condition that is caused on the Continent.

The most awful responsibility is resting upon the Government in deciding what to advise the House of Commons to do. We have disclosed our mind to the House of Commons. We have disclosed the issue, the information which we have, and made clear to the House, I trust, that we are prepared to face that situation, and that should it develop, as probably it may develop, we will face it. We worked for peace up to the last moment, and beyond the last moment. How hard, how persistently, and how earnestly we strove for peace last week, the House will see from the Papers that will be before it.

But that is over, as far as the peace of Europe is concerned. We are now face to face with a situation and all the consequences which it may yet have to unfold. We believe we shall have the support of the House at large in proceeding to whatever the consequences may be and whatever measures may be forced upon us by the development of facts or action taken by others. I believe the country, so quickly has the situation been forced upon it, has not had time to realise the issue. It perhaps is still thinking of the quarrel between Austria and Servia, and not the complications of this matter which have grown out of the quarrel between Austria and Servia. Russia and Germany we know are at war. We do not yet know officially that Austria, the ally whom Germany is to support, is yet at war with Russia. We know that a good deal has been happening on the French frontier. We do not know that the German Ambassador has left Paris.

The situation has developed so rapidly that technically, as regards the condition of the war, it is most difficult to describe what has actually happened. I wanted to bring out the underlying issues which would affect our own conduct, and our own policy, and to put them clearly. I have put the vital facts before the House, and if, as seems not improbable, we are forced, and rapidly forced, to take our stand upon those issues, then I believe, when the country realises what is at stake, what the real issues are, the magnitude of the impending dangers in the West of Europe, which I have endeavoured to describe to the House, we shall be supported throughout, not only by the House of Commons, but by the determination, the resolution, the courage, and the endurance of the whole country.

LATER IN THE DAY SIR EDWARD ADDED THE FOLLOWING:

I want to give the House some information which I have received, and which was not in my possession when I made my statement this afternoon. It is information I have received from the Belgian Legation in London, and is to the following effect: *"Germany sent yesterday evening at seven o'clock a note proposing to Belgium friendly neutrality, covering free passage on Belgian territory, and promising maintenance of independence of the kingdom and possession at the conclusion of peace, and threatening, in case of refusal, to treat Belgium as an enemy. A time-limit of twelve hours was fixed for the reply. The Belgians have answered that an attack on their neutrality would be a flagrant violation of the rights of nations, and that to accept the German proposal would be to sacrifice the honour of a nation. Conscious of its duty, Belgium is finally resolved to repel aggression by all possible means".* Of course, I can only say that the Government are prepared to take into grave consideration the information which they have received. I make no further comment upon it.

'In Continuing & Grateful Memory'
THE MENIN GATE

With an introduction by Major Tonie and Mrs Valmai Holt this fascinating three volume book (1,100 pages) contains nearly 1,500 individual cameos of those commemorated on the Menin Gate together with its history, plus a lot, lot more. The books are profusely illustrated with portraits, contemporary drawings, photographs, diagrams and maps. They are an essential guide when visiting Ypres, the Salient or the Western Front. Trace the footsteps of many of those who made the ultimate sacrifice and put a face to a name on the memorial — those awarded the Victoria Cross winners together with stories of a wide selection of famous sportsmen, poets, musicians. Also included are those who were 'Shot at Dawn'. It makes compelling reading.

"... one of the most fascinating set of books I have read and so moving."
John Gilbert-Jupp

"... it really brings the names on the Menin Gate to life."
Barrie Dickman

"... the detail included is incredible, I learned so much."
Peter Amory

Order on line visit: www.remembering1418.com
or send a cheque payable to 'W P Foster'
for £75.00 plus £6.75 p&p to: IC&G, 15 Cress Way, Faversham, Kent ME13 7NH.

'In Continuing & Grateful Memory'
THE PLOEGSTEERT SECTOR

This 502 page book includes profusely illustrated cameos on five hundred individuals who are commemorated on the Ploegsteert Memorial or buried in the surrounding twelve cemeteries, together with a detailed tour of the sector to accompany the text (and a photographic tour of the inaccessible parts of Ploegsteert Wood); the history of the Christmas Truce; General Erich Ludendorff's history of the German Spring Offensive; and general tourist information to assist the visitor.

The Ploegsteert sector is a fascinating area to visit. It first came to public prominence as the centre of the Christmas Truce in December 1914 but the desperate fighting that took place prior is often overlooked as most concentrate on the First Battle of Ypres that raged only a few miles to the north. The sector was active throughout the war although it was not involved in a major action until 1917 during the Battle of Messines and again during the German Spring Offensive in April 1918.

Order on line visit: www.remembering1418.com
or send a cheque payable to 'W P Foster'
for £25.00 to: IC&G, 15 Cress Way, Faversham, Kent ME13 7NH.

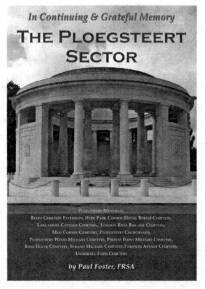

"I WAS THERE!"

During the First World War and in its immediate aftermath a large number of books based on letter and diaries of those who were killed were published. Many of them were private publications compiled by their immediate family and are no longer available. After some consideration I selected a series of such books and faithfully reproduced the original. Where appropriate, I have added contemporary illustrations and photographs. In each publication an additional section has been added that provides a series of cameos on a selection of those mentioned in the text that significantly adds to the appreciation of events discussed in the letters and diaries.

The books are filled with fascinating details often missing from other publications and puts you in the front line with the troops looking at the war through their eyes and recorded at the time.

Order on line visit: www.remembering1418.com
or send a cheque payable to 'W P Foster'
for £75.00 plus £6.75 p&p to: IC&G, 15 Cress Way, Faversham, Kent ME13 7NH.

THE LETTERS OF ARTHUR GEORGE HEATH
6th Battalion Queen's Own
(Royal West Kent Regiment)

 Lieutenant Arthur Heath volunteered on Thursday 20th August 1914 and his letters home and to his friends begin from that date. They chart his training in England, leaving for France and then serving in northern France in the trenches. His letters reflect the optimism felt by so many men and then the reality of life at the front. Lieutenant Heath was killed in action Friday 8th October 1915 at Loos. The original book was published by his family in 1917. In Part II there are cameos on thirty four personalities mentioned in his letters. 162 pages — **£7.99**

ACTIVE-SERVICE DIARY
1st Battalion Irish Guards

The letters of Lieutenant Teddy Shears cover the period from Monday 22nd January 1917 to Wednesday 4th July 1917 when he finally was able to serve in

France. Teddy left with a draft and you follow him into the front line where his optimistic and cheery letters provided a detailed experience of an officer and his men. Teddy served on the Somme and on the Salient where he was killed when hit by a shell splinter. The original book was published by his parents in 1919. In Part II there are cameos on twenty personalities mentioned in his letters. 104 pages — £7.99

DENIS OLIVER BARNETT, IN HAPPY MEMORY
Artists Rifles and Leinster Regiment

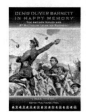

Denis Barnett volunteered and enlisted in the Artists Rifles. He left for France on Monday 26th October 1914 and served with them until he was commissioned on Saturday 9th January 1915 the Leinsters. Denis served in northern France and on the Ypres Salient where he was mortally wounded and taken to Poperinghe where he died on Monday 16th August 1915. The original book was produced by his family shortly after his death. In Part II there are cameos on over twenty personalities and events mentioned in his letters. 220 pages — £9.45

A MEMOIR, EDWARD WYNDHAM TENNANT
4th Battalion Grenadier Guards

Edward 'Bim' Tennant was the son of Edward, Baron Glenconner and Lady Pamela. The family was part of 'the establishment' and very well connected. He was much loved by his mother who produced the original book in his memory and traces his life from a baby, his school life and then as a soldier in France. It also contains many of his poems including those written in the trenches. The book is highly detailed and provides a fascinating insight into the attitudes of society in Edwardian Britain, Bim's family life and friends (many of whom were killed in the war), his schooling and the excitement of a newly commissioned officer going to war. Bim was killed on Friday 22nd September 1916 on the Somme and he is buried in Guillemont Road Cemetery together with many of his friends and contemporaries. In Part II there are cameos on fifty-eight personalities mentioned in his letters. 358 pages — £11.99

GILBERT WALTER LYTTELTON TALBOT
7ᵗʰ Battalion Rifle Brigade

 The story and letters of Gilbert Talbot, in whose memory 'Talbot House' was named in Poperinghe, is fascinating. Many visit both 'TOC H' and Gilbert's grave in Sanctuary Wood but know little about the man himself. His family were aristocratic and he had a traditional upbringing for a boy of his background. He became President of the Oxford Union and a glittering career in politics beckoned but his life ended at Hooge on Friday 30ᵗʰ July 1915. The letters and well written commentary are exemplary that any student of the First World War should not miss. The original book was produced by his father in 1917. In Part II there are cameos on thirty-one personalities mentioned in his letters and much more.
132 pages — £7.99

SOLDIER AND DRAMATIST,
BEING THE LETTERS OF HAROLD CHAPIN
Royal Army Medical Corps

 This book of letters from Harold Chapin to his mother, wife and son provide an interesting slant on the First World War. He was an American, a well-known actor, an author and a playwright. At the outbreak of war he volunteered and enlisted in the Royal Army Medical Corps serving in France from March 1915. Although not in the front line manning the parapet Harold undertook dangerous and important work at the front. His cheerful 'newsy' letters are full of fascinating details that fill in many gaps when learning of life on the Western Front in northern France. Harold's service was cut short when he was killed during the Battle of Loos and is now commemorated on the Loos Memorial. In addition to Harold's letters in Part II provides information on four of his plays and an appreciation by E B Osborn.
186 pages — £7.99

LETTERS OF CAPTAIN SIR EDWARD HULSE
1ˢᵗ and 2ⁿᵈ Battalion Scots Guards

Edward Hulse became the 7ᵗʰ Baronet on the death of his father in 1903 at the age of thirteen. He was educated at Eton College and went up to Balliol. Apart from running his estates Edward was an officer in the Coldstream Guards from 1912 before transferring to the Scots Guards the next year. He went out to France with the BEF at the outbreak of war and served with the 1ˢᵗ Battalion until November

1914 when he transferred to the 2nd Battalion Scots Guards. His account of the 'Christmas Truce' at Ploegsteert is often quoted and referred to — his original letter forms part of the book. It is a fascinating history that traces the many actions from Mons to Neuve Chapelle where he was killed on Friday 12th March 1915. In Part II there are cameos on fifty-eight personalities mentioned in his letters.

170 pages — **£8.45**

LETTERS FROM FRANCE – A D GILLESPIE
Argyll & Sutherland Highlanders

Douglas Gillespie was an intelligent young man who was educated at Winchester and New College, Oxford. He was well travelled and but for the First World War he was expected to become an accomplished lawyer. He was commissioned and left for France in February 1915. He served on the Ypres Salient and in northern France being killed on Sunday 26th September 1915 during the Battle of Loos. His long and detailed letters provide an intimate view about life in the trenches. The original book was published by his family in 1916. In Part II there are cameos on twenty-eight personalities mentioned in his letters.

228 pages — **£9.45**

THE LETTERS OF GEORGE BRENTON LAURIE
1st Battalion Royal Irish Rifles

Lieutenant Colonel George Laurie born in Canada who became a professional soldier. He was gazetted to the Royal Irish Rifles in September 1885, the last officer to be commissioned in the Army with the rank of Lieutenant. He served with them in Gibraltar, Egypt, Sudan, Malta, South Africa, Ireland, India and Aden before the First World War. He was appointed to command the 1st Battalion in 1912 and took them to France in November 1914. He was in the front line and participated in the 'Christmas Truce'. He was killed on Friday 12th March 1915 during the Battle of Neuve Chapelle. His fascinating letters from a senior front line officer are packed with information and cheery news from the trenches. The original book was compiled by his wife in May 1921 and dedicated to his three children. In Part II there are cameos on sixty-two personalities mentioned in his letters and notes on some of the events.

214 pages — **£8.45**

LETTERS TO HIS WIFE, WAR POEMS AND OTHER VERSES - ROBERT ERNEST VERNÈDE
12th Battalion Rifle Brigade

In this publication I have combined two of Ernest's books, *'Letters To His Wife'* that was published in 1917 and covers his life in the First World War, and *'Poems and Other Verses'* that were written during war were published in 1920. Ernest was a popular author who published his first novel, *'The Pursuit of Mr Faviel'*, in 1905. Ernest was keen to play his part in the war but due to his age he had been turned down several times. Eventually he was able to enlist in the Public School Battalion, Royal Fusiliers, and whilst training was sent for officer training. In November 1915 Ernest left for France and he served in northern France, the Ypres Salient, the Somme and was killed on the opening day of the Battle of Arras.

His wonderfully individually styled letters, coupled with his poems, makes a terrific read. In Part II there are cameos on twenty-eight personalities plus notes on events mentioned in his letters coupled with information on his novels.

232 pages — **£8.45**

RICHARD VINCENT SUTTON, A RECORD OF HIS LIFE
1st Life Guards attached Guards Machine Gun Regiment and Staff

Sir Richard Sutton, 6th Baronet, or 'Dick' as he was known to his family and friends, inherited his title at a very young age. This wonderfully produced book was shortly after his death that covers his life from birth. His first letters are from Ludgrove Preparatory School and contain some of his little sketches he sent home.

Dick went out to Belgium in October 1914 and soon saw service at the First Battle of Ypres. He continued to serve with the Life Guards until he joined General Sir Henry Rawlinson and served on his staff until at his own request he returned to the front with the Guards Machine Gun Regiment. Dick survived the war only to succumb to influenza and died on Friday 29th November 1918.

In Part II there are cameos on eighty-five personalities plus extensive notes on events mentioned in his letters.

318 pages — **£10.99**

A Memoir – Julian & Billy Grenfell and Francis & Riversdale Grenfell

The book amalgamates two publications on the Grenfell cousins, Julian and Billy, Francis and Riversdale. The four of them would give their lives for King and Country during the first year of the First World War with Francis winning the Victoria Cross and Julian the Distinguished Service Order. Julian was a poet who wrote the well-known poem '*Into Battle*' amongst many others.

Julian, 3rd Baron Grenfell, who was named after his illustrious relation, has kindly written a fascinating introduction to the publication, that provides a contemporary and valuable insight to the family.

Their separate but intertwined lives prior to and during the war provide a fascinating insight into the attitudes of society, the language and a way of life that vanished at the conclusion of the war.

Within ten months the four of them had been killed after seeing the horrors of the First World War from the beginning. Riversdale was the first to die on Friday 4th September 1914 and in 1915 Francis died on Monday 24th May, two days later Julian succumbed to his wounds on Wednesday 26th and finally Billy who was killed on Friday 30th July 1915. We will never know what contribution they would have made to society like so many, their promising futures were cut short.

In Part III there are cameos on eighty-six personalities plus extensive notes on events mentioned in his letters.

322 pages — £11.99

In continuing & Grateful Memory
Specialised Battlefield Tours

I began organising battlefield tours to the Western Front in 1981. In the early years I enjoyed taking veterans back to where they had served on the battlefields, from Ypres to the Somme. Many of them had never previously returned to the battlefields they had left at the end of the First World War — sadly those opportunities no longer exist.

The fully-guided specialised tours normally are for four or five days. We stay in a high standard of hotels (based in central locations), with all meals, museum entrances *et al* included. (The only additional costs are for personal drinks and single room supplements.) The tours welcome everyone and we provide time to accommodate individual requests and visits. We cater for all levels of knowledge — from the expert to the first-time visitor.

The main aim is that you enjoy your trip; also that you will improve your knowledge, visit new places, return feeling you have received good value for money — then come back again on another tour!

Each year a tour Ypres for 11th November has become an institution which includes, in addition to tour of the Salient and the ceremonies in the town, a Remembrance Day Reception and Dinner with an after-dinner speech. The tours throughout the rest of the year are based on specific battles, places and personalities with new tours added each year. An full information pack with notes and maps support the tour.

If you would be interested in joining a forthcoming tour and would like further information please contact me:

email: remembering@btinternet.com

post: c/o 15 Cress Way, Faversham, Kent ME13 7NH

I look forward to the opportunity of meeting you on a tour.

Paul Foster

Lightning Source UK Ltd.
Milton Keynes UK
UKOW03f0824100214

226186UK00001B/36/P